*The Specter of Democracy*

# Books by Dick Howard

*The Development of the Marxian Dialectic* (1972)

*The Marxian Legacy* (1978)

*From Marx to Kant* (1985)

*La naissance de la pensée politique américaine* (1987)

*The Birth of American Political Thought* (1989, translation of 1987 with new Preface and Afterword)

*The Politics of Critique* (1988)

*Defining the Political* (1989)

*From Marx to Kant* (1993, revised and expanded of 1985)

*Political Judgments* (1997)

*Pour une critique du jugement politique* (1998)

*A l'origine de la pensée critique. Marx* (2001)


# Editor

*Selected Political Writings of Rosa Luxemburg* (1971)

*The Unknown Dimension: European Marxism Since Lenin* (with Karl E. Klare) (1972)

*Serge Mallet's Essays on the New Working Class* (1975)

# *The* SPECTER OF
# Democracy

Dick Howard

*Columbia University Press    New York*

Columbia University Press
*Publishers Since 1893*
New York    Chichester, West Sussex
Copyright © 2002 Columbia University Press
All rights reserved

Library of Congress Cataloging-in-Publication Data

Howard, Dick, 1943–
   The specter of democracy / Dick Howard.
      p. cm.
   Includes bibliographical references and index.
   ISBN 0–231–12484–8 (cloth : alk. paper)
      1. Democracy.  2. Marx, Karl, 1818–1883—Political and social views.
   I. Title.

JC423 .H7536   2002
321.8—dc21                          2002018889

Columbia University Press books are printed
on permanent and durable acid-free paper.

Printed in the United States of America
*Designed by Audrey Smith*

10 9 8 7 6 5 4 3 2 1

# Contents

# Introduction: Why Should We, and How Should We, Reclaim Marx?

Imagine that Karl Marx had sat down in 1847 and written, "A specter is haunting Europe, the specter of democracy." Would *The Communist Manifesto* that he published in February 1848 read so very differently from the now classic text that has been said to have changed the world? Recall some of the ringing phrases from Marx's description of the rise of the bourgeoisie and the capitalist world it created. He portrays the bourgeoisie as "revolutionary" because it has "put an end to all feudal, patriarchal, idyllic relations." It has "stripped of its halo every occupation hitherto honored," and "torn away from the family its sentimental veil." Its great productive force, surpassing the pyramids, aqueducts, and cathedrals, has shown "what man's activity can bring about." In a famous sentence, Marx sums up his praise for this capitalist revolution: "All fixed, fast-frozen relations . . . are swept away, all new formed ones become antiquated before they can ossify. All that is solid melts into air, all that is holy is profaned, and man is at last compelled to face with sober senses, his real conditions of life, and his relations with his kind."[1] Granted, this is not a description of democracy that can be found in political science textbooks; it is a tense portrait of social relations that must seek constantly a stability that will always exceed their grasp. It represents a historically unprecedented form of human coexistence no longer based on the principles of unity, stability, and community but instead accentuating a dynamics of difference, uncertainty, and individualism. Such are the social relations of democracy, a mode of living that is as much a threat to any established order as Marx's communist revolution was supposed to have been.

The claim of this book is that, whatever his intentions, Marx did announce that the specter of democracy is haunting Europe. To justify that claim, I have to explain first of all why he—and those who later claimed his legacy—did not understand the radical implications of his work. That is why the first part of the book examines Marxism and the intellectuals. While it is true that Marx considered the working class to be the agent of the coming revolution, the theoretical basis of this assertion appealed to minds primed to receive it and eager to translate it immediately into their own practice. That is why it is tempting to identify the intellectual with Marxism, at least after fascism had discredited right-wing theorists (to the point that even Heidegger's French disciples tended to assimilate his thought to a leftist critique of capitalism). While it is not false, such a generalization reaches too wide. The first part of the book illustrates both the attractiveness of Marxism to intellectuals and the ways in which some of them learned how to use Marx not only to criticize Marxism but to recognize the radical implications of democracy. Particularly in the French case,[2] this could take place only after the historical uniqueness of another type of new social relations was recognized: the critique of totalitarianism (which is not just another tyranny) made clear the radical nature of democracy—which the emergence of totalitarianism shows to represent a challenge not only to the established order but to itself as well. Totalitarian ideology, after all, claims that it incarnates the true realization of democracy when in fact it is the attempt to overcome the creative instability characteristic of democratic social relations typical of modernity.

Why did Marx and his successors misunderstand his basic insight? The title of *The Communist Manifesto* suggests one reason. Marx's goal was to make manifest a reality that was maturing in the womb of capitalism; the communists were to be the midwives of history. Communism would put an end to a savage history of class struggles that had divided humanity against itself. Because Marx was looking for a solution, he could not recognize that democracy posed to humankind new problems that could not be solved without putting an end to democracy itself. As if he intuited the threat posed by this new political form, Marx tried to anchor its reality in the economic relations of capitalism, which would produce its own proletarian "grave-diggers." This project made some sense in the nineteenth century, when a growing urban working class challenged the justice of the new economic system. But the effects of twentieth-century totalitarianism make clear that the economy cannot be isolated and treated as if it were the determinant cause of social relations. The totalitarian seizure of power precedes its use of this power to impose its will on socioeconomic relations. This autonomous political intervention is not admitted by the totalitarian regime, which denies its own political nature by claiming to express only the necessities of a history whose interpretation it monopolizes. In this way, totalitarianism is the antithesis and negation of democracy, whose problematic achievements stand out more sharply in its light. As such, totalitarianism can be defined as an *antipolitics*.

This theoretical claim can be illustrated by two personal experiences.[3] I went to Paris in 1966 to discover the radical political theory that I thought was missing in the United States. At my first Parisian demonstration against the Vietnam War, I was caught up in the speaker's world historical perspective; immersed in the flow of his rhetoric, I was a moment late in registering my applause when I noticed that he too was applauding. This was no egoistic individual expressing mere opinion; his applause signified that his words came from elsewhere, from society or History even. The speaker (whose name I have long since forgotten) was making manifest a Rationality that, because it was shared by all humanity, could draw each individual out of alienated private life into a greater community. This meant that he did not have to take personal responsibility for a judgment that could be debated; he was deciphering History for an anonymous public that he did not need to convince rationally to accept its revelation. The speaker was not only a caricature of Hegel in the role of Secretary to the Absolute Spirit; such an attitude is what permits the totalitarian machine to function. The irony is that he thought he was refusing the arbitrary egoistic regime of the bourgeoisie when in fact he was delivering himself, powerless, to an even more powerful arbitrary rule, that of a totalitarian society that takes itself as the Last Judgment of History.

This anecdote suggests that totalitarianism is not imposed by force on an innocent, democracy-loving population. A second experience, not long after that Parisian demonstration, illustrates the necessity to choose actively democratic politics. I became friendly with some dissident students in Prague in 1967, before the attempt to create from the top down a "Socialism with a Human Face" was crushed by the 1968 invasion by the Warsaw Pact. These students explained that they had gotten into trouble because they had organized a demonstration against the Vietnam war. I didn't understand: wasn't their government opposed the war? Yes, but *they* had organized the demonstration, not the government. Independent activity was a threat, autonomy a danger, and self-organized groups a menace. That is why the invasion of August 1968 was probably unnecessary; the party-state knew already that it could not risk abandoning its control.[4] But the same reasons explain why, despite the repression imposed after 1968, many Czechs (and other East Central Europeans) refused to accept the *Gleichschaltung* that sought to eliminate all independent organization. The resistance that culminated in the revolutions of 1989 was a manifestation of the clash of democratic self-organization with totalitarian power. The defense of civil society against the omnipresent state demonstrated again the radical challenge that democracy poses to *any* established order. Indeed, when the old order fell in 1989, the civil societies that had united in solidarity against it found that their own divisions, which were set aside in the struggle against the totalitarian state, emerged nearly as soon as their victory was confirmed.[5] Democracy is a challenge even to itself.

If democracy is indeed the specter haunting Europe, it clearly does not represent the kind of real force that Marx saw incarnated in the rising working class that capitalism was creating in ever greater numbers and equipping with an ever more powerful machinery of production. If democracy does not have the same kind of world historical role that Marx postulated for communism, what *is* democracy? What is its historical place? In what sense is it truly new? And how can its novelty be understood?

Although he is not directly treated in this book, Tocqueville provides a useful insight. At the outset of *Democracy in America*, he insists that equality is the new principle that separates democracy from all preceding societies, which, in one or another manner, were based on a hierarchy assumed to be natural and immutable. Tocqueville calls this equality a "generative fact," whose widely diverse effects he then follows in his still readable study. As opposed to Marx, Tocqueville does not treat equality simply as a material fact (or a goal to be realized). Its function can be called *symbolic*, and its results exist in the sphere of meaning.[6] The idea of a symbolic institution of a society can be understood by comparison to attempts to describe the way political culture influences social relations. The symbolic is concerned with the philosophical creation of social meaning, whereas political culture is treated as a causal factor to be studied empirically in order to ensure that there exists a material or social foundation of meaning. The symbolic institution of meaning is the presupposition of political culture, which rearranges and adapts the symbolic to fit empirical conditions.[7] This distinction permits an interpretation of the difference between traditional societies and modern democratic societies. Traditional societies are characterized by the fact that the symbolic institution that generates meaning (e.g., the gods) is assumed to be external to the society, which therefore cannot change it. They are societies without history, seeking only to reproduce themselves. Modern democratic societies have overcome such external sources of meaning, but this victory of enlightenment is ambiguous since it means they have to generate their own meanings from within themselves—and they can change these meanings or organize competition for such change. That is the task of democratic politics in a society that creates its own historical dynamic. It is also why "all that is solid melts into air." But the quest for solid foundations in a modern society whose future must remain open is also the source of the antipolitical or totalitarian threat.

While the encounter of Marxism and the intellectuals in part 1 of this book concludes with the passage from the critique of totalitarianism to the politics of democracy, democracy is defined there only in the categories of political philosophy and illustrated by contrast to the varieties of antipolitics.[8] Part 2 attempts to fill in the picture of democracy and to explain some of the difficulties in the practice of democratic politics. It develops the distinction between a *democratic republic* (toward which French politics has tended historically, at least until some recent developments) and a *republican democracy* (which represents the historical form adopted but never theorized at the time of the American Revolution). This conceptual framework is not identical with the familiar characterization of the French Revolution as oriented to social transformation while the American Revolution remained (self-)limited to the political sphere.[9] The difference between the symbolic and the empirically real suggests the need to look for a unifying principle in the experiences of both political societies. The French had to legitimate the overthrow of a political society unified by its monarchical institutions; to do so, they had to oppose a new unitary principle to the old order. This meant they could leave no place for particular organizations such as political parties, and the same unitary principle militated against judicial autonomy.[10] Yet it is just this judicial autonomy and the development of a system of political parties whose competition is accepted as legitimate that characterize the practical results of the American Revolution. The French democratic republic assumes that society only acquires its true unity by being integrated within the republican state, whereas the American constitutional republic guarantees the autonomous self-management of individual and social relations.

The two contrasting political histories that were inaugurated by revolutionary breaks with traditional societies make clear that democracy is not defined by fixed institutional structures (such as elections, checks and balances, or judicial autonomy) but depends rather on the meaning that individual actors attach to their social relations. But the institution of meaning is not a one-time affair that lasts forever; it must be constantly renewed and always runs the risk of temporary failure and even self-destruction. That is why the chapter that intervenes between my presentations of the historical paths of French and American democratic politics (chapter 10) points to the ways in which the two histories tend to overlap, interrelate, and intersect. It shows also how these histories cast new light on the tired contemporary quarrels between liberals and communitarians, both of whom prove liable to the reproach of antipolitics. Similarly, the reconstruction of the political dimension of American history is followed by an attempt (chapter 12) to explain the emergence of a kind of political-religious fundamentalism that is at once contrary to the American vision of democracy and yet contained within it as a latent possibility, just as the French democratic project came to be identified with the communism inaugurated in 1917. Once again, "all that is solid melts into air." Democracy is not a solution (comparable to Marx's communism); it poses problems not only to the established order but to itself. The French got it right with their quest for the unitary democratic republic (which is not quite identical with socialism), but so did the Americans with their discovery of the politics of republican democratic diversity (which is not quite identical with liberalism). The challenge is to hold on to the unity that animates the one without losing the diversity preserved by the other.

The return to Marx in part 3 is now prepared. It might seem that the demise in 1989 of so-called really existing socialism and the dissolution of the Soviet Union would permit a rediscovery of Marx as a political thinker unencumbered by the historical mistakes of those who claimed to be his heirs. If that were my intention, I could have gone directly to work, without the theoretical and historical preliminaries in the first two parts. But while there is much to criticize in present-day socioeconomic relations, I leave that criticism to others. My project instead is somewhat paradoxical—at least at first glance. Rather than directly recover a political Marx, I stress the importance of the philosophical Marx in order then to open the path to politics. The events of 1989 permit the rediscovery of a Marx who is first of all a philosopher. Although Jacques Derrida's *Specters of Marx* seemed to return to the philosopher as well, his goal was more immediately practical: to undercut the self-certainties of the times. I want to show that *Marx's inability to recognize the democratic political implications of his own analysis was due to his own philosophical rigor.* Marx tried mightily to radicalize Hegel by doing what I call (in chapter 13) philosophy by other means. Where Hegel appealed to reason, Marx appealed to the material world—but, like Hegel, he searched for the traces of reason incarnated in that world.[11] That is why he could not recognize the democratic political implications of analyses like those in *The Communist Manifesto*. The economy, class struggle, the proletariat: these realities were what Marx thought would realize philosophy and put an end to history. Once again, it would be too easy to criticize Marx retrospectively; it is more important to reconstruct the rigor of his search, to watch him revise his analyses from one work to the next, to articulate the unity of a life's work that didn't either shy away from the political arena or hide behind facile rhetoric.

The presentation of Marx in chapter 13 has another ambition. Just as the specter of democracy showed its radical potential as well as its self-destructive possibilities only against the backdrop of totalitarianism, so the political problems posed by modern democratic society can appear as problems but also as appeals to creative intervention only against the backdrop of Marx's systematic philosophical achievement.[12] As with the encounter of Marxism and the intellectuals, this philosophical project has to be reconstructed in order for political theory to be freed from its sway. It is not any more legitimate or useful to imagine simply that Marx was wrong (or stupid, or worse) than it is to assume that totalitarianism is imposed on an unwilling people by a foreign conqueror. It is more fruitful—and more consonant with Marx's own favorite method of immanent critique—to assume that there are reasons that Marx misunderstood himself and that these reasons must be understood before it becomes possible to right the errors. That is why the conclusion of the book returns to the beginning (to the question of Marx and philosophy) rather than proposing a new political project, as if humanity were only awaiting new marching orders to achieve its destiny. Democracy is not a natural condition of humankind; nor is it inscribed in the inevitable course of human history. Democracy cannot exist without democratic citizens, individuals conscious of the perils as well as the pleasures that it offers. In this sense—to paraphrase a slogan dear to Marxists[13]—*there can be no democratic practice without democratic theory*. An analysis of democracy that starts from a critical rereading of Marx not only transforms our understanding of Marx's theory but also calls our attention to the difficult dual status of democratic theory, which opens toward both politics and antipolitics.

The adventure and the danger opened by modern democracy lead me to conclude with a promissory note. I do not want to leave the impression that the theoretical arguments presented here have no immediate political implications. During the time that I was writing this, I also wrote more directly political articles, contributed shorter political commentary, and was often interviewed about current political developments. To have added that material to this book would have made it more complicated than it needs to be; it is better to reduce my thesis here to a clear and concise theoretical presentation. However, modern technology provides a way to offer the reader access not only to these earlier political writings but also to my ongoing attempts to apply the understanding of democracy as radical and my critique of the various forms of antipolitics (including those that shocked the world on September 11, 2001)[14] to current events. I will therefore post the earlier articles, as well as future contributions, on my Web site: *ms.cc.sunysb.edu/rhoward.*

It remains for me to thank all the usual people, who know what I owe them, but most of all Jennifer Crewe of Columbia University Press (and her two anonymous reviewers), who was convinced by the very rough and approximate set of materials that I presented as the first version of this project. She encouraged me (with a contract!) to continue, and, when I was in the midst of the far more vast rewriting than I had intended and was lost in my own systematic web, she unpacked the project, showed me the broad lines that were important, and made it possible to produce this work. The book would not exist without her help. Thanks also to Paul Berman for a final critical reading that got many things right.

It will be clear to the reader how much I owe to Claude Lefort and to the late Cornelius Castoriadis, whose absence I still feel. I also owe a debt to the people whom I have known in the context of the journal *Esprit*, above all to Olivier Mongin and Paul Thibaud. I regret that I cannot reprint here the chapter in *Defining the Political* in which I tried to explain (already in 1978!) the uniqueness of that journal, which had just begun its antitotalitarian, democratic turn. I should thank also Bernard Perret, who double-checked the reading of French economic theory that I propose in the appendix to chapter 9, "The Burden of French History." And there are also my German partners, particularly Sigrid Meuschel and Hermann Schwengel. But this book emerges from an international dialogue and debate, whose participants are too numerous to be listed individually. I have been fortunate since the earliest experiences (some of which I have described in this introduction) to share in the experience of something like an international new left. I hope that this volume will contribute to our collective project.

Thanks also go to those who forced me to write earlier versions of some of these chapters, all of which have been revised, extensively in most cases, for this volume.

"Marxism in the Postcommunist World" was a lecture at the annual summer school of the Moscow School of Social and Economic Sciences in June 1998. The theme was chosen by the students and faculty of the school. It was published in the Australian journal *Critical Horizons* 1, no. 1, in February 2000. A modified French version appeared in *Transeuropéennes* in the fall of 1999.

"Can French Intellectuals Escape Marxism?" was a talk organized by Lawrence D. Kritzman at Dartmouth College. A first version was published in *French Politics and Society* 16, no.1 (winter 1998). A revised German version appeared in *Kommune* 16., no. 6 (1998). A French version appeared in *La Nouvelle Lettre internationale*, no. 1 (fall 1999).

"The Frankfurt School and the Transformation of Critical Theory into Cultural Theory" was published in an early version in *Cultural Horizons*; a revised German translation appeared in *Kommune* 18, no. 8 (2000).

"Habermas's Reorientation of Critical Theory Toward Democratic Theory" presents ideas that I developed first in "Law and Political Culture," *Cordozo Law Review* 17, nos. 4–5 (March 1996), and then in a shorter review of Habermas in *German Politics and Society* 15, no. 1 (spring 1997).

"The Anticommunist Marxism of *Socialisme ou Barbarie*" began life as a short contribution to Lawrence D. Kritzman, ed., *The Columbia History of Twentieth-Century Thought*, forthcoming from Columbia University Press. It has been expanded and developed here.

"Claude Lefort's Passage from Revolutionary Theory to Political Theory" combines an essay for *The Columbia History* with the *laudatio* for Claude Lefort on his receiving the Hannah Arendt Prize of the city of Bremen. It also adapts material from chapter 8.

"From Marx to Castoriadis, and from Castoriadis to Us" was presented in a French version at a conference organized in Paris in 1999 to commemorate Castoriadis's death; it was reworked for a conference on Castoriadis organized by Andreas Kalyvas at Columbia University in December 2000. No version has been previously published.

"From the Critique of Totalitarianism to the Politics of Democracy" was part of a lecture given in Paris in June 1999 at the Institut des Hautes Etudes de la Magistrature to a group of French judges.

It was rewritten for publication in *La revue du Mauss*, no. 16 (2000). The English translation here has been extensively revised.

"The Burden of French History" began life as a lecture in German to a group of French and German businessmen in February 2001 at the Frankreich-Zentrum of the University of Freiburg. I have radically revised it in the meantime. A shorter English version appears under the title "From Republican Political Culture to Republican Democracy: The Benefits and Burdens of History" in *French Politics, Culture and Society* 10, no. 3 (fall 2001).

"Intersecting Trajectories of Republicanism in France and the United States" develops arguments presented earlier under the title "From the Politics of Will to a Politics of Judgment: Republicanism in the U.S. and France," in *Internationale Politik und Gesellschaft*, no. 4 (2000).

"Reading U.S. History as Political" was a lecture at the Collège International de Philosophie in 1987, which was published in the *Revue française de science politique* 38, no. 2 (April 1988). It is reprinted in *Pour une critique du jugement politique* (Paris: Cerf, 1998). An English translation of it serves the afterword to *The Birth of American Political Thought*. It has been radically revised and expanded (and retranslated) for the present volume.

"Fundamentalism and the American Exception" was a talk at a meeting in Paris on problems of fundamentalism organized by the Friedrich Ebert Stiftung and the Fondation Jean-Jaurès. A short version appeared in *Fundamentalism and Social Democracy* (Bonn: Friedrich Ebert Stiftung, 1996); an expanded version was published in *Etudes* in November 1996. A German variant appeared in *Kommune* 14, no. 11 (1996). The present version started with a translation from the French by Julie Sadoff, which I have expanded and adapted for this volume.

"Philosophy by Other Means?" was written for this volume. It is based on a much longer essay published in Alain Renaut's five-volume *Histoire de la philosophie politique* (Paris: Calmann-Lévy, 1999). With the help of Eric Cavallo, that article was reworked; a somewhat different version appears in *Metaphilosophy* 32, no. 5 (October 2001): 463–501.

*The Specter of Democracy*

# I

# Marxism and
# the Intellectuals

# CHAPTER I

# Marxism in the Postcommunist World

If we could agree on what "Marxism" is—or was—then the task of evaluating its possible future in the post–cold war world would be relatively simple and noncontroversial. But there is no agreed definition of Marxism. There used to be something more or less official called Marxism-Leninism, and, as opposed to it, there was something called Western Marxism, which had its roots in the Hegelian and Weberian rereading of Marx that was initiated by Georg Lukács in *History and Class Consciousness* (1923), developed by the Frankfurt School's program of critical theory, and thematized in Merleau-Ponty's *Adventures of the Dialectic* (1955). There was also a related debate that peaked in the 1960s concerning the priority of the orientations of the young and the mature Marx, the humanist philosopher as opposed to the historical-materialist political economist. Although other distinctions and debates within the family could be introduced—for example, Austro-Marxism with its stress on the nationality question or Gramsci and his concern with culture and hegemony—it is best to begin from a simple dichotomy: on the one hand, there is the reading of Marx that can be generally put under the notion of historical materialism, and, on the other, there is a more philosophical and dialectical interpretation. Since 1989 the first form of Marxism has been rendered obsolete by the demise of Communism; it wagered on history, and it lost its bet. But where does this leave the other variant of Marxism? Can it, or must it be able to, provide the historical orientation that began as the strength but was ultimately the weakness of the deterministic model offered by historical materialism?

Philosophical-dialectical Marxism can be characterized by two interconnected methodological assumptions. The first is the notion of immanent critique. Many commentators have noted that nearly everything Marx wrote, at all periods of his life, was titled or subtitled "a critique." For example, Marx discovered the revolutionary potential of the proletariat in his critique of Hegel's *Philosophy of Right*. Later, *Capital* did not propose a theory of socialism—that misreading may have been a factor in the ill-advised practice of those who came to power claiming to introduce socialism by applying categories used in Marx's critique of capitalism to build what they hoped would be a different future[1]—instead, *Capital* presents a critique of capitalist political economy whose radical implications were drawn by means of an immanent critique showing the rich potential created but not realized within that mode of production. This idea of immanent critique leads to the second methodological assumption. I just referred to capitalism as a "mode of production." That, however, is the language of historical materialism. It would be more true to the philosophical-dialectical Marx to speak of forms of social relations. That is why *Capital* does not begin with an analysis of the process of production but with an analysis of the commodity form and its metamorphoses. I will return to *Capital* later. For the moment, I want to stress Marx's method. Social relations are interpreted as the expression of practical relations among human beings. Although they don't do it as they please, notes Marx in *The 18th Brumaire*, men do make their own history. The potential that the immanent critique uncovers is not of merely theoretical interest; it has practical applications and makes possible social change. This, rather than a politics of will or a voluntarism that ignores material constraints, is the implication of Marx's demand, in the famous eleventh thesis on Feuerbach, that philosophers not restrict themselves to contemplating the world but seek instead to change it.

I propose to address the question of the place of Marxism in the postcommunist world in three steps. First, I consider some of the temptations that have arisen in the West, where many creative left-oriented thinkers have attempted to find alternative variants of Marxism, all of them more or less adopting the orientation developed by Western Marxism that I have called here philosophical-dialectical. I title this first section "Replacing Marxism . . . with Marxism" because all these attempts fail to develop the kind of practical-historical orientation that was at least attempted by the now discredited historical-materialist kind of Marxism. The extreme implications of this approach come with Adorno's negative dialectics and Marcuse's existential Great Refusal in *One-Dimensional Man*.[2] Second, I propose a reconstruction of Marx's work that takes into account the problems addressed by historical materialism. I call this section "Realizing Marxism . . . as Philosophy." The Marx who emerges from this second step in the argument is a fascinating philosopher, but he remains a philosopher who, however self-critical, is unable to go beyond the mode of immanent critique to invest his philosophy in the historical world in which we live. Third, I attempt to sketch briefly a New Political Manifesto, suggesting that the "specter" haunting Marx's Europe—and our own—was not the proletarian revolution that would finally put an end to a history of class struggle but the advent of democracy. If this intuition is plausible, it will suggest a way to reread Marx so that his contribution can be made fruitful in the contemporary world. The basic insight of the philosophical Marx was seen correctly by Lukács: Marx replaced the Hegelian idea of Spirit with the material proletariat understood as the subject-object of history—as a product of historical development that, because it is a subject and capable of autonomous action, can become the author of its own history. What I call the political, or democratic, Marx is neither so ambitious nor so Hegelian. To put it perhaps paradoxically, the political Marx seeks to maintain the conditions that make possible the immanent critique and practical engagement that characterized the philosophical Marx sketched in the second part of this discussion. Pace Leo Strauss, democracy is the condition of possibility of philosophy.

## REPLACING MARXISM. . . WITH MARXISM

Marxism in the postcommunist world could be thought of as a theory happily rescued from the weight of a failed experiment. Many

Western leftists found themselves caught in contortions, attempting to put the blame on Stalin—often less for Stalinism and its totalitarian domestic misdeeds than for its abandonment of world revolution in favor of creating Socialism in One Country. That approach made it possible to remain an anticapitalist, to accept something like the historical vision of *The Communist Manifesto* (and perhaps even the *Economic and Philosophical Manuscripts of 1844*) while jettisoning the baggage of the determinist breakdown theory attributed to *Capital*. Happy tomorrows could still be hoped for, while the exploitation of today could be condemned not for what it actually is but from a broader theoretical and historical perspective. It is, after all, quite satisfying to couch one's criticism in an all-encompassing theoretical system. From this point of view, one can predict that since capitalism, its crises, its inequalities, its exploitation and alienation remain with us, Marxism in the postcommunist world—at least in the West, which had no experience of what was euphemistically called really existing socialism—may find itself on a far more solid terrain than was the case in the years following if not the invasion of Hungary in 1956 at least those following the invasion of Czechoslovakia in 1968 and the Brezhnev years of stagnation.

But the attempt to claim that the "essence" of Marxism was betrayed by its "appearing form" (to use the Hegelian language of Marx) does not explain why, 150 years after *The Communist Manifesto*, the revolution Marx was waiting for has not appeared. The essence of an essence is to appear, and if appearance betrays the essence, perhaps one has misunderstood the nature of that essence. It is no doubt true that the cold war was not so much won by capitalism as it was lost by the existing form of socialism.[3] Meanwhile, capitalist crises recur, inequality increases glaringly, the third world remains marginalized. Capitalism has few grounds for satisfaction. And it is easy to find passages, chapters, articles, and books from Marx and Marxists to explain the miseries of the present. But what does that prove? If I appeal, for example, to "Wage Labor and Capital," while you turn to the "Anti-Dühring" and someone else invokes Lenin's "Imperialism," while her friend prefers Hilferding's "Finance Capital," what has been gained? We have each adverted to holy text, but none of this explains the dynamics of the present. Each of our claims remains static, structural, and in the last resort antipolitical because it leaves no room for active intervention and no justification for action. At best, this kind of interpretation gives subjective satisfaction, encouraging the belief that one is on the right side of history, which, as Fidel Castro famously said at his 1953 trial after a failed revolt, eventually will absolve us and forgive our trespasses. Despite those who interpreted Marx as predicting a breakdown of capitalism (via the "law of the tendency of the rate of profit to fall" in volume 3 of *Capital*), Marx was concerned with the dynamics of capitalism as a new type of social relations. For *The Communist Manifesto*, all history, after all, is a history of class struggle.

Still, there will be those who will hold on to their Marx. The first among them will be (or will remain) the Trotskyists.[4] Despite the greatness of Trotsky's phenomenology of the Russian Revolution, he remained a structural dogmatist.[5] In a memorable phrase, he asserted that when the artillery man misses his target, he doesn't blame the laws of physics. But is Marxism a theory like those of the natural sciences? Was the basically good and justifiable revolution of 1917 deformed, isolated, and forced into a Stalinist Thermidor? Doesn't Trotsky violate his own Marxist dogma when he blames the person of Stalin for the debacle of Soviet Marxism? Nonetheless, there is something comforting in the Trotskyist position, which will continue to find adherents after 1989 because it unites the reassuring claims of a structural account of capitalism with a criticism of the supposed Stalinist deformation of the promise of 1917.

The problem with attempts to save Marxism from the demise of "really existing socialism" is that they cannot reply to the objection from Karl Popper: that it is nonfalsifiable. It remains as a horizon, a framework or narrative that can internalize contradictions as simply stages in a presumably necessary historical development. This is the case even of Rosa Luxemburg, the spontaneist, who insisted that "only the working class can make the word flesh." This most militant of activists was content to have refuted Eduard Bernstein when she showed that his reformist socialism contradicted the text of Marx. Rosa Luxemburg, the theorist of the Mass Strike, whose final article from the ruins of a failed revolution affirmed that "revolution is the only kind of war in which the final victory can be built only on a series of defeats," could be perhaps even more than Trotsky the model of a post-1989 Marxist. Defeat in the class struggle was for her only a stage in the learning process that would necessarily lead to the final goal. How can she be proven wrong?[6]

The criticism of nonfalsifiability leads to another critique of Marxism, represented in the West by the often impressive textual accounts of Robert Tucker and many others: that it is a new religion. In the hands of a critical historian such as Jacob Talmon, this becomes the reproach that Marx belongs to a long millenarian tradition. At its best, this becomes a positive philosophical claim in Ernst Bloch's *Prinzip Hoffnung*, a kind of wager that humanity cannot but constantly seek reconciliation with itself and with nature. It is not always clear what is Marxist in this honest and admirable utopian position. Marx, after all, claimed not to be a utopian (and his historical-materialist heirs took him literally). In the remarkable, and often neglected, third part of *The Communist Manifesto*, Marx tried to reconstruct the history of socialist utopias to show how they were logically and historically *aufgehoben*, united and made whole in his own position. If it is to be more than a pious wish, this kind of religious-utopian position—which, as such, will certainly remain present after 1989—has to show how the utopias that have come and gone over the 150 years since the *Manifesto* are part of a historical logic of the type that Marx presented in 1848. In this way, it would avoid the nonfalsifiability of the Luxemburgian "defeat as the basis of victory." But then it becomes open to the reproach of being a totalizing historical metaphysics similar to the Young Hegelian theories whose overcoming—in *The Holy Family* and *The German Ideology* of 1845/6—led Marx to formulate his "science."

In this case, however, the renewed Marxism has to refute the objections of Habermas: that it is economist and determinist in its orientation and neglects the other domains of human social interaction. Habermas's *Knowledge and Human Interests* (1968) showed clearly that the materialist philosophy of history that expects social (and human) transformation to follow directly from the material-technical advances of capitalism is one-sided. It is guided by a type of cognitive interest that stresses technological progress and necessarily neglects the spheres of social interaction and human self-liberation. Habermas's *Theory of Communicative Action* (1981) takes his argument beyond the model of the individual social actor to integrate the linguistic turn that points to the primacy of dialogical relations in the development of social rationality. But the upshot of Habermas's theory is that the Marxian project is simply the completion of the project of the Enlightenment. Thus, for example, his first attempt to deal with soviet-type societies, in the wake of 1989, was entitled *The Catch-up Revolution*.[7] Perhaps this saves the Marxist baby, but it subsumes it under a historical or idealist project that Marx explicitly claimed to overcome.

Marx's advance over Enlightenment theories was his insistence on class struggle and his recognition (e.g., in his critique of Proudhon in *The Poverty of Philosophy* [1847]) that history advances through contradictions and by means of negations. Marx's theory of the revolutionary proletariat was certainly the key to this theoretical insight. But today it is hard to recognize Marx's proletariat in our new world order. The polarization of two classes has not occurred (and Marx seemed to have recognized this in the incomplete chapter "Classes" that concludes the third volume of *Capital*). Even before 1989 many in the West sought to reconstitute the proletariat by other means. In France, Serge Mallet and André Gorz talked about a "new working class," while Italian theorists sought to reconstitute the "total worker" to whom the third volume of *Capital* refers somewhat vaguely. In the United States, attempts were made first to rediscover a "history of class struggle" that had been supposedly suppressed by the reigning ideological consensus among historians and social scientists. The idea was that if one could show that there had been constant struggles of workers against bosses, perhaps a defeated working class would gain self-confidence and undertake new struggles. Other Americans sought to broaden the notion of the proletariat, including in it blacks, minorities, women, homosexuals. When it became unclear how these strata (or status groups) could ally with one another, the turn to cultural studies was made: a cultural unity would replace the working class as the new proletariat.[8] Somewhere, somehow, there needed to be an opposition, a negation to negate the negation. Alas, it remains to be discovered.

There are no doubt other strategies that could be invoked in the attempt to redeem Marxism by a better Marxism. So-called analytic philosophers have attempted to justify one or another aspect of the Marxian corpus, while the deconstructionists take a leaf from Jacques Derrida's rehabilitation of the (hard to recognize) "specter" of Marx. Others continue to hope that the struggle against globalization will produce the new agent of revolution. What is lacking in all these approaches is serious consideration of the philosophical theory by which Marx was led to his practical insights. It is this philosophical project that permitted him to make the empirical and analytical discoveries that lost their critical thrust as they came to be part of the Marxist vulgate. Separated from the philosophical endeavor, these insights lose their immanent dynamic as well as their utopian horizon; they are reduced to mere criticism or to naive utopianism. The proletariat becomes merely labor-power, exploited by capitalists as the source of surplus-value; the philosophical critique becomes a positive statement to be studied for its own sake. Yet the philosophical Marx saw that this proletariat had achieved a certain measure of freedom (compared with the serf, for example); this liberty, however, is alienated and can become aware of itself only as economically exploited. If only the second part of this claim is stressed, the immanent historical dynamic of Marx's theory is replaced by static complaints of victimization, and the practical result is self-righteous commiseration. In the end, this leads to the replacement of autonomous praxis by the conscious intervention of the political party, completing the cycle that began with the rejection of Leninism by Western Marxism. To avoid this (unhappy) conclusion, Marx's philosophical project needs to be rethought.

## Realizing Marxism . . . as Philosophy

If Western Marxism seems to find itself driven to adopt political conclusions that clash with its original intentions, a consideration of Marx's own attempt to overcome the immanent limits of philosophy reveals a similar paradox. Marx was essentially a philosopher; this was his strength but also explains his political weakness. His entire work can be seen as the attempt to realize the task proposed in a note to his doctoral dissertation, which his editors have titled "The Becoming Philosophical of the World as the Becoming Worldly of Philosophy."[9] Put simply—as it was for Marx at this point—the idea is that Hegel had elaborated a rational system that explained that the actual is rational and the rational is actual (as Hegel put it in the introduction to his *Philosophy of Right*) but that the actual German world of Marx's time was miserable, chaotic, and impoverished. It was necessary to show two things: that philosophy had to occupy itself with the world in order to realize itself (to actualize itself, in Hegelian language) and that the world had to become philosophical, that is, rational, if this realization of philosophy were to occur. We can reconstruct briefly the steps in Marx's evolution in terms of this two-sided problem (whose two sides, philosophy and the world, themselves turned out to be dual by the time of Marx's "solution" to his dilemma in the economic critique in the *Grundrisse*).

There is first the critique of Bruno Bauer's proposed solution to the "Jewish question." Mere political emancipation does not suffice because, as seen in the contrast between the French and American Declarations of Rights and their reality, these rights become defenses of what has come since to be called possessive individualism. The reason for this inadequacy is that the societies that proclaimed these universal rights were still burdened by the legacy of feudalism; hence the universal rights in fact universalized a society based on inequality.[10] There needed to be a change in the social relations in civil society. As a result, Marx's "Introduction to a Critique of Hegel's *Philosophy of Right*," after showing how philosophy had to become worldly—coining now well known phrases such as "the critique of the weapons becomes the weapon of critique"—went on to discover the proletariat as "the nothing that can become everything," the "class that is not a class," which is thus the material basis of the world's becoming philosophical. (The proletariat is what Lukács and Western Marxism called the subject-object of history.) Two features of Marx's account need to be stressed. He insists that the proletariat is an "artificial formation" that differs from simply the poor or the oppressed, implying again that his immanent critique is concerned with dynamics, not statics. And he adds that there needs be a "lightning of thought" that strikes in this "naive soil of the people" to awaken its emancipatory possibilities. The first of these points suggests to Marx the need to turn to political economy; the second refers to what was later called class consciousness, which Marx analyzed first under the Hegelian category of "alienation."

The *Economic and Philosophical Manuscripts of 1844* can be seen as the development of these two insights. The first manuscript is Marx's initial attempt at understanding political economy. He wants to show how this "artificial formation" (the proletariat) comes into being and acquires legitimacy. Alienated labor is shown to be the basis of private property, which is in its turn the source of social division. The account is supplemented by the third manuscript, which develops what Marx calls "the greatness of Hegel's *Phenomenology*," namely, its insight into the creative role of labor. It thus appears that it is the labor process that produces in the proletariat the capacity to realize its own destiny—the equivalent of the "lightning of thought." The broader philosophical project is evident throughout the text, for example, in the discussions of "generic being" and in the insistence that "the science of nature becomes the science of man while the science of man becomes the science of nature." All these famous aphorisms are variants on the theme of alienation and its philosophical overcoming that will make the world philosophical. But this philosophical project now leads Marx beyond the realm of philosophy; he now has to do philosophy by other means.

Marx was not satisfied with the *Economic and Philosophical Manuscripts*, which remained unpublished. He and Engels then wrote *The German Ideology* (again unpublished). That massive tome develops, on the one hand, the philosophical-historical reasons that would explain the emergence and transcendence of capitalism. The problem with this theory, which is based on the primacy of material labor, is that the lightning of thought is replaced by a materialist assertion of historical necessity (which Marx would reaffirm in the preface to the 1859 *Toward a Critique of Political Economy*, a text that became canonical in the Leninist-Stalinist vulgate). On the other hand, *The German Ideology* contains other, more fruitful insights, for example, into the dialectic by which labor creates new needs that in turn create new types of labor on a progression that concretizes what Marx had called in 1844 "the greatness of Hegel's *Phenomenology*." But these insights disappear in the next canonical text: "Wage Labor and Capital" (1849), Marx's first major economic analysis.

Before Marx could work out his own dogmatic philosophy of history, history intervened. *Class Struggles in France* (1850) attempts to explain the 1848 revolution and its failure. However remarkable some of Marx's insights, what is striking is his attribution to the proletariat of a historical wisdom that prevents it—after the June days—from falsely intervening at the wrong historical moment. The proletariat remains present in the drama like the "specter" that Marx invoked at the outset of *The Communist Manifesto*. This is another case of Marx's nonfalsifiable historical vision. He applied the insight from "On the Jewish Question" according to which a mere political revolution was insufficient in order to make sense of the unexpected revolution that broke out in 1848, but he could not predict what would become the subject for analysis in his next major essay: the coup d'état of Louis Bonaparte in 1851, which put a final end to the hopes awakened in 1848. If *Class Struggles in France* denounced the illusion of politics, *The 18th Brumaire* (1852) was an account of the politics of illusion. Beneath the memorable rhetoric encapsulated in such phrases as "the first time is tragedy, the second time is farce" and "men make their history but they do not make it as they please" lay Marx's assumption of a historical necessity that would impose itself come what may. The statue of Napoleon would fall with the next economic crisis, concluded Marx optimistically. The politics of illusion and the illusion of politics would be dissipated by sober reality of the kind Marx had depicted in *The Communist Manifesto* as dissolving "all that is holy" and leaving the proletariat at a (Hegelian) *hic rhodus, hic salta* that would finally make the world philosophical as philosophy become worldly.

The political conclusion that Marx seems to have drawn from these historical events was to intensify the economic study that gave rise to the *Grundrisse* and *Capital*. But before integrating these economic analyses into the philosophical account, the third of Marx's historical essays on French politics should be mentioned. The Paris Commune is often seen by Marxists as the "finally discovered form" in which the class struggle can be brought to its conclusion. But Marx's argument is more ambiguous. It seems to be a praise of direct democracy. Yet Marx calls the Commune the "form" in which the class struggle can be fought out openly. This form—like that of the commodity that is analyzed at the outset of *Capital*, as I will suggest in a moment—could be interpreted from the perspective of a democratic politics. For Marx and the Marxists, however, it appeared to be a solution, not the condition of the possibility of a solution, because it seemed to represent the unity of philosophy and politics, reason and the world.

The same ambiguous relation between economic and political analyses is seen in Marx's account of the second stage of mature communism described in the 1875 *Critique of the Gotha Program*: Marx makes things too easy for himself when he claims that when the "springs" of wealth flow freely, the inequalities of bourgeois society will be overcome. He should have remembered his own account of the continual dialectical development of new needs in *The German Ideology*. Indeed, Marx ought to have known better since in this same *Critique* he denounced Lassalle's so-called iron law of wages by comparing its political claims to those of a slave who, when his fellows have finally rebelled, writes that "slavery must be abolished because the provisioning of slaves in the slave system cannot exceed a certain low minimum." This reflection suggests the need to look more closely at what can be called the idealism of Marx, for it seems to be a denial of the causal primacy of material economic conditions.

When one looks at the status of Marx's mature economic theory, it turns out to be not really economic at all. The labor theory of value makes sense only from a sociological standpoint—guided, however, by a philosophical quest. Why does volume 1 of *Capital* begin with the commodity form? After all, it was production that was central to the historical-materialist vision of *The German Ideology* and the work that followed it. The chapter in *Capital* that makes the transition from the analysis of the commodity form to an analysis of production contains the surprising comment that the exploitation of labor-power is not unjust (nor is it just: a class struggle will decide). This suggests that Marx is still operating in terms of immanent critique rather than seeking to formulate a positive science. Capitalist development is part of the process by which the world becomes more rational. As in *The German Ideology*, the proletarian selling his labor-power is freer than the serf. But how can he use that freedom? After extensive criticism of the capitalist abuse of the length and intensity of the working day to increase production of absolute surplus-value, Marx returns to the method of immanent critique in his explanation of what he calls relative surplus-value. He shows how cooperation, manufacture, and modern industry are increasingly productive stages of a mystifying alienation that gives the impression that capital's contribution justifies the benefits it draws from this advance in capitalist rationality. This inversion is simply a material form of the theological mystification that the young Marx had criticized in Bruno Bauer and the Young Hegelians. But the mystification here is real: capital is not just an alienating projection of the powers of man or an imagined deity; it is the reality of human alienation. The worker is reduced to a cog in a machine that, guided by the capitalist and applying science, increases productivity—in the words of the *Manifesto*—to "heights hitherto un-envisioned." Will there follow a dialectical *Aufhebung* through which the proletariat will reclaim the fruits of its increasingly rationalized labor? Where will it come from? Volume 1 of *Capital* (which I have just summarized) gives no answer; it concludes with a criticism of "so-called primitive accumulation." But why conclude with what, historically, was the starting point of capitalism? What happened to immanent critique? Why the discussion of the commodity form? Neither positive science nor historical analysis, *Capital* is Marx's attempt to do philosophy by other means.

The transition from volume 1, whose subtitle is *The Immediate Production Process of Capital*, to volume 2's account of the circulation of capital is explained in an unpublished manuscript entitled *The Results of the Immediate Production Process*. This missing link makes clear that Marx did not intend to explain economic production for its own sake; his concern is with the process of social *re*production. Marx's theory is not reducible to economics as a science of production.[11] The commodity that emerges from the capitalist production process is formally different from the commodities that entered it: it is a social—and capitalist—commodity; it must circulate and find its buyer. How this occurs is traced in the (quite boring) second volume of *Capital*. More interesting is its consequence in the third volume, which treats the process as a whole, including competition among capitalists. Here, after some 375 pages, we find the infamous "law of the tendency of the rate of profit to fall." But the presentation of this "law" is followed by another 500 pages that meander through landed and financial (or money) capital. What role do these play? Why does the third volume conclude with the incomplete chapter on classes? Why didn't Marx simply stop with the falling rate of profit? What is revolutionary about *Capital*? The answer to the last question, which is the key to the others, is quite simply that it is philosophy that, for Marx, is revolutionary. This conclusion is suggested as well in the well-known pages of the *Grundrisse* that still seem to be prophetic today.

To make a long story as short as possible:[12] Marx predicts that the growth of the forces of production will reach a point at which production based on exchange-value breaks down of its own accord (because of the huge increases in productivity resulting from the application of science that make the contribution of human labor, which is the basis of exchange-value, minimal). At that point, the

reduction of necessary labor time will make possible the free development of the individual. The measure of wealth will no longer be
labor time but disposable time. What is more, at this stage of productive development the product ceases to appear as the product of
an individual worker; its social character becomes evident. And at
that point the individual recognizes that the free time he now has
available to him in the new capitalism is not his own but that which
comes to him as a member of the collective social workforce. To put
it in rigorous Hegelian-Marxist terms: Two commodities face one
another, capital and labor. Each of them is in turn dual: each has a
use-value and an exchange-value, and these come into contradiction
with themselves. Capital can no longer function in terms of
exchange-values, nor can it properly develop the use-value of the
great productive forces it has created (since to do so would be to
break out of the capitalist mode of production based on the constant
increase of exchange-value). Labor on its side is no longer necessary
as exchange-value, and yet as use-value, in the new and clearly
socially interdependent forms of scientific production, its role is
reduced asymptotically. There are thus contradictions on both sides,
and so, as the English version of *Capital* has it, the "integument must
be burst asunder"—or, in a more Germanic formulation, *Aufgehoben*.

For the philosopher, these pages are sheer pleasure. For the political thinker, either they describe one of those utopias whose eternal
attractiveness—and ineffectiveness—I sketched earlier, or they are a
sign that the visionary who could foretell trends of capitalist social
(and not simply economic) development was at a loss as to what to
do about these trends. Indeed, at another point in the *Grundrisse*,
Marx criticizes Adam Smith for not understanding that labor must
be made attractive at the same time that it cannot be "mere fun,
mere amusement, as Fourier . . . conceives it."

But enough of Marx philology. There is no need to discuss the
harried question of whether Marx thought, ultimately, that freedom
was to be found in work or beyond work: he thought both and
couldn't make up his mind, even in the space of a single text. Let this
stand as the final demonstration that Marx was and remained a
philosopher and that this is indeed his virtue, so long as one doesn't
try to make his philosophy into what it cannot be (despite the pleas
of Adorno and the Frankfurt School): a politics.

## POLITICIZING MARXISM

Marx was too good a philosopher. After 1989 he needs to be turned into a political thinker. This could start, as I suggested previously, from his analysis of the Paris Commune as the "finally discovered form in which the class struggle could be pursued to its end." The first draft of *The Civil War in France* also contains the significant observation that all previous revolutions had only strengthened the state,[13] although the published text concludes from this only the need to destroy the old state. This neglects the possibility that the state could be reused for other ends, as suggested by Marx's claim that the Commune was the "form" in which class struggle could be fully developed. But rather than engage in more Marx philology, I want to propose a different approach to the question addressed here, beginning from the program developed in *The Communist Manifesto*.

At the time of the collapse of communism, I proposed that we had found ourselves finally freed from "two hundred years of error."[14] The year 1789 marked the advent of democracy as a political problem posed by the new social conditions created (or, in Marx's eyes, consecrated) by the French Revolution. The institutionalization of the rights of man presupposed the destruction of the traditional cosmos in which each person had his and her place, in which society was conceived of as a structured organism, and where politics were not society's concern (which is why Marx's unpublished 1843 critique of Hegel's theory of the state could mock the old regime as a "democracy of unfreedom" based on a "zoology"). Society did not then have the means to act on itself. The French Revolution inaugurated modern politics by creating the conditions for the possibility of democracy: the rights of the autonomous individual had to be coordinated with his coexistence with other individuals in a society that is able to determine for itself its vision of what political theory since Aristotle has called the "good life in the city." But democracy is not a solution; it is a problem, inseparably philosophical and political. After 1989, when its reified opposition to communism no longer made it into an unquestionable value, its problematic nature could and should again become manifest.

In this context, I am struck by the absence of "communism" from the central arguments that constitute the first, and most substantive, part of the *Manifesto*. Marx praises the revolutionary nature of capitalism—its revolutionizing of traditional society and constant revolutionizing of itself—and he stresses that it is at the same time producing its own grave diggers. The picture painted is similar to that in *Capital*, which of course is subtitled *A Critique of Political Economy* rather than something like "A Handbook for the Communist Future." But this poses the questions: What then is the famous "specter" invoked in the prefatory remarks to the *Manifesto*? How will it become flesh? What are its politics? Or does it simply obey structural necessities in becoming what it must become?

The "communist" as a political actor enters the argument only in the second part of the *Manifesto*. He is said "to have no interests separate and apart from those of the proletariat as a whole" and not to form "a separate party opposed to other working class parties." And of course communists, who represent universal justice, are also said not to "set up any [particular] sectarian principles of their own." What distinguishes the communist is that he is an internationalist and—more important—he represents "the interests of the movement as a whole." The ability to do this is not the result of "ideas or principles" but "merely express[es], in general terms, actual relations springing from an existing class struggle." This claim is politically seductive because of its philosophical sophistication.

This philosophical argument seems to me to be dangerous. It would be reformulated later, in Lukács's *History and Class Consciousness*, as the idea of "ascribed class consciousness," which became the basis of the "substitutionism" that justified Leninism and Stalinism (which claimed to act in the name of the "true" interests of the class, even when they acted against its immediate or conscious interests). Claude Lefort sees this communist militant as a new gestalt in political theory (although one might see him as a return of the idea of the "selfless servant" of Plato's philosopher-king). The hubris of the communist is breathtaking. He becomes a kind of materialist version of the Hegelian Secretary to the World Spirit. What is troubling here is not the claim that theory can pierce beneath appearances to get to their structural foundations; that is the presupposition of any theoretical argument. I am bothered more by the fact that the resulting communist politics is based on a denial of itself as political, of its responsibility for its theoretical claims and practical aims. There is no autonomous place for politics in this world historical theory; its goal is to transcend any particular politics . . . and to realize a philosophical project over the heads (or behind the backs) of the participants. Its justification lies in its claim to transcend their (alienated) self-consciousness in the name of the really real truth. It is politics as antipolitics.

The foundation of Marx's antipolitical politics had been laid already in the essay "On the Jewish Question," particularly in its critique of the Declaration of the Rights of Man and of the Citizen. The achievements of the French Revolution were devalued by being placed under under the rubric "bourgeois"; the political problems posed by the advent of the individual as a bearer of rights (which could be expanded, since these rights now had no transcendent foundation as they did in the old order) were translated to the economic sphere, which quickly replaced the never further defined "civil society" that Marx thought for a moment he could take over and adapt from Hegel's earlier analysis of it. The path to historical materialism was opened.

But Marx's argument can be said, paradoxically, to be itself bourgeois, typical of two hundred years of bourgeois domination. After all, it is the capitalists (or bourgeois) who stress the primacy of the economy and for whom labor is the source of value. No Greek or Christian could have said such a thing. Moreover, the bourgeoisie has never been unequivocally democratic; all institutional advances in democracy have come as it makes forced concessions to social movements. What characterizes bourgeois politics is rather its constant attempt to deny the autonomy of politics—an autonomy that is the precondition of democracy. Thus the invisible hand of classical liberal economics is based on a structure identical to that of Marx's philosophical antipolitics. The free market is supposed to do in its unconscious way what the planned communist society will do consciously. Does the difference make a difference? In both cases, politics is rejected, and responsibility and judgment are subordinated to supposed impersonal necessity.[15]

Rereading *The Communist Manifesto*, one wonders why Marx didn't notice this. The reason is suggested in its often-neglected third part, which reconstructs and denounces the antipolitical implications of the various utopian socialisms current at the time. Although Marx reconstructs their appearance and the progress that each represents—as stages leading to his own synthesis—he doesn't reflect on their antipolitical character. This neglect provides the occasion for reflecting on the issues that might be proposed by a New Political Manifesto that has become necessary now that 1989 has consigned Marx's philosophical vision to the world of utopia.

The first part of the *Manifesto* presented the self-revolutionizing, globally corrosive, yet creatively self-destructive capitalist production process and the forms of social relations that it at once produced and destroyed. But the *Manifesto* began with the promise to explain the "specter" that was threatening the established order in Europe. The philosophical-materialist interpretation of this claim implied that it was capitalism-as-dialectical, capitalism-as-pregnant-with-communism—rather than the particular or arbitrary political action of "the communists"—that is the self-negating principle of modern society. The problem with this interpretation is that it leaves no place for politics or political responsibility; it is antipolitical."The" revolution is the antithesis of politics. Its supposed necessity is explained structurally, leaving no room for autonomous political agency.

Could one, however, accept Marx's philosophical insight into the need to make use of both critique and science without seeking their dialectical unity as he did? Instead of identifying the "specter" with capitalism-as-dialectical-self-overcoming-leading-to-the-communist-synthesis-of-the-world-as-philosophical-and-philosophy-as-worldly, why not analyze the social relations and political problems of democracy as what was—and is still—haunting Europe? The self-revolutionary nature of capitalism would be replaced by the emergence and—with Hannah Arendt—constant (possibility of the) reemergence of democratic demands.[16] Unlike capitalism-as-dialectical, such a democracy is not a thing or subject that moves history, like Hegel's Spirit or Reason, according to an immanent logic particular to it. As I have noted, the rights that make democracy possible have no external guarantee or foundation; their existence cannot be justified philosophically. They depend on politics, which, as democratic and autonomous, both presupposes these rights and must reaffirm them constantly. This paradoxical circularity—as opposed to the dialectical unity sought by Marx's philosophy—means that members of even an incomplete democratic society do have something to lose beside "their chains."[17]

The paradoxical political structure of democracy, whose forward march—but whose defeats and disappointments—would be cataloged in the first part of a New Political Manifesto, has implications for the style in which it would be written. This would affect the second stage of the argument. It would be self-critical and dialogical because it cannot repeat Marx's appeal to historical necessity but must accept responsibility for its judgments as its own.[18] Hence the equivalent of Marx's "communist"—who never identifies himself as the author of the *Manifesto* but who seems rather to be a secretary taking dictation from History—would be the political critic who self-consciously assumes that most philosophical of rights: the right to be wrong, which is the precondition for thinking at all. This right to be wrong is of course not an invitation to error and categorically not a justification of error. But it does imply a certain caution about truth claims. Joining Marx's insight into the commodity form with Max Weber's more general analysis of the antinomic structure of modern rationality,[19] the democratic critic cannot operate with the goal of producing a unified society in which the particularity of politics and personal interest is forever made impossible. That is the lesson of the revolutions of 1989. But what then is the foundation for a democratic critique?

The third part of a New Political Manifesto would part company with Marx's attempt to show that all previous doctrines lead toward and are contained in his theory. Instead, it would analyze the history of two hundred years of error—that is, of antipolitics—in the form of free markets, planned economies, nationalist identity politics or social-democratic technocracies, and legalistic codifications or appeals to judicial intervention to overcome political impasses. This analysis would not interpret these antipolitical choices as determined by an economic mode of production. It would follow, for example, suggestions from Polanyi's *The Great Transformation* but also numerous hints in Marx's *Grundrisse* to show how the different forms of antipolitics are in reality the results of implicit political choices, of actions (or omissions) that may not fall into the domain formally called "politics" but affect the relations of individuals to one another and to society as a whole.[20] This implies that political critique of social injustice—rather than economic criticism of exploitation—is the foundation of democratic politics. It does not mean that politics (even democratic politics) is an end in itself. A

New Political Manifesto would praise democracy as Tocqueville praised it, "not for what it is but for what it leads people to do [*ce qu'elle fait faire*]."[21] In this way, political critique is not restricted to the sphere that political science defines as politics. Rather, it is concerned with the foundation of social relations themselves.[22]

The New Political Manifesto would reject Marx's goal of finally realizing the conquests inaugurated by the French Revolution by adding a social dimension to the merely formal political rights won in 1789. Democracy is not a set of formal institutions that must acquire a social content in order to be realized; that was Marx's initial error when he first criticized democracy in "On the Jewish Question." That path leads to the creation of what the former Soviet empire labeled "democratic republics." The lesson of 1989 is that such democratic republics—as well as the dream of direct democracy—are simply another manifestation of the antipolitical attempt to avoid facing up to the challenge of modern democracy. Based on the protection of individual rights while seeking at the same time and for just that reason the common good, democracy is a problem, and democratic politics consists in maintaining that problem, not in solving it once and for all. Only under such conditions can the struggle against forms of injustice—which are not limited to the economic sphere—have hopes for success. Capitalism from this perspective is just another antipolitical form of politics; criticism of it is based not on the "chains" it imposes but rather on the responsible freedom it denies as its logic imposes itself.[23] But is such denunciation sufficient to delineate a politics, which was, after all, the achievement of the historical materialism deduced from *The Communist Manifesto*? It is that achievement, however, that is put into question by the revolutions of 1989.

Marx's political philosophy was based on the immanent philosophical-dialectical critique of capitalist social relations. After the end of the totalitarian claim to realize democracy, it is an immanent critique of democracy, not of capitalism, that is now on the agenda. But that critique cannot make the philosophical-dialectical claim that Lukács, correctly, attributed to Marx, because the challenge of democracy is not based on the emergence of a new subject of world history. Democratic citizens must assume responsibility for their political choices, including the choice not to seek to make a revolution and—what comes down to the same thing—the choice not to seek to realize democracy because that is, paradoxically, the only way in which democracy can be preserved. By abandoning the kind of totalizing philosophy that motivated Marx, the New Political Manifesto could salvage a part of the Marxian legacy by showing the need to make the transition from philosophy to politics and, from there, to rediscover the challenge of political philosophy.

# CHAPTER 2

# Can French Intellectuals Escape Marxism?

Although the title of this chapter poses a question, and its analysis will be descriptive, the conclusion is prescriptive. I will offer an argument that explains historically, sociologically, and philosophically the attraction of Marxism in France, the intellectual options that choice entails for those whom I broadly term "communist" (following Marx's own description in *The Communist Manifesto*), and the strength and weaknesses of their position.[1] Finally, I will point to some indices of the emergence of another intellectual style, one that I find more attractive and have labeled elsewhere a "politics of judgment,"[2] to which I will return later in this volume. Although I begin with a comparison of the American and French intellectual, I am not concerned here with the American case, in part because the left/right split in the United States has been supplanted by debates between the center and the right and in part because the intellectual in American political life has been marginalized as a result of the cultural effects of the cold war. I present my arguments in the form of eleven theses—the parody on Marx's *Theses on Feuerbach* is of course intended. Unintended but unavoidable is the technique so well applied by old-style Marxist intellectuals: the amalgam. I am painting a group portrait, not referring to specific cases, which nonetheless fit more or less well the big picture described here. My definition of that creature called "the intellectual" appears in the sixth thesis, with reference to Emile Durkheim's interpretation of the Dreyfus affair.

1. *French and Americans as intellectuals represent two styles: one moral, one political.* In the United States, as in France, the intellectual is a specialist of the universal in a double sense: (a) concerned with everything; and (b) claiming universal validity for his or her arguments. But in the United States the intellectual tends to be a moralist (not a technocrat or pragmatist, as is sometimes claimed, for in either of those cases universal relevance is absent). Moreover, in the United States the intellectual not only tends to stand in opposition to the powers that be but also—and this is a uniquely American phenomenon—stands opposed to the public, from whom she or he does not expect immediate understanding or support. In this the intellectual may be taxed as being elitist and in fact may be—consciously or not. Yet at the same time the American intellectual tends also to be a populist, believing that people are basically moral and susceptible to appeals to their "better angels." Such populism, however, is not a politics but a morality disguised as politics. As a result, even when intervening in so-called political matters, the American intellectual is not a political actor and contributes little or nothing to the understanding of everyday politics. (Of course, exceptions leap to mind, but aside from lawyers, whose role was noted already by Tocqueville, the only significant social category that is excluded is the social scientist, whose brief moment in the sun during the Great Society was perhaps irreparably harmed by excessive promises and inadequate delivery, for example, in the misnamed War on Poverty.)

In contrast, the French intellectual is a political animal, and even his moral interventions contribute to defining the political by directing the framework of debate. Further, the French intellectual can be on the right as well as on the left, whereas the American intellectual has tended to stand on the left wing of the political spectrum. (When American intellectuals appear on the right, as did the neoconservatives in the 1980s, this is said to be less the result of a change in *their* values than a reaction to the antics of the left, which is accused of betraying *its* values.) This political positioning is due to the relation of intellectuals to the revolutionary traditions that underlie the political cultures of the two countries. These traditions explain not only the moralism of American intellectuals but also the reasons they have been only rarely tempted by the Marxism that until recently was a looming presence in French politics. Americans are not inherently more moral than the French. They are the products of a different history (see, e.g., chap. 10, "Intersecting Trajectories of Republicanism in France and the United States").

2. *Historical changes may have made the French intellectual obsolete.* After World War II, not only was antifascism de rigeur, but the inglorious demise of the Third Republic and the shameful Vichy regime discredited even more moderate political orientations, leaving only the left standing tall. The credibility of socialism and communism eroded over the years, but Marxism seemed untouched by this decline; as a theory, it could be exempted from the historical accidents that distorted its practical realization. But after the seemingly incomprehensible and certainly unexpected collapse of the East European sister states, followed by the demise of the Soviet Union in 1991, the reality of the failed experiment could no longer be denied. The question is, why had so many been blinded for so long? François Furet tried to suggest an answer in his suggestive study *Le passé d'une illusion.*[3] But his allusion to Freud's psychoanalytic account of the roots of religious belief does not take account of the reality of the illusion, which was not simply the product of arbitrary faith. And in any case the decline of Marxist beliefs had clearly affected the French intellectual community some fifteen years before the fall of communism, when Solzhenitsyn's *Gulag Archipelago* appeared. It was at this time that French political thinkers discovered liberalism, while the philosophers seized on the idea of human rights. The philosophers, always the leading group in France, sought to give their new conceptual orientation a political twist, demanding a moralization, particularly of international politics, that contrasted with their previous distrust of the motives of state actors. The political liberals also turned to ethics, but their contribution was apparently more modest, challenging the state's administrative power in the name of citizen participation in controversial decisions.

These changes have led to a surprising number of translations of apparently quite technical American philosophical works, which are nonetheless read in a French political context. The quality of this reception varies (although the vitality and engagement of the recent work of Paul Ricoeur, who returned to France after many years teaching in the United States, should be noted). More significant is the persistence of a political interpretation of the new French concern with ethics. This can take the extreme form that some criticize as "rights-of-man-ism," whose absolutism in its new cause may be simply a reformulation of the absolutism that refused to allow the "accidental" forms of totalitarianism to infect faith in Marxism. Such extremes, whether or not they are typical, can often point to analytically fruitful paths of inquiry.

3. *The French intellectual is not Marxist; French culture is*. Americans, particularly those who came of age during the heyday of the new left, tend to think of French intellectuals as functioning within and developing the legacy of Marx. In fact, however, it is hard to think of important French contributions to Marxism. Some would say this is due to the pressure for conformity exercised by the Communist Party, which drove, for example, Henri Lefèbvre from its ranks while taming a former surrealist like Louis Aragon. The one systematic attempt to develop the philosophical bases of Marxism, Sartre's *Critique de la raison dialectique*, had little influence, and its promised second volume was published posthumously (as the engaged author toyed with Maoist activism).[4] The other serious philosophical confrontation with Marx, in the pages of the then little known journal *Socialisme ou Barbarie*, led its leading figures, Cornelius Castoriadis and Claude Lefort, to a severe critique of Marx's premises and to the elaboration of their own political theories, whose principal concern was the radical nature of the democratic demands that Marx neglected. The most systematic study of Marx remains *La pensée de Karl Marx*, published first in 1957 by the Jesuit Jean-Yves Calvez, who was the leader in the Catholic-Communist dialogue of the times. Other confrontations with Marx, such as Derrida's post-totalitarian *Specters of Marx*, reflect more the idiosyncrasies of their authors, although Michel Henry's phenomenological rereading stands out, as does Jean Baudrillard's *The System of Objects* (written before the author developed his unique persona). This is not simply a historical irony; it points to the way Marx is present among French intellectuals.

If Marxian theory is not a major contributor to French philosophical life, Marxism even today plays a central role in its intellectual culture. The American is often surprised by the almost casual allusions to concepts such as class struggle, bourgeois domination, or capitalist exploitation that remain background presuppositions apparently in no need of elaboration. The reason for this influence lies partially in French history (to which I return in chap. 9, "The Burden of French History") and partially in the fact that Marx's most accessible and most political writings concerned French history.[5] This deeply political understanding of their own culture explains French mockery (and mock horror) of the invidious "political correctness" by which Americans tend to distinguish themselves: the French assume they have bigger fish to fry, their republican universalism standing in sharp contrast to American democratic particularism. The same overheated stress on the political may explain as well the relative social underdevelopment of French feminism (although the recent law insisting on parity of male and female candidates for office may introduce social change through political means). But there is a positive side to this political orientation: its presence throughout society explains the ability of French intellectuals to get a public hearing for their criticisms—since the general assumptions of Marxism, if not the theory of Marx, have seeped into the soil of French culture. As opposed to their American counterparts, French critics are not condemned to moral appeals from the wilderness.

4. *The French intellectual illustrates Marx's presuppositions.* The metaphor of the "soil of French culture" alludes to a passage in which the young Marx, after discovering the revolutionary nature of the proletariat (in the 1843 "A Contribution to the Critique of Hegel's *Philosophy of Right*. Introduction"), insists that the "the lightning of thought" must strike "this naive [proletarian] soil of the people" for human emancipation to be realized. This "lightning of thought" would be brought, Marx argues in *The Communist Manifesto*, by the communist armed with an understanding of the necessary course of world history. This communist, as Claude Lefort has argued, represents a new gestalt in political history, a figure who is paradoxically both within history and yet able to rise above it and account for its inevitable progress.[6] The communist assumes that radical potential is constantly present, needing only the spark of consciousness to be awakened. American left-wing intellectuals since the 1960s have tried to operate on this assumption, first seeking to revive (or recover) a forgotten tradition of working-class struggle, then turning to ethnic histories to stake out a wider terrain,

and finally broadening their reach to the field of "culture" in order to find within society the agent capable of transforming it. Alas, the results have been only the development of academic specialties (e.g., cultural studies) whose political translation is an identity politics that evokes little response in the wider public and whose results are only a disguised and cheapened form of interest politics.[7] Some French intellectuals make similar presuppositions, a legacy of Marxism found in the positioning of sociologists like Pierre Bourdieu and those who join him in supporting what they take to be a "social movement" that is finally manifesting itself in spontaneous surges like the strikes of 1995.[8] Most, however, do not. Yet their interventions resonate with the public in a way that makes the American jealous . . . and curious.

In this context, it is useful to recall the French intellectual who in the 1960s, while remaining a faithful member of the Communist Party, did introduce a philosophical reflection on Marx: Louis Althusser. Althusser's basic intuition was expressed in his insistence that a so-called epistemological rupture (*coupure épistémologique*) separates the "humanism" of the young Marx, which finds its expression in the still idealist notion of "alienation," from the "scientific" Marx of the mature economic work, which discovers a "new continent" on which to establish that communism of the future. Althusser's contribution belonged to the general cultural movement through which the purported science of structuralism, the analysis of processes-without-a-subject, conquered French intellectual life by means of a paradoxical process of self-denial. The structuralist intellectual rejected the possibility of conscious political intervention to bring about social change while at the same time, and on the same basis, grossly inflating that same role, which was now seen as safe in the hands of the scientist. As in the case of Marx's communist, the intellectual was thus placed at once inside and outside of history. The resulting position is apparently modest in its denial of so-called bourgeois subjectivity, but in fact it expresses the greatest hubris of all: the claim to knowledge of historical necessity.

There was something undeniably appealing about this stance; the ambitions of the teach-in, that political exercise invented by contemporary American intellectuals trying to face up to the Vietnam War, seemed modest in comparison with the certainties of structuralism. It is no accident—as the Marxists like to put it—that the structuralist intellectual was at home in the world of the communist. But it was also not surprising that after May 1968 many of Althusser's young disciples adopted the voluntarism of Maoist politics: the step from a vision of processes without a subject to the primacy of radical will demanded only an inversion of values, not a political analysis.

5. *The French intellectual tradition is broader than its communist deformation.* The hubris of the communist entails a denial of personal responsibility (which explains the political dishonesty and lack of principle that have marked that tradition, which purports to take into account only objective necessity). But the French intellectual tradition—dating at least to Voltaire's "écrasez l'infâme," prolonged in the nineteenth century by Zola's "J'accuse," and continued in the twentieth century by Péguy, Simone Weil, and even at times Sartre and Beauvoir—did accept moral responsibility. The typical intellectual intervention was not the scientific analysis but the petition, the pamphlet, the open letter; it was literary (in the tradition of the *moralistes*) rather than technical or pragmatic. But this intellectual tradition had its own difficulty in linking moral critique to political responsibility. Tocqueville's analysis of the French Revolution memorably criticized the philosophes for not understanding the practical imperatives that a government must face; their moralism made impossible the successful closure of the process begun in 1789. More recently, Reinhart Koselleck's *Kritik und Krise* analyzed the intellectual's role in the formation of public opinion before the French Revolution. He argued that the basis of the power of intellectual critique was the fact that its moralism expressed implicitly a political program that either dared not speak in its own name or was unaware of its own political premises. As a result, the old political order could not combat it, yet when it came to power it was unable to give itself stable institutional form. A similar point is made by François Furet's analysis of the contribution of Augustin Cochin to understanding the political dynamics of the French Revolution.[9] What is significant in the present context, however, is that despite the accuracy of this criticism the French intellectual's moral intervention did find a public and political echo in a way that similar action by the American does not (or does only exceptionally). An intellectual tradition had come to exist in France, rooted in its "soil." The question is: Why? What makes the French intellectual a public intellectual?

6. *The French intellectual is a social creation.* The intellectual emerges as a social type only when there exists a public receptive to his words. Emile Durkheim's remarkable "Individualism and the Intellectuals" illustrates the point.[10] The Dreyfusards were accused of questioning the authority on which the political unity of the nation depended; their insistence on the sole authority of reason was said to ignore the weight of traditional institutions (such as the army) that were needed to hold in check the forces of modern individualism. Durkheim's reply stressed not only this attitude's philosophical roots in Rousseau and Kant but also its foundation in the Declaration of the Rights of Man and of the Citizen and in the moral catechism of the Third Republic. But he went further. Individualism is the religion of man "in the ritual sense of the word"; it is sacred; and it must be defended in the same way that a believer reacts to the profanation of an idol. Such individualism admittedly puts "la personne humaine" above the state and allows no compromise with its practical claims. But this does not mean that the rights of the collectivity are ignored, in theory or in practice. Kant's defense of the autonomy of reason produced not only Fichte, who was already "quite impregnated with socialism," but also Hegel, who produced Marx; and Rousseau's individualism was complemented by a "authoritarian conception of society" that led to the French Revolution, which was "above all a great moment of national concentration." In short, for the philosopher of the "social fact," the moments of individualism and social solidarity are mutually reinforcing poles, and the analyst of the social division of labor warns that an attempt to restrain the development of individualism would only reintroduce conformism, which is no pillar of national strength.[11] The intervention of the intellectuals in the Dreyfus affair cannot be explained simply by their sympathy for the victim, continues Durkheim; nor does it result from their fear that they might be treated in an equally unjust manner. Turning the tables on his traditionalist and nationalist opponents, Durkheim insists that the social basis of the "religion of the individual" means that if such affronts to the individual are unpunished, the very existence of the nation is threatened. Since what is shared by modern France is the religion of the rights of man, the violation of Dreyfus's rights is a threat to the community, while their defense by the intellectuals reaffirms the glue that binds together a society founded on the ideas introduced to the world in 1789. On this, no compromise is possible.

Despite his stress on the social roots of modern individualism, Durkheim concludes on a note of political engagement whose similarity to that of Marx and the communist is striking. The individualism of the eighteenth century has to be brought up to date, he insists. At its origins, it was only negative, a liberation from external political bonds. This emancipation brought freedom to think, write, and vote, but such political freedom is a means, not an end; its value depends on how it is used. With the foundation of the Third Republic, says Durkheim, new barriers fell; but his generation did not know how to use its freedom, which it turned against its fellow citizens to reinforce social division. Durkheim is not advocating that the clash of interests be ignored; the sociological intellectual wants to use his new freedom to ameliorate a social machine that is "still so harsh on individuals," while seeking to realize what Durkheim's use of quotation marks clearly recognizes as Marx's principle of " 'to each according to his labor.' " This would be the true realization of the individualism inaugurated in 1789, organizing economic life and introducing greater justice into contractual relations. This achievement is not preordained, as in Marx; it is the result of political intervention—which is made necessary by social conditions. The present crisis, Durkheim affirms, has "returned to us a taste for action." Our enemies are strong only because we are weak, but they are only "men of letters seduced by an interesting theme" that is but an abstraction that will not permit them to hold back the masses "if we know how to act." Although he does not go on to explain "how to act," one can assume that Durkheim's new social science would be the source of the needed advice. But that new science itself has not only social roots; its discovery that individualism is the principle that binds together modern society implies that the freedom that permits the intellectual to "act" has its own roots in a political phenomenon: the French Revolution.

7. *The uniqueness of the French Revolution is its incompleteness.* François Furet's final reflections on the uniqueness of the French Revolution, published posthumously,[12] underline the fact that this revolution had to confront a question that neither the Glorious Revolution in England nor its American successor had faced: the religious question. France had not had a Reformation; church and state were bound in a theologico-political unity that neither side could break. Unable to invent a satisfactory political solution, the French

made politics itself into a religion. The explanation of this claim provides a pessimistic political complement to Durkheim's sociological optimism founded in the modern religion of the individual. For Furet, the revolution presented an "a-religious character" because "the promise of a good society is no longer written in sacred texts, as in the English case, or in a harmony of the political and the religious, as in the American example, but depends only on the development of history." The philosophes were not only individualists and intellectuals; they were the most radically antireligious participants in the European Enlightenment, and the revolution continued their work, despoiling that pillar of the ancien régime, the Catholic church. But it was then forced to confront "for the first time all of the dimensions of the dilemma of modern liberalism, which supposes that social and political life no longer entails any common belief shared by the citizenry since each citizen is the master of what are considered to be only his 'opinions.' No revolution prior to the French had to face this collective spiritual deficit, which would become the common destiny of modern societies." Rather than follow the recommendations of the optimistic sociologist, the pessimistic critic of communism as an illusion (in *Le passé d'une illusion*) draws together his analysis of our century with his life work on the political nature and legacy of the French Revolution: "From this point of view, Voltairean deism, parliamentary Jansenism, the Savoyard vicar, the natural religion of the physiocrats, the esoterism of the Masons are all of a piece: they consecrate political expectations more than they form collective beliefs." Indeed, Furet returns (implicitly) to his own past as a Communist who left the party after 1956 when he concludes by admitting the accuracy of Marx's critique of the French "illusion du politique." But the fact that the political goals sought by the revolution were illusory does not mean that they are not effective in producing real political action. Their illusory nature does, however, mean that the political action is condemned to fail—and condemned also to be taken up again, over and over.

8. *Denial of the uniqueness of the French Revolution leads to the emergence of the communist as intellectual.* Furet's analysis shows that the revolution was condemned to failure. But this failure—and the repeated attempts to realize the revolution's promise—are the basis of what is known as "French exceptionalism." This unique history

created the conditions for the emergence of the critical intellectual; it made him—and later her—part of the fabric of modern French history. In effect, if present conditions do not correspond to the universality of the revolutionary republican vision, criticism becomes a republican duty, and the critic does not stand outside society but claims only to express what is "in itself" or implicitly already present in the fabric of that historical society. This political claim has a similar structure to the social claim of the communist. The painful ethical decision faced by the American intellectual who must decide to stand up for right and rights even against the majority does not trouble the intellectual heirs to the French Revolution. (This is no doubt one reason why ethical theory—as opposed to the catechism of republican morality—was little developed in France.) What is more, the public to which the intellectual addresses his criticism was formed by the same self-critical tradition and is therefore receptive to the critique. The same historical structure explains why right-wing political intellectuals could also flourish in France; they stood at the other pole of the debate, putting religious or nationalist values where the republicans stood on their own promise of individual rights.

The failure to reflect ethically on the republican morality presupposed by the critical intellectual led to a denial of the uniqueness of French political culture, which explains the emergence of the communist, who claims to represent the necessary development of world history. There are both logical and historical grounds for this shift in orientation. Logically, the critic had to presuppose that the revolutionary project was realizable; otherwise, the critical mission made no sense, and there was no reason to expect that the message would be received by public opinion. Historically, a transference of the republican faith to the Russian Revolution of 1917 made that event appear—despite what some came to admit were its "deformations"—to be the continuation of the republican project. There is no need to rehearse here the historical basis on which this belief was edified, but precisely because it was edifying, because it satisfied the essentially religious nature of the French "politics of illusion," it retained its power over the imagination of generations.[13] During the interwar years, left and right could both criticize a so-called bourgeois republic that had bled France during the long war from 1914 to 1918 and then lacked the strength to rebuild it at its close. After

1945 intellectuals of the left supported the party of the working class, whose resistance to Fascism supported its claim to be the rightful heir of the republican revolution. Anticolonial agitation made the mental gymnastics more difficult during France's Vietnam and then Algerian wars, but anti-imperialism could claim that the French Empire, like that of Bonaparte, was a betrayal of the revolutionary legacy (although others could claim the opposite and compare Napoleon's failures to Stalin's successful extension of the Soviet imperium). When the invasion of Hungary drove many from the Communist ranks in 1956 and the "fraternal" intervention in Czechoslovakia in 1968 drove out still more, most continued to consider themselves part of the original project, sometimes rebaptized as "Euro-Communism" or even the "Third Way."

9. *The "service public" is the expression of the uniqueness of the French Revolution.* At the end of his essay, Furet argues that the Third Republic sought "an end to the revolution marked, or at least promised, by a new sacral power—but a secular [*laïque*] power—because the instructor had replaced the priest." This shift signifies also that the nature of the intellectual has changed. How does the primary school teacher become a sort of intellectual? What kind of intellectual has emerged here? His—and only later her—task was to carry the civilizing mission of the republic to the countryside, realizing its universal message. Following Tocqueville, Furet stresses the religious element that animates this secular politics: "It is the universalism of 'civilization,' faith in progress, the emancipation of the human species." Belief in this secular trinity endures today; it underlies worries about threats from the European Union and the Euro, and it explains the masses who went to the streets in December 1995 to protest the government's attempt to reform an antiquated and indebted social security system. Paul Thibaud, the former editor-in-chief of *Esprit*, draws the implications of this secular trinity in an important essay:

> The French public service is a sentiment, or even a belief, which unites three attitudes or orientations: the spirit of the Enlightenment that inspires technicians who seek to demonstrate progress and bring it to the people by innovative activities; the desire of politicians to have access to the means to intervene in society, particularly in projects of urban planning and modernization; and a quasi-liberal mode of working that is

regulated by fixed procedures that are not dependent on the whims of petty bosses, an illustration of the value of autonomy that is treasured by the *Homo republicanus* who made public service a national ideal.

Thibaud's replacement of the third term, the "emancipation of the human species," by "a quasi-liberal mode of working" announces the transformation of the *Homo republicanus* into the modern liberal individualist. It is thus no surprise that Thibaud concludes that the republican synthesis has come to an end; that is why his essay is titled "Réapprendre à se gouverner" (The need to relearn self-government).[14]

10. *The role of the intellectual as public servant has become problematic.* The inherited notion of the service public was not incompatible with the self-conception of the communist as intellectual. The inherent goodness of the gift of civilization brought to those who have been deprived of it cannot be put into question; it participates in a necessary progress whose intellectual origin lies with the antireligious Enlightenment and whose political realization began in 1789. This intellectual project is a "public service" whose messengers stand, modestly, in the service of the public, which is expected to recognize in them its own needs. Denouncing its enemies, articulating its nascent but inchoate demands, refusing to compromise with injustice, this "public servant" has been derided as the "intellectuel pétitionnaire" who claims to lend voice to the voiceless. At its best, public service is a noble calling, an admirable vocation, a form of Weber's ethics of conviction. This allusion to Weber suggests, however, an implicit criticism: the intellectual abandons the ethics of responsibility. But Weber (whom the French have only recently come to know, in large part thanks to Raymond Aron) knew that the ethics of responsibility is burdened with its own one-sidedness. The question of responsibility has to be formulated differently for this case. What is striking is that there is no connection between the intellectual's work (*oeuvre*) and the work (*travail*) of the intellectual.[15] The importance of this distinction becomes clear in the second interpretation of the intellectual as public servant. In this case, the universality signified by the collective category "public" is challenged; the dual nature of the intellectual (whom my first thesis defines as concerned with everything while claiming universality for his judgments) becomes truly ambiguous. The public servant has the

task of serving the Republic, whose identity with the public has become problematic.

The critique of totalitarianism that belatedly seized French intellectual life with the translation of Solzhenitsyn's *Gulag Archipelago* (in 1974) led some to rediscover the importance of the ethical reflection that appeared unimportant to the republican political project (these were the so-called new philosophers, although one could doubt their newness as well as the naive simplicity of their philosophy); others were led to reexamine the problematic nature of modern democracy (as was the case for *Esprit* and the more liberal *Commentaire*, founded by Raymond Aron). Both styles of reflection of course could appeal to the French Revolution, whose Declaration of the Rights of Man had declared also the rights of the citizen without worrying about their compatibility. While the reexamination of the roots of democracy has been more important (since the new philosophers' tended more toward moral exhortation than political analysis), its significance lies in the quest for a philosophical foundation for political analysis. Returning to the classic Greek tradition, democracy is interpreted as a regime, a set of individual and social relations united by the world of meaning that attaches to them.[16] The idea that meanings are not inherent in things shatters the pretension of any positivism (including that of historical materialism) and opens to criticism all aspects of human life, public as well as private, suggesting the possibility (and necessity) of uniting the ethical, liberal, and republican dimensions of political life. The foundation of intellectual critique is no longer a public that is presumed to be waiting for the Word that enlightens and thereby liberates. Whereas Furet's politics-as-secular-religion was condemned to illusion, democratic politics—which refuses traditional religious transcendence and presupposes a Reformation—is liberated by this supposed illusion, that is, by its own impossible but always renewed self-affirmation. In this way, the modern individual whom Thibaud rightly saw replacing the classical *Homo republicanus* acquires the role of the critical individual stressed by Durkheim's sociology. If the intellectual is to serve that individual, he or she can only do so by strengthening individuality, not by acting in the place or name of this or that individual or category of individuals.

11. *The intellectuals have tried to change the world; the point, however, is to interpret it.* The old French intellectual whom I contrasted at the

outset to his and now her American cousin will survive as long as the communist interpretation of the legacy of the French Revolution remains alive. Its paradoxical foundation is its modest (!) assumption that it is only giving voice or bringing to consciousness what is already dormant in the soil of history. This means that its professed goal of changing the world is self-contradictory, since it is in fact only making explicit what was implicit in existing society. Its politics is an antipolitics: a refusal of responsibility and the expression of an inability to live with that other legacy of the French Revolution—the indeterminacy of democratic politics, which must be constantly interpreted anew and can never be finally fixed or repaired. Responsibility is the axial category for the intellectual today; judgment rather than the expression of revealed truth is its manifestation. To interpret the world is first of all to put it into question, to doubt its fixedness and solidity, to go beyond its appearing forms. This implies acceptance of the possibility of error—more, the affirmation of the right to err and the need to confront others in public debate. This has not been the traditional stance of the French intellectual. But in the world of modern individualist democracy, it is the only practice open to the intellectual—that is, to the critical intellectual who is not content with the world as it is.

Whether globalization will make national boundaries and traditions irrelevant in the long run may be an empirical question. The process after all was analyzed more than a century ago by Marx, who saw it as the precondition for the (communist) realization of the French Revolution. That Marx's French followers continue to hold on to their inherited national mission shows only that their Marxism lacks the imaginative courage and capacity for judgment that makes reading Marx still rewarding even while the work of his French adepts has been quietly left—like Marx's own *German Ideology*—to "the gnawing criticism of the mice" (as Marx put it in the autobiographical sketch that he published in the 1859 preface to "Toward a Critique of Political Economy"). The certainty that the world needs to be changed has led to an inability to interpret it that condemns the self-declared revolutionary's political project to vanity precisely because of its supposed modernity.

CHAPTER 3

# The Frankfurt School and the Transformation of Critical Theory into Cultural Theory

The appeal of the Frankfurt School's critical theory to a young leftist of the late 1960s was based on a paradox expressed in the practice of both critical theory and the leftist. On the one hand, modern capitalist society seemed able to co-opt protest by integrating it into the dynamics of competitive business, creating a demand for the newest, most advanced, and most risqué products (a trend that continues today as cultural rebellion has became the motor of consumer society). On the other hand, that society was characterized by a spirit of revolt against its "one-dimensional" reduction of all use-values to their economic exchange-value that devalued politics and consecrated the tenets of liberalism (a trend that continues in the form of the reaction against globalization). In this context, a legacy from the past called "critical theory" appeared as a kind of guideline that pointed beyond the poles of integration or nihilism. This was all the more persuasive because established theory in those days had forgotten its past; its pragmatism led it to fight the War on Poverty without looking beneath its surface manifestations to see the embedded roots that made the metaphor of war a disguise for political vanity. Critical theory, a politics of theory and an appeal to the history of theory rather than to real history, seemed to offer an alternative that the leftist could seize. This choice was based on a paradox that the young leftist did not see. Its premise was that modern and capitalist society is impervious to external interventions that seek to change it; theory was the only legitimate practice in such a situation, and politics then became the politics of theory. That meant that in making this choice the left would necessarily cut itself off from the popular base on which political success depended. Such was the price, and paradox, of radical politics.

Frankfurt School critical theory fit perfectly into this situation. It was radical in its very modesty. It sought to formulate the kind of immanent critique that Horkheimer and Marcuse had proposed as the alternative to the contemplative and static perspective of traditional theory.[1] The goal was to demystify a reified or alienated society whose institutions are separated from the lived experience on which they nonetheless depend. This type of immanent critique assumed that theory had practical import when it could uncover and point to—and thus liberate by making self-aware—the emancipatory potential that is hidden or frozen in the external frame of a mindless machinery. Immanent critique in this sense was not far from the Enlightenment tradition typified by Kant's imperative to "free oneself from a *self-incurred* immaturity."[2] But to be effective in the postwar climate, such a political critical theory would have had to pay as much attention to the logic of the political as the critical philosophers paid in 1937 to the logic of the concept. What kind of liberation could come from philosophical self-awareness? The basis of the turn to critical theory was the instinctive rejection (or even repulsion) of the actual political system. Liberation became an end in itself, and by a short-cut that would prove costly critical theory itself came to stand for or to replace politics. *The politics of theory replaced the theory of politics*. This gesture was justified by the famous aphorism that forms the first sentence of Adorno's *Negative Dialectics*: "Philosophy, which once seemed overtaken, remains alive because the moment of its realization was missed."[3] Today, the pendulum finally has swung so far that the politics of (critical) theory has become the aesthetics of postmodernism. The critical political project of the Frankfurt School has disappeared. Ironically, its moment too was missed.

By the 1980s, long after the new left was itself only an object of study if not a myth called "'68," critical theory was defined in the university as the province of literary—or, more broadly, cultural—theory. This shift was not simply the result of campus politics or bureaucratic convenience (although these were also involved). The theoretical premises of the old Marxist critical theorists lent themselves to the transformation; co-optation was not imposed on them by malicious forces (such as their old enemy, the logic of capitalist reification). Their paradoxical but self-defined revolutionary politics was based on a desire to overcome politics, to avoid being contaminated by interest so that pure goals would not be realized by compromised means. The critical theorists advanced a politics based on the hatred of everyday politics, and their disdain for politics had good theoretical reasons. In its place, radical politics and aesthetics were treated as if they were identical; both were defined, without further ado, as critical because they represented goals that were distinct from quantitative and calculating interests of capitalist social relations: aesthetics and aesthetic politics were critical because they dealt with values, with quality and culture rather than the mechanics of civilization. If it is said that this attitude comes from German romanticism, the reply is that Marx too shared in that tradition. A contemporary analogy can be used to make the case for this identification of different domains. The critical aestheticism as politics resembles the claims of contemporary postmodernists: postmodernists are modernists who hate modernity, just as the old critical theorists were political thinkers who hated politics. This kinship appears most saliently in the literary style and especially the musical likes (and dislikes) of Adorno.[4]

But analogies are often excuses for oversimplification, and the history of the Frankfurt School presents a more complicated picture. It suggests either that the political project of the old Frankfurt School be revivified—or that it should at least be given a proper burial, under its own name. The same goes for the Marxism of which it considered itself the dialectical heir.[5] But that leaves open the question of whether there is still a place for a critical theory today. What might such a theory look like? What would it do? The history of the Frankfurt School provides some useful paths for thinking about these questions.

Was the disappearance of the political dimension of critical theory necessary? There is no doubt that the intention of the founders was political; critical theory was an academic code name for Marxism.[6] The interest of Rolf Wiggershaus's fascinating history of the Frankfurt School is that it follows the founding intuition of the Marxist philosophers who sought to unify their passions under the title "critical theory" as they encountered a world whose advent they could not imagine: the America of exile and the painfully democratizing West Germany of the return, where the lessons of exile had to be brought into harmony with the need for the self-creation of a new generation (and a new left).[7] The encounter draws out and makes explicit an ambiguity that increasingly took the form of a brittle paradox whose original dynamic tension gradually was lost as critical theory became a "school." Wiggershaus cites the preface to Horkheimer's early, highly personal volume, whose title is deliberately dual (*Dämmerung* [Dawn and decline], 1934): "This book is obsolete," writes Horkheimer. But, he continues, "the ideas . . . may perhaps be of interest later."[8] Wiggershaus stays on the case, following both the ideas and the career of critical theory and the critical theorists' Institute for Social Research. Horkheimer's ideas did seem "of interest" to the student movement of the sixties, whose adoption of them, however, seemed to him a betrayal. The former critical Marxists now seemed opposed not just to radical but even to social-democratic politics.[9] This shift has to be explained. What did the critical theorists mean by "politics," and what makes this political theory "critical"?

With the return to Germany, Adorno came to play the dominant theoretical role while Horkheimer was busied with administrative integration of the old institute into the new West Germany. (This was no small task; Horkheimer's contribution to the new Germany should not be underestimated, but it is not clear that this activity followed directly from his critical theory.) Compromises seemed necessary; funding came from sources that were at times part of the integrated opposition's social forces and at other times directly from business interests within a stabilized postwar social-market economy. As opposed to the social scientific turn of the institute staff, Adorno's increasing use of the essay form appealed to opinion beyond the lecture hall. This was not simply a question of style, nor was it a sign of revolt. Wiggershaus tries to show that "the essay was for [Adorno] the form of free thought." But how did this free thought contribute to critical theory? Wiggershaus's illustration of

Adorno's use of it is telling. "I consider," writes Adorno, "the survival of Nazism *within* democracy as potentially more threatening than the survival of fascist tendencies *against* democracy." What could this hyperbolic claim, by a principal author of *The Authoritarian Personality*—the pioneering study of the advent of fascism within democracy—mean in the new West Germany? Wiggershaus is charitable almost to a fault; he suggests that its lack of a determined referent points to the insufficiency of the original intuition that was at the foundation of critical theory. Essayistic insights based on "intuitive chance readings and his own experiences and associations" are "a utopia . . . which [Wiggershaus insists] must be translated into an empirical form of knowledge capable of making use of the successful discoveries of organized science in all their breadth while providing science with fresh horizons to produce more specific, and at the same time more cautious discoveries and applications."[10] The old critical theory showed signs of its age and could not read clearly the signs of the new.

With this observation of the shifting object of critical theory, Jürgen Habermas enters the picture. But one may wonder whether the picture was changed by this new presence, whom Wiggershaus presents in a chapter title as "a social theorist at the Institute at last, valued by Adorno but," the title continues, "seen by Horkheimer as too left-wing."[11] "Left wing" turns out to mean, for Horkheimer, whatever threatened the continued existence and dignity of *his* institute. But Horkheimer's personal whims (and ambitions) do not explain how and why critical theory lost its radical political roots. It is significant that Wiggershaus's introduction of Habermas refers to the entry of a social theorist "at last" into the stable of critical theory. Was this a sign that the political string had been played out? The institute had been doing social science in the empirical studies that permitted it to keep its financial coffers full; now it seemed to recognize the need to turn to social theory. The shift was not made explicit, but its existence needs explanation. What did Adorno "value" in Habermas? Did the empirical studies point toward the need for a new theoretical framework in which the place of politics would be diminished?

Wiggershaus makes the reader aware of the idiosyncrasy of Horkheimer's personal politics and of the lengths to which his function as chief bureaucrat and/or entrepreneur of the Institute for

Social Research could take him—in power struggles over the direction of research, in choosing to support or reject research projects,
or in compromising with the authorities in the restored West Germany. Horkheimer's treatment of Herbert Marcuse during the exile
years in the United States, for example, is shocking in its manipula-
tions. While it is nice to know that theoretical heroes also have clay
feet, such character traits are not simple quirks of personality or
responses to the pettiness of office politics. Besides institute politics,
the Frankfurters, particularly during their exile years, were concerned with the political world around them. Wiggershaus nicely
restores to the institute's history such truly political thinkers as
Franz Neumann and Otto Kirchheimer. Kirchheimer's earlier
attempt to make a critical use of Carl Schmitt's criticism of parliamentary democracy in order to formulate politically a "left-Bolshe-
vism" had led to an incisive debate with Neumann, who had been
chief lawyer for the Social Democratic Party.[12] But Wiggershaus
doesn't take the occasion to question how this debate reflects the
clash between the utopian dimension of critical theory and its implications for actual politics. For example, he fails to follow up a (dis-
sembling) letter in which Horkheimer explains to Marcuse that his
decision to work on the anti-Semitism study (with Adorno) was only
another way of pursuing the project (shared with Marcuse) of a critical theory of politics. Marcuse had proposed that the critical study
of democracy might be an appropriate way to combine the analysis
of social problems with the development of new questions of theory.
Horkheimer replied simply that "for certain reasons [not explained
further in the letter], we dismissed that possibility."[13] The biogra-
pher here concentrates on the politics of theory while leaving the
reader to speculate about the nature of a critical theory of politics
that in principle was the presupposition and goal of the shared
research interests of the Frankfurt School.

The actual politics of critical theory was based first and foremost
on the steadfast and steady insistence on the power of negativity.
The faint optimism about the role of theory—as critical—in the passage cited earlier from the preface to *Dämmerung* had disappeared
completely by the time of Horkheimer's apocalyptic "Authoritarian
State" of 1940, whose brutally pessimistic vision of a history that had
produced two authoritarian states seemed to allow for no exit from
the nightmare.[14] From the initial refusal of a reified history of phi-

losophy, to the critique of the totally administered society, to the critique of psychological forms of adaptation and denial, to Adorno's essayist freedom, the slogan *nicht-mitmachen* was the imperative that protected the theory (and thus the theorists) from any possible conformity, while holding open the space that makes critique possible.

Admirable as the attitude may have been, this politics of the negative entailed theoretical and practical difficulties. Its presupposition and its political self-justification are the idea of a Reason that transcends the strategic and reified capitalist instrumental logic that devalues political projects by integrating them into a manipulable administered world from which there is no escape. Once again, the romantic roots of this presupposition are undeniable; it could also adopt a messianic religious coloration in, for example, Benjamin, Adorno, and (more surprising) Horkheimer himself. More important, this option for (uppercase) Reason, Romance, or Religion entails the sacrifice of (lowercase) politics. The imperative of negativity that founds critical theory devalues the merely empirical world, which can be "saved" only by an immanent dialectical (or mystical) method of critique that finds a Reason that underlies the reasons offered by empirical social science caught up in the quotidian world. The original paradox returns: saving the power of the negative implies that theory is itself a politics and that the politics of theory is all that remains for radical thought. This is the theoretical ground that underlies the pessimism that gripped the Frankfurters, and it may also be a partial explanation of their successors' choice to pursue the politics of theory within the university.

The imperative of negativity has another consequence for the critical theory of politics: its protagonists become ipso facto part of a (self-declared and self-reproducing) elite defined by its self-proclaimed capacity to pierce beneath the surface of the administered world of reified relations. True to the Marxist analysis of commodity fetishism, the Frankfurters' conception of the relation of theory and practice privileged the former even while appealing for the latter. But ironically (or paradoxically), the practice—or praxis—to which they appealed was in the end the practice of theory, the exercise of negativity, the utopian longing for Stendahl's "promesse de bonheur" that Marcuse was fond of invoking. Again, the critical theory of politics and a certain vision of the aesthetic tend to be fused in a unity that destroys the ability of each to recognize its difference and the specific domain of legitimacy of its propositions. While the often-cited Hegelian claim that "all determination is negation" can be defended, it does not follow that all negation is determination. Just as the best can show itself the enemy of the better, so the promise of happiness that turns us away from the false allure of commodity culture can prove itself to be a false promise, a pious longing or self-satisfied self-denial.

It is no surprise that Adorno and Horkheimer never found themselves at home in American culture. But it is surprising that nowhere in their criticism of that all-purpose bogeyman called "America" do they make reference to that other aristocrat who formulated a critical theory of politics against the backdrop of the vulgar American practice of democracy (nor is Alexis de Tocqueville mentioned in the index to Wiggershaus's book). Yet the Frankfurt-schooled reader of *Democracy in America* is struck by Tocqueville's account of the "mediocrity" of Americans' democratic passions, their pragmatic lust after the mere appearance of life, the manipulability that makes them now pacifist and self-seeking, now bellicose and roiling in idealistic rhetoric that carries them beyond themselves. Despite the similarity of their descriptions and of their critique, the Frenchman developed a critical theory of politics—of democratic politics—while the Germans' theory gave rise only to a politics of critique.[15] Why did critique replace politics? The question does not concern only the biography of the Frankfurt School; it defines also our postmodern world where critical theory has become literary criticism while politics disappears from the curriculum not only in the university. The fault does not lie with the Frankfurters, but their rigorous and consistent option for the negative, their refusal to *mitmachen*, makes the career of their developing critical theory a telling symptom of the temptations that accompany a certain style of theory that is still with us.

Horkheimer's constant concern to constitute a school, a collective project that would express a shared vision, could and did lead to administrative nastiness, trickery, editorial manipulation, and worse (as noted above in regard to relations with Marcuse). But it did produce a unified product (even if, as Dubiel shows,[16] it went through three distinctive phases before the return to Germany, and, as Wiggershaus demonstrates, it could retain its theoretical coherence on the return to Germany only by freezing theoretical developments and sponsoring the most bread-and-butter empirical research).[17]

The need to maintain a school entailed an option for theory even at the cost of ritualizing its critical function. This helps explain why Habermas was "too left-wing" for Horkheimer: he was a threat to the unity of the school not only because of his attempt to renew the Marxist theory that the founders thought they had outgrown but also because of his relations to the Social Democrats and even more because of his concern to dialogue with the rebellious youth movement, the SDS.[18] The production and maintenance of a school of theory came at the price of rigidity, fixation, and exclusion of debate. Theory became its own politics; self-critique was too risky a venture for a school of theory, even when it defined itself as critical. Again, this turn cannot be attributed to some sort of character fault of Horkheimer or of the others. Some might attribute it to the bitter experience of Fascism or of the two totalitarianisms criticized by Horkheimer in 1940; others would look to the experience of U.S. exile, whose theoretical culmination in Horkheimer's *Eclipse of Reason* applied the imperative of negativity to American pragmatism, but with the explicit proviso that "the author is not trying to suggest anything like a program of action. On the contrary, he believes that the modern propensity to translate every idea into action . . . is one of the symptoms of the present critical crisis."[19] Nonetheless, Wiggershaus's history suggests the need to ask whether there was something in the initial project, in the basic critical intuition, that could explain this unexpected and unintended end.

The young leftist reader who encountered critical theory in the 1960s is shocked to read a history of the gleanings of daily life at an institution called the "Frankfurt School." A rebel by nature, that reader wonders whether the creation of a school was worth the trouble it took? Were the results of that effort compatible with the intentions of its creators? The conclusions to which Wiggershaus is led suggest a positive answer insofar as the influence of the Frankfurters on both the analyses and the action of the student movement in West Germany contributed to the democratizing of a culture and society that had emerged from the experience of Fascism and war largely intact. Of course, many other factors contributed to this process, not the least of which were the developments of a modern capitalist and consumer culture and society. The fact that the school could maintain itself and continue to have influence has an explanation that goes deeper than just biographical description. It was presented in Adorno's aphorism at the beginning of *Negative Dialectics*, which suggested that theory is critical and political because the moment of its realization has been missed. Once that assumption is made—and it is an assumption—then those who are disposed to be critical and political will unite around the negative politics of critical theory, which will not need the kind of office politics described by Wiggershaus to maintain its hold in the universities. The young leftist will remain caught unhappily between an all-consuming capitalist culture and a self-satisfied politics (or posture) of negativism.

The difficulty has its basis in the concept of critique itself. Its identification with the negative leaves aside the original Frankfurt School insight (that came from Hegel and Marx) into the need for immanent critique. That orientation seems to have disappeared gradually with the loss of faith in the project of human self-liberation that culminated in Adorno and Horkheimer's *Dialectic of Enlightenment* (1947). The door through which postmodernist cultural theory came to replace critical theory as political was opened. But the cultural "democratization" that followed their return to Germany had political implications that the Frankfurt School could not see. My earlier allusion to Tocqueville suggests that a critical theory of democracy would have to treat the autonomy of the political sphere as the moment of negativity that cannot be co-opted into the new global world in which (not only geopolitical) boundaries are increasingly porous. This is what makes possible the changes sought in culture and society: the political is always present within modern societies, just as early critical theory assumed Reason to be present if latent. This political explanation of critical negativity avoids the temptation that justified first the optimism and then the pessimism of the old critical theory that appealed to a Reason discovered by an immanent (cultural) critique. The temptation for critical theory is to transform the negativity of Reason into a foundation that, in principle, can become positive. That was just what Marx did when he explained that "reason has always existed, but not in a rational form."[20] Cultural critical theorists in the university combine Marx with the Frankfurt School in the affirmation that it is just these non-rational forms that become the positive expression of critical theory. The autonomy of politics is forgotten; immediacy and surface appearance are equated with democracy, which in this way loses its critical potential.

The paradox from which I began can now be restated, and the apparent similarity of the Frankfurt type of critical theory and its academic homonym disentangled. Radical political theorists who have no intuitive feel for politics and who implicitly express a kind of aristocratic disdain for it feel an obligation to be critical. It is not surprising that their critical practice takes the form of a politics of theory. But the politics of theory can be practiced according to different rules. The critical theory of democratic politics that is lacking today cannot be provided by the postmodernists' happy frolicking on the surfaces, as if a democratic praxis were simply the spontaneity of men and women suddenly freed—how? by decree?—from the constraints of what Jean-François Lyotard denounces as the *grands récits* that tell the story of Humanity as it progresses from one preordained phase to another. Lyotard's debt to *The Dialectic of Enlightenment* is obvious; his proposition aims also to negate Kant's critique of "self-incurred immaturity." But does the negation of the *grands récits* imply simply their replacement by the nonrational (which Lyotard calls a *différand*)? Postmodernism too is a politics of theory, but it cannot replace a critical theory of politics (as Marx reminded his contemporaries in 1843, when he insisted that "the weapon of the critique cannot replace the critique of the weapons").

Postmodernism in its various forms is critical in the sense that it opposes another reality to the accepted social vision of what counts as real. But in doing that, it is a positive theory, not a critical theory. The opposition of one reality to another produces at best a criticism; it is not the kind of immanent critique that the original intuition of the Frankfurt School sought to actualize in its quarrel with modern capitalism and capitalist social and cultural modernity. The problem for such an immanent critique is that it apparently can be maintained only by the kind of heroic abnegation that the Frankfurters expressed in their *nicht-mitmachen*. But heroes tire, disciples falter, attitudes harden as the institute becomes a school, undertaking perhaps what sixties' radicals began defining in the seventies as a "long march through the institutions" in the hope that in that way at least the essential would be preserved. But there is another way to save critical theory; ironically, it is one to which Marx alluded in a preparatory note to his doctoral dissertation when he suggested that, like Themistocles, the philosopher must know when it is time to found "a new Athens on the sea, on another element."[21] This "other element" that can permit critical theory to pursue its uneasy path at a distance from the illusory charm of aesthetic fancy and the sticky necessities of globalizing society is the sphere of the political, whose autonomy stands at just that point of immanent negative distance that a critical theory presupposes, needs, and must be able to maintain.

# CHAPTER 4

# Habermas's Reorientation of Critical Theory Toward Democratic Theory

Despite Max Horkheimer's fear that he was "too left-wing" to inherit the legacy of the Frankfurt School, Jürgen Habermas has modernized the tradition of critical theory just as the original Frankfurters sought to modernize Marxism: by criticizing and thereby reaffirming in his own way the premises from which the founders began. This achievement has not always been understood by his audience, despite a remarkable series of successes, each one crowned by a theoretical work of synthetic breadth and theoretical depth. Typical was the case of the book that was his Habilitationsschrift in 1962, *Structural Change of the Public Sphere*,[1] which joined American sociological research with German philosophy and Enlightenment politics to create the notion of a "public sphere," whose emergence, ripening, and potential withering Habermas traced. Although this work has come to be recognized as a fundamental contribution to democratic political theory, Habermas had to leave Frankfurt for Heidelberg in order to receive university recognition for it. Even though he would later modify some of his theoretical claims, he never renounced what he already called the project of enlightenment, in which understanding comes about through engagement in the public space.

Ever the public intellectual, Habermas published a collection of his early essays under the title *Theory and Practice* (1963),[2] placing himself squarely in the tradition of Western Marxism, for which neither theory nor practice can be understood in isolation from the other. This was a reaffirmation of the older Frankfurt tradition that the first generation had abandoned and the younger generation of students who would become the new left tended also to reject—although the older group took the side of theory, the younger that of practice. Habermas would abandon neither. But it was with the younger generation that the public intellectual soon found himself in conflict—with its theory (such as it was) and especially with its practice. For the representatives of that generation, Marxism was a theory that was supposed to offer the basis of a positive recipe for social transformation, whereas Habermas's long essay on Marxism, written in 1957 and published in the German edition of *Theory and Practice*,[3] stressed that it can be understood only as critique. As for their practice, Habermas saw in it only an illusory revolution or the illusion of a revolution (*Scheinrevolution*); participating in one of their congresses in 1968, he even went so far as to denounce a "left fascism."[4] The same year, Habermas published the first systematic synthesis of his vision of critical theory. Its title, *Knowledge and Human Interest*,[5] expresses his insistence that knowledge is not the possession of a neutral, disincarnated spectator: its acquisition is guided by the practical interests of the active subject.

With the death of Adorno in 1969, Habermas (who had become quite friendly with Herbert Marcuse) was the uncontested master of critical theory. He became the director of a research institute in Starnberg and assembled there a talented and diverse group with whom he began the work of solidifying critical theory into a social analysis with empirical consequences. The political climate in West Germany was bitter, polemical, and at times paranoid; the legitimacy of the institute was soon challenged. Habermas took it upon himself in 1973 to synthesize the diverse research projects that had been undertaken, presenting his results in a book entitled *Legitimation Problems in Late Capitalism*.[6] Whereas *Knowledge and Human Interest* had pinned its critical hopes on an "emancipatory interest" that produces a kind of knowledge that neither is instrumental nor aimed simply at social adaptation but is liberating in the same way that psychoanalytic knowledge frees the subject from internalized fetishes, the new book looked to social interaction for its critical foundation. Habermas distinguishes four potential types of crisis that can and indeed have affected capitalist society: economic, administrative, motivational, and legitimatory. Capitalism can be said to have entered its late phase when it has worked through the first three of these crises. Legitimation, which neither concerns individual motivation nor reflects contradictory systematic imperatives rooted in the economy or the state, is the critical social resource that capitalism cannot reproduce on its own.

This empirically based analysis of the source of capitalist crisis needed a theoretical foundation, which Habermas provided in the two-volume *Theory of Communicative Action* (1981).[7] The linguistic turn proposed in this two-volume reexamination of the foundations of critical theory had been foreshadowed by the shift from the emancipatory interest of the individual to the social interactions that resulted in a crisis of legitimacy. While some were unhappy that in this new synthesis the philosopher seemed to have overcome the social theorist and the moralist had replaced the political thinker (as the analytic philosopher triumphed over the continental theorist), Habermas drew other conclusions and turned to other projects. He dissolved the institute at Starnberg and returned to teach in Frankfurt.

More than a decade later Habermas published *Between Facts and Norms* (1992).[8] The book's subtitle clarifies its focus: it offers "contributions to a discourse theory of law and democracy." Although the original Frankfurt School had included two legal theorists (Franz Neumann and Otto Kirchheimer), their work remained on the theoretical periphery of the prewar production of the Frankfurt School. After the war, when both remained in the United States, their work did not become an essential part of the arsenal known as the Frankfurt School, whose works were becoming well known in the 1960s through pirate editions that were made necessary by the refusal of Horkheimer to allow reprints.[9] While left-wing jurists in West Germany did publish a serious journal called *Kritische Justiz*, it was not seen as an organ of Frankfurt-style critical theory. What is significant in Habermas's latest venture is his attempt to use the "discourse theory" developed in the study of "communicative action" in order to contribute to both law and democracy, whose interdependence recalls the earlier concern to unite theory and practice. This new project is all the more provocative because the downfall of what West Germans had come to call "really existing socialism" occurred while Habermas was working out his theory. Although he includes one appendix dating from 1990, Habermas's project seems to have been unaffected by these events, which, one would have thought, influenced the received understanding of the nature of both democracy and law—particularly for someone who, like Habermas, had always identified himself as a Social Democrat concerned with the development of what he theorized as the public sphere.

Habermas did publish essays on the great changes that were taking place—changes that he did not hesitate to label "revolutions." He collected a small volume of his essays in 1990 under the somewhat odd, perhaps condescending title *Die nachholende Revolution*.[10] The title essay, which suggests that these revolutions were seeking only to "catch up" (*nachholen*) to the West, claims that Eastern Europe has only to realize the enlightened ideas that were put into practice at the glorious dawn of 1789. (These "ideas of 1789" are the object of a second appendix published in *Between Facts and Norms*.)[11] Habermas's prescription is not surprising: he admitted in an interview with the Polish former dissident Adam Michnik that he had never written on communism or even on Stalinism because he did not think they were important.[12] Despite this lack of interest, the essay was concerned with more than just the "catch-up revolution"; its title refers also to "the need for a revision by the left." That revision concerns in particular the fundamental place that must be given to both democracy and human rights in the theory and practice of those who partake of the legacy of "the ideas of 1789." Habermas insists that these basic demands can be realized only within a certain type of liberal state—called in German a *Rechtsstaat*—that guarantees not just the rule of law (which need not be democratic) but ensures the maintenance of what might be called a republican or "constitutional" state (which encourages participation by means of what Habermas elsewhere calls "constitutional patriotism"). It is plausible that Habermas could have learned these lessons much earlier, from a critical engagement with the varieties of really existing socialism. But he didn't. This makes it all the more remarkable that his conclusions are in many ways—although not in language or explicit form of argument—similar to those the French left came to learn through its critique of totalitarianism.[13]

The law is portrayed as an institution standing "between facts and norms." It has a force that is both symbolic and real. A valid law in a democracy has to be able to call on the coercive force of the state to ensure its factual existence at the same time that, in everyday life, obedience is assured because citizens accept its normative character. Similarly, rights are both the expression of existing social relations, which they validate, and the articulation of normative expectations about social relations that ought to be. The polarity recalls the earlier formulations of the relation of theory to practice. But the linguistic turn has added nuance to the analysis. Now it is seen that we can distinguish between social relations as observed by the social scientist who describes a series of facts whose existence can be empirically validated or falsified and the same social relations as understood by the participant who is caught up within those same facts. In a democratic society, the participant expects the facts that are encountered as constraints also to be normatively legitimate as the result of a political process that satisfies procedural criteria that can be described empirically by an observer as present or absent. This example enriches the framework. It suggests both that analysis of the facts affects the claim to normative validity and that the assertion of normative validity can never be absent from the stance (or what Habermas, in *Knowledge and Human Interests*, called the "cognitive interest") that thinks it is only describing the world as it is. In this first sense, then, Habermas remains firmly within the framework of the Frankfurt School of critical theory: he too moves constantly between facts and norms, never abandoning either, constantly concerned with their interaction.

But the old Frankfurt School was at the outset Marxist inspired, always violently critical of bourgeois society, and in its later phase quite sensitive to the destructive paradoxes of a "dialectic of enlightenment" through which Reason's quest for purity and certainty turns into a form of self-domination and willful blindness. Habermas, on the other hand, seeks to realize the project of enlightenment, whose transformed public sphere he had criticized and then interpreted as producing an emancipatory interest before reaffirming his commitment to "the ideas of 1789" in the new book. He had explained his differences with the old school in the concluding chapter of volume 1 of *The Theory of Communicative Action*, which returned to the tradition of Western Marxism under the title "From Lukács to Adorno: Rationalization as Reification." The linguistic turn that recognizes that subjectivity is always intersubjectivity permits what Habermas calls his postmetaphysical modern philosophy to recognize that the paradoxes of the dialectic of enlightenment were the result of its basic assumption that knowledge is produced by the relation of an isolated subject (or consciousness) to an objective world. This linguistic turn is developed further in *Between Facts and Norms*, which claims to be both a "discourse theory of law" and a "communication theory of society." Its implication is first of all that every time we speak to someone, we make a set of "counterfactual" assumptions about the person whom we address: that she is rational, that he is not deliberately trying to deceive, that words mean the same thing for both of us, and so on. These counterfactuals are norms; if we did not assume their validity, we could and would not speak.[14] The immanence of these norms in all speech acts can come to play a role similar to the immanent critique that the Frankfurt School derived from Marx's critique of capitalism.

The interrelation of facts and norms that the linguistic turn reveals is not present only in the world of the philosopher. As noted, facts are revealed to the observer, norms to the participant, but of course in social relations each of us has to play both roles. When we turn to the law, we have to ask, what kinds of participation are necessary in order to ensure the normative validity of the observed legal facts? The answer will describe the conditions that constitute democratic participatory social relations. This democratic society can in turn become an object for observation, and the question naturally arises as to the conditions that give normative validity to that society. Presumably that legitimacy would be provided by something like what Habermas calls a "democratic culture," but it is not clear what is meant by this concept or how it comes to exist. Its relation to the earlier concept of a public sphere is not developed. Does it refer to a society that is based on and honors liberal rights of the individual? Or does not such a democratic culture depend on the presence of a community that gives it shape and constancy? This dilemma recalls the quarrel between liberals typified by John Rawls and his communitarian or "classical republican" critics; it forms another leitmotiv of Habermas's theory. Is it the case that individu-

als have rights—even if only in the form of private or negative liberties—that no political or legal measure can violate? Or do individuals have rights only because of their membership in a community, in
which case the community is justified in abrogating some rights if
that is judged necessary to the preservation of the sovereign community? A similar problem is posed by the question of the relation
between rights as liberties and rights as social (or economic) entitle-
ments. Habermas's goal is to overcome these dichotomous formulations by elaborating—and illustrating by means of a condensed
reconstruction of the evolution of feminist politics—what he calls a
"proceduralist paradigm" that can take into account both aspects of
the dual function of the law.[15]

What holds together a society caught between fact and validity?
How can the constant oscillation from one perspective to another be
overcome without having recourse to some transcendent values such
as those offered in traditional societies by metaphysics, religion, or
morality? In *The Theory of Communicative Action* Habermas had
offered a double explanation of the unity of modern postmetaphysical societies: they are held together, on the one hand, by the functioning of "systems" that follow their own logic with no need for
human intervention—as is the case for the market, which is steered
by money, and for the bureaucracy, which is steered by power—or
they maintain themselves, on the other hand, through the reproduction of an intersubjective "lifeworld" that has to be protected
against "colonization" by the impersonal and instrumental logic of
said impersonal systems. The place of the law in this picture was not
clear: it could function as a self-contained system that can be
described by an observer and whose task is to fix individual expectations and limit the burden of personal uncertainty; or law could be
seen as the articulation of the intersubjective norms that underlie the
lifeworld and formulate the background consensus unifying its
members. The equivalent of a Marxist or critical-theoretical crisis
theory could then emerge insofar as the institutions of a paternalist
welfare state use legal (systemic) forms to intervene in the lifeworld,
drying up its collective resources and destroying its coherence. Politics such as those of the then-vibrant "new social movements" of the
period when Habermas was writing could serve as practical illustrations of this theoretical exercise in immanent critique.

Habermas's revised approach to the law cannot be explained simply by the changed political conjuncture in which social movements are no longer so important. Yet it is worth noting that the first appendix in *Between Facts and Norms* is an essay written in 1990 titled "Citizenship and National Identity." It begins from the new problems posed not only by the end of the Soviet bloc but also by the supranational institutions of what was once only a common market and now claims to be a European Community, as well as by the waves of immigration and the attendant demands for asylum that challenge the universalistic principles of constitutional democracies that nonetheless feel the need to protect their particular forms of life. Habermas appeals neither to facts nor to norms in the face of these practical difficulties. His new theory takes advantage of what he calls the "hinge" function of the law: the fact that it attaches two poles while being identical with neither. Democratic law depends on the participation in its elaboration of all those who are affected by it; in this sense it is part of the lifeworld, which it serves to reproduce. On the other hand, the formal structure of the law means that it must obey systemic requirements such as constancy and predictability, and in this sense it functions as a system that must run without human intervention. How do the two functions of the law relate? The opposition between the formality of the law and the demand for substantive justice could lead to what Weber called "kadi-justice," which is able to take into account the particularity of a situation only by separating the judge from the procedural restraints needed to avoid arbitrariness. Or it could take the form of a lifeworld refusing to be "colonized" by the imposition of administrative and judicial codes. Neither reaction is modern, nor democratic in Habermas's sense of the concept. He introduces two other metaphors to explain his proposals: democratic politics functions according to the model of a "siege" or a "sluice." Democratic political actors do not seek to take over the state for their own purposes (as if democracy were only a means to an end distinct from it); they aim to convince the state to take into account their points of view. Since the state is a system that makes use of the medium of the legal form in order to administer society, a democratic political society has to speak to it in a language that can be "heard" by the impersonal state system. And that language is none other than the language of the law, understood now—of course—in its normative role as lived by and from the standpoint of the participants in a democratic society.

These metaphors of a "siege" and "sluices" describe an interaction that articulates the hinge function of the law at the same time that they help to explain that democratic culture about which neither liberals nor communitarians could agree. The legal language through which democratic society has to formulate its norms in order to be heard by the state provides what Habermas calls a "countersteering" that leads the society to modernize itself by adopting and elaborating institutional forms that make explicit the norms that previously only had the status of taken-for-granted (traditional or metaphysical) norms existing in the unarticulated background consensus of the lifeworld. When society is forced to articulate formally and to justify rationally to the observer the presuppositions that constitute it as a particular society—which define its own conception of the good life, so to speak—it can be said to modernize itself in the sense that what it took as unquestioned presuppositions now must be justified and can be criticized. Habermas does not identify the democratic or liberal culture that is crucial to his theory with either rights-first liberalism or the communitarian alternative. Instead he identifies the procedural means (the countersteering that replaces the dialectic of enlightenment's dead ends) by which democratic culture can come into being and develop itself explicitly. And, significantly, his exploitation of the dual nature of law makes it clear that a democratic culture does not have to abstract from or fear co-optation by the state. The state cannot be eliminated, as some devotees of a directly democratic lifeworld would have it. The public sphere (or what is often called civil society) cannot exist on its own.

The use of the legal hinge permits Habermas to avoid a dilemma that results from his recognition of the role of the modern state (and, more generally, from his use of systems theory to account for the complexity of modern societies). It might appear that impersonal, self-reproducing systems are immune to democratization and that attempts to introduce greater social justice into state decision making or to adjust market mechanisms to ensure real equality among citizens are not just impossible but actually threatening to the smooth functioning of the social system. While it is true that Habermas's theory rules out utopias such as workers' self-management, its implications for progressive politics are, as he says, those of a "radical democrat" (he no longer talks about being a Social Democrat in this context). Precisely because the state or administrative or market systems must be regulated by the legal form, they can be influenced by social demands that, on their side, make their own use of the legal form in order to be heard. Indeed, the more the apparently impersonal systems that regulate society become subject to law—rather than the playthings of arbitrary decision by those in power—the greater the chances of affecting their democratic accessibility and, it can be hoped, their ability to ensure social justice.

It does not suffice to say that law is democratic simply because society or those members of society directly concerned by a decision take part in its formulation (the latter clause is necessary because one can, for example, use labor law or even the labor contract within a firm to ensure or increase its democratic nature). Indeed, there is a sense in which democracy has to be self-limiting in order to succeed in maintaining itself as democratic: this is what the practical need to speak to the powers within the system(s) in the formal language of law implied. More concretely, the state system is needed to ensure the conditions in which democracy can be realized. The republic is the precondition of a democracy, which in its turn validates or legitimates that formal republic. The point can be illustrated at the level of constitutional law as well. When the sovereign people gives itself a constitution it thereby puts limits on itself, defining the rules or norms (or procedures, as Habermas prefers to say) in terms of which laws and legal actions will be considered valid. This structure can be described factually by a political scientist or sociologist. That leaves open the question: what makes it, for the participants, normatively valid? And this is only the first step; a series of validity questions follow: How does adjudication acquire its democratic legitimacy (assuming that one does not want to accept a paternalistic or kadi-court)? How do ordinary legal discourse and adjudication relate to questions of constitutional decision making? When it comes to practical politics, we know that the law is supposed to be neutral with regard to the participants, but we know too that—as is the case with the contract between worker and capitalist, for example—some actors start with a structural advantage, such that the principle of "treating equals equally" could be interpreted as recommending a non-neutral stance, say, in questions of affirmative action.[16]

A critical theory of democracy, beginning from the distinction of fact and norm, must confront countless concrete problems, and Habermas takes up, regroups, and articulates more than I can even allude to here. What I should mention, however, is that the concept of a public sphere (*Öffentlichkeit*) that Habermas had developed in 1962 is reformulated radically by the "discourse theory" approach in order to take into account the necessarily pluralistic and complex character of modern societies. This is where Habermas's "proceduralist paradigm" enters his argument. A brief characterization of the challenge that it poses is necessary before coming to a final reflection on what it is that makes Habermas's theory "critical" and why that qualification is important today.[17]

Habermas insists on what he calls the "equiprimordiality" (*Gleichursprünglichkeit*) of rights and democracy. In modern postmetaphysical societies, rights are legitimate only insofar as they are posited in the democratic participatory discourse of all those concerned by their existence. Rights are not something that one has in the way one has a thing—indeed, strictly speaking (pace Locke), a thing becomes my property only through intersubjective agreement. This analogy suggests that, just as the contract through which I acquire a property may be deemed illegitimate (if it resulted from an asymmetry in the power relation between me and the previous owner or if one of us lacked some relevant information, etc.), so too the democratic participatory discourse that defines rights is itself an agreement to respect certain procedural characteristics whose definition, it should be underlined, depends in turn on the same democratic participation that it seeks to make legitimate. The interdependence of participation and procedure is only a reformulation of the hinge: procedures defined by participants at once make further participation legitimate even while the legitimate participants can agree to change the rules that made them legitimate participants (e.g., amending a constitution). We return to the oscillating structure that defined the relation of fact and norm, but now, on the basis of the discourse theory, we see why Habermas's subtitle applied it to both "law and democracy." Their relation now can be seen to imply that, because the legitimate presence of each as a fact is the prerequisite for the other's normative validity, each of them is reinforced by the imperative presence of the other. And the nub of the procedural paradigm will consist in establishing the means to conserve their equiprimordiality. In this way, the liberal or democratic culture that was central to Habermas's project is conserved, reinforced, and made more rational.

This claim poses a final question, illustrating once again the uneasy relation of Habermas to critical theory from which this discussion began. In a reply to participants in a symposium on *Between Facts and Norms*, Habermas writes that "even if readers do not always see the 'end of critical theory' in this project, they frequently think it defuses the critique of capitalism and just gives in to political liberalism."[18] This was indeed the claim that has been presented here—but with the qualification that the result of this project will strengthen liberal culture. Habermas rejects both sides of the liberalism/communitarianism polarity, even while recognizing the element of truth in each. What makes his theory critical lies at a deeper level than a practical program for social change. His inclusion of the appendix on the "ideas" of the French Revolution suggests that he does not situate his theory in the Marxist or communist historical perspective that seeks the realization of the French Revolution. The import of the French Revolution for him lies in the challenge that it posed—and still poses two centuries later. As long as critical theory is not implicitly identified with Marxist theory that is still looking for its ersatz proletariat and as long as Marxist theory is not oriented toward the realization of a revolution that will overcome opposition by uniting once and for all fact and norm, what Habermas has done is to demonstrate why and how, since 1789 and all the more after 1989, "democracy" is that which founds any theory that can claim to be critical. This simple truth may get lost in the vast and complicated (sometimes passionately exciting, at others pedantically satisfying) edifice that represents Habermas's newest proposal for a modern and synthetic critical theory. It will be interesting to see whether the French, to whose conclusions it is so close despite its foreign conceptual language, will be able to understand it.[19]

# CHAPTER 5

# The Anticommunist Marxism of
# Socialisme ou Barbarie

The journal *Socialisme ou Barbarie* came to the attention of a wider public only after some of the leaders of the May '68 movement, especially Dany Cohn-Bendit, had explained its influence on them. The journal, like the political group that published it for sixteen years, during which forty issues were published—first bimonthly, then quarterly—placed itself explicitly out of the mainstream of organized left-wing politics. Only some three hundred copies of each issue were printed, and the journal finally ceased publication in 1965 after a final split within its ranks when its critical Marxism turned finally into a critique of Marxism. Attempts to reconstitute it during May '68 failed, however much its initiators found the May events to be a confirmation of their basic political orientation. Its leading members—Cornelius Castoriadis, Claude Lefort, Jean-François Lyotard, and Daniel Mothé—continued its project in their own ways.[1] But their experience with the journal—and with the political actions that the group undertook—should not be neglected by those who know only their later work. In the wake of 1989, their immanent critique of communism is more relevant than ever, as is their passage through Marxism to its internal self-critique. Although the historian may find their fears sometimes exaggerated (a third world war was expected) and their hopes often hypertrophied (projecting their own vision onto the participants in the struggles they chronicled), the journal showed a remarkable ability to sense the importance of what was historically new and ripe for the future. It is this feature that is most impressive for those who come to reread it today.

From its first to its last issue, the cover of *Socialisme ou Barbarie* presented the journal as an "organ of critique and revolutionary orientation." Its cofounders, Castoriadis and Lefort, were dissidents from the Trotskyist Fourth International. As the editorial statement in the first issue (March–April 1949) explained, it was "no accident" that critics of Stalinism would become Trotskyists, but it was also "no accident" that they would in turn challenge the Trotskyists' inability to confront "the fundamental problem of our epoch: the nature of the 'workers' bureaucracy and especially its Stalinist form." This bureaucratization, the editors insisted, could not be explained as a simple accident or the result of constraints imposed by enemies; its durability in the Soviet Union, its spread to Eastern Europe and to China, and its domination of the Western workers' movement pose the question "of the evolution of the modern economy, of the signification of a century of proletarian struggles, and, in the last instance, the revolutionary perspective itself." But the journal insisted that it would address these theoretical questions from the perspective of practical activity. That, after all, was the position of Marx himself, which the journal claimed to represent and to carry on in the postwar world. That is why the journal was published by a group of political activists offering both critique and practical orientation.

The interrelation of theory and practice returns frequently in the pages of *Socialisme ou Barbarie*. The group's political constitution, which was published in the second issue, explains that members would meet monthly in plenary sessions and that public meetings would be held after the publication of each issue. New members would join by invitation, after which they would have to take part in an educational program; they would have to agree with the programmatic orientation of the leadership, accept collective discipline, and pay dues that would serve to finance the publication of the journal. This rigorous discipline led to vigorous disputes, notably in 1952 (no. 10) between Castoriadis (writing under the pseudonym of

Pierre Chaulieu) and Lefort (whose pseudonym was C. Montal). Lefort finally left the group in 1958 on the grounds that it had become a minibureaucracy whose organization made impossible the very proletarian spontaneity that it claimed to represent. Lefort's explanation of his decision was published as "Organization and Party" (no. 26, 1958); it was answered by Castoriadis's aptly titled polemic "Proletariat and Party" (nos. 27–28, 1959), which reaffirmed the basic position taken by the first two issues of the journal.

The claim to represent the "vanguard" of the future revolution posed the theory-practice problem directly. The revolution was to be worldwide (without it, the journal maintained during its early period, "barbarism" would emerge in the form of a third world war). Hence the journal devoted much effort to following events outside France and sought to maintain contacts with the few groups that had similar orientation, such as those animated in the United States by C. L. R. James and Grace Boggs. They sought allies among the Italian followers of Bordiga, the Dutch followers of Pannekoek and the Council Communists, and radical elements in the British shop-steward movement. Following Trotskyist practice, many authors wrote under pseudonyms (although Castoriadis, as a foreigner in France, was forced to do so). In the same way, when they published lists of respondents to funding appeals, they listed only initials or thanked "a comrade from . . . ." This anonymity was a protective device (against the thugs of the Communist Party), but it had a theoretical import as well. It implied that the journal presented truth, which is universal, rather than expressing opinion, which is particular. But despite the suggestion that theory was international and universal, this did not reflect a devaluation of practice and its implications.

The international orientation of the vanguard was maintained throughout the life of the journal, although the accent shifted as the journal developed and refined its understanding of the specificity of modern society. The critique of Soviet-type societies was constant and wide-ranging; Castoriadis-Chaulieu (who worked at the time as a professional economist in Paris for the OCED) demonstrated at length the emergence of a new form of economic exploitation in "The Relations of Production in the Soviet Union" (no. 2, 1949), while Lefort analyzed the persistence of "Stalinism without Stalin" in the wake of Khrushchev's Secret Speech at the Twentieth Congress of the Soviet Communist Party in 1956 (no. 20, 1956–1957). Eastern Europe was not neglected, particularly with the emergence of the challenge of Tito's autonomous course and later with the revolts in East Germany and then Poland and Hungary. Signs of change and alliances were sought in the West as well. The first six issues of the journal carried a translation of Paul Romano's "The American Worker," while later issues examined the implications of strikes in England and Belgium, as well as developments in France. Starting in 1955 Jean-François Lyotard was charged with the task of analyzing the war that led finally to Algerian independence in 1962.

The practice of the vanguard in this context consisted in criticizing false idols while demonstrating the actual creativity of which the revolutionary movement itself was supposedly not aware, in the quite Leninist expectation that this information would encourage a self-conscious continuation of previously spontaneous action. The goal was to combine class analysis with a critique of its bureaucratic deformation; class analysis alone was insufficiently alert to political choice, while critique of the bureaucracy ignored the issues of power that a future revolution (which they expected) would have to confront. The line between the two aspects of the analysis was often difficult to draw and was subject to revision. When, for example, did the authentic revolution of 1917 undergo bureaucratic deformation? Not only was there room for debate, but the journal would later question whether the Russian events were ever truly revolutionary. How could one justify Algerian independence while warning (presciently and trenchantly) against uncritical support for the National Liberation Front? At first, it appeared that economic conditions could supply the criterion permitting evaluation; later, politics acquired a broader definition and an autonomy from the supposed economic infrastructure.

Another task of the vanguard also emerged in the pages of *Socialisme ou Barbarie*: to furnish the tools with which to understand what was revolutionary about existing conditions. Considering themselves the true heirs of Marx, the group began from the premise of a historically inevitable proletarian revolution. The Soviet Union was seen at first as a form of bureaucratic (or state) capitalism; it differed from the West only in the class that did the exploiting.[2] In a quasi-Hegelian but very Marxist mode, it even appeared that revolution might advance more rapidly in the Soviet world, since a higher stage of alienation had been reached there because of the experience of bureaucratic deformation; that world would not fall victim to legalistic illusions but would recognize the need for its own self-organization outside any institutional framework.[3] Thus the journal's reaction in 1956 to the Polish October reforms and then the Hungarian revolution was euphoric (but not uncritical, particularly in the Polish case, which simply exchanged the national Communist Gomulka for the Stalinists who had been in power).

It became clear, however, that even so-called true Marxist theory was insufficient as a weapon for the vanguard. As the editorial to the first issue had already stated, "The classical claim [that there is no revolutionary practice without revolutionary theory] only makes sense if we understand it to mean 'without the *development* of revolutionary theory there can be no development of revolutionary practice.' " The "development" of theory poses the question, is the path that leads to the new position what is fundamental to the politics of the group, or are the theoretical results what is primary? At least concerning the final phase of the journal's life, the theory seems to have been more important. For *Socialisme ou Barbarie*, "development" of theory on the basis of experience led it, finally, to the explicit abandonment of Marxism's claim to be a radical theory, a decision that was explained at length in Castoriadis's article series "Marxism and Revolutionary Theory," published in numbers 36–40 under the pseudonym Paul Cardan (and later published as the first half of Castoriadis's presentation of his own positive version of a truly revolutionary theory in *The Imaginary Institution of Society*). The series was controversial within the group, and its appearance was no doubt one of the reasons the journal ceased publication.

The vanguard can also play a role closer to that assumed by aesthetic avant-gardes: it warns against the repetition of the old and advocates looking for signs of the new (and it does so without appeal to a pregiven teleological vision of history's course). This alertness to novelty marks the entire course of *Socialisme ou Barbarie*. Its vision of proletarian revolution stressed the spontaneous creativity of the working class, not only in moments of effervescence such as the strike waves that sustained its revolutionary hopes but even more in the daily experience of production. The contributions of Daniel Mothé, who joined the group in 1954, reflecting on his experiences at the Renault factory in Billancourt, were central to this analysis. Mothé made clear not only that production-line workers were not dumbed down by exploitation but that they were alienated by the bureaucratic domination of their creative initiatives. But the domain in which the journal tracked everyday creativity was not limited to the work experience. As early as 1952, a short article pointed to the problems of youth, a new social category whose importance emerged in modern capitalist societies. In 1959 a special section was devoted to the avant-garde author Benjamin Péret. Later that year (in no. 31), the journal began reviewing films, starting with Godard's *A bout de souffle*, while the same issue noted the significance of what it called the "sit-down" of black American students in Greensboro, North Carolina. In 1963 special attention was directed to the problems facing youth; Mothé wrote about the situation of young workers, and the psychoanalyst Alain Girard coauthored with Castoriadis (writing as Marc Noiraud) an article on "sexual education in the USSR." A regular feature entitled "Chronique du mouvement étudiant" was inaugurated in the same issue that published the first installment of Castoriadis's final critique of Marxism. The last two issues of the journal commented on the significance of the Berkeley free speech movement and on the civil rights movement in the United States, reprinting selections from Hal Draper's "The Mind of Clark Kerr" and David Riesman's *Lonely Crowd*. Creativity and autonomy, not the material necessity that underpinned Marxism, became the dominant concerns. It is easy to see how the combination of Castoriadis's critique of Marxism and the aesthetic reevaluation of creativity would appeal to those who would be leaders in May '68.

Jean-François Lyotard retrospectively stresses this more aesthetic function of a vanguard in the reflections that accompany the republication of his articles on Algeria in *La guerre des Algériens*.[4] Lyotard compares the practice of the group to that of psychoanalysis, calling it a free listening that remains attentive to contemporary struggles in which what Marxists had called "exploitation" takes the form of the intractable (*l'intraîtable*): that which resists incorporation into the system and manifests itself as creativity. But Lyotard argues that this resistance and creativity can no longer be attributed to a collective subject whose role is to realize History; the signs of the new to which *Socialisme ou Barbarie* remained alert culminate rather in what he later called the postmodern condition. The aesthetic function of the political vanguard also explains the group's brief collaboration with the situationists in the early 1960s, when attention had turned to the problems of youth. That short-lived adventure seems to have broken down when it became clear that the situationists were more attuned to the aesthetic and *Socialisme ou Barbarie* to the vanguard.

It is not correct simply to claim that the sixteen years of *Socialisme ou Barbarie* followed a path from the most authentic and rigorous Marxism to the most authentic and rigorous critique of Marxism's presuppositions. That is how many who discovered the journal after 1968 came to see it. But such a view takes for granted the autonomy of theory; it supposes that critique comes from within theory or at best from a comparison of theory with reality. One of the group's basic principles, on which Castoriadis particularly insisted, was to assert that Marx meant just what he said when he claimed that what made his theory revolutionary was its intimate connection with a reality that would be changed by virtue of its being correctly understood. When that change remained absent, revolutionary theory had to draw the conclusions that followed from remaining faithful to Marx's principle—and abandon Marxism. Thus while it is true that the polemics that often filled the pages of the journal vigorously criticize contemporary theorists—Serge Mallet, Alain Touraine, Michel Crozier, Sartre, and more generally those whom Lefort labeled "the progressive intellectuals"—these critiques were not intended to raise intellectual capital; they were made from the standpoint of the creative practice on which *Socialisme ou Barbarie* insisted. Precisely because they took seriously Marx's claim to formulate a theory that is inherently revolutionary, they were able, as Daniel Mothé suggests in his obituary for Castoriadis,[5] to maintain the autonomy of thought itself in a French left dominated by the mentality of Stalinism to a degree that today is too readily forgotten. This was no small accomplishment.

There is another way to characterize retrospectively the project of *Socialisme ou Barbarie*. Castoriadis put it simply in a conversation many years ago: they found the thread of bureaucracy and simply continued to pull on it, from critiquing the Soviet bureaucracy, to the relations of production that it institutes, to modern capitalism in its difference from the classical mode of production analyzed by Marx, to a reified thought claiming the status of theory when it is simply subsuming the new under already given categories. This intellectual movement reflects not only a change in the empirical object of analysis. In an interview with the mimeographed journal *Anti-mythes* in 1975, Lefort explained that "it is the belief . . . in a general formula for organizing society that I criticized as illusory by showing that it was the basis on which . . . the power of the bureaucracy was built, and that to break with it—*to attempt to break with it, for this is a break that has constantly to be repeated* [emphasis mine]—is the basic condition of a struggle in all fields, against actual or potential forms of domination." The italicized passage suggests that the adventure of *Socialisme ou Barbarie* concludes with the movement from a critique of bureaucracy to the critique of totalitarianism; with that, the theory of revolution inherited from Marx is transformed into the quest for autonomy on all planes of life, in theory as in practice, for the society as for the individual. That is why the journal's founders could continue their intellectual and political contributions long after the demise of their collective project and why they can—and should—still be read after 1989.

*Socialisme ou Barbarie* did not solve the theory-praxis problem that has haunted Marxists since the work of the founder. It showed, through multiple analyses of politics, economics, social relations, and cultural practices, that there is no unified solution, as Marx's conception of revolutionary theory presupposed. As the theme of autonomy came increasingly to replace the concept of revolution, the way was prepared for the participants in the journal to face up to the project of democracy that would institute the creativity on which they laid such stress. As Castoriadis, the Greek primus inter pares of the journal after Lefort's departure, came increasingly to realize, autonomy is a concept developed in Athens; it designates the act by which an individual or a group gives itself its own laws (*autos-nomos*). What could better incarnate the spirit animating *Socialisme ou Barbarie* than an antinomic quest for autonomy? Such a quest, rather than the theoretical result at which it arrives, can serve better to define political praxis in a modern democracy. If *Socialisme ou Barbarie* did not formulate this insight explicitly, the work of the journal makes possible its formulation today.

# CHAPTER 6

*Claude Lefort's Passage from Revolutionary Theory
to Political Theory*

When he learned that I was to deliver the traditional *laudatio*
when he was awarded the Hannah Arendt Prize for Political
Thought by the city-state of Bremen in 1999, Claude Lefort
reminded me jokingly that his work did not end with *Socialisme et
Barbarie*.[1] It was easy to meet that request but harder to write the
*laudatio*, which went through three radically different drafts. The
trick is to explain the association of the recipient with the principles
behind the award (in this case, with the political thought of Hannah
Arendt; this was easy enough); then to explain the great worth of the
recipient's work (which had to be reduced to digestible portions for
a general public); and finally to associate oneself and the public in a
shared sympathy with the recipient. This last task is the most difficult and explains why my drafts were so different from one another.
The solution that I finally adopted was to ask at the outset of the *laudatio* why it was necessary to bring an American to Germany to
praise the work of a French political thinker. Why was Lefort's work
not well known or studied in Germany? There seem to be three reasons: in Germany, moral philosophy has replaced political philosophy, properly speaking; in Germany, politics tends to be reduced to

its sociological foundations; and in Germany, given its history, a political thinker for whom democracy is a problem rather than a solution swims against a powerful tide.[2] Because the temptation to identify political theory with moral theory or to reduce it to sociology, as well as the idea that democracy is a political remedy for all problems, are not typical only of German intellectual life, it is worth looking more closely at these rather distinctive and provocative philosophical and political standpoints.

Claude Lefort was a student of Merleau-Ponty in high school, became his friend, and joined him at *Les Temps Modernes*. There, Lefort's critical articles were published (with some reluctance) until his fierce polemic against Sartre's philocommunism, which coincided with Merleau-Ponty's exit from the journal he had cofounded with Sartre. Lefort later edited Merleau-Ponty's posthumous works *The Visible and the Invisible* and *The Prose of the World*. Their shared interests were evident in Lefort's early philosophical essays on ethnology and sociology, which were later republished in *Les formes de l'histoire* (1978), and in their interrogation of painting and literature, documented in Lefort's essays republished in *Sur une colonne absente* (1978), whose subtitle is *Écrits autour de Merleau-Ponty*. Lefort adopted and adapted Merleau-Ponty's phenomenological vocation and vocabulary as his own work matured. But the "master" (*maître*), as Lefort has said, knew how to avoid the "position of a master." It was Merleau-Ponty who suggested to the young *lycéen* that with his interests and character he would find it interesting to read Trotsky. The master was right: Lefort became an engaged militant in the Fourth International. His own philosophical adventures with dialectics had begun.

Lefort cofounded (with Cornelius Castoriadis) an oppositional faction within the party before leaving the Trotskyists in 1948 to create the journal *Socialisme ou Barbarie* and the movement whose aims it expressed. This political and intellectual project was unified by its quest for a leftist critique of what its members saw as the bureaucratization of working-class politics, internationally and domestically. To remain within the left in postwar France meant using Marx against the orthodoxy of the party Marxists while insisting on the autonomy of the proletariat as the agent of revolution. The claim of the party to know what is best (i.e., what is "historically necessary") for the workers led Lefort to criticize Trotsky's defense of the Soviet Union in spite of Stalin, which Trotsky had based on the ground that the infrastructure of socialism had been created by the nationalization of property in the USSR and the realization of communism depended only on liberation from bureaucratic "excesses." After Khrushchev's 1956 denunciation of Stalin at the Twentieth Congress of the Soviet Communist Party, Lefort's "Stalinism Without Stalin" showed that the changes proposed were only a modification rather than a serious transformation of the new form of domination that had taken root in the wake of the 1917 revolution. Lefort still applied Marxist categories to his analysis, arguing that the party's seizure of power followed by its use of that power to transform social relations constituted a new form of class exploitation. After the strikes and protests of the Polish workers, also in 1956, led to a change in party leadership there, the Hungarian revolution the following month seemed to confirm the possibility of autonomous working-class activity. Lefort could still think of his theory as revolutionary because it was in accord with the interests and actions of the proletarian class that had inaugurated these radical actions.

While Lefort could explain the installation of the bureaucracy as a new dominant class in the USSR by his creative use of Marxist categories, this left open the question of why Western workers and intellectuals were blind to this deformation. It posed the more serious question of why they followed their own Communist Parties when no constraint to do so existed. The answer to this question would lead Lefort away from his belief in the essentially revolutionary vocation of the proletariat. A first step had been taken in his devastating critique of Sartre's 1952 essay "The Communists and Peace." Lefort had little trouble showing that Sartre misunderstood Marx's idea of proletarian revolution, and the nicely titled "From the Reply to the Question," his response to Sartre's counterpolemic, was even more convincing. But the problem was not philological (although Lefort showed himself to be a superior reader of Marx); Sartre did not see that the question was philosophical. Its most succinct formulation is found in Lefort's critique of the "method of the progressive intellectuals." As with the Communist Party that claims to know what is best for the proletariat, these self-defined progressive intellectuals assumed that it was their duty, when the Polish and Hungarian workers asserted their autonomy in 1956, to explain the "political necessity" of the repression of that claim as a result of superior world historical necessities of which the class could not be aware. It was as if the role of the intellectual were to be the mouthpiece of History rather than to voice a critique of injustice and oppression. The philosophical consequence of the appeal to History's necessities is that the progressive intellectual is incapable of recognizing the new because he denies the possibility of historical creation. A decade later, after May 1968 had undertaken its own historical creation, Lefort published a short article in *Le Monde* reaffirming this critique against those hoping for a "resurrection of Trotsky" as the positive result of what some thought would be the first step toward a new French revolution.[3]

Lefort's understanding of historical creation was phenomenological. In the first phase of his development, the central category was experience: he argued that its richness and ambiguity, its mixture of determination and creativity, could become the basis of the self-organization of the proletariat. Lefort still believed in revolution, and his argument developed the dialectics that could lead to overcoming alienation (positing, for example, that the Stalinist experience could be seen as a stage teaching the proletariat the need to rely only on itself).[4] But Lefort's phenomenological analysis of political experience led to a further conclusion: his comrades at *Socialisme ou Barbarie* were guilty of the same claim of knowing what is best for others that had been the basis of the critique of Bolshevism.[5] After an earlier break in 1952, Lefort finally left the group in 1958, explaining in "Organisation et parti" why he had joined like-minded friends to form a new political group that resolved to put itself at the service of the spontaneity they saw as essential to true revolution.[6] But he continued to learn from experience; by 1960 his answer to the question "What is bureaucracy?" recognized that the belief in workers' self-management was based on the illusion that perfect transparency of motive and action as well as a completed rationality were possible.[7] This led in turn to a revision of his earlier phenomenology of proletarian experience. Returning again to Marx—as he has done constantly[8]—his doubts were confirmed in the 1965 lectures at the Sorbonne in which he analyzed Marx's move "from one vision of history to another."[9] Despite Marx's vision of a humanity progressing from one mode of production to another as the class struggle moves toward its climax, a closer reading shows that Marx recognizes the existence of novelty and innovations that no material necessity can explain; such is indeed the case with the advent of capitalism. Whereas previous societies were organized around their own self-preservation, this new social formation differs insofar as it seeks constantly to expand, to innovate, to increase its reach. As Marx himself defines it—for example, in *The Communist Manifesto*— capitalism is revolutionary; it defiles "all that is holy," including the customs and traditions that ensured the reproduction of previous social forms. At the same time that it cannot be explained by the preexisting economic infrastructure, capitalism seems to create the material conditions for its own reproduction. In this way, capitalism finds itself doing what traditional societies do (i.e., making possible their own reproduction) even while it is explicitly oriented toward growth and change. How can such a paradoxical society be understood? How can historical creation be explained? What kind of explanation is needed? Read as a philosopher, Marx poses the problem; the solution remains to be found. Lefort came to recognize that it entails a reinterpretation of the nature of politics and the institution of democratic politics.

Lefort's massive study *Le travail de l'oeuvre: Machiavel* (1972) and his participation in a collective republication and commentary on La Boétie's *Discours sur la servitude volontaire* (1976) seek to unearth the roots, and dangers, of the fascination with the political. He begins from a historical analysis of the "name and representation" of Machiavelli, which serves as a preface to the reconstruction of eight typical and at first convincing interpretations of Machiavelli's work. Read closely, each of these loses its initial plausibility for the same reason: its pretension to know what Machiavelli really said, or meant to say, or ought to have said. Turning to *The Prince* and *The Discourses on Livy*, Lefort clarifies his title: the work (*travail*) of the *oeuvre* results from its very indetermination (which is not the same as arbitrariness); the *oeuvre* retains its power to enlighten just because it cannot be made univocal. Lefort is developing here the intuition that guided his critique of the bureaucratization of politics; the work of the Machiavellian *oeuvre* constantly undermines any attempt to know, once and for all. There can be no overarching theory (what Merleau-Ponty called a *pensée de survol*), disconnected from and standing above its object, whose objective existence can be fully known. In the language of phenomenology, the noetic intentional act cannot be united with the noematic object of knowledge. Yet the desire to find such a place, freed from the threat of temporality and the emergence of the new, is constantly present. Moving back to Marx once again, in an essay entitled "The Genesis of Ideology in Modern Societies" (1974), Lefort sees that this desire to avoid the threat of the new becomes the secret motivation of what Marx came to understand in his critique of ideology. As opposed to the usual vision that reduces ideology to the contradiction between ideas and the supposedly real or scientific infrastructure, Lefort shows that Marx did not have a fully developed concept of ideology that he applied to an already existing reality; he discovered rather the effects of ideology through his analysis of the new relations of modern society.[10] Lefort demonstrates the same process of discovery in Machiavelli, in La Boétie, and, returning to the theme two decades later, in the "modernity" of Dante's *On Monarchy*.

Lefort's studies of centuries past are exercises in reading: reading texts, deciphering signs of what the author sought in vain to master, comparing texts with their later reception, but also reading the supposedly real and the historical novelty that challenges its certainties and calls for interpretation, as it existed for the author but also as it awakens our curiosity by putting into doubt our own certitudes. Each of these interpretive ventures is animated, moreover, by a concern with politics "here and now," as Lefort repeats on the last page of *Machiavel*.[11]

Lefort's abandonment of the goal of proletarian revolution and its dream of the "good society" did not mean that he accepted the existing political order. Always alert to signs of the new, he rejoined Castoriadis (and Edgar Morin) to publish—in late May '68, while the strikes were still taking place—*Mai 1968: La brèche*.[12] The next year, he joined his former student Marcel Gauchet on the editorial committee of the journal *Textures*, in which he published an essay that was the first step in a new stage of his development. "On Democracy: The Political and the Institution of the Social" (1971) was based on notes transcribed by Gauchet from Lefort's lectures, which Lefort reworked. Reunited with Castoriadis, who also joined the editorial group of *Textures*, along with Miguel Abensour and Pierre Clastres, both of whom also participated in the collective work on La Boétie, this group founded a new journal, *Libre*, in 1977. Its ten issues widened and deepened the implications of the earlier critique

of totalitarianism that took on a more philosophical cast while opening the investigation of democratic politics as a renewal of critical
radicalism. As the new journal was being created, Lefort published
in *Textures* the first part of what became his next book, *Un homme en
trop* (1976), a philosophical reading of Solzhenitsyn's recently translated and much contested "literary investigation," *The Gulag Archipelago*, a book denounced by many (who read only its first volume)
as the expression of a religious reactionary.[13] The "excess man" of
Lefort's title refers both to the simple man, the *zek* imprisoned in the
camps who must be separated from a society that seeks to become
transparent to itself (or to its rulers) by eliminating not just enemies
but "parasites," and to the "Egocrat" who arrogates to himself a
vision of historical necessity and, what is more, the power to imprint
it in the real. Lefort's reading of totalitarianism has now left the flat
terrain of sociology; his later readings of Orwell and Rushdie are
anticipated by the confrontation with Solzhenitsyn.

Lefort was becoming known to a wider public in a France whose
intellectual climate, always heavily influenced by political debate,
was beginning a process of change that would overcome the unquestioned hegemony of the Marxist left. He published a collection of
the essays that had led him away from Marxism, as *Eléments d'une critique de la bureaucratie* (1971), and another volume, *Les formes de l'histoire* (1978), that collected his early ethnographic essays together
with the fruits of his renewed study of Marx from the transitional
period of the 1960s. He had left the University of Caen for a position at the Ecole des Hautes Etudes in Paris, where his weekly sem-
inars became an influential part of the shifting scenery.[14] After
another rupture with Castoriadis brought the adventure of *Libre* to
an end, Lefort began writing in *Esprit* and founded his own journal,
*Passé-Présent*. The title of that short-lived journal suggests one of the
unifying themes of Lefort's work: the presence of the past, like the
*oeuvre* that challenges the certainties of the present.

In the French context, the living past was of course the French
Revolution. Lefort's attraction to the revolution was more complex;
he was drawn by the attempts of its nineteenth-century heirs—liberals, such as Guizot; republicans, such as Michelet or Quinet; and
democrats, such as Tocqueville—to understand the fundamental
indeterminacy that the revolution introduces in the very attempt to
interpret it. The *oeuvre* of these liberal, republican, and democratic

readings of the very revolution whose ambiguous presence called for them makes clear a fundamental insight: what is taken to be real is in fact instituted, and—since reality is not caused by some necessity external to it—this institution is symbolic. The roots of this formulation go back to Lefort's philosophical-ethnological studies from the 1950s that showed the necessity of a shared framework of meaning as the symbolic instance that institutes a society as *this* society, one in which the licit and the illicit are lawfully regulated in a manner that gives a particular society its unity and sense.[15] This symbolic institution can be called "the political," as distinct from the particular political life that it institutes by making visible what was previously invisible at the same time that, in an apparent paradox that is quite familiar to the phenomenologist, it makes itself invisible as the act of institution. The symbolic function of the political is to institute what a society takes as real. But, as with ideology, to be effective the political has to hide its own creativity from itself.

Lefort had now elaborated the concepts needed to understand the uniqueness of democracy, which he had intuited at the time of his break with Marxism but could not then formulate. The symbolic institution of society in previous social formations depended on an external or transcendent source: gods of various kinds, tradition, or the appeal to the nature of things.[16] This external source of legitimation for the social order began to change with the formation of modern monarchies. Lefort turns to Ernst Kantorowicz's analysis of *The King's Two Bodies*, which shows how and why the absolute monarch was understood as incorporating in his mortal body the immortal body of the kingdom. This is the sense of the popular cry "The King is dead; long live the King," which implies and affirms that society never dies; it reproduces itself over and beyond the actions and the diverse interests of its mortal inhabitants. But the overthrow of the ancien régime institutes a new form of social division; the old hierarchical unity disappears with the monarch, as does the representation of a society whose immortal being and sense could be preserved across space and time. Society is forced to seek its unity from within itself at the same time that its members must take responsibility for their own individuality. But this quest is doomed to failure. Even if society were to succeed in giving itself a government that expressed popular sovereignty, that government would face two equally impossible choices: it could rise above the actual society and (try to) represent the general interest—in which case it would become external to the individuals whom it was supposed to represent; or it could seek to compromise with the plurality of individuals—in which case it would lose the generality that the political institution of shared meanings is supposed to represent. This implies that the institution of democracy neither results from the action of government nor is the expression of the unitary will of the sovereign people. Its institution must remain invisible; its divisions must be made to appear natural, taken for granted. This, again, is a form of ideology—which can now be seen to exist *only* in democratic societies, which must seek their legitimation within themselves.[17] Democracy secretes ideology to hide from itself the radical indeterminacy that is its foundation. It seeks to render innovation impossible, to put an end to history, to hide the basic division of society in a representation of its natural unity. The political implication is that democracy must come to understand that it is based on the recognition of conflict, the admission that the society is divided and must remain divided. The idea of class struggle is thus reformulated as the question of the legitimacy of social division. The overcoming of class division sought by Marx and claimed by totalitarian societies is in fact the elimination of democracy.

Lefort knew of course that his argument for democracy as radical politics would be criticized by those who claim to represent the left. He had taken up their challenge already in the preface to *Eléments*, pointing out that since power cannot be legitimately exercised by either the government of the moment or the united people, democratic civil society is thereby separated from the state and becomes the basis for a challenge to the totalitarian project. He returns to this issue in the introduction to *L'invention démocratique* and in an essay in that volume that tries to pinpoint the political role of the "invisible" symbolic institution, "L'impensée de l'Union de la Gauche."[18] How could French Socialists unite with a Communist Party that only paid lip service to the critique of totalitarianism, denouncing so-called excesses as if they were merely regrettable accidents and reproducing in this way what Lefort had previously criticized as the "method of the progressive intellectuals." The implication of this behavior is not only that the Communists are not committed to democratic politics; despite their professions of democratic faith, the same holds de facto for the Socialists, whose failure to understand was evident in their justification of the alliance. The weight of this critique became apparent a year later, when the National Committee of Solidarity in Poland and dissidents elsewhere in Eastern Europe built their resistance to totalitarianism around the demand for the "rights of man." How could these "rights," whose "merely formal" and so-called bourgeois character was famously denounced by Marx's essay "On the Jewish Question," become the basis of a radical politics? Marx's critique, Lefort counters, neglects the political dimension of politics; he had no concept of the symbolic institution of society; his Young Hegelian conceptual critique ignored the phenomenology of actual experience. The right to privacy, for example, might well justify private accumulation in capitalist reality, but compared to the arbitrary nature of the absolutist state, this right was in practice the precondition of political action, the ground for freedom of association, the basis on which further rights could be demanded. With this, Lefort takes a step beyond his claim that democracy is made possible by the overthrow of the ancien régime. The institution of such rights from within society, the declaration of what Hannah Arendt (whose work Lefort had not read at the time of his earlier critique of totalitarianism) called "the right to have rights," is the foundation of democratic politics.

But democratic politics are not instituted once and for all.[19] The same revolutionary event that overthrew the visible power of the monarch and made possible the institution of democracy also makes possible totalitarianism, which is not just an extreme form of despotic arbitrariness. Lefort's 1948 critique of Trotsky had already underlined the implications of Trotsky's casual remark that while Louis XIV could merely say, "L'état c'est moi," Stalin's claim was even more radical: "La société c'est moi." The analysis of totalitarianism must be reactivated once more.[20] The fact that Lenin had defined a Bolshevik as a "Jacobin working for the proletarian cause" (in "One Step Forward, Two Steps Back" [1904]) poses the question of the nature of "the revolution in the French Revolution." Lefort's answer again points to its inauguration of the world of the modern individual coupled with the destruction of the old, unified hierarchical cosmos. But the revolution was not a single, unified event. Its lurching passage from phase to phase was marked by attempts to bring it to an end; yet that end would have brought with it the elimination of politics, the erasure of social division, and the creation of a new unity.

The modern individualist world can no more be mastered than could be the *oeuvre* of Machiavelli. What is this modern individualism? Lefort turns to Tocqueville, questioning the passage "De l'égalité à la liberté" in the American context. The usual reading sees equality as what Tocqueville himself called (in his introduction) a "generative fact" founded on the natural equality of conditions on the new continent. This natural equality is said (in volume 1) to at once make possible liberty but also to threaten it; it eliminates hierarchy by making individuals equal, but it thereby produces the tyranny of opinion: the constant love of equality is said to overwhelm the ephemeral desire for liberty and to call for a "tutelary state" that Tocqueville sees as a dangerous and new political formation. But this reading (which relies on volume 1)[21] suggests too quickly the kinship of democracy and totalitarianism, as if the former led of its own nature to the latter, such that totalitarianism was not the result of a political choice and struggle.

The simple reading of Tocqueville as predicting a democratic despotism reduces him to a mere sociologist. Lefort's critique of totalitarianism is that of a philosopher. But its political relevance should be stressed as well, especially after the fall of Communism. Totalitarianism was not historically necessary, but it was not an accident, and its disappearance does not signify the triumph of a pure democracy that only had been waiting to be freed from a repressive state. When the progressive intellectuals finally rallied to antitotalitarianism, they tended to turn away from politics, adopting an ethical absolutism typified by the so-called new philosophers, as if philosophy had to avoid compromise and experience to remain pure. Referring often only implicitly to his contemporaries, Lefort is merciless with their intellectual laziness, moralizing self-satisfaction, unthinking modishness, all combined with a positivism that calls itself science. Yet his readings of the great works of the past (starting with Machiavelli, then Marx, and now Tocqueville) are attentive to what necessarily must escape even the rigorous experience of thought: the indetermination of being, the ambiguity of the relation of liberty and equality, the creativity of history. Addressing a group of new recruits to antitotalitarianism concerning "la question de la démocratie,"[22] Lefort points out that while Tocqueville saw the ambiguity of the new democracy—law is strengthened because it appears as the expression of the collective will, but it imposes increasingly uniform norms on individuals within that collectivity—he did not see that this ambiguity is itself ambiguous: as in Lefort's critique of Marx on the rights of man, Tocqueville forgets that law gives the individual also the right to demand new rights, giving content to democratic demands. Tocqueville's blind spot may have been due to political prejudice, admits Lefort, but it is also the sign of an intellectual resistance to the uncertain adventure of democracy even in democracy's most self-critical analyst. But perhaps the fault lies not with Tocqueville but with his reader, whose quest for a scientific interpretation of democracy induced a self-willed blindness. Can the philosopher escape from his own short-sightedness?

Asked to contribute to an English collection entitled *Philosophy in France Today*, Lefort stressed the question mark in his title: "Philosophe?"[23] With his concern with politics, history, literature, and their reciprocal interactions with one another, he doesn't fit into the usual professional pattern. But what then is philosophy? he is led to ask. He admits that he has no answer. He knows that it can manifest itself in works that do not know that they are philosophy, such as those of Michelet or Tocqueville. But the fact that he has no answer doesn't mean that the question is vain. What is vain is the claim that the question has disappeared, for that converts an interrogation into an affirmation or, rather, into a negation. In fact, Lefort finds the path to an answer in Tocqueville, as he explains in "Réversibilité: La liberté politique et la liberté de l'individu," the essay that accompanies the study of equality and liberty that led to his question.[24] The author who had the audacity to say that "whoever seeks freedom for something other than itself is made to serve" was curiously unable, says Lefort, to recognize that he who seeks truth for anything other than itself is made to believe—and thus to serve. Lefort could have been speaking of himself. Only as philosophers, convinced not that we have the truth but that the truth is precisely what none of us can have but all of us seek (and are tempted to delude ourselves into thinking we have), can we actively criticize the world in which we live and liberate the signs of the new from the temptation of repetition that is the mark of ideology.

CHAPTER 7

# From Marx to Castoriadis, and
# from Castoriadis to Us

Some decry the sixties generation as hedonistic and blame it for
the social laxity that has given us culture wars and increasingly conservative government. I remember it rather for the attempt to create the politics of a new left. That project, I have been arguing in this
book, remains on the contemporary agenda. But in order to reclaim
it, it is necessary to understand where it went astray and to see
whether it can be reconstructed on another foundation. As it happens, this project coincides in many ways with Cornelius Castoriadis's own political development. To illustrate the overlaps (without
denying the differences), a few introductory remarks are useful.

It was clear that the new left had to distinguish itself from the old,
but this was not easy in America at a time when its anticommunist crusade (which was not confined to the excesses of McCarthyism) was
still part of the recent present, the universities were still oriented to
the liberal consensus, and monolinguism prevented access to the various dissident left traditions.[1] I had the good fortune to travel in Eastern Europe and become friendly with some young Czech dissidents;
that experience inoculated me against the enemy-of-my-enemy arguments that led many in the new left to adopt an *anti*-anti-communist

politics whose consequences were an inability either to discuss foreign policy issues critically (not the least of which concerned the kinds of revolutionary regimes created first in Cuba and then in Vietnam and Cambodia) or to enter into serious debate with an older generation of leftists that warned against a naive populism symbolized by the self-identification of the new left as a "movement" rather than a specific political project. But it is only fair to say that I too felt the need to find a true Marx who, I assumed, had been distorted either by opportunist ruling cliques in the so-called socialist world or oversimplified by transforming dialectics into a banal reduction of politics to economics. It was in this context that I accepted a proposition by Karl Klare to coedit with him *The Unknown Dimension: European Marxism since Lenin*.[2]

To discover the authentic Marxist kernel that would be the basis of a radical critique of a society whose flagrant injustice was evident not only in its Vietnam adventure but especially on the home front, where the civil rights movement had already awakened new political engagements, it seemed necessary to find an alternative to Leninism. (We had no idea at the time that there could be a revolutionary tradition that was not indebted to Marx.) The grounds for Lenin's creation of a unique kind of political party were explained in *What Is to Be Done?* Lenin argued that the working class on its own could develop only simple, self-interested "trade union consciousness," whose particularistic limitation had to be overcome in order to create truly revolutionary "political class consciousness." But the result of Lenin's emphasis on the party as the consciousness of the class was to destroy the spontaneous self-organizational character of working-class activity. This critique of Leninism had been made before, by Social Democrats, who considered themselves still to be working for socialist goals, and by liberals, who did not. What we wondered was whether it was possible to retain the radical political project of Marx (as we understood it) without accepting the stagnation of Leninism. It was for this reason that I convinced Karl Klare that we needed to include a chapter on the group Socialisme ou Barbarie. Through contacts with the clandestine movement against the war in Vietnam, I was able to meet first Claude Lefort and then, in Lefort's study, Cornelius Castoriadis.[3]

I was at this time also involved with the project of *Telos*, a quarterly publication begun by the graduate philosophy students at Buffalo but quickly joined by others. It can fairly be said that *Telos* represented, in its first decade, the theoretical self-education of a new left. The journal began from phenomenology; Husserl's late manuscript *The Crisis of European Sciences* showed that the lifeworld of human experience was the foundation without which the abstractions of modern science became an end in themselves that could be misused and manipulated. This criticism of the abstractness of modern science became the basis for a broader critique of the alienated, reified, formalized, or one-dimensional world of contemporary capitalism.[4] A few issues later, the journal discovered Lukács's *History and Class Consciousness*, with its Hegelian-Marxist interpretation of the proletariat as the revolutionary subject-object of history; two issues later came a debate with Karl Korsch's *Marxism and Philosophy* but also the recognition that this author—whose Hegelian-Marxism had been condemned by the Communist Church, as had Lukács's work—did not go to Canossa and renounce his own work but adopted an increasingly independent radical ("council communist") orientation. New discoveries continued in *Telos*—through Gramsci, the Frankfurt School, and on to the early Habermas. It was at this time that I proposed translations of Lefort and Castoriadis. The debate over whether to do so went on for more than a year. All the journal's previous critical adventures had remained within the orbit of Father Marx; now the proposal was to criticize the foundations of his gospel. Castoriadis's critique was particularly radical and disturbing; it questioned the basic ontology of the master. This challenge to a group of self-professed radical leftists—who were pursuing their education in public but were also (relatively) sophisticated philosophically and reading these new texts in the original (and publishing them in often awkward translations!)—was a threat. Still, the translations finally appeared.[5]

In the next quarter century, Castoriadis's work appeared with growing frequency in English translation, and he lectured increasingly at American venues. He no longer stands as a critic of Marxism; as it should, his critique developed into a positive philosophical system, with applications to the natural and social sciences as well as to psychoanalysis. Has he been understood? It's hard to say. He wanted recognition from his equals. A final anecdote is telling in that regard. At the time that I wrote the introductions to Castoriadis and Lefort for *Telos*, I found myself at a dinner party in Paris with some

American academics, as well as Julia Kristeva and Philippe Sollers, the editor of the very chic and very avant-garde (and at the time very Maoist) journal *Tel Quel*. I objected to some of their political stances, invoking arguments from both Castoriadis and Lefort. Kristeva and Sollers had heard the names but didn't know the work. Could he read my introductions? asked Sollers. "Certainly" was my response. Some two days later came an offer to translate and publish my essays. When I told this to both Castoriadis and Lefort, their replies were identical: not in the journal of those *crapules*! Recognition of that fashionable kind was no more desired than recognition was accepted as a good in itself. Castoriadis was, I think, inspired by the same motivation that drove the new left: the leitmotiv of his systematic philosophical work was the critique of heteronomy in order to realize the autonomy and the creativity that make humans the inventors of their own history.

## From Marx to "Revolutionary Theory"

The title of this section alludes to the fact that, in spite of his devastating critiques of Marx and Marxism, Castoriadis constantly returned to Marx. On a first reading of "Marxism and Revolutionary Theory," the 1964–1965 essay that elaborated polemically the consequences of his twenty years of critical engagement with Marx seems to conclude with a definitive rejection of what the author calls Marx's "metaphysics." But a closer look at the arguments suggests that Castoriadis's title should have read: "Marxism *or* Revolutionary Theory?" In effect, Castoriadis abandoned the former in order to remain faithful to the latter (and thus to Marx's project). But this leaves unexamined the question of what makes a theory revolutionary? And by implication it poses the question, did Marx have a correct intuition, even if he followed it badly? If that is the case, can we remain Marxists? How?

The Marx whom Castoriadis rejected claimed to be a "revolutionary theorist." This meant that his theory was intimately bound up with "the standpoint of the proletariat" (Lukács), which incarnated the conditions for the practical overcoming of the contradictory circumstances of its own birth. The proletariat was understood as the product of past historical progress that could, by becoming self-conscious and aware of its own blocked potentiality, overcome the limits on its creativity imposed by class society. In another of Lukács's phrases, the proletariat was the "subject-object of history." Marx was able to discover the radical essence of the proletariat because he rejected what Lukács called the "contemplative" and external stance of philosophy. Merleau-Ponty nicely labeled this philosophical attitude a *pensée de survol*, flying above and gazing down on its object, whereas revolutionary praxis must adopt an immanent critical-historical engagement whose results cannot be separated from its theoretical premise. This engaged position is not without risk. Castoriadis takes Marx at his word; he accepts Marx's wager on history—and accepts history's verdict. There is no more use in claiming constantly "conditions are not yet ripe" than in blaming betrayal or human weakness for the failure to win Marx's revolutionary wager. Marx bet on history, and he lost. To continue to hope for a future revolution would be to read Marx as merely a contemplative philosopher; it would be, Castoriadis implies, necessarily to misread him.

Restoring Marx's original historical project permits Castoriadis to lay the foundations of his own revolutionary theory. This explains why he reprinted "Marxism and Revolutionary Theory" as the first part of *The Imaginary Institution of Society*, which was published a decade later (1975). But what is revolutionary about Castoriadis's own theory? Does he too, like Marx, bet on history? How do the two parts of his book fit together? He had suggested that Marx's intention to go beyond a contemplative or metaphysical account of a real history guided by the logic of an immanent telos was correct but that the Marxism that emerged was unfaithful to Marx's radical intention. But Castoriadis refuses to simplify: really existing Marxism cannot be rejected as a (conscious or unintended) betrayal of Marx. Subjective factors explain nothing of any significance. One can only conclude that there must have been a problem with Marx's understanding of the revolutionary project itself. It is necessary to return to the original question to seek a better way to pose it—or to find the question that made possible that first question.

An essay published not coincidentally in the same year (1975) that saw the appearance of *The Imaginary Institution* took up the challenge of defining what counts as revolutionary under the title "Valeur, égalité, justice, politique: De Marx à Aristote et d'Aristote à nous" (Value, equality, justice, politics: From Marx to Aristotle and from Aristotle to Us).[6] This return to the Greeks[7] makes clear Castoriadis's recognition of the need to create a non-Marxist understanding of revolutionary theory. The essay begins with a long citation from Marx's analysis of commodity exchange in volume 1 of *Capital*. Marx praises Aristotle's "genius" that permitted him to grasp the paradoxical foundation of the exchange relation by means of a notion of "value" as that which represents or stands for "a common substance" that accounts for (or even constitutes) the equality of the otherwise unequal things exchanged (for if the things were equal, why would they be exchanged?). But, adds Marx, Aristotle could not go further in his analysis; he could not understand that this value represents "abstract human labor" because "Greek society was based on the work of slaves." This invocation of a historical fact implies that History (understood as progress toward complete social self-understanding) only makes possible the revelation of the secret of exchange to the residents of a capitalist society that has developed completely its economic basis. Castoriadis criticizes this claim as Marx's "metaphysics"; it transforms capitalism, a particular historical society, into the incarnation of a telos that makes possible a correct reading of all past History. The result of Marx's misguided assumption is that not only does the present lose its uniqueness; the past also loses its autonomy and indeterminacy. The implication of Castoriadis's critique is that for a theory to be revolutionary, both its relation to history and the nature of the historical world must become explicit. The teleological assumption that history can come to an end, that (class) contradictions can be overcome, and that society can know itself fully and completely, leaving no space for indetermination, must be abandoned. What can be put in its place? Is revolutionary theory simply the critique of a metaphysical understanding of history?

While Castoriadis never abandoned the critical engagement with Marx that drove him (starting in the second part of *The Imaginary Institution*) to make explicit his own conception of revolutionary theory, the growing preoccupation with the Greeks inaugurated by "Valeur, égalité, justice, politique" suggests what the internal evidence of his own theory (and the political history of our times, from which—like Marx—he never separated his thought) amply confirms: that for Castoriadis *revolutionary theory came increasingly to be identified with democracy.* This suggests that the kind of criticism Castoriadis addressed to Marx would not be different from the kind of criticism he would address to democracy. Democracy too can become a metaphysics. It too can take itself as representing the telos of History, the self-transparency of society to itself, and the end of contradiction and opposition. Rather than solving the riddle of history, both democracy and Marxism pose more new problems than they resolve older ones. Neither the democrat nor the Marxist can eliminate indeterminacy from history; neither can do away with the need for political judgment, which must always assume the possibility of error and the need to take responsibility for its claims. Like Marx's theory, democracy can fall victim to hubris and refuse to recognize the need to set limits on itself (for such self-set limits are not the denial but rather the affirmation of autonomy). This danger becomes clear when one turns again to Castoriadis' critique of Marx.

## Elements of the Critique of Marxism

At a first level, Castoriadis demonstrates the internal contradictions of Marx's claim to have gone beyond philosophy to establish a new science. Perhaps the most telling illustration of this point is his critique of Marx's claim to demonstrate the necessary breakdown of capitalism as the result of the so-called law of the tendency of the rate of profit to fall. Because surplus-value can only be produced by labor-power, whose value (as "variable capital") decreases relative to the value of the constant capital invested in large-scale modern industry, Marx demonstrates that the rate of profit must sink (on the basis of complicated calculations of the transformation of value into price, whose determination depends on the average profit of each capital remaining equal, since Marx makes the neoclassical assumption that markets are free and open and money is fungible). Even if the so-called scientific validity of the labor theory of value is accepted (in spite of the metaphysics involved in the transmutation of concrete labor into something like an abstract substance parceled out among commodities to be exchanged), this law assumes that the value of constant capital invested in machines and raw materials remains fixed, and it makes the same assumption about labor-power. In so doing, it neglects in both cases the social and historical (and human) factors that enter into the relations of production. It does not consider the possibility of the discovery of new raw materials or resources or the invention of new machines making older ones obsolete (regardless of the value they still incorporate).

More important for Marx's basic claim is Castoriadis's demonstration that the labor theory of value itself abstracts from what was otherwise the basis of Marx's entire historical theory: the class struggle that, presumably, can have the effect of raising or lowering the value of labor-power and therefore that of its materialized product when one or the other class is in the ascendant. Despite these criticisms that aim at the heart of Marx's economic claims, Castoriadis treats Marx with the same respect that Marx reserved for Smith and Ricardo: he doesn't denounce these internal contradictions as the product of an apologetic ideology said to reflect a personal bias but tries to understand the real historical root of the inconsistency of an innovative thinker. The supposed logic of class struggle is based on a theory of history that assumes, as in Marx's critique of Aristotle, that capitalism represents the complete (but still alienated) development of society's human capacities. As such, it eliminates the indeterminacy of the past; it assumes that humans only can know what they truly are when the economy (of which they are the producers) becomes socially dominant. But this implies that capitalism is not a particular, historically specific social formation; instead it is understood as the actualization of what was only potential in all previous social formations. As such, its particular logic is identified with logic *tout court*; its notion of science is not understood as specific to particular, historically given social relations but is generalized through its identification with technology to become *the* proper way for humans to relate to, and to understand, the natural world. The quantitative relations of equivalence exchange impress their mark throughout the society and are taken as the proper model for all social relations. And so it is, finally, that Marx's quest for a scientific theory appeals to the existence of a "substance" called value that would be at once historically specific and yet general and present in all societies, that is concrete and yet abstract, the individual output of the worker that is only made possible by social conditions. Why assume that such a substance, which Castoriadis calls "metaphysical," actually exists? Why make Homo economicus the truth of Homo sapiens?

This critique of Marx's metaphysics had already been developed in "Marxism and Revolutionary Theory"; the contrast to Aristotle now makes clear that it had political consequences that went beyond the negative conclusions concerning Marx and Marxism. Aristotle was not trying to discover a scientific theory of economics; he wanted to understand the political foundation holding together a society composed of heterogeneous and thus unequal actors. Not only does Marx neglect the distinction between the realm of necessity that governs the household (*oikos*), which is populated by women and slaves, and the domain of freedom that is the city (*polis*); he also fails to recall Aristotle's concern not to confuse the logic of production, which must obey external necessity, with the freedom of action, which is governed by a type of political reason. That Marx misunderstood Aristotle's philosophical intention is evident not only in the inconsistencies of his labor theory of value; his political misunderstanding also becomes apparent when he returns to Aristotle in the 1875 *Critique of the Gotha Program*, which was a direct intervention in the practical political choices of the German Socialist Party. When it comes to the question of the kind of equality to be sought under socialism, Marx's analysis proceeds as if the value that is to be distributed equally were somehow knowable in advance, as if it were fixed and given as a natural product, transcendent and immune to historical change. But the famous solution promised by communism—"From each according to his abilities, to each according to his needs"—presupposes not only a society of abundance, whose existence would not so much solve as dissolve the problem of equality; it also assumes that what each gives and receives is in some way commensurable, without ever explaining (or even recognizing the need to explain) how this commensurability (which Aristotle discussed as "proportional equality") is attained. More important still, the resolution of the problem of equality by the production of physical abundance seems to suppose the transcendence of "bourgeois" law (as it exists in the stage of formal equality that characterizes the "first phase" of socialism). This could have the dangerous implication that Marx's goal is the transcendence of law and, with it, of politics.

The critique of Marx that emerges from this contrast to Aristotle results in two related claims. First, Aristotle's philosophical theory has political consequences because it takes into account the social-historical character and resulting lack of univocal determination implicit in the Greek distinctions between *nomos* and *physis*, *doxa* and *aletheia*, being and appearance. As a result, Aristotle seeks not a science but a theory of judgment, a *phroneisis* that makes possible the kind of political intervention that Marx's "revolutionary theory" sought in vain because its claim to necessity and universality made it a metaphysics that had no room for the freedom of action needed for politics. Second, the basic "values" that bind together a society—that is, the justice and equality that are joined to value and politics in the title of the 1975 essay—are posited *politically* through what Castoriadis calls the "foundational enigma," whose basis is the apparently contradictory fact that a society can only exist as such on the basis of some commensurable values but at the same time these foundational values must be continually posited by the same society whose existence they ensure. In the one case, the shared values appear to be *nomoi*; in the other, they tend toward the material necessity that defines the pole of *physis*. While no society can imagine itself to be totally arbitrary, none can exist if its being is determined simply and completely by nature. Confrontation with this "enigma"—a term favored by both the young and the mature Marx—is a fundamental condition of the possibility of "revolutionary theory."

## Rehabilitating Marx as a Philosopher

While one might speculate as to whether the demise of communism coincides with the triumph of liberal capitalism, giving a final proof that history has (or has not) refuted the author of *The Communist Manifesto*, it is certain that the new world order that has put democracy at the top of the global agenda has also increased the actuality of the revolutionary theory of democracy sought by Castoriadis. It has done so, however, by focusing attention not so much on Marx the revolutionary as on Marx the philosopher, who now must be read in a new light, much as Castoriadis reads Aristotle and the Greeks against the background of the enigma of Greek democracy. For example, instead of denouncing the scientistic illusion presented by the law of the tendency of the rate of profit to fall, one should ask why Marx's demonstration of that particular law is followed by nearly five hundred pages of text analyzing the problems of interest and rent on land before the argument finally collapses entirely in the (incomplete) chapter on classes. Marx's demonstration of the absurdity of capitalist social relations in his account of interest as the solipsistic appearance of "money producing money" and his critical analysis of how the apparently self-evident explanation of the sources and distribution of income within capitalist society by the "Trinity Formula" (land, labor, capital) breaks down in the face of the actual divisions of capitalist society in fact recall more the careful analysis of Aristotle than they do the certainties proclaimed by the Marx Castoriadis convincingly criticized. Despite their scientific pretense, these analyses recall the young Marx's notion of an "immanent critique" that, he wrote in 1843, "would make these petrified relations dance by singing before them their own melody." But the young Marx too was in search of a revolutionary theory and should not be separated so neatly from the mature theorist he would become. The artificial distinction of the two phases does serve, however, to recall the need to read Marx's work as that of a philosopher.

The philosophical Marx, like the young Marx, remains a Hegelian. He is concerned constantly to join together a "phenomenology" of appearing relations with a "logic" that demonstrates the categorical relations that unite these appearances.[8] Even his "scientific" theory of capitalist economics reproduces the basic structure of Hegel's dialectical logic: volume 1 of *Capital* presents "the immediate process of production," volume 2 analyzes "the process of circulation of capital," and then volume 3 unites them in "the process of capitalist production as a whole." This Hegelian revolutionary, moreover, claims to show the necessary demise of capitalism in an inspired passage from the unfinished manuscript known as the *Grundrisse* that demonstrates how and why advanced capitalism overcomes (*aufheben*) its own economic premises doubly, both on the side of labor and on the side of capital. In this way, Marx is suggesting that economic development does not take place autonomously within its own sphere. His argument suggests the need to rediscover the place for political intervention that was covered over by the apparent domination of the economy in capitalist society—a domination that proves only the self-alienation of the citizens of that society.

The way in which the philosophical Marx makes room for the autonomy of politics can be seen in an incomplete manuscript, published in 1933 but widely available only in the mid-1960s under the

title "The Results of the Immediate Production Process." This manuscript presents a chapter the was to have formed the transition from
volume 1 to volume 2 of *Capital*. Its contribution can be summed up
simply: Marx recognizes that the commodities that enter into the
circulation process are no longer "immediately" given physical
products but now have been transformed into commodities contain-
ing something that has been socially created—what he calls surplus-
value (but which need not be understood as a substance). This means
that not only does capitalist society constantly transform itself (and
thus open itself to further transformation) but—as Aristotle had
insisted—economic processes have to be understood within the context of social reproduction. This more philosophical vision of the
place and nature of economic relations suggests that the status of
Marx's "scientific" economic theory is not that of a science and still
less that of a "revolutionary theory"; its relevance rests with its contribution to political theory. Its implication, from this perspective, is
the denunciation of a society that denies its own political foundation, treating its shared values as if they were naturally given, *physei*,
and therefore eternally and unquestionably valid. Marx the philosopher meets here with Castoriadis the "revolutionary theorist."

These philosophical reflections on Marx's economic masterwork
lead to a further query: why is *Capital* subtitled *A Critique of Political
Economy*? What does Marx mean by "critique"? The usual interpretation, since Lukács's *History and Class Consciousness*, points to the
notion of "immanent critique" that Marx called for in his 1843 essay.
Castoriadis doesn't stress this concept—perhaps because he tends to
identify Marx's scientism with a materialist Hegelianism that
assumes that beneath appearances there exist realities just waiting to
be liberated by the weapon of materialist science. But when it is
applied to the philosopher Marx, immanent critique could develop
some of Castoriadis's own insights. It rejects the metaphysical
assumption that false appearances must give way to true realities,
recognizing both that the appearing world is always open to question and that the ability and need to pose questions open the individual to the possibility of error. This means that the immanent critique is founded on the primacy of judgment and the responsibility
that each of us must assume for our judgments. It follows that politics is the domain not of truth but of its representation, and this
problem of representation is yet another formulation of Castori-

adis's insistence on the "foundational enigma" that poses the values that account for what a society accepts as relations of equality and justice. And, as we have seen, political theory seeks to understand the existence and reproduction of these values, and—we can now add—political practice is what makes possible the reproduction (or transformation) of those values.

## Marx and the Immanent Critique of Democracy

Marx the philosopher is not incompatible with Castoriadis the revolutionary theorist. Marx's treatment of "capitalist production as a whole" in volume 3 denounces the illusory self-representation of capitalism (for example, in the phenomenon of competition, which is the true analytic contribution made by the demonstration of the so-called law of the falling rate of profit). It criticizes the hubris that admits no limits to the "production of money by money" in the form of (self-referential or solipsistic) interest-bearing capital. It is not the mechanistic economic breakdown theory that is crucial to Marx's critique of capitalism; Marx's utopian vision is found in the double movement of self-overcoming portrayed in the *Grundrisse*, where the internal self-contradiction of capitalist social relations is shown to destroy their presuppositions, making possible (although not necessary) the emergence of new forms. When these insights are put into the context of the need for capitalist society to ensure its own social reproduction, the usurpation of the properly political institutional function by the mechanics of the economy becomes evident. At this point, the path to immanent critique is opened. But this does not yet delimit the spheres to which that critique can be applied (and those where it cannot be applied, since self-limitation is essential to autonomy).

Although *The Critique of the Gotha Program* posed the question of the nature of the shared values that at once constitute and are instituted by society, Marx's solution to the problem of equal sharing of these values avoided the institutional—the political—problem by assuming that in communist society the "springs" of wealth flow freely. But at another point in his critique, when he refutes Lassalle's "iron law of wages" that is supposed to bring about revolution because the workers can never share fully in the growing wealth they create, Marx is less materialist. He sees the role and place of autonomy, even though he never uses the term. "It is as if, among slaves who have at last got behind the secret of slavery and broken out in rebellion, a slave still in thrall to obsolete notions were to inscribe on the programme of the rebellion: Slavery must be abolished because the feeding of slaves in the system of slavery cannot exceed a certain low minimum!" Castoriadis could not have said it better. But more can be said.

Castoriadis also criticized Marx's materialist recourse to flowing "springs" of wealth for avoiding the political problem of the institution of society. The locus classicus of this critique is Marx's vision of the Paris Commune as a direct democracy that is the "finally discovered secret" to the riddle of history he had sought since his youthful critique of Hegel's theory of the state in 1843. In fact, however, Marx described the Commune more precisely as "the finally discovered *form*" (my emphasis) in which the class struggle could be played out. Class struggle, however, is not an elemental, material fact (despite Marx's coquetry with Darwin). When Marx writes, in *The German Ideology*, that the first form of this opposition is in the relation of man to woman, he is adopting a crude positivism. Groups may coexist while ignoring one another's existence and remaining quite indifferent to what a later analyst might see as opposition between them. Like society itself, the existence of class struggle depends on a shared value, a political framework through which the classes are able to represent to themselves their own position in relation to other classes. Such a framework is provided by democratic institutions that permit the flowering of difference within a universe of shared values. It is this creation of shared values that would be the achievement of the Commune that permits what Marx thought would be the final phase of the class struggle. But Marx's vision of democracy is not developed further; he treats its appearance in the Commune just as he treated it in the 1843 critique of Hegel: as a solution that puts an end to what he and Castoriadis have called the "enigma" of history.

These two illustrations of the way in which the philosophical Marx and the "revolutionary theory" of Castoriadis begin to dovetail explain the move proposed by my title "From Marx to Castoriadis, and from Castoriadis to Us." By rereading Castoriadis's critique of Marx we are brought back to the question of Marx's relevance to our contemporary situation. That is why I have suggested that the "specter" Marx thought was haunting Europe is not the reality of a communism that is materially overcoming the class struggles that shaped the course of history. Rather, the "specter" represents democracy. As a specter, it is a representation of itself and of the shared values that society gives itself in order to become what it is. When "all that is solid melts into air" (*Manifesto*) as capitalist economic relations begin to take hold, society needs to represent to itself such shared values in order to make sense of the diverse social relations that constitute it. Such values can be purely economic, masking their properly political institution under the guise of naturalness. But they can also be posited politically, as *nomoi*, whose character, however, is not simply arbitrary. The legitimation of such democratic political values is the domain to which immanent critique properly belongs. The idea of an immanent critique of the natural world (or of economic relations that are considered to be natural) makes no sense. The task of immanent critique is to avoid the reification of the political by making clear the philosophical choice that lies at what Castoriadis called its "enigmatic foundation."

The immanent critique of Marx has thus provided the foundations for a critical evaluation of democracy, and it is not surprising that Castoriadis returns repeatedly to both of them. Capitalist economic relations and democracy are related, but they are hardly identical. When he reflects on the relation of theory to the revolutionary project, at the end of "Marxism and Revolutionary Theory," Castoriadis returns to the institutional dimension of political thought. He compares it to our relation to language, which at first appears as something external and alien. But in fact our relation to language is more intimate and more paradoxical. Language permits us to say everything or anything at all; it determines what can be said while providing at the same time the possibility of free speech. "Alienation," he concludes, "appears *in* this relation but alienation *is not* [identical to] this relation—just as error or delerium are only possible *in* language but *are not* [identical to] language."[9] By the same token, capitalist economic relations can appear within democracy, but the two are neither identical nor related by any necessary causal or logical chain. Just this is, in the last resort, also the claim of the philosophical Marx whose achievements we can appreciate today because of Castoriadis's devastating critique of that Marx's revolutionary pretensions. The revolutionary critique of the revolutionary philosopher makes clear the relation of philosophy to the political quest for autonomy. Democracy constantly activates that quest by undermining all attempts to give it a fixed and univocal definition that would assimilate it to the world of *physis* rather than admit that its dependence on representation binds it unalterably to the appearing world of the *nomoi* where political judgment cannot be replaced by the appeal to scientific determinism.

CHAPTER 8

# *From the Critique of Totalitarianism to the Politics of Democracy*

Should a critique disappear when its object is no longer present? Although politicians and journalists still use the concepts of fascism and communism rhetorically, perhaps taking the precaution of adding a "neo-" to cover their embarrassment, nearly no one any longer admits adhering to either, and neither does anyone seriously think that they will return any time soon. But of course no one thinks that the Roman Empire—or the Roman republic—will return soon, which doesn't prevent learning from those experiences. And there are those, still a minority, who believe that the only way to interpret the U.S. Constitution is by reference to its authors' supposed original intent. I use the terms "experience" and "intent" to stress that the study, and the critique, of totalitarianism does not belong to the domain of objective science based on neutral observation of nature or culture; it is philosophical—and therefore political, in a sense that I will define in the process of this analysis. Indeed, the critique of totalitarianism can serve as an introduction to modern political philosophy insofar as the immanent critique points beyond itself toward an understanding of the political problems confronting a democratic society that cannot take for granted its own foundations.

In the past—for example, with the emergence of Italian Fascism—totalitarianism (a term that the Fascists appropriated for themselves)[1] presented itself as a political project worthy of replacing a corrupt and venal democracy that not only unleashed a foolish and self-destructive "total" war but privileged only those who were already established. For their part, Leninists explained that there can be no omelettes, or happy tomorrows, without breaking some eggs. Stalin would later explain that the only way to ensure that the state will wither away is to strengthen it to the maximum in order to reshape society in its image. But those times have gone; experience has made us more cautious, less rash or adventurous. Yet saying "those times have gone" only seems to express fatigue, a loss of tension that doesn't explain anything. Moreover, what "experience" has made us more cautious, wiser? What could we in the West, who have always lived in democracies, have experienced of totalitarianism? What kind of wisdom have we learned from the experience of others? Can that new knowledge serve as the basis of a political thought or action, or is it simply a kind of resignation in the face of the massive fact—whose explanation is left to the political scientists—that democracy seems now to reign globally and without contest? But anyone could have seen well before 1989 that, if this victory was not preordained, certainly totalitarianism was a declining force, both politically and ideologically.

I am not worried that the capitalist democracy that stands alone on the global stage will somehow lose its footing (even if some of the new democracies may confront serious difficulties, stemming in part from their insufficient economic development, itself a product of political failures). My fear is rather that it will weaken gradually as a growing public apathy makes democracy a private personal experience rather than a site of public action, with the result that democracy will lose its signification and "capitalist" will stand alone, justified only by its (unequal) material results. In the post-1989 world, interest has been reduced simply to economic interest—which is not the same as individual interest, which must be understood as the modern form of autonomy.[2] Economic interest should of course not be ignored, nor is its pursuit dishonorable. Its place was suggested by Hannah Arendt who, in *The Human Condition*, the philosophical-political project that followed her still-provocative *Origins of Totalitarianism*, stressed the Aristotelian distinction between (economic) production, which is ruled by necessity, and (political) action, which is the domain of freedom. It is that domain of political freedom that is lost (or perhaps voluntarily abandoned, or exchanged for a kind of security that is taken to be a greater good) in totalitarian political regimes as well as regimes whose politics are determined by economic necessity. The result is what I call the antipolitics of capitalist democracy. This does not imply that capitalism is simply a different form of totalitarianism. It does, however, provide a starting point for a political and philosophical reflection on the actuality of the critique of totalitarianism after 1989.

It might be objected that public participation is itself typical of totalitarian societies, which are based on mass mobilization, the refusal to separate the private from the public, and the constant concentration of unified opinion. But that observation is static; it neglects to ask how the phenomena it describes came into being. The observer places himself outside the thing observed, neglecting to take into account the experience of the participant. If it is granted, as it must be, that totalitarianism is not imposed by force on unwilling participants,[3] then the meaning of their experience must be explained. That is why Hannah Arendt recognized that the precondition for the totalitarian politicization of society, which must in turn be reproduced in order for the regime to remain in power, is the atomization and breakdown of social solidarity and its replacement by private anomie. It is not enough to describe the process by which totalitarianism is reproduced institutionally; the experience of its subjects must be explained as well.

An aphorism of Arendt's friend, the critic Harold Rosenberg, casts light on the process that needs to be explained. The political activist, he suggests, is an intellectual who doesn't need to think. Of course, the activist uses his intellect, argues, studies the facts closely, but this is only to justify the party line, which he or she does not determine. The party line is general; the task of the activist is to apply it to the particular issue at hand. The activist gains certainty and security in this exercise because he avoids the need to think the snovelty of the situation he confronts. This experience is not limited to the activist in totalitarian societies. Claude Lefort points to a similar observation by the nineteenth-century political thinker Edgar Quinet, who critically analyzed the process by which courageous affirmation of freedom in 1789 could be transformed, a decade later, into self-willed servitude to Bonaparte.[4] The similarity of the two types of experience—which Lefort often describes by appropriating La Boétie's expression "self-willed servitude"—suggests that the emergence of democracy and that of totalitarianism are related. But before jumping to conclusions, it should be noted that the activist as an intellectual who doesn't think is not so different from the capitalist relentlessly pursuing economic self-interest, for whom intelligence is vital but stands in service to a goal that cannot be challenged. These analogies do not imply identity, but they do incite one to further thought.

My concern with political participation results from an attempt to understand the loss of the signification of the political in modern democratic society. The political, formulated as a substantive noun, refers to the process or structure through which everyday interactions among persons and interests acquire a sense or meaning that is not immediately apparent in their naked being. The priority of the experience of meaning and its connection to the specific forms taken by the political constitutes a guiding thread in the work of Claude Lefort. Starting from a Marxist critique of the Soviet bureaucratic deformation of political life, Lefort was led to pose the question of totalitarianism for its own sake and, more important, the question of the relation of totalitarianism to democracy. This path is also significant because it takes into account the need to adopt a critical stance toward both totalitarianism and the political domination of the logic of the capitalist economy. Lefort's analysis of democracy does not treat it as what Marx called "the solution to the riddle of history." Lefort is painfully aware of the antinomies of modern democracy, its fragility as well as its charm, and he is as painfully aware of the same characteristics on the side of totalitarianism. His most recent book, *La complication* (1999), was occasioned by his fear that a new complacency has emerged, one that sees totalitarianism as a mere accident, a temporary event on the broad canvas of historical progress of which democracy is the natural underpainting. The same worry is still evident in his most recent work, including the lecture in which he comments on Harold Rosenberg, noted above. His recognition of the need to try again and again to describe the uncanny logic that intertwines democracy and totalitarianism makes Lefort's analysis of them both all the richer.[5]

## Why Did the Critique Fall from Favor?
## Questions of Method

The concept of totalitarianism gained popularity rapidly after World War II, but it lost its currency rather quickly. This was due only in part to the fact that it served both as an analytic category and as a (rhetorically) political one. This dual usage could be easily seen through, but other problems were more complicated, more philosophical. Was a new form imposed on social relations by the political seizure of power, such that the state was used to impose social changes; or were the social changes generated from within society, for example, by economic pressures; or were they a response to the stresses and strains of rapidly modernizing old European polities? Such was the question of the social scientist. Was the new, all-embracing society a reaction against the democratizing trends that had grown constantly if unsteadily since the Atlantic revolutions; or did it result from the inability of the old ruling classes and institutions to confront the challenges of the modern lifeworld? This was the challenge to the historian. Or did totalitarianism represent a new political form that differed from the classical models of despotism and tyranny familiar since the Greeks? This more philosophical question had radical implications; it implied not only the need to rethink the nature of political life itself but suggested also that the post-totalitarian world could not simply return to the old ways of doing things, as if the totalitarian interlude were simply an accident along the well-traveled highway of progress toward modernity. The advent of totalitarianism put into question not only the positivism of social science but the teleological representation of history that is its (unspoken) premise.

The first to use the concept of totalitarianism critically were anti-Fascist and anti-Nazi refugees who had remained part of the non-communist left and sought to use the concept against both left- and right-wing forms of totalitarianism.[6] In the case of the Frankfurt School's Max Horkheimer, this leftist orientation had as its complement the insistence on the need to criticize capitalism as well. Although Horkheimer and Adorno, in the *Dialectic of Enlightenment*, abandoned economic criticism for a broader, and historically universal, analysis of the constant presence of a darker side of Reason that accompanied each apparent step toward human emancipation, the turn to cultural criticism was a minority reaction to the analytic challenge of understanding fascism.[7] The majority of left-oriented critics held on tightly to their critique of capitalism, as if the radical novelty of the two totalitarianisms threatened not only their political hopes but also their ability to situate themselves in their world. But this way of saving their sense of self came at the cost of misunderstanding the new political world that challenged them.

Many left-wing antitotalitarian anticapitalists hesitated to use the concept, fearing that it could only play into the hands of a right wing whose goal is to delegitimate any politics that attempts to achieve a real and substantive social equality they consider more important than a freedom that is in the last resort simply formal and abstract. After all, the concept of totalitarianism was defined—or at least consecrated in the academy—by the theses of Brzezinski and Friedrich in the early fifties, and this codification would then serve as the basis of the American anticommunist offensive in the hot period of the cold war.[8] The CIA is said to have financed the Congress for Cultural Freedom in order to spread that critique of totalitarianism and thereby close off any temptation to seek a third way that would avoid the polarities of the cold war.[9] Even the work of a philosopher as scrupulous as Hannah Arendt fell victim to this Manichaean interpretative framework. The reception of her *Origins of Totalitarianism* and then of her *Essay on Revolution* was muted in the fifties: the first work was criticized for placing Nazism and Stalinism in a common framework; the second because it analyzed what would later be called the egalitarian social "slippages" of the French Revolution while highlighting on the contrary the originary political creation produced by the American republic.[10]

The justification of the refusal to take seriously the critique of totalitarianism was the need to maintain a critical standpoint from which to criticize the present while making room for the possibility of a real justice in the future. And who could disagree with such a goal? But what is the present that is being criticized? What is the future that is promised? What is the justice that is to be achieved? How can one answer if one doesn't accept the massive reality not only of totalitarianism but of the support—often unconscious or passive but nonetheless real—that the totalitarian temptation found in the heart of the Western democracies? Such, for example, was the politics of the anti-anticommunists. One cannot forget, after all, that the totalitarianism that was imposed over there, far away, knew quite well how to profit from the goodwill (and self-deception) of too many within the Western democracies. The promises that even many critics saw in "really existing socialism" do not offer a sufficiently critical definition of the present, the future, or the social justice to be won.

Others today go to the other extreme; they refuse the critique of totalitarianism on the grounds that it is no longer relevant. Not only does totalitarianism belong to the past, they insist; it was only an "illusion" (Furet) or a simple "ideology" (Malia). But, as the oft-quoted Santayana famously said, we must study the past in order not to be condemned to repeat it. Of course one doesn't study that past with Ranke, to fulfill the positivist dream of finding out *wie es eigentlich gewesen ist*; rather, it is the constant reinterpretation of the past that shows its actuality in our thoughts and in our actions. Of itself, the past is passed, dead, without meaning; it comes alive only in contact with present history and those who are involved in its making. So it is also with totalitarianism and its critique.

The progressives who reject the critique of totalitarianism on the grounds that it would harm the good cause thus involuntarily bear witness to the actuality of that critique. They don't deny that totalitarianism existed, but they pretend that it was only an accident, a detour on the road to the happy tomorrows. To resume the critique would be to reopen the wound, and it would also assume that evil doesn't belong only to the past, that it is also part of the present. This attitude, interestingly, is not so far from the presuppositions of contemporary critics like Furet and Malia. That is why Claude Lefort recently returned to the critique of totalitarianism. His title, *La complication*, expresses his goal: complication has to erase the oversimplification that treats the present as if it were only a present, transparent to itself, univocal in its signification. It is too easy to preserve one's good conscience, to pretend that we now know, finally, what needs to be avoided, to claim that the error was only subjective, that we will know in the future how to behave. The error, however, is not reducible simply to "stupidity" (Glucksmann); it is rooted in history, and that history endures in the present.

The situation could be described differently. Perhaps it is the illusion that is past, but the thing itself has not disappeared. To speak here of a "thing," however, already expresses an erroneous understanding of the object of the critique of totalitarianism. It assumes that the reality of totalitarianism was a set of institutions, or behaviors, or other objective facts. But the reality is more difficult to grasp; to do so, one needs to adopt a phenomenological approach that avoids the one-sided standpoints of either the supposedly neutral outside observer or the participant in the process itself. What appears to the observer cannot encompass the sense the participants attribute to their actions, but the sense the participants intend to activate may not be congruent with the effects they produce. How can these two necessary standpoints be united?

The concept of illusion, like that of ideology, assumes that there is somewhere something that is real that one was led—why?—to mistake, to ignore, or to distort. Like the old-fashioned critique of ideology, the critique of totalitarianism would be a therapy, a learning to see what is truly real, whose goal is to correct the subject's near- or far-sightedness. This implies that the real remains what it always was: the object of a science or perhaps of a technique. The totalitarian error was subjective and in principle something temporary that can be corrected at little cost. (But why would people not once again fall into error?) More significant, this account denigrates human intelligence since the responsibility for error is put exclusively on the subject, while it implicitly treats the real as merely a passive substratum. Of course, people can err, we all have illusions and are tempted by ideologies. But history and politics are not so one-sided; they form a "flesh" (Merleau-Ponty) that acts as much as it is acted upon, that demands that we reflect on it at the same time—and because—we are part of it. After all, to do philosophy—and to do politics—implies that we put into question what only appears to be really real, that we interrogate it, and, if it seems necessary, that we correct it. And this implies that we give ourselves the right to be wrong. To think, after all, is to seek the truth while taking on the risk of being wrong, of erring.

This new totalitarian phenomenon that resists static definitions appears at the same time that the nature of the political is transformed by the birth of democracy. One aspect of democracy is the realization that human intervention can transform reality. It is important to take the terms literally: to transform reality is not simply to modify it, rearrange it, make it better, or correct it; those actions seek to adapt the real to an already given model, whether it be Platonic Ideas, natural Laws like those of science, or even the so-called laws of History. As opposed to such premodern projects, democratic politics becomes possible (and necessary) when there are no more preexisting models, when the individual has to take responsibility for his actions, to justify them by their own results, and to act such that the goal sought and the action undertaken are each their own origin. This indetermination of the democratic form of politics means that both the actor and the action, the subject and its object, the individual and society are thrown into doubt. That is why a democratic political philosophy calls on the method of phenomenology: the intentional act constitutes its object at the same time that, if it is not to be arbitrary, the same intentional act is also constituted (or called forth) by its object, from which it cannot be separated. This is an uncomfortable indetermination from which the individual seeks instinctively to free himself. This instinctive reaction to indetermination is not explained by the "bad faith" defined by Sartre's existential phenomenology—whose subjectivism hides an implicit positivism; it has a deeper ontological ground, one that recalls the late Merleau-Ponty's analyses of the interplay between the visible and the invisible.[11]

These preliminary methodological reflections should be completed by a brief reference to the final stages of the critique of totalitarianism as it became belatedly popular in France. It was taken up by a media-savvy group calling themselves the "new philosophers"—often ex-Maoists whose eyes had finally been opened by the (or, more precisely, their) discovery of the gulag—who drew radical consequences from their new certainty. They applied the label "totalitarian" to any political project, reasoning that by its very nature politics seeks to impose a conception of the future. The result of this reasoning was a sort of "angelicism" that argued that the only good politics is an antipolitics. The translation of this standpoint, by André Glucksmann, was an "Eleventh Commandment," whose injunction is the Hippocratic imperative: Be sure to do no harm to anyone. Glucksmann's personal manner of acting on this premise was often based on good political instincts, as early as his famous petition concerning the boat people, later in Vukovar, and today in Chechnya. But it is not always clear how his action and his theory relate to one another.[12] Others who had been made sensitive to the new reality contributed to the widespread public sensitivity to the horrors taking place in the former Yugoslavia, succeeding in turning French diplomacy away from its traditional Serbophilia.[13]

All these recent criticisms of totalitarianism share an important methodological characteristic: the critic stands outside the criticized phenomena; he arrogates to himself a position that guarantees a kind of epistemological innocence from which to describe a world of sheer contrasts in which the grays of reality find no place. Such a picture opens to an understanding neither of the present nor of a possible future. In this context, a return to the old Marxist method of "immanent critique" makes explicit the interdependence of the subject with its object while seeking to understand not only the objective conditions of the possibility of critique but also the conscious mode of transforming the appearing reality. Even if it is no longer possible to be a Marxist, it is nonetheless the case that today one cannot avoid confronting Marx's philosophical rigor in the attempt to rediscover political thought.

## How to Take Up Marx Today

What do we find when we return to Marx, who is so often blamed for the disasters of totalitarianism (and who is not innocent of them, even if the responsibility falls rather on those who didn't know how to read him)? Lefort was a Marxist, in his own manner, and he has never abandoned that inspiration, to whose source he has returned several times in order to refresh his arguments and his own self-understanding—a fact that not only points to the seriousness of his engagement with these problems but also indicates that he recognizes and is provoked by the seriousness of Marx's questioning itself. It is Marx, not Marxism, to whom he returns, but the exercise is not academic; it is lived experience, history and its novelty, that motivates the return.

As a serious Marxist, Lefort obviously could not avoid the encounter with Trotsky, already during the Occupation. This led him to an intense political activism in the Fourth International, followed by a rupture consummated in 1948 by the cofoundation (with Cornelius Castoriadis) of the group Socialisme ou Barbarie. A first summary of his engagement and break with Trotsky and Trotskyism was published that year in *Les Temps Modernes*, under the title "The

Contradiction of Trotsky." The contradiction that Lefort under-lined was central to the Trotskyite political standpoint. The assump-tion that led to the founding of the Fourth International was that the proletariat was by its very nature revolutionary and that when it escaped from the ravages of Stalinism, it would need to find a "truly" revolutionary party to which it could turn for orientation. Lefort's critique of this assumption already showed a characteristic typical of his analyses. He was not attacking a merely subjective error; he sought to show how Trotsky's earlier participation in the creation of the Leninist-Stalinist party, and the justifications that he gave for this participation, could only blind him to the fatal role that this party incarnated without being aware of it. Trotsky's "truly" revolu-tionary party would produce the same alienation as the Leninist party before it. The analysis, in other words, is already two-sided, or phenomenological, concerned with both the subject and its object. But Lefort's assumptions are also Marxist, wagering still on the rev-olutionary capacity of the proletariat that, once it frees itself (or is freed) from the constraints imposed by the Stalinist leadership, will show itself to be in its very essence revolutionary—and able to organize itself without the mediation of a party.[14]

This first analysis was developed by Lefort in the following years through a continued critique of Soviet society as well as a critical analysis of Western societies. Lefort started from Castoriadis's demonstration that the USSR represents a new social formation that cannot be identified either with "state capitalism" (where the party would play the role of the nonexistent Russian capitalist class) or with a superstructural deformation of a society whose socialist char-acter is said to be guaranteed by the fact that private property no longer exists there (as the Trotskyists claimed). He then sought to evaluate the new forms of class division that emerged in the USSR and particularly the new dominant class incarnated by the party bureaucracy. At this stage, Lefort takes for granted the existence and dynamic role of classes and class struggle, as well as the idea of a pro-letariat that is naturally revolutionary and whose passivity could only be explained by the tactics—of which the purges represented only the most obvious manifestation—of the new dominant bureaucratic class. The implications of the claim that the USSR represented a new social formation had not yet been fully realized; the existence of a truly real infrastructure that needed to be brought to light was still presupposed. But that infrastructure was, in a sense, already double; it was composed, on the one hand, of the proletariat as the revolutionary subject and, on the other, of the reality of bureaucratic domination. Thus in 1956, with the publication of Khrushchev's secret report to the Twentieth Party Congress, Lefort published in *Socialisme ou Barbarie* an article titled "Stalinism Without Stalin" that sought to demonstrate the continued existence and domination of the bureaucracy and the methods that permitted it to remain in power as the "leading party," whose role in preserving the unity of Soviet society justified its position. In this way, Lefort was insisting on the reality of totalitarianism above and beyond the person of the "Little Father of the People"; the party itself was part of the reality of Soviet society. On the other hand, the outbreak of revolution in Hungary in the autumn of that year seemed to be a demonstration of the revolutionary reality of the proletariat and its ability to manage its own affairs; the creation of workers' councils showed that the proletariat could get rid of—indeed, that it spontaneously distrusted—the party and its claims to leadership.

The key to the analyses of totalitarian society was therefore the power of the bureaucracy, an insight that seemed to be validated by the known facts. The temptation was therefore to apply the same analysis to capitalist society, while insisting there as well on the self-organizing capacity of the proletariat. Lefort had already laid the groundwork for this approach in the elegant phenomenological analysis of "proletarian experience" published in 1952 in *Socialisme ou Barbarie*. And of course the author of that magisterial analysis could only be shocked when, shortly thereafter, he read the encomium to the Communist Party (without which the class supposedly could not recognize itself for what it is) that Sartre presented in *Les Temps Modernes* under the telling title "The Communists and Peace." Lefort's reply, published in the same journal in 1953, went to the heart of Sartre's argument while picking up a theme he had already alluded to in his analysis of Stalinism. Sartre's premise was the *idea* of the unity of the working class rather than its everyday experience; as a result, his analysis insisted on the idea of that class as a "pure act" separated from the material and social conditions that produce it. Because of this separation, the working class depends on the presence of "its" party in order to exist as a being for itself. Sartre's violent polemical reply to Lefort suggested that the criticism struck a nerve; it was met by another challenge from Lefort, whose title suggested his argument: "From the Answer to the Question."

What question was Lefort referring to? A somewhat later essay, published in 1958 as a critique of "The Method of the Progressive Intellectuals," shows that the question Lefort was driven to formulate depended on a deepening of the analysis of totalitarianism. Lefort sets himself again in opposition to the political-theoretical line of *Les Temps Modernes* that, in seeking to justify Gomulka's return to power in Poland on the back of, and at the expense of, a working-class rebellion, put itself, so to speak, in the position of the press secretary of History. Lefort was challenging a vision of history and historical progress that supposes that the intellectual can have knowledge of the telos and goals that give that history its sense. This would put the intellectual in a position to judge and/or justify practical decisions taken in the midst of political uncertainty where the future remained open. Denouncing this intellectual pretension, Lefort was able to clarify his concept of totalitarianism as a new social formation, making clear that it could not be reduced to the results imposed by a power whose foundation is either bureaucratic domination (a reality that exists but has to be put into its proper context) or the division and diversion of a proletarian class that, once the cumbersome bureaucracy has been eliminated, would easily rediscover its real unity. Totalitarianism incarnated a new *sense* of the real and thereby a new reality. This new argument challenged the attempt to apply the critique of the totalitarian bureaucracy to capitalist society (as in convergence theories popular in political science at the time) because it is now clear that the two types of political system are not merely variants of a common material social formation. This conclusion was clarified in "What Is Bureaucracy," which Lefort published in the journal *Arguments* (along with essays on the same theme by Alain Touraine and Michel Crozier) in 1960. The ground was prepared for a new stage in the analysis, one where the philosophical foundations of the sociological analysis would become more explicit.[15]

## With Marx Beyond Marxism

The Marx to whom Lefort appealed during his first period was the revolutionary Marx, the voice of the proletariat and critic of social division. That Marx would soon give way to a Marx more concerned with the theory of history and, for that reason, more philosophical. This new style of questioning was influenced by the political experience that led to Lefort's definitive break with the group Socialisme ou Barbarie. He came to recognize that, however creative its activity and however iconoclastic its theoretical work, its acceptance of the Leninist-Trotskyist role of the party inflected its analyses in a way that it could not eliminate.[16] This small union of the faithful understood itself, in Lefort's language, as the immortality of the "revolutionary body" that had been usurped by Stalinism. But in reality the group functioned like a microbureaucracy, with a division between the leaders and the followers, who only executed tasks that were given them, and with a manipulation of meetings, the separation of the different spheres of activity, the control of information concerning the functioning of the apparatus, and especially a stereotypical discourse that proved to be impermeable to events that put into question or challenged either its theory or its practice. What was remarkable in this manner of functioning, the height of its self-illusion, was that this microbureaucracy had no material foundation whatsoever. The power of its leaders depended on their control of information, their mastery of the proper language, and their ability to inscribe each and every fact, of whatever type, into a sort of mythic history. This bothered Lefort all the more, because he himself had a certain power in the organization for just these reasons. If things were this way inside Socialisme ou Barbarie, how could one claim to analyze bureaucratic domination in the Soviet Union according to a schema that only saw there a deformed version of class struggle? It was clearly necessary to take up again the reading of Marx while giving up the immediate hope for a proletarian revolution. But that sacrifice had to be justified philosophically—for one doesn't change one's analysis simply for conjunctural reasons.

A first step toward this new reading of Marx had been taken with the critique of the progressive intellectuals, who claimed to know the truth of history and who used that "truth" to justify a practice that at best adapted to the temporary situation or at worst became simply opportunist. But it was Marx himself who affirmed, in *The Communist Manifesto*, that the superiority of the Communist Party over all the other parties claiming to represent the proletariat consists in the fact that it knows the ends of history. It was therefore necessary to return to Marx to try to understand the roots of that claim, whose effects were felt also in the practice of the group Socialisme ou Barbarie, which because of this theoretical assumption proved to be blind to new facts that could have put into question its theory.[17]

How, then, can one discern the newness of the new? How can one avoid the return to repetition?[18] How can theory open itself to temporality? These questions that Lefort has to confront as a result of his abandonment of the idea of an essentially revolutionary proletariat will continue to concern him. Later, in 1979, he adopted as the title of a collection of his essays *L'invention démocratique*. But before turning to the meaning of that title—is it democracy that is invented, or democracy that is itself inventive?—it is necessary to consider the results of Lefort's rereading of Marx at the end of his first period. It should be noted as well that this was not his only rereading of Marx and that his reading is not simply pragmatic. For example, in a short essay on *The Communist Manifesto* published in 1986,[19] Lefort stressed the eerie strangeness of Marx's literary style: the presence of a voice that speaks from nowhere and claims to speak the truth, as if it were reality itself that was expressing itself. The author of this political thought disappears; he is only the path or the voice (*la voie, ou la voix*) through which truth makes itself "manifest." But this fundamentally antipolitical view of history is not the only one that is presented by Lefort's rereading of Marx.

Retrospectively, it is clear that Lefort had seen the need to challenge Marx's understanding of the meaning of history for a long time without it having become the center of his concerns. His reflections finally crystallized in the lecture course he presented at the Sorbonne in 1965. These lectures were published first in mimeograph form by students attending the course; Lefort reworked them for publication only in 1978, when they appeared in the same collection—*Les formes de l'histoire: Essais d'anthropologie politique*—that contained his earlier essays putting into question (without mentioning it directly) the simple linear vision of history accepted by Marxist orthodoxy.[20] The relation of these earlier essays to the rereading of Marx is clear from the title chosen by Lefort: "Marx: From One Vision of History to Another."

The distinction between a representation of history as continuous or cumulative as opposed to a concept of history as marked by moments of discontinuity, rupture, or invention is clear in Lefort's renewed consideration of Marx. The standard presentation of Marx that proposes an inevitable movement through which the forces of production develop and progress constantly in fact coexists with the idea of a radical historical rupture that explains the advent of modern capitalism. What is the source of such a rupture? Returning to Marx's writings, Lefort is struck by the presence of both an interpretation of the world that seeks to discover its material foundation and a reading of that same world that underlines—starting from the famous analysis of the "commodity fetishism" in *Capital*—the power of the social imaginary. Lefort asks, how can we reconcile the Marx who appeals to Darwin with the Marx who swears by Shakespeare? The answer lies with Marx himself, says Lefort—who had just finished editing Merleau-Ponty's posthumous *The Visible and the Invisible*, in which the philosopher proposes a phenomenological reading of history as a sort of "flesh" while insisting at the same time on the concept of "reversibility." More precisely, it is not so much the answer that one finds with Marx but a reformulation of the question that would determine Lefort's new reading of totalitarianism.

From this point, the terms of the analysis change. Lefort is no longer looking for the totalitarian deformation of an always possible revolution whose agent remains the proletariat, which has only to be freed from the weights and constraints that prevent its self-realization. That old image is based on the idea of a subject "in itself" that has to become "for itself" (i.e., self-conscious) in order for history to find its happy end(ing). That image postulates that totalitarianism is the other, the enemy from which one has to free oneself—as if totalitarianism had been imposed from outside, in spite of the efforts of the (good) subject or at least without its having contributed to its own self-abasement. (It should be noted in passing here that this vision of totalitarianism in fact reproduces the totalitarian structure that, as I will show in a moment, cannot do without the representation of external enemies in order to justify its grip on the social.) This dualistic interpretation is the product of a conception of history that is continuous and teleological. But such a conception contradicts itself: it postulates the end of that history whose contradictions are supposed to guarantee the revolutionary transcendence of its contradictory foundation. Its success would bring with it the seeds of its own (totalitarian) failure.

Rereading Marx draws attention to another dualism. On the one

hand, there exist societies whose history appears immobile, repetitive, oriented to simple self-reproduction. These are all precapitalist societies. One of them presents a curious problem for the Marxist *doxa*: "Asiatic" despotism, in which economic relations clearly
depend on the intervention of political power. This puts into question the notion that political superstructures depend on the economic infrastructure.[21] Marx seems less concerned by this anomaly
than by the phenomenon of the immobility of a historical society.
He returns to it repeatedly, but he does not manage to explain it.
The assumption that such societies must somehow be the theater of
a hidden class struggle leaves him paralyzed. He turns with a certain relief to capitalist history, which, for its part, is structured by a
progressive temporality that is constantly oriented to the production of the new. This permanent innovation that produces the
mobility of capitalism constitutes what Lefort calls a "quasi-anthro-
pological" revolution in human relations whose political translation
is the advent of modern democratic society. The question that
arises at this point is, what is the source of this mutation? It clearly
defines the historical uniqueness of capitalism. And set against the
description of the variety and permanence of immobile societies, it
in turn poses the question of its own stability. Is capitalism, and the
possibility of democratic social relations that accompany (while not
being necessarily identical to) it, a historical aberration? Can the
fall back into the repetitive vision of a society without history be
avoided?

Lefort takes as the guiding thread of his renewed analysis of totalitarianism the question of the historicity of history, the relation of its
mobility to its immobility, as it appears in the phenomenon of ideology. He begins by noting that Marx did not apply the concept of
ideology to a pregiven capitalist reality. That would suppose that
Marx knew already what was the essence of that reality and what was
only its appearance. This first point makes it clear that ideology also
differs from religion, for example, insofar as religion too explicitly
postulates a beyond that is supposed to give meaning to the world.
In doing this, religion shares with precapitalist societies a repetitive
structure: both of them conjure away the threat of change, the
uncertainty of history, the threat of novelty that defies tradition.[22]
Ideology comes to exist only within a capitalist society that cannot
seek its legitimation by the repetition and reproduction of the Same;

such a society is undermined by its immanent temporality; it is constrained to produce from within itself the representation of what it is supposed to be. Ideology is thus immanent to capitalism insofar as capitalism is a uniquely historical society; one could nearly define capitalism as incarnate ideology. But Lefort will show how the ideology immanent to capitalism is constantly put into question by its own immanent temporality.

The general structure of the ideology is rather simple, even though its forms are diverse (and deserve a more detailed presentation).[23] Lefort first defines what he calls bourgeois ideology. Confronted by the constant changes that its capitalist industry introduces into society, the bourgeoisie seeks to eliminate the resulting uncertainty by proclaiming the eternal validity of values (such as the family, the nation, labor, etc.). These values are supposed to be immanent to society; their function is to give general meaning to their constantly changing particular manifestations. But the constant movement imposed by capitalist innovation on society ultimately challenges the fixity and permanence attributed to these values, which, as a result of the constant criticism, appear now as simple empirical claims. They lose their legitimating symbolic function such that, for example, the family appears simply as the reification of a specific form of family life imposed by a dominant class. The bourgeoisie may then attempt to save its claim by appealing to science. In this case, the value will be represented as a formal and universal rule that is possessed by a master—for example, the rules of grammar. But it is nonetheless necessary that the rule be proven valid in spite of the constant changes in society. The master will thus have to speak, to coin phrases, to use language to create meaning. But the rule is by definition abstract; its application will therefore produce either formulaic banalities, or, if it does produce meaning, a closer look will show that it had to infringe on the formality of the rule to do so. In either case, bourgeois ideology is again put into question. But it is not yet defeated. It can appeal to other values—for example, it will redefine the domain of applicability (claiming, for example, that the norms of the family do not apply only to heterosexual couples), or it will conjure up more precise and better defined rules (such as distinguishing the diverse grammars of the sciences and of cultural forms). Nonetheless, the instability that emerges in spite of all attempts to master instability and close off innovation finally puts into question the validity of bourgeois ideology. Its critics imagine and work toward overcoming the contradiction between a formal universality (of the value or rule) and its always particular realization by means of the invention of a new unity. With this, the temptation of totalitarian ideology appears on the horizon.

The totalitarian ideology whose historical genesis Lefort sketches is not identical with totalitarianism. Indeed, the failure of the totalitarian project does not put an end to the ideological form of totalitarianism. As a reality, totalitarianism shows itself to be always unstable, constantly forced to reaffirm itself by integrating otherness, whereas totalitarian ideology is a new way of seeking to put an end to the historicity of history, and thus of modern society, by showing its immanent meaning. As opposed to bourgeois ideology, which postulates values or rules that (like religious values) are explicitly different from the social reality they are supposed to legitimate, totalitarian ideology claims that its society carries within itself its own legitimacy.[24] This legitimacy is obviously not that of capitalism as an economic system; the claim concerns rather the implicit and repressed historical truth that is carried by capitalism but whose effects transcend it. Lefort's return to the analysis of the Marxist vision of history and its immanent telos was essential to the further development of his theory: Totalitarian ideology, and its agents, do not seek to bring totalitarianism into being—quite the contrary! They sincerely want to take into account objective necessity; they want to realize humanity, to overcome alienation and class contradictions, to reconcile society with itself—to put an end to what Marx called "pre-history" and its painful class struggles. Those who are tempted by such goals—and we all have been and will be again, at one time or another—will, hopefully, abandon them when confronted with their real consequences. Nonetheless, others, who are ready to break a few eggs in order to prepare the omelette of history, will make it a virtue not to hesitate when the stakes for humanity appear to be so high and the rewards so great and gratifying.

It is not necessary to carry the argument further here. Two lessons can be drawn from what has been said. On the one hand, capitalism and totalitarian ideology have a common source, they share a foundation: that dynamic, mobile history that carries the constant threat of the new. On the other hand, we do not yet understand why and how really existing totalitarianism comes into existence. We know that its seed (or ideological possibility) is born with modernity and the capitalist revolution, but we don't know what revolution is needed for it in turn to overcome and eliminate capitalism. Indeed, it is necessary to underline the fact that this analysis of the shared substance of bourgeois and totalitarian ideology in no way claims that capitalism and totalitarianism are identical.

## THE MEANING OF HISTORY

The analysis of the historicity of capitalism and the ideological attempts to conjure away its effects remains caught up in the premises of Marxism. Because the historicity that constantly produces the new is explained with reference to the structure of capital, the meaning of history is reduced to its material or economic foundation. That premise now has to be put into question. Lefort does so by returning once more to Marx himself, taking up the analysis of the Asiatic despotism that was one of the immobile forms of precapitalist modes of production. In effect, Marx recognizes that societies of this kind are given their material form by the political institutions whose power the society thereby reproduces. What is striking here is that Lefort's description of totalitarian power in the USSR had presented a similar type of socioeconomic relations resulting from the imposition of political power. After the coup d'état—which is what it was—brought the Bolsheviks to power in 1917, the party became the absolute master of Russia. The new power then set about creating a society that reflected its own nature and thereby reproduced its power. It did so by eliminating competing parties, then through internal purges of the party itself, and then through the massive induction of new party members who owed their position and influence to the newly established system (this was the so-called Lenin Levy preceding the Thirteenth Congress, at which Stalin's power was solidified). Now solidly in power, the process continued with the restructuring of the economy, the urbanization and industrialization of the country, and the gulags and the secret police. The new masters of course claimed to be orthodox Marxists and insisted that their actions were dictated by the priority of the economic sphere, but their practice belied their theory. The Russian

Revolution was a political revolution whose effects were economic and social, not the inverse.

The analogy to Marx's account of Asiatic despotism conceals as well as it reveals. It doesn't explain either the contradictions that would undermine the new society from within before leading to its disappearance or the spectral actuality of the totalitarian phenomenon even after the disappearance of its material incarnation. The analogy is in fact only a reformulation (without the revolutionary hope) of what Lefort had shown already in his earlier analyses of Russian totalitarianism. That materialist analysis was not false—which is why Lefort uses it in *La complication* to criticize those idealists who interpret totalitarianism as either an "illusion" or a simple "ideology." But it is incomplete. The Asiatic seizure of power was certainly a violent exercise of force, but if it were only that there would be no reason to fear a return of totalitarianism and nothing to learn from analyzing it. A further step is needed in order to eliminate a final remnant of Marxism: the idea of the determination "in the last instance" by the economic. The difference between precapitalist and capitalist social formations lies not only in their historical temporality but in the fact that the source of meaning in precapitalist societies is explicitly external to social relations, whereas capitalist society produces its significations from within itself. This poses the question of the meaning of the revolution—and the birth of capitalism was a revolution, not a coup like the Bolshevik revolution—that Marx reduced to the material and apparently natural emergence of capitalism. When this question is answered, it will be possible to understand why the concept of ideology is not simply applied to a reality that is assumed to be distinct from it and why ideology is not the result of the stupidity of the people who are duped by those who use ideology to rule the world. At the same time, it will be clear that science will never be able to replace philosophy for those who want to understand and intervene in contemporary political life.

The example most often used to illustrate Marx's critique of ideology, and its relation to the birth of capitalism, is his analysis of the French revolutionary Declaration of the Rights of Man and of the Citizen in the essay "On the Jewish Question." Marx describes French society as freeing itself from the yoke of a feudal monarchy only in order to impose on itself, unintentionally, the chains of capitalism. Capitalist relations are described as having grown up within the womb of the old feudal society; the revolution sets them free from hierarchical constraint and naively codifies them in the Declaration. This simple description of historical change needs to be looked at all the more closely because the metaphor of a revolution ripening within the "womb" of the old society is also applied by Marxists to the transition that will lead from capitalism to the radiant future—as if that future itself were simply another type of material economic relations. This metaphor also justifies the role of violence ("birth pangs") and the intervention of the party (as "midwife" of history).

Lefort takes up Marx's argument in the essay "Politics and Human Rights," published in 1980 in the journal *Libre*.[25] The Solidarnóse movement in Poland had come to represent a new kind of radical demand, one that appealed to human rights and did not seek state power as their presupposition. The influence of Marxism was still sufficiently strong that many French found it difficult to understand the radical implications of this different understanding of the political. Lefort begins by insisting that Marx's analysis is not false, but it is incomplete because Marx misunderstands the political meaning of human rights. Indeed, Marx is not even true to his own method insofar as he criticizes these rights as if they existed only as ideals rather than as a practical reality lived by those who affirm these rights. From this practical perspective, for example, Marx is wrong to reduce liberty to the guarantee given to a monad separated from other men; nor is security just the protection of private property that justifies the power of the police. The lived reality of these rights, and their contrast to the rigid constraints of hierarchical society, shows that liberty is also the freedom of opinion and the liberty to express that opinion—an opinion, moreover, that is not a form of private property but rather exists only insofar as it has free access to a public sphere whose existence therefore must also be guaranteed. Similarly, security is experienced as a guarantee against arbitrariness, which is clearly expressed in the presumption of innocence and its protection granted by the law. Marx's criticism doesn't see the new possibilities of political action that these rights make possible; he sees instead only the reality of ideology.[26]

Marx's blindness is explained by the economic reductionism that serves as both the foundation of his theory of history and its justification. But this theory is not only circular, presupposing what it needs to prove; it is also challenged by the very phenomenon that it seeks to explain: the political. Rather than focus attention on the supposed protocapitalism taking root within the ancien régime, Marx should have recognized and taken into account the absolutist character of that political regime. Absolutism was a regime in the classical philosophical sense of the term; it was not just an economic mode of production but encompassed the entirety of social life. A political regime is defined by a principle (or, with Montesquieu, a "spirit") that determines the meaning of all levels of social life. Absolutism—which is not totalitarianism—was a type of regime in which the principles of power, of knowledge, and of the law are condensed in a single place; they are incarnated in the person of the King, who is himself the embodiment of the Nation.[27] Because these three principles (without which no society can exist) are unified symbolically in the body of the King, they are explicitly recognized as external to the society to which they give meaning. Their monarchical incarnation was challenged by the revolutionary assertion of rights belonging to "man."

The three principles (of power, knowledge, and law) are present in every society because every society must have a legitimate form of power (since decisions cannot be imposed by force or violence), society must produce knowledge defining its nature (because arbitrary action by members would potentially endanger social unity), and it must regulate relations among men and women by legal means (since there must always be a distinction between what is licit and illicit). The three principles need not be condensed in one representative. If they are, and their unity is then broken as their incarnation is denied, the nature of the regime changes: it undergoes a revolution. At that point, the demand for the rights of man emerges. The liberty that guarantees the free expression of opinion puts into question the idea of a monopoly of knowledge; henceforth, knowledge must be determined collectively, and its claims can be challenged. Legal protections and the presumption of innocence imply the rejection of arbitrary laws; the law henceforth must be the same for everyone. As for power, which is supposed to ensure the unity of society, it appears to return to the Nation, which must find a way to use it legitimately. But that legitimation will henceforth be put into question constantly by the other two principles, knowledge and the law, which have become autonomous and separate from one another as a result of the revolution that overturns absolutism.[28]

This revolution of the rights of man that makes possible the democratic project produces precisely the unmasterable temporality that haunted the historic vision of Marx. But this impossible mastery is no longer based on competition among capitalists; that competition, rather, is the result of this new temporality. The revolution that puts an end to absolute monarchy (and to its ultimately religious legitimation) *disembodies* the locus of power. The Nation does not have control of its own body; the determination of the embodiment of the Nation remains always an issue for the political. In other words, this revolution creates the conditions of the possibility of modern politics. From now on, political choices will acquire legitimacy by appealing to a Nation whose complete determination is never pregiven. The will of the Nation is constantly reproduced, and it is always open to challenge. As a result, the place of power is henceforth empty. This means that the principles of knowledge and those of the law, which remain separate from power and from one another, can in principle never be fixed. Power continues to exist, of course, but the struggle for its determination does not take place only at the level of the material state. Since knowledge and the law are in principle always open to debate, they too will continue to be the object of competition. The democratic adventure does not take place only at the level of power; knowledge claims are constantly challenged, and the law is applied to new domains where it must invent new norms defining the licit and the illicit. The multiplication of the types of legitimacy that Lefort found in bourgeois ideology no longer appears as the attempt to put an end to history; it now acquires a positive import insofar as it preserves the indeterminacy and indeterminability of democratic society.

But the immobile history that was incarnated in the absolutist regime is not thereby abolished; it remains present as the dream of a lost unity.[29] Living with indeterminacy is a source of anxiety; democracy is inherently unstable, indeterminable. Attempts will be made to re-create unity, to find a worthy (symbolic) representative of it. These efforts result from the need to give meaning to the void that results from the disembodiment of power (and the competition for its determination), to understand the meaning of a unity that is always on the horizon but can never quite be domesticated. This is the meaning of the history of modernity—a modernity that is not so much capitalist as it is political and democratic. Because this meaning is nowhere fixed or incarnated, because it is revolutionary, the ideological structures that Lefort analyzed earlier will return, but this time they will be mobilized to understand the political process by which really existing totalitarianism both emerged (in its Communist form) and then collapsed with a rapidity that surprises the materialist but not the philosopher.

## The History of Meaning

The reason that totalitarianism cannot be reduced to Asiatic despotism is that the power that is reflected in it is not based on force and even less on arbitrariness—although both of them are present in existing totalitarian society. Totalitarianism is revolutionary because it seeks to create and install a new meaning in the place of the historical indetermination that opened the path to the democratic revolution. This implies that, as revolutionary, totalitarianism doesn't embody a fixed essence that can be determined once and for all. That is why political science cannot define it. The difficulty in understanding the Soviet Union once the "thaw" following the death of Stalin eliminated the canonical criteria of the Friedrich-Brzezinski model is well known, and I have already discussed Lefort's earlier attempts to analyze these changes. What is now clear is that attempts at definitions fall short because each judges from a position external to the phenomenon it describes; they want to present a positive structure, to circumscribe its boundaries and its frameworks.[30] But the phenomenon at issue concerns meaning, and its newness cannot help evading all these attempts to encompass it. Because meaning is disembodied and exists only as symbolic, and because it must always seek—always in vain—to embody itself somewhere, it is necessarily open to a history without end and without ends. The problem of embodiment, which found its unity in the absolute monarch, provides a guideline for Lefort's analysis of the potentialities contained in totalitarianism.[31] The deformation of the political imposed by totalitarianism results from its claim to realize the meaning of history by putting an end once and for all to the indeterminacy of democratic politics. The analysis of this paradoxical political engagement, which denies itself in order to realize itself, is in turn an interpretation of democracy that confronts democracy's creative capacity but also the traps that it carries with it.

Totalitarianism does not lend itself to a positive sociological or economic analysis because the concept designates the meaning of a political regime, not its temporary institutional form. An analysis must try to understand the principle that gives totalitarianism its form and then explain the origin of that principle, as well as the work that it performs in really existing totalitarian society. This principle was implicit in the previous account; it is the principle of unity. More precisely, it is the idea of the embodiment of the people-as-One (*peuple-Un*) that represents a response to the disembodiment inaugurated by the democratic revolution. The argument avoids the temptation to treat that unity as abstract or as located outside the new society. That was the case in precapitalist societies, which were unified by a religious representation of their principle. The unity sought here is presented explicitly as immanent to the society, and it appears at several levels, which are not necessarily compatible with one another. On the one hand, the void left by the disappearance of the unifying representation of the body of the King must be filled by finding a way to embody the Nation. But, on the other hand, since the disembodiment of power has destroyed its unity with the principles of knowledge and of the law, the new unity must be achieved across a proliferating diversity that results from the multiplication, diversification, and competition of the domains of application of law and of knowledge. The Nation has to be represented at one and the same time as unitary and plural, a homogeneous association of citizens coexisting as a heterogeneous multiplicity of interests and individuals.[32]

Bourgeois ideology tried to compensate for the internal contradictions between the universality of its normative claims and the particularity of their realization by a sort of preemptive move beyond this immanent contradiction. As a result it enriched society not only materially but also and especially spiritually by multiplying kinds and domains of knowledge in order to find potential universal norms that could correspond to the particular claims that the old norms could not justify and by producing, for the same reason and by a similar process, new forms of law and new images of justice. Lefort's analysis of the positive implications of the revolution of the rights of man can be seen as a testimony to the achievements of bourgeois society. But the same movement that produced these results shows that this society in quest of its lost unity suffered from alienation, just as the young Marx (who also thought bourgeois society, as capitalist, prepared a revolution by virtue of its positive achievements) predicted. The disembodiment of power frees civil society and the individuals who inhabit and produce it. These individuals are no longer attached, they become abstract, and it is not only Marx who criticizes the abstraction and formality of a democracy in which the will of the Nation is supposed to determine itself by the vote of atomized individuals, desocialized and separated from any community. It would appear that the overcoming of alienation defines the distinction between bourgeois and totalitarian society. But Lefort had shown the inadequacy of this Marxist understanding of the task of politics. His argument develops instead the implications of the symbolic dimension of the political.

When the principles of power, knowledge, and law were represented as if they were condensed in the body of the King, those principles were not assumed to exist in the reality of a particular king. The body of the King represented their symbolic unity. The cry "The King is dead, long live the King" expresses this idea that the mortal body of this or that monarch is not identical with the King, let alone with the Nation that the monarch symbolizes. A distinction is made between the visible and the invisible, a sort of doubling of the mortal and the immortal, a difference between what is instituted and that which institutes it. As opposed to the Marxist vision, there is a distinction between the head and the members of the body of society. As I noted earlier, the disembodiment of power by the bourgeois (or French) revolution destroys this symbolic function, and the task of bourgeois ideology is then to reinstitute or resymbolize unity and embodiment. But just as the master can only show the real effectiveness of the rule by giving a particular instance of its validity—whose particularity refutes the rule's claim to universality—so too the exercise of power risks appearing as particular and thus as contingent or even arbitrary; indeed, it risks being identified simply with those who are exercising it today, losing its symbolic function as a result. When this happens, power is faced with what Machiavelli recognized as the greatest of all threats to its reign: hatred, ridicule, and disdain.

At this point, the actual revolutionary seizure of power appears on the horizon. Bourgeois ideology has shown itself to be more than just an ideology: it now appears as a mask for force and violence. Its symbolic effectiveness is destroyed, illusions are stripped away. But this does not mean that the old Marxists were right when they criticized bourgeois ideology by pretending to know its real, material foundation. The interplay between the symbolic and the real is more complex. The difficulty is not that reality loses its power to unify the society; rather, it is the symbolic that loses this power—and that is something quite different. This distinction becomes clear in the analysis of the principle that forms totalitarianism as a regime.

The foundation of totalitarianism is the representation of the people-as-One. This is the principle that gives meaning to the new social regime. The sociologist, the positivist Marxist, or the historian may see here the principle of the overcoming of class division. But the principle of totalitarianism makes a broader claim than the quest for a classless society; it wants to eliminate *all* forms of division—except, as was noted earlier, that between the people and its enemies, between the internal and the external. This later division is permitted precisely because it is necessary for the affirmation of unity. The representation of unity would not be effective without the idea of the enemy, which has not only to be constantly overcome but to be constantly reproduced—even if only in the form of those whose neutrality makes them merely lukewarm. This constant reaffirmation of unity is necessary because there is of course division in totalitarian society, if nothing else the distinction between the party that occupies the state apparatus and the society it governs. But that division must be hidden; better, it must be pushed to the outside such that all criticism, any hint of autonomy, appears as a threat to the unity that is the immanent principle of the new society. The symbolic dimensions of knowledge and of the law are integrated into this unity. The unified totalitarian society is represented as homogeneous and as transparent to itself; this latter characteristic means that it can know itself fully and thereby give itself its own law without having to have recourse to the Other (more precisely, to any sort of otherness, uncertainty, or doubt); the Other is the enemy who is, in principle, external and therefore need not be accommodated.

For all this insistence on unity, it is clear that, from its very origin, totalitarianism is undermined by contradiction and threatened by the division between the dominant party and the society. The threat is the greater because the very principle of this society makes this division unrecognizable to it.[33] The society is represented as a body that maintains its identity—better, its health—by the feverish rejection of all otherness. As Solzhenitsyn noted in *The Gulag Archipelago*, it is no accident that Lenin designated the enemy as a parasite and political activity as a sort of social prophylaxis. Totalitarian society is characterized more generally by a contradiction between its being and its appearance, between the reality of division and the imaginary representation of unity. But this contradiction does not condemn it; societies can live, and indeed even prosper, despite this type of contradiction. That was the case for bourgeois society, whose constant effort to overcome such contradiction was the source of its richness. The reflection on totalitarianism has to be taken to a deeper level.

The unity that is constantly reproduced by the repression or denial of otherness appears as a process without a subject or agent that sets it into motion. It governs itself by means that it itself produces. Of course, the party is the principal actor in this process, and the people it dominates are not blind. But what the people see is determined by the principle of unity, which blinds them to division. The role of the party is not hidden; it is underlined, glorified, and inscribed in the constitution. The role and place of the party are justified by the interplay of the representation of the body and of embodiment. The party is identified with the people-as-One because it presents itself as the representative of the proletariat that in its turn represents the essence of the people. The party thus does not represent itself as a separate reality that would exist for itself, with its own interests, within a plural society; rather, it claims to represent the very identity of society. More than that, the party also presents itself as the guide and the conscience of the proletariat and, through the proletariat, of society itself. The result is apparently identical to the structure incarnated by the ancien régime: the party claims to be the head of which the society (the people-as-One) is the body.

Although the political principles of absolutism and totalitarianism insist on the principle of unity, there is a crucial difference between them. The absolutist regime is structured symbolically from the top down; the totalitarian regime builds itself from the bottom up. The representation of the party works by means of a series of identifications: the people and the proletariat, the proletariat and the party, the party and its leadership, the leadership and the leader, whom Lefort defines with Solzhenitsyn as the "Egocrat."[34] Each identification is based on the representation of an organism that is at once the totality and, insofar as it is separated from that totality, the agent that institutes it, gives it its identity, embodies its essence, knows its truth, and expresses its law. But, whereas the absolute monarchy could claim to unify power, knowledge, and law because it presented itself only as a symbolic power, this new series of identifications claims to legitimate the principle of the unity of power-knowledge-law in the reality of the party. This is why the unity that the party imprints on society cannot be challenged: that unity is taken to be the real reality of the society over which it exercises its power.[35] The ancien régime was challenged when it lost its symbolic status and appeared simply as arbitrary, factual domination. Totalitarianism in principle unites the symbolic and the real, leaving nothing outside itself, but this strength turns out to be the source of its impressive weakness once the unity of the fortress is breached.

The principle that determines the identity of totalitarian society claims really to exist as immanent to it; its function is to set into motion the process without a subject that is said to be the self-management of a society that finds unity beyond its divisions. The result is that legislative or judicial activity is not understood to be the result of a choice among other possible choices. If it were a choice, it could be put into question, but that would destroy the unitary claim. Hence, government must be the very expression of reality. In the same way, knowledge can be understood only as the reflection of a reality, of which it, this particular bit of knowledge, incarnates the unitary essence, or the self-transparency of reality to itself. Self-management, transparency of reality, legislative and judicial actions that leave no room for individual judgment or arbitrary decisions: all these are only the articulation of a unity that is in principle already there. This picture explains why the representation of the totalitarian principle can be attractive.

This happy harmony is deceptive, however; its consequences are not what it intends. Because it cannot accept division, totalitarian society is closed to the new; it denies the unexpected and is unfriendly to creation. Its attempt to combine a realist discourse with the constant reaffirmation of unity leads it to misunderstand its own weaknesses (which of course are not all the result of an evil other). The claims made by unitary discourse to articulate the reality of the real can go too far, extending their pretensions to the point of absurdity (for example, Lysenko and the claims of socialist genetics), such that they appear as merely the discourse of power. Now, power becomes anything but symbolic; it is a particular power, open to mockery, to hatred—or to the politics of human rights of those dissidents who speak the reality that is concealed from those who hold power by their own unitary and identitary discourse. From this can arise a kind of solidarity that makes the fragility of the unitary materialism evident to all. The grounds of the failure of Gorbachev's perestroika and more particularly of glasnost are easily understood; both policies can be seen as attempts to restore the unitary discourse by making it correspond to the real. Gorbachev's reforms were not intended to eliminate the totalitarian system; his goal was to repair the ship while keeping it afloat.[36]

The totalitarian principle has many resources and can adopt different forms. The attempt to reform the Soviet Union drew on another possible strategy, articulated around one of the central elements in totalitarian antipolitics. The party is of course composed of activists who are convinced by its self-representation and its vision of the unitary society. The first chain of identifications that justify totalitarian logic was based on the representation of society as a body. The failure of this logic of embodiment makes room for another image, that of society as an organization: organized and organizable. Society is now analyzed by a scientific-technological method for which society appears as a multitude of individuals and groups organized by a division of social labor. As opposed to the disembodiment characteristic of bourgeois society that frees each sphere so that it can develop its own logic before the unity of the society is produced by the invisible hand of the market, totalitarian society claims to be thoroughly and completely organized. But organized by whom, and to what end? The answer determines the meaning of the question: because it is organized, society is in principle also organizable. The party activist will therefore have a double function: he must be at one and the same time an organization man, integrated into the party organs and dependent on them, and also an organizer, a social engineer constantly active, agitating, intervening in all aspects of society. How can the activist be at once integrated within the total society and yet the agent that makes the society what it is? When society was understood in terms of the image of the body, the activist did not face this problem. He was absorbed by a "we" that spoke through him; he identified with the party, which represents the body of the people at the same time that it provides a head that gives society its self-consciousness and identity. But that option has been challenged; the activist now faces a society that is in principle organized and yet in need of organization. The metaphor of a "transmission belt" conveying instructions from the center to the periphery is joined to the metaphor of an "engineer of souls" who decides how society will be produced. The implications of both metaphors are disastrous for the totalitarian-unitarian project. Both the party whose orders are being transmitted and the activist-engineer have placed themselves outside society. It now is clear that the power exercised on a society treats the society as passive matter that, like clay, is there to be organized. The party reveals at the same time its own feet of clay.

The triumph and the failure of totalitarianism can be understood, finally, as part of a history of the meaning of the political. That history proceeds from the symbolic embodiment of meaning incarnated by the absolute monarch, to its disembodiment within democratic society, and finally to the attempt to restore meaning through the totalitarian fantasy whose confusion of the symbolic with the real dooms it. This history is not a linear sequence whose logic is pregiven; it does not predict particular events and even less explain the invention of new meaning. It proposes only a critical interrogation that tries to make comprehensible the meaning of both the events and the invention. Nothing makes necessary the creation of totalitarianism—bourgeois ideology can continue to function[37]— and nothing ensures that totalitarianism will adopt the forms described in this reconstruction of its itinerary. Its principle could attempt to represent itself differently—for example, in nations whose newly acquired democracy emerged from the demise of communism and its empire or in those whose secularization process has taken a course different from the Western model's. Just because the totalitarian principle was not necessary and its manifestations were malleable, its return cannot be excluded. Clearly, modern democracies unsure of their own legitimacy are structurally conducive to its ideological form. Empirical inducement is added by the presence of increased global economic inequality, social exclusion, and the shameless arbitrariness of the political establishment. Who would not wish that things change, and radically? But the revolutionary temptation must be resisted; democracy can be realized only democratically. But that realization is not an end in itself or a mere formality.

## IN PRAISE OF DEMOCRATIC INDETERMINATION

Democracy inaugurates a history without end and without ends. Its advent makes possible the emergence of capitalism, but the two are not identical. The democratic revolution furnishes the framework within which capitalism can take hold; capitalism presupposes democracy, not the inverse. Capitalism's emergence is one result of the process by which bourgeois ideology is forced to open new domains of value and to invent new rules to take account of particular phenomena that cannot be squeezed under the already given norms. The economic, with its own lawfulness and norms, comes into being just as do such domains as the law, the sciences, autonomous art, and the like. This process, whose basis is the disembodiment of absolutist society and the separation of the domains of power, knowledge, and law has remarkable similarities to the one Marx describes in *The Communist Manifesto*. What Marx came to suspect—that the capitalist economy had come to replace the political[38]—explains also the emergence of the totalitarian temptation (which Marx did not suspect).[39] Totalitarianism represents an antipolitics in the same way that the unilateral domination of the economy does; both are antidemocratic in denying the differences among power, knowledge, and law. Antipolitics has been the omnipresent shadow across the political history of meaning; its principle of unity cannot tolerate the complexity, indetermination, and ambiguities that condemn the individual to judge and assume responsibility for such judgment. This indetermination, the negation of the totalitarian temptation, makes possible democracy.

The framework of meaning defined by the political is not itself the object of everyday politics. It defines only what can be called the symbolic or cultural parameters within which issues and institutions acquire political significance. The question posed at the outset—whether totalitarianism is to be understood as the politicization of all spheres of life, or whether it depends rather on the privatization and atomization of a mass society—can be analyzed from this perspective. If totalitarianism represents antipolitics, and if it is not forced on an unwilling society but is the expression of that society's own self-image, it could only emerge when the disappearance of all external legitimation (be it traditional or religious, mythical or natural-scientific) has left society to fend for itself—that is, created a society that is through-and-through political. Such a society is political because it must itself produce the meanings that legitimate the existing forms of power, knowledge, and law. The politicization of society is in principle characteristic of democratic societies, not of their totalitarian enemy. In a democracy, it is in principle always possible for a domain of life that seemed immune to politics to lose its neutral status and become the object of political interrogation. Natural characteristics such as age, gender, or the family have undergone this process in recent years. The refusal to accept such democratic debate about aspects of social relations explains why totalitarian societies are and maintain themselves as privatized, atomized societies for which political judgment is a threat. It explains also why the critique of the totalitarian temptation remains actual in modern democracies whose conservative instincts rule out debate about issues that could become contagious. Conservatism is of course not totalitarian, but because it tends to be antipolitical, the analysis of the political history of meaning warns against it. But liberalism, with its stress on the unconditional and indiscriminate validity of human rights, could be accused of a similar conservatism. A return to the concept of human rights will make clear why the proposed democratic means to realize democracy, the resistance to the revolutionary temptation, is not an option for the status quo.

Faced with the indeterminacy of democracy, the quest for an ultimate foundation of social life becomes more than a philosophical speculation. But the actual discovery of such a foundation would eliminate the democracy that made necessary the search. The kind of foundation that would avoid such an antipolitics would have to be itself inherently democratic, proliferating even while it unifies. Lefort's

analysis of human rights fulfills this criterion. Lefort offers a phenomenological analysis that works from the perspective of the participants'
experience. The account underlines a triple paradox. First, a democratic society is composed of individuals who are free and equal in
their rights. As such, this society is in principle one and homogeneous.
But because it is individuals who are equal and free, this (political)
unity exists only in principle; in reality, inequality or restricted freedoms may threaten social unity. Hence human rights cannot be
defined in advance, as if they were fixed properties possessed by individuals. Nor can these rights be defined by those who hold power.
They are in principle open to indefinite extension and modification.
Second, while these rights belong to humans, the fact that no power
grants them means that individuals, or their representatives, are
responsible for defining them. The ability to articulate rights, however, is itself a right (as the history of struggles for suffrage suggests).
This means that the act of claiming rights and the rights that are
claimed are but two sides of a single action. It is that action by which,
one can say without fear of paradox, rights proclaim themselves. Once
again, this interdependence of the intention and the intended object
means that there can be no preestablished limits on what will count as
rights.

The third facet of this paradox draws the first two together.
Although these rights seem to concern only the individual as a private person, when they are considered within the framework
defined by the critique of totalitarianism, their impact is political in
a way that a liberal would not recognize. The affirmation of the private sphere reaffirms a basic premise of democracy; it means that no
power can claim to regulate society as a whole. To insist on the
sanctity of the private does not entail anything more than this democratic claim; it does not define what will count as private in a given
society. The sanctity of the private is the precondition of the public
use of rights that maintains what Lefort calls "transversal" relations
among individuals who are independent of external power. In this
way, individuals establish their identity through social interactions
that are autonomous (not monadic, as Marx thought). This is why
the French declared the rights of man *and* those of the citizen. My
right to free speech cannot exist without your right to listen to me,
to read me, or to join with me in an association. As a result, the public space is enlarged. This triple paradox makes clear furthermore

that the principle of the rights of man exists as symbolic; no concrete institution can exhaust that principle, and none can claim to represent it once and for all. It is a principle inherent in democratic politics, and it is manifest in each specific manifestation of a democracy at the same time that it guarantees that none of these manifestations can for that very reason ever claim to be a definitive definition of the institutions of democracy.

While human rights are an essential element of the indetermination of democracy, democratic politics is not defined by the actual struggle for rights as they are defined at one or another historical period. Of course, politics may seize upon the degree to which the norms asserted as human rights are less than adequately realized. It may also argue that certain material or institutional transformations are necessary for the realization of rights that are part of the constitutional consensus (or an empirically defined Rawlsian overlapping consensus). Political science and institutional sociology can make a contribution to this critique. But their contributions have meaning only insofar as they take into account the philosophical logic of the democratic structure of the political. If they ignore the need for this philosophical reflection, they risk becoming victims of the totalitarian temptation, whether they intend to or not. These empirical sciences may even, without reflecting explicitly on the meaning of their action, make human rights into an absolute.[40] A positivist politics is from this perspective not different from a moralist politics: both are forms of antipolitics. The critique of totalitarianism warns against either, while pointing to their methodological error: both assume they can fly above reality, look down on it as if they were neutral observers who could describe its true structure, and dictate actions on that basis, regardless of the perspective of the actual participants.

The analysis of totalitarian reality becomes increasingly philosophical because the phenomenon described is not simply a historical accident. That is why the critique casts light also on problems faced by the post-totalitarian present. This claim should not be confused with the one criticized by Lefort at the end of his Marxist period, when he termed the progressive intellectuals activists whose teleological vision of history made it unnecessary for them to think. The error of these progressives was not only that they sought to justify present choices with reference to a future they assumed they knew; their political error had a philosophical source. Their supposed knowledge prevented them from recognizing the historical innovation that accompanies the invention of democracy. This philosophical blindness is shared with another type of progressive political attitude, that of the positivist, for whom it suffices to compare ideas with their actual realization in order to awaken the desire for action. Modeled on the Enlightenment criticism of religious mystification, this approach to political life forgets that the modern world is in principle secular; private religious practice is of course not forbidden in secular democracies, but their public life is not determined by religious principles. The problem with this position lies with its assumption that the observer can know the really real and compare it to its discursive representation. As with Marx's *Manifesto*, the claim is that social reality is in itself determinant and open to univocal knowledge. The critique of totalitarianism should have laid to rest this philosophical presupposition as well.

Democratic indetermination and philosophical critique are two sides of the same political coin. Both have positive implications precisely because and insofar as they retain a sense of themselves, that is to say, of their limits. To overcome indetermination by the attainment of univocal unity or to attain the hard ground of philosophical certainty is, as the young Marx liked to say, a victory that is at the same time its own defeat. It is the indetermination of social conditions that ensures that whatever inequalities and limits on liberty may empirically exist will be challenged again and again from different points of view as different perspectives are invented. Similarly, philosophical critique is not just the result of a choice by an individual subject to challenge the certainties that no one else questions, an arbitrary measure by a private individual. Philosophical critique in turn arises because reality calls for this kind of individual engagement; if it were not for this material and social imperative, the critic would have no hope that the critique would be heard by others, shared, and eventually developed together with them. Democratic indetermination and philosophical critique show themselves to be the presupposition of the triple paradox of human rights that transforms them from the liberal property of a private *homme* into the political engagement of a public *citoyen*. The democratic project is not a solution to the miseries of humanity, another variant of the idea of revolutionary immanence embodied in the proletariat. The democratic project is, however, necessary for the indetermination that is in turn the precondition for the democratic project. This circle, rather than the progressive teleology of the Marxists, is virtuous because self-expanding.

# PART 2

# Republican Democracy
# or Democratic Republics

CHAPTER 9

## *The Burden of French History*

Marx called France the political nation par excellence, as compared to economic England and philosophical Germany. But Marx arrived at his mature theory only after a stern critique of a "merely political" view of revolution. And some of his most important insights are developed in analyses of the failures of revolution in France. While Marx's observation is insightful, the theoretical conclusions he drew from it are problematic. The monarchy in France was not absolute because it was all-powerful or arbitrary; its power came from the means by which it dominated all spheres of life, transforming an administrative and territorial entity into a political nation. In the wake of the Revolution, the republican tradition became equally absolute; it came to define what the French mean by the political (a concept different from what Anglo-Saxons define as politics). Today, globalization (in its various meanings) seems to threaten the power the French attribute to the political. Either the nation-state, whatever its history, will simply be unable to resist the untamed logic of the global culture and the world economy, or the French tradition will contain resources permitting it to transform itself internally in order to provide a unique way to deal with the changed environment. Is the priority of the political a benefit or a burden?[1]

The French political tradition is also challenged from within. The bitter quarrels over political legitimacy that began in 1789 are said by many to have ended when the left came finally to power in 1981 (or when it cohabited with the right, in 1986).[2] Yet this political success has not eliminated a crippling social anomie, designated by the category "exclusion." Exclusion does not refer simply to economic conditions; it suggests that the republican political project has not been realized.[3] An ambiguity in this project is revealed by this new economic situation. The republican quest for national unity is threatened constantly by the appearance of particularity; the obligations of the citizen clash with the rights guaranteed to the individual. When the economic conjuncture was positive, both the state and the individual could be satisfied. When conditions worsened, the difficulty was hidden by an aversion to the (Anglo-Saxon) vision of an independent judiciary imposing its will in the place of the general will. That attitude has changed as political scandals have undermined the legitimacy of the political elite while permitting the judiciary to acquire a new independence. As a result, individual claims against the state have acquired increased legitimacy.[4] Such rights are not welfare grants from on high; they permit the kind of self-activity that in principle could integrate the excluded. If this process is successful, it will transform the inherited French political culture into a republican democracy that may indeed be able to face up to globalization.[5]

## The French Revolution and the Primacy of the Political

The French Revolution sought to replace one form of unitary sovereign power by another. Drawing on the analogy to Christ as the head of the Church Universal, the absolute monarch was the head of the nation, whose permanence transcended in principle his merely temporal activity. But the terms could be inverted. Court life, with its culture of conversation and *politesse*, reached its heights under Louis XIV. This culture was political only by default; it had been made possible by the destruction of all autonomous political life (whose feudal particularity hindered the political progress of national unification). The Sun King's domestication of his nobility in the artificial and formal world of Versailles, at a safe distance from the people of Paris, was a triumph bought at a price that would be paid with the Revolution.[6] The unitary political culture of the absolute monarchy could be challenged only by an equally unitary political claim. It was this challenge that determined the dynamics of the relation of forces after 1789. In retrospect, social and material interests appear important, but they acquired salience only within the framework of the revolutionary contest between unitary values. Over time, "the" Revolution became the primary value. It was feared by its enemies (who created the category "conservative" to justify a political vision that had never previously needed to be named) and adored by its friends (who invented the category "reactionary" to excommunicate those who would not join in its worship).

The political importance of the quest for unity was evident from the very onset of the Revolution. Even before the meeting of the Estates-General, Sieyès had answered his own question, "What is the third estate?" by demonstrating that those who had been "nothing" under the old order must now become "everything." This logical demand took a step toward realization when the representatives of the three Estates swore the Oath of the Tennis Court, affirming that they spoke for the nation and that they would not separate until its will was realized. The first of many difficulties was foreshadowed when the National Assembly became a Constituent Assembly. Its majority sought to create a constitutional monarchy, reuniting the monarchical head with the national body. This project went aground on the question of the royal veto power. Opponents voiced for the first time the fear of judicial independence when they argued that a veto would permit the king to nullify the unitary popular will. They carried the day, producing the first exiles from the victorious Revolution. The dilemma was patched over by the Constituent Assembly, but it reemerged under the Legislative Assembly and became an explicit contradiction with the king's flight and his capture at Varennes. The inevitable result was dissolution of the Legislative Assembly and the calling of a constitutional convention that proclaimed a republic founded on the "general will" to replace the now disqualified monarchical claim to incarnate the nation. The Revolution had now truly begun. Its end was not in sight. The radical Jacobin constitution of 1793 was placed in a sacred ark, to be put into practice only when "the" Revolution had been realized. The relation among the revolutionary republic, its constitutional foundation, and its political representatives was troubled, uncertain, and marked by suspicion from the outset. The fact that it had real enemies only magnified the fear of "the" enemy, against whom one always had to be on guard.

The quest for unity provided its own momentum. The choreography was simple and repetitive: opponents denounced as belonging to the ancien régime were identified one after the other and eliminated. The aptly named Comité de salut publique was given a mandate for the salvation of "the" Revolution. Again, the quest for unity produced new divisions. From the audacious Danton to the anonymous Parisian militants around Hébert, all had to be sacrificed so that the Revolution could appear in its fullness. Then came Thermidor. Called the triumph of the reaction, it in fact confirms the unitary logic governing the Revolution. Although the revolution had "eaten its children," it had also overcome all domestic opposition and defended itself from external danger. The Thermidorians were themselves revolutionaries; they were members of the radical convention, who had voted death for the monarch. Their coup was a product of their fear that Robespierre and his allies represented a threat to the unity of the Revolution. The orator whose power came from his ability to speak as the incarnation of "the" Revolution—as the King had spoken for the Nation—appeared to his revolutionary enemies as the leader of just another faction.[7] The (again, well-named) "Directory" that now assumed power sought unity by declaring that the Revolution had been realized. Nonetheless, differences emerged, and renewed purges were supplemented by electoral manipulation to prevent the appearance of opposition. The Directors could not direct the Revolution; their particular interventions discredited them. The coup of the 18th Brumaire was based on a new claim to revolutionary legitimacy, as much political as it was military. Napoleon's defense of "la patrie en danger" was joined to the expansion of the Revolution to realize "la grande Nation." The Consulate was replaced by the Empire, whose fatal march across Europe externalized the quest for unity that had appeared in 1789. Unable to manage the forces he had inherited and magnified,

Napoleon was ultimately the victim of the unmasterable revolutionary quest for unity.

The Restoration, imposed by defeat, did not bring back the absolutist unitary vision of the political, despite the attempt by Louis XVIII to impose the Charter of 1814. Louis succeeded only in provoking the spirit of the Revolution, which reemerged in the astonishing events of the One Hundred Days, when France united with the emperor only to be defeated at Waterloo. But the Revolution was still not dead. The restored Bourbon monarchy was short-lived because it lived in fear of the revolutionary ghost; its passage of a repressive press law finally called forth a revolution in 1830, bringing its Orleanist cousin to the throne. The new monarch, whose ancestor had adopted the name Philippe Egalité in his failed attempt to unite monarchy with revolution in 1792, could not expect support from the legitimists he replaced. He banked rather on a legacy from the empire, the Napoleonic Code, with its codification of private rights. The republican quest for unity was softened by this separation of public and private life and the legitimation of private interest that it entailed. The private quest for enrichment (and the vices accompanying it) was challenged in February 1848 when another revolution demanded the return of the republic. The attempt by some supporters to define republican unity as "social" led to division in the ranks, and the radicals who took to the streets in June were crushed. The moderate republicans now governed, but their rule was haunted still by fear of revolution. New divisions appeared, paving the way for another Bonaparte and then another empire, whose decisive defeat at Sedan (in 1870) made way (after the suppression of the Paris Commune)[8] for a third attempt to realize the republic. But this Third Republic only seemed to close the history of "the" Revolution.[9] It had not achieved the unity sought since 1789. Its history repeats the old political conflicts, now represented by different actors.

This compulsive repetition of hardened political logic over the course of a 150 years demands explanation. In France, the concepts of left and right, and their unbridgeable opposition, were defined by support for, or fear of, "the" Revolution. This meant that each political stance sought to incarnate the unity of the nation. In so doing, each was following the same divisive logic that animated its predecessors in the originary revolution. On the left, statist Jacobins fought decentralizing Girondins, while both opposed the voluntarism of Hébertists and the conspiratorial plots of Babeuvists, and all of them denounced the compromises of reformers who looked to the English model of a division of powers. Captives of their imaginary historical self-understanding, each faction denounced the propositions of the others by pinning on them a label inherited from the past. The dance of division could continue because the legacy of the first revolution was a binary political logic so universal and crystalline that it could subsume any political content. Its result is most clear in the republican left's inability to forge justifiable compromises, which was both cause and effect of the imperative of unity. Potential allies appeared "objectively" to be supporters of the old order. Revolutionary unity excluded plurality. Rigorous in its logic, the republican left was ruthless in putting it into practice, to the point of becoming a threat to itself. The best became the enemy of the better.

Historians too (who became political actors as a result of this logic) saw the world through the eyes of their iconic representatives. Lamartine and Louis Blanc, for example, had been allies before breaking with one another over the "social" republic of 1848; it was no surprise that their well-received historical studies of the Revolution adopted Girondin and Jacobin stances, respectively. The history of the Revolution remained alive and contested in the present. Political divisions among the founders of the Third Republic were foreshadowed by Edgar Quinet's attempt to demonstrate that republicans need not accept or try to repeat all aspects of "the" Revolution (e.g., de-Christianization, the Terror, or revolutionary war).[10] Because it was unfinished, and stood at the origins of modern France, the history of the Revolution remained embattled territory. Within the Third Republic, Jean Jaurès offered a synthetic "socialist" history to legitimate his Socialist Party in its contest with his orthodox Marxist (Guèsdiste) rivals. The moderate republican politicians who created the first official chair of the history of the Revolution made sure that it was given to Alphonse Aulard, who presented the Girondin vision of events. After the Russian Revolution, Albert Mathiez countered with a rehabilitation of Jacobinism, whose adherents have held the Sorbonne chair since that time.[11]

The right (which was created by the Revolution) has not been immune to a similar compulsion to repeat old battles. The conflict over the royal veto was led by those who envisaged the creation of a constitutional monarchy on British lines. After their failure, Lafayette attempted his own synthesis after his moment of glory at the Fête de la Fédération of 1790. The greatest challenge was the attempt by the Orleanists to join with the Revolution. These failed syntheses from the right had successors who were most visible in the revolutions of 1830 and 1848. While the supporters of the Bourbons adopted the title "Legitimists," that concept in fact expressed the shared political goal of the right. The difficulty was that, with the exception of the Bourbons, the others on the right accepted the legitimacy of at least the first phase of the Revolution, which had put into question the unitary claims of absolutism. This basic split meant that the groups on the right would remain unable to unite in a common cause other than opposition to a specter called "the" Revolution. That is why the legacy of Bonaparte remains ambiguous, representing a potential legitimacy for the left as well as the right.[12] Bonaparte was the revolutionary who put an end to the evil by-products of revolutionary anarchy. As Marx rightly saw, this ambiguity permitted the nephew, Louis Bonaparte, to ride the revolution of 1848 to take power in an empire that did not appear usurped or imposed on society.

Two political-intellectual orientations escaped at least in part the compulsive repetition of revolutionary politics: liberalism and utopian socialism. The heirs of the Anglophile constitutionalists seized the occasion of the revolution of 1830 to pass from opposition to power. Led by François Guizot, to whom Marx famously gave credit for first recognizing the importance of class struggle in world historical development, this liberalism appealed for support to a new bourgeoisie that had been liberated from feudal corporatism by the Revolution. In this way, French liberalism could also lay claim to the revolutionary (but not the republican) legacy. As opposed to the competing republicans and antirepublicans, liberalism's debt to the Revolution is not political; it is sociological. Guizot designates the new bourgeoisie as "les capacités" and suggests that liberal politics has a negative goal: to free these new social forces from the fetters of political constraint. This explains the famous imperative attributed to him: "Enrichissez-vous!" With society rather than the state in command, unity is expected to find its own, economic path. This unspoken return of the republican concern with unity was shared with liberalism's arch critic, utopian socialism, which draws on the same sociological insight into the new capabilities unleashed by the overthrow of the old regime. The utopian socialists, beginning with Saint-Simon, were willing to give politics its place—as long as those with the proper abilities were in charge. Despite their turn to sociology, both political theories are thus also infected by the republican legacy of the Revolution.

The French politics of historical repetition is both explained by and in turn explains a remarkable blindness to the evolution of social reality. The logic of pure politics remains dominant because it recognizes nothing outside itself that could impose a different form of behavior. Fascinated by its own purity, it has no reason to look to society. If the liberals and utopians seem to escape, that is because they do not succumb to the worship of "the" Revolution as a unitary whole. The stress on unity implies that politics cannot accept the legitimacy of its opponents. As a result, it cannot understand or situate itself; when it encounters difficulties, it blames them on the malevolent enemy who advances under the guise of friendship or on the neutral whose lack of real enthusiasm is a hidden obstacle. This self-assured politics cannot see itself for what it is in actuality (as opposed to what it wishes to be); it takes its wishes for reality, believes its own claim of identity with the nation, blinding itself to the reality that it merely represents a particular political choice. Such political solipsism is unable to recognize the reality of society—its changing historical development and its internal divisions. Together with the unitary representation of "the" Revolution, this solipsistic politics explains why political parties are treated as threats to republican unity; they stand for the intrusion of social particularity into the domain of the political.[13] The logic of the political first defined in the Revolution continues to justify its own eternal recurrence.[14]

Despite this solipsism, obsessive repetition, and social blindness, the legacy of the Revolution has a dynamic character; although repetitive in its form, French history did not stand still. This is the result of the impact of the values that the Revolution consecrated as the rights of man and of the citizen. Inscribed in the preamble to its constitution, these rights are at one and the same time proclaimed by the citizens of the French nation and declared to be universal rights belonging to all men, regardless of their national or social characteristics. Like the republic, these rights are assumed in principle to be universally valid but not yet fully realized. This dual status contributed to the almost religious zeal with which "the" Revolution was received by its supporters and hated by its opponents; the universal values it promises are in principle capable of indefinite extension (for example, to all women). The tension that binds a universal principle to its temporary realization lends a dynamic character to the static cycle of political repetition. That is why French history is political history, and France is obsessed by this history. But it is a doubled, illusory, and self-mystifying history. As with the republican historians, the past is studied not for what it actually was but in order to find past values (such as the rights of man) whose proclamation forms part of the logical progress toward the future realization of the republican revolution. As a result, the historical dynamic that is produced by the tension between the universal and the particular, between principles and their temporary realization, is not real; the historian presupposes what he wants to prove, and the history described is in fact a history that is prescribed. The French obsession with history turns out to be a kind of narcissism whose results contribute to the maintenance of the politics of repetition.[15]

The dynamics introduced by the demand for rights suggests an explanation for the lack of concern with *democracy*'s contribution to the republican political project. If the republican principles of the Declaration of the Rights of Man and of the Citizen were truly realized, democracy would be substantively achieved by overcoming the opposition of (private) man and (public) citizen. This means that democracy is an end of politics rather than a means that affects the nature of the end sought. Democracy appears to be the social result of a political process rather than being itself a form of political action. In practice, democracy means division, it thrives on competition, and it thereby furthers the particularism that threatens the universal republic. The argument seems logical: since democracy is an end, the republic must be the means to its realization.[16] But this claim neglects the question of the means for the realization of the republic itself. The problem was not simply theoretical; the unavoidable lesson of French history is the difficulty of passing from the overthrow of one regime to the stable realization of another. It became a very practical (and difficult) matter when Prussia's victory in 1870 destroyed the Second Empire. Political power was vacant, but the republic that replaced it was explicitly provisional, and the assembly elected under the aegis of this republic had strong monarchist leanings. Skillful maneuvering by Thiers and the quarrel of the pretenders to the throne led finally to the constitution of the Third Republic in 1875, more than four years after the end of the Empire.

The new republic undertook a process of modernization that recalls the political achievement of the absolute monarchy in creating a nation from a collection of territorial properties. The achievement is captured in Eugen Weber's classic phrase: "peasants to Frenchmen." The method employed is epitomized in the introduction of universal education associated with the name of Jules Ferry.[17] The republican theory of educational progress reformulates the historical tension that animated the Declaration of Rights. As in the case of rights, whose universality must be assumed before each individual citizen affirms them himself, this educational theory assumes that the student is capable of appropriating the general knowledge encapsulating the best of human history. The fact that not everyone will realize fully this knowledge does not disqualify either the knowledge or the student seeking to acquire it. Rather, it points to a second assumption of the educational theory, which explains how it provides the means to realize the republic: Universal education for all will result in the production of a republican elite without which the shared and universal republican historical project cannot be developed further.[18] This elite is not conceived as separate from the nation; like the republican general will, it is rather the essential realization of the nation, bringing to fruition republican unity. Universal education means that anyone can become a part of this elite, which is not a self-perpetuating aristocracy. It works for the good of all even though not everyone is a part of it. Once again, democracy is the end sought by the republic, not the means to its realization. More than a century later, and in a new republic, this form of republican modernization would face unexpected problems.

The republican elite is designated as the *service public*, France's specific form of political administration. As an agent of social modernization, this political elite has had a crucial role. Legitimated by the universal educational opportunities offered to all and confirmed by competitive exams open to all, it is an uncontested meritocracy. But its success contained the seeds of its own failure. The initial successes were based on an education that permitted all to attain basic skills (and the historical-political knowledge needed for citizenship). Over time, the skills needed to adapt to society increased; higher education of greater numbers was needed, and offered. As was the case elsewhere, it was necessary to open higher education to increasing numbers. As the university came to be seen as the ticket to social success, the difference between the republican elite and the society it was to serve became less evident. The elite feared being leveled down, while the increasingly educated public saw no reason for its political exclusion. Reforms were needed, but the inherited republican principles (and the vested interests that skillfully appealed to them) seemed to make change impossible. May '68 brought a brief glimmer of hope that was soon extinguished. After a first failure by the Socialists to reform the system, their very republican minister of education, Jean-Pierre Chevènement, let the symbolic cat out of the bag in November 1985 when he proclaimed the goal of 80 percent of each class successfully passing the baccalaureate exam required for university admission. This, it now appeared, was the reality of the republican form of democracy: a leveling social equality whose denial of the difference that legitimated the republican elite destroys the raison d'être of politics.

The argument that the successful republic has undermined itself calls attention to the strength as well as the limits of the French logic of pure politics. The complete realization of the republican project would overcome the tension between the universality of rights and their particular realization; that is why republican politics is not foreign to the socialist vision of Marx. But the divisions and stubborn resistance of social reality cannot be ignored. This social resistance cannot be reduced to a reflection of the macroeconomic difficulties facing advanced capitalist nations that try to maintain a welfare state in the face of high unemployment, an aging population, and a fluid global market for capital funds. As at the time of the French Revolution, the political salience of such social facts depends on the framework in which they come to the attention of the public. If the educational system is to be reformed and the dignity of the *service public* reestablished, participation of society in the political republic is needed. That democratic complement to the republican vision is implicit in the French adoption of the broad label of exclusion to designate the difficulty the nation faces. To understand the force of this concept and its relation to contemporary democratic demands, it is necessary to return again to French history—starting now from the Socialist victory in 1981, which was said to put an end to the revolutionary quest for a realized political republic that the Third Republic only began.[19]

## Translating Social Issues into Political Practice Before *1989*

The program on which François Mitterrand and the Socialists were elected was—socialist! In light of the persistence of the republican political vision, this surprising option for socialism needs explanation. It is true that many aspects of the program, such as the educational reforms that would integrate into the national educational system the Catholic schools whose separate existence was deemed a residue of the ancien régime, were indeed reflections of the republican tradition. The old reflexes were still present too in the party's vocabulary; for example, at its victory celebration in October 1981 at Valence, the party's general secretary, Paul Quilès, demanded that "we should not say like Robespierre at the Convention 'Heads will roll'; we should say which ones, and say it quickly."[20] But adherence to the economic socialism of the platform was a disaster. The stalled economy was to be restarted by increased demand resulting from raised wages and benefits at all levels, plus the addition of a fifth vacation week. The state also undertook a 100 percent nationalization of a collection of major industries, with the result that some 24 percent of all workers were directly on the government's payroll. This Keynesianism in one country failed. Inflation resulted in falling production and rising unemployment, followed by three devaluations of the franc; finally the government had to abandon "socialisme à la française."

Two questions follow from this inglorious episode, whose further details and tactical abandonment can be left aside here. (1) Why did the left opt for these ritualized socialist economic measures when it was clear that the Thirty Glorious Years (*les trente glorieuses*) that had modernized French capitalism had come to an end in the period following the 1973 oil crisis? After all, from the point of view of socialism, it was the weakened economy that brought the left to power.

The answer depends on an ideological compatibility of this kind of socialism with a specific interpretation of the republican project that had traditionally defined the left. The source of that ideology needs to be explained. (2) What would become of the left once its socioeconomic project had proven itself to be unrealizable and the market had seemingly had its way? If the old republican alternative based on the centralizing rationality of an elite administration was not politically viable, what could replace it for a people whose culture had been historically overdetermined by the political? Could it be renewed on the strength of its own virtues, by being combined with a democratic project that would emerge as a potential replacement for the old elite that had lost its pertinence in the modernized French republic?

The left in France cannot be identified with the cause of socialism or with the Socialist (or Communist) Party.[21] Because the revolution preceded the emergence of what the nineteenth century called "the social problem," the left was identified as the party of the republic. The republican cause was presented first of all in the fight for universal (male) suffrage rather than for immediate social change. Insofar as society was at all considered by republican politics, it was denounced as complicit with the old order (which is one reason that male suffrage was sought: women were thought to be in the thralls of the church, itself a weapon of the reaction). Later republicanism could of course take a radical form, transforming the fight against privilege into a struggle for social equality. But not all republicans would go so far (as was seen in June 1848); as a result, the left was subject to splits and factionalism, since the domain to which equality was to apply remained open to dispute, ranging from electoral participation to social justice. Even when it was socially radical, early republicanism was led by an elite that sought to use the power of the state to impose the universality of the law for the good of all. This mode of political intervention meant that republicans who were concerned with social betterment had to choose whether to enter into compromises with other, less radical factions in order to acquire some power to effect some good or to remain principled but powerless. When they did enter such compromises—for example, after the failed workers' rising in June of 1848 or in the tense years when the Third Republic was being established—they were accused of compromise with the old order.

Their dilemma became more painful as industrial growth produced an ever-larger urban working class and a more glaringly prosperous capitalism. How could the republicans retain their political project in the face of rising social injustice? What stance could they take with regard to projects for social reform?

The situation was no less difficult for the newly created Socialist parties. Their socialism had to overcome the republican political blindness to social problems if it was to find a hearing in French political life. The concept of class meant they spoke explicitly for only a part of society; class-based politics appeared to be inherently dogmatic and antirepublican. The Socialists could argue that they were seeking nothing different from what the radical republicans of 1848 sought: to restore political unity by overcoming social divisions. But the radicals had been defeated in 1848—although the indecisiveness of their moderate former allies had paved the way for Bonaparte's coup. The problem returned each time the possibility of reform through compromise seemed possible. How could social reform be justified by republican political means? Either republican politics debased itself by defending the cause of a particular interest, or the reform proved to be only a partial realization (and a weakening) of the social cause that justified it. This structural dilemma of French socialism explains why, after the Russian Revolution and creation of the Third International, an explicitly Communist party was created after the scission that took place at the Socialist Congress of Tours in 1920, setting the stage for a fratricidal competition for the proud heritage of the republican left. The terms of the competition were constantly renegotiated, but both parties seemed to find the heritage worth fighting for.

This structural dilemma explains the importance of ideology, and particularly of Marxism, for the French left. If a republican government forms alliances to rule jointly through compromise, each participant has to be able to distinguish itself and legitimate its choices. When Marxism became the dominant ideology of the workers' movement with the creation of the Socialist International in Paris in 1889—not incidentally, the centenary of the French Revolution—each decision had to be justified with reference to that theory. The same was true when a faction within the party sought to influence other members or the party line or even to found a new party. (This meant that the theory could never develop further as a theory, for it was by definition the criterion by which other theories were evaluated and criticized. That is why the French contribution to Marxist theory is so limited despite the crucial political role of that theory. It also explains why the French understanding of Marxist theory is often limited to the ability to cite from various collections of *Morceaux choisis*. Finally, it suggests why Marxism attained such cultural currency in France.) This central role of Marxism as ideology also meant that political participation by workers tended to be sparse; their concerns were more immediate and often better addressed by trade union activity. As a result, the leaders of the Socialist Party tended to be representatives of the kind of intellectual elite typical of the republican tradition. The model was Jean Jaurès, who managed to ally socialism to the republican tradition by his decision to involve the party in the Dreyfus affair when the competing socialist factions considered the injustice done to the Jewish captain to be simply a matter for the bourgeoisie to fight out among itself.[22] The model persisted in the interwar years in the person of Léon Blum, who distinguished the (republican) exercise of power from the (socialist) conquest of power, which was to be prepared by its exercise.

The ideological maneuvers and compromises that sought to paste together the goals of the socially oriented left with the republican tradition were already being denounced in the nineteenth century by an antiparliamentary left that became solidly implanted. The best-known figure in the early period is Proudhon, who insisted that the artisan workers had to organize their own salvation outside the framework of parliamentary politics. Toward the end of the century, as union organization (and industrialization) proceeded apace, self-managed Bourses de Travail—distinct also from the capitalist Bourse, or stock market—became rallying points competing with the organized parliamentary socialists for the attention of the workers. The strength of antiparliamentary sentiment was evident when the CGT (General Confederation of Labor, created in 1895 by a fusion of the self-managed Bourses with the traditional trade unions) rejected the proposal for a fusion with the parliamentary socialists at its 1906 congress in Amiens. Independence from political parties has remained a foundation of French trade union action.[23] It is a proud autonomy that can also trace its origins to the oppositional *journées* of the Revolution. This is another reason it has been difficult to invent a French version of a reformist, social-democratic politics of compromise similar to that of other modern democratic industrial societies. Although Proudhon's artisans were long ago replaced by an industrial working class and then by a new working class, the idea that political affiliation depends on economic class remains strong.

A further aspect of the antiparliamentary tradition is more dangerous. It can make room for an antidemocratic, chauvinist, mean-spirited temper that was present already in some of Proudhon's work and has developed since his time. This is where the far right[24] meets the far left, whether at the time of the Dreyfus affair, during the confused Depression years, with the acceptance of the Vichy regime, or after the war in the movements of Poujade and later Le Pen. This unintended and unexpected meeting of opposites is made possible by the devaluation of the republican ideal. It was that republican ideal that constrained the socialists to try to work within the parliamentary republic while simultaneously defending the interests of a particular social class. Only in this way, it appeared, were reforms possible. But these same reformist compromises also provided grist for the antiparliamentary mills put into action by antipoliticians of the left or the right. The only way out of this dilemma was through the appeal to ideology as a justification proving that the compromise is called for by the doctrine itself. *This explains why the French Socialists entered government in 1981 with a platform that was socialist.* They had formulated a "Common Program" with the Communist Party, which could provide them with the ideological legitimation that would make their parliamentary politics credible.[25]

Now that the question of why a socialist platform was adopted in 1981 has been clarified, it remains to consider what conclusions can be drawn from the failure to unite the republican and socialist programs. The facts are simple enough. At first, attempting to make a virtue of necessity, the Socialists tried to reconcile the rigor of the market's laws with the universality of republican law. They also attempted to use "Europe" as the kind of motivating ideal that "the republic" had represented in the creation of the Third Republic. This resulted only in the Acte unique européen of 1985, which was a modest attempt to make possible a renewal of Keynesianism on a more defensible, Europe-wide scale.[26] None of this prevented the defeat of the Socialists in the 1986 parliamentary elections. But the right, still haunted by its antirepublican traditions, went too far too fast. Over-confident, it sought to emulate the antistate radicalism of Reagan and Thatcher. This permitted President Mitterrand (whose term ran until 1998) to adopt the role of arbiter standing above the passions and interests of politics; he made himself a republican monarch, transforming the "cohabitation" of left and right into a realization of the unity long sought by the republic. As a bonus, the radicalism of his opponents permitted Mitterrand to present himself as a Socialist simply by defending the mixed economy. This prepared his reelection in 1988. Tellingly, his new campaign did not appeal to socialism or even draw on the resources of the Socialist Party; his platform was presented in a public "Letter to All the French," in which he proposed a politics of "neither-nor": neither nationalizations nor privatizations. The realized republic appeared to be pacified.

However remarkable Mitterrand's personal success, it poses a question about French political culture today. Mitterrand understood that the Socialists' victory was based on the unique political structure introduced by the Fifth Republic. The direct election of the president (and the power accorded him) changed the rules of the political game. The old SFIO had decomposed as the Algerian war became more poisonous. The primacy of economic development implied by its Marxist ideology let it hope that it could have it both ways, arguing that it was the duty of France to remain in Algeria in order to develop the economic basis for an autonomy that would gradually bring independence. That may have been plausible abstractly, or in the long run, but politics is a dynamic process in which there is more than one actor. The demise of the Fourth Republic, and de Gaulle's acceptance of Algerian independence, created the conditions needed for rebuilding French socialism. Its strategy remained oriented to winning state power; its ideology was largely unchanged, but its tactics were modified. Mitterrand recognized that the need for a runoff election if no presidential candidate won an absolute majority in the first round could be used to his advantage. In 1965 he was able to gain the support of a broad republican as well as socialist left to win 45 percent in the runoff. (Such support is the result of what is designated candidly as *discipline républicaine*, which permits the elector to vote for a particular party in the first round while assuming that the good of the nation will motivate his final decision.) After the failure of the divided left even to place a candidate in the runoff in 1969, Mitterrand's earlier success provided the legitimacy needed to create a new Socialist Party (PS) at Epinay in 1971 and to impose himself as its leader.

Electoral tactics are not the only explanation of Mitterrand's success. Although he had not been a socialist, he was able to impose his leadership over the moribund SFIO because of a second modification brought about by the constitution that created the Fifth Republic. The electoral rules that Mitterrand had used so well in 1965 also changed the relation of the leader to both his party and the electorate. The direct election of the executive meant that there was no longer a need for party activists (and lower elected officials) to act as mediators between the candidate and the public. A new logic emerged. The party became an instrument at the service of its candidate, on whose success the fate of its members depended. The imbalance between the summit and the base was increased by the subordination of the elected representatives in Parliament to the powerful executive, which had the effect of denying elected members of the party any autonomous power that could be used to rein in the party leader. Parliamentary or social republicanism now gave way to a new political form, a kind of plebiscitary democracy that is often designated as a "democracy of opinion."[27] Mitterrand proved a tactical master of the new rules. Only one dimension escaped him: as with the old parliamentary socialists, he was forced to justify his compromises by appealing to the still-dominant Marxist ideology—with the disastrous economic consequences of 1981–1983.

The concept of a democracy of opinion designates the establishment of a direct relation of the politician to the electorate, unmediated by particular political institutions. This relation is created with the aid of modern techniques of communication, whose use is of course not unique to France. More particular to France is the relation between the democracy of opinion and the political phenomena that Yves Mény analyzes under the title *La corruption de la république*.[28] The corruption that is peculiarly French is not that of individuals using public office for private gain; that kind of illegality exists no doubt in all political societies. The French kind of corruption is more philosophical; it refers to the rotting from within of the foundational principles (or virtues) of a society. This kind of corruption is particularly dangerous in a nation that conceives of itself as republican. Corruption of the republic (which paves the way for individual corruption) sets in when activists play a decreasing role, while communications specialists become more important, and politics becomes increasingly expensive as a result. The finances needed for a campaign cannot be raised from members' dues. Other sources of revenue must be found. Lobbying firms (which the French call "bureaux d'expertise" or "bureaux d'études," on the assumption that expert knowledge represents no particular interest) are created by the political parties, at both national and local levels. These party-dependent firms can then overcharge their clients, recycling into the party's coffers taxpayer (or private) money that was factored into the cost of a new school, public facility, or rezoned land.[29]

When the French use the concept of a democracy of opinion, there is an overtone of critical distance that expresses disdain sometimes for the role accorded to mere opinion, sometimes for the role of democracy. But it is precisely the new role of public opinion that explains the denunciation of political corruption. The practices that have come to light in recent years are not new, nor are their uses limited to a single party. But they were long overlooked in part because of the lack of independence of the French judiciary and in part because of the complicity of the politicians themselves.[30] It is not just the (undeniable) courage of investigating magistrates that has brought about a change. The system itself creates the conditions that challenge its legitimacy. Public opinion loves scandal; investigative journalism (which has not been typical of the French press) needs leaks to feed that opinion, while investigating magistrates can recall the outraged cries of the public when their political superiors try to restrain their zealous pursuit of corruption. As a result, citizens who are reduced to spectators by the new political institutions are now able now to see the corruption of political life; the cynicism that results is not the kind of virtue needed to maintain a republican society. Yet the goal of the journalists and of the magistrates is to restore that republican political system. It is not clear which tendency will predominate: private cynicism or the renewal of republican virtue.[31]

Despite much talk and some limited reforms, a trait typical of French political life that dates back to the monarchy has been strengthened by the Fifth Republic: the "*cumul*" (accumulation of functions). A successful French politician must occupy positions at both the national and local levels; indeed, it is wise to have an official role at many (public, semipublic, and private) levels between the two extremes. This practice is said to be functional for all concerned. As a representative of the locality, the politician can intervene with the national government to get help, and as a participant in the national government, the representative brings an appreciation of local particularities, permitting efficient administration. In this way, the *cumul* ensures what the logic of French republicanism calls "*la synthèse.*" (Other political logics might recognize here a conflict of interests.) This synthesis not only unites the different levels of political intervention; it also provides a second mediation, between the local electorate (or particular interests within it) and the powerful state bureaucracy (whose task is to translate the universality of the law for application to particular cases by means of so-called *décrets d'application*).[32] This second synthesis is needed in order to make the bureaucratic machine function smoothly while taking account of particularities that fall outside the generality of the law. At the same time, however, it weakens the ability of the state to exercise its centralizing legislative power.

The interplay of these two aspects of the *cumul* contributes to the depoliticization that accompanies the democracy of opinion. On the one hand, the elected national representative has little reason to be present in Paris, where his (and increasingly her) interventions count for little in a parliament that is subordinated to the executive who controls the destiny of the party and where the bureaucracy jealously protects its autonomy from party politics. The ability of the representative to intervene meaningfully depends on the control of a slice of local power that can be made useful to the national party. This gives the national representative a positive reason to cultivate the home turf, with the result that Parliament is weakened further, attendance decreases, and political committees are left in the hands of experts and a small coterie of political leaders. (The power of such leaders explains another peculiarity of French politics: the "parachuting" of a national figure into a new local electoral district, which is expected to support the outsider because this will bring national influence that even a popular local leader could not attain easily.) These conditions affect also the elite of the *service public*, whose ability to serve the public is weakened by the second aspect of the *cumul*, which ensures that local particularity is taken into account. As a result, the elite becomes demoralized, and, in a society where private and monetary advancement has become increasingly important outside as well as within politics, increasing numbers are leaving for private industry.[33] Elite abstention from politics nourishes in turn the cynicism of the democracy of opinion.

The general corruption of the republic produces the conditions that lead to the denunciation of the particular practices of corruption that empty republicanism of its meaning, destroying the ideals it carried and the political style that made its citizens more than just privatized and atomized individuals. This denunciation of corruption may be a sign that republican ideals are not dead. But it may also create a public of cynics who are not just apolitical but strongly antipolitical. The replacement of political activism by expertise in communications techniques is only the external manifestation of a deeper rot. France was a nation built around politics and the expectation that problems could be solved in the political arena. When that belief disappears—even if the belief was based on an illusion— the society finds itself without a rudder. The antipolitical vein that has been present in French life since the revolutionary *journées* gains strength. So-called social movements return—for example, in the massive strikes of December 1995 that led to the fall of the right- wing prime minister, Alain Juppé.[34] These social movements are not necessarily on the side of the progress identified with the left, as was evident with the rise of Jean-Marie Le Pen's National Front (abetted by Mitterrand's cynical electoral tactic of 1986, when he introduced proportional representation in order to divide the right). The danger is that such movements and their advocates, most notably in *Le Monde diplomatique*, plead the cause of the victims, happy to take the side of the oppressed, while idealizing conditions that supposedly existed before the economy became global and social relations were monetarized. This too is part of the corruption of the republic, whose vision of political justice was never oriented to a mythical past.

The regeneration of French republicanism will depend on its success in reforming itself as a republican democracy. As has been seen, democracy in France was traditionally understood as the result of republican politics, an end not a means. This attitude began to change at the same time that the Socialists were joining with the Communists finally to conquer state power. A so-called second left led by Michel Rocard emerged within the Socialist Party to challenge its statist and centralizing presuppositions. It was joined by those for whom the movements for human rights in Poland and increasingly across Eastern Europe represented a renewal of the meaning of political participation. Assuming that the Soviet Union would never permit them to seize state power, these movements sought to organize the autonomy of civil society against the state. The support for these East-Central European struggles from self-identified leftists was significant; it distinguished the French left from other lefts in the capitalist world that were more ambivalent about the nature and future of "really existing socialism." This political orientation in part emerged because the critique of totalitarianism arose much later in France than elsewhere. It contributed to the unique French reaction to the translation of Solzhenitsyn's *Gulag Archipelago*—although the impact of the book's revelations (and political arguments)[35] depended also on the fact that the French Communist Party had appropriated the mantle of the radical republic, which it combined with an antiparliamentary populism (and a legend of antifascist resistance) to make itself a cultural power even though its real political weight was small and growing weaker. As a result, the French critique of totalitarianism was a self-critique of its own tradition. This self-critique of both the republican and the socialist elements of French political culture, combined with the new appreciation for a self-organizing civil society, has made possible a reevaluation of the place of democracy.

## TOWARD A REPUBLICAN DEMOCRACY?

The new attitude toward democracy had another antecedent: May '68. The events of that May of course meant many things to many different people, which is no doubt why one of the most memorable slogans affirmed that "it is forbidden to forbid." In the present context, it was another step toward the end of French socialist illusions. The mass demonstration of a million people on May 13 passed under the balcony of Mitterrand's political vehicle of the moment, the FGDS (Fédération de la Gauche Démocratique et Socialiste), without a serious glance, while consigning to the tail of the march the "Stalinist scum" (*crapules staliniennes*), who were desperate now to board the speeding train they had done their best to sabotage. At the end of the demonstration, an old question reemerged: what is to be done? Those who cried, "A l'Elysée!" were dismissed as anarchists. Those who took themselves (and history) more seriously had a different idea. As strikes continued to paralyze society, a demonstration on May 27 at the Charlety stadium was attended by the respected former republican prime minister Pierre Mendès-France. Could he be brought temporarily to power, a French Kerensky leading a "February revolution," until new Bolsheviks (or a rapidly maturing proletariat) could overthrow him?[36] History did not repeat itself. A country had been paralyzed, revolution seemed at hand, and then, with a speech of the president (and his visit to French military bases in Germany), it was over. Now the right could send its millions into the street. Less than a month later, it won a massive 358–127 majority in Parliament that for historical French memories recalled the "Chambre introuvable" elected after the Restoration of Louis XVIII.

Lessons had to be drawn, and they were. Many activists sought to continue their struggle, joining the Trotskyists and Maoists or even hoping to radicalize a Communist Party whose role during the events was hardly glorious (but whose presidential candidate in 1969 scored 21.5 percent to the Socialist's 5 percent). But their hard work with a lack of noticeable progress gradually forced many to recognize the truth of their own experience (and that of French political culture): 1968 was not the beginning of a long struggle toward revolution; *1968 was the demonstration that revolution is not possible in modern society*. This is one reason that in France, as opposed to Germany or Italy, no serious leftist group argued that terrorism represented a viable political method.[37] It is also part of the explanation of the turn to ethics that came to replace the political project.[38] This ethical option did not have to be antipolitical; the demand for the rights of man had been an animating factor in the self-organizing civil societies of Eastern Europe. Ethics could contribute to a renewal of republican values, as in the case of André Glucksmann, who abandoned his Maoism to bring together Sartre and Aron in support of the Vietnamese boat people and has remained the ethical conscience of political engagement. Similarly, the young doctors who founded Médecins sans frontières were former sixty-eighters who didn't forget their political past. Their first intervention, during the Nigerian civil war (or Biafran struggle for independence), showed that they were aware that formal neutrality under the guise of ethical evenhandedness can hide a real bias constituted by facts on the ground. For the same reason, later French leftists did not just protest the massacres at Vukovar or Srebenica; they analyzed and condemned the responsibility of the Milošević regime. The ethics embodied by this republican left is individual but not individualistic (which may be one reason that John Rawls for so long remained untranslated into French).

The politics of the post-1968 left had theoretical roots as well. The publication of *Mai 1968: La brèche* underlined the rupture that the new movement introduced into the tradition of socialist politics. Its three authors, Edgar Morin, Claude Lefort, and Jean-Marc Coudray (a.k.a. Cornelius Castoriadis), draw positive consequences from their critique of Marxist politics. Lefort and Castoriadis had been Trotskyists who came to see that their Marxist search for the material basis of Stalinism brought to light a paradox: those conditions had been created by the *political* seizure of power by the Bolshevik party. For his part, Morin had drawn similar conclusions from his exclusion in 1951 from the Communist Party that he had joined during the Resistance. The radical rethinking of the nature and goals of political action undertaken in the enforced isolation of the French ultra left permitted these three authors to recognize that 1968 could not be recuperated by the old order whose self-declared foes in fact had a stake in its maintenance. The formerly isolated critics began to find a public. Morin's *Autocritique* (1958) was republished in a mass edition in 1970, at the same time that a twelve-volume edition of Castoriadis's essays from *Socialisme ou Barbarie* began to appear. The impact of this critique was double. The Marxism that had frozen into an ideology of political legitimation was thrown into question. As a result, Marx became again a critical philosopher, although explicit reference was no longer useful since Marxism had been denounced as ideology. But if Marxism could no longer serve to legitimate political choices, some replacement had to be found. Ethics was one candidate, human rights a second, democracy became a third.

The path by which the French left came to place its hopes in political democracy colored its understanding of the term. The critique of Marxism and its totalitarian reality put into question any doctrine (including aspects of the republican tradition) that laid claim to be the incarnation, essence, or true unity of the people or nation. Moreover, the critique of Soviet pretensions to being a true democracy made it clear that institutions alone cannot create or ensure the maintenance of a democratic society. Democracy could not be taken either as what Marx liked to call "the finally discovered secret" of historical evolution, as if it could put an end to all societal ills. These three critical insights pointed to the fact that democracy is a problem; it is not a (static or univocal) solution to social or political difficulties. This understanding of democracy as a problem was confirmed by French history, whose compulsive and repetitious course it also helps clarify. Democracy can be seen as the attempt to formulate the conditions in which the differences that were wrested from the unitary culture of the ancien régime can not just coexist but enrich each other. (In this way, the theory of democracy could be made compatible but not identical with aspects—including the self-interested economic motivation—of the French liberalism typified by Guizot.) These democratic differences are not comparable to the fixed and permanent status marks of a hierarchical society; they are differences that coexist within a field whose foundation is the principle of a basic equality of rights. Although the right to difference that is the precondition of democracy was made possible by the Revolution, republican (and later socialist) political culture sought constantly to eliminate it. That is why these republican and socialist goals can only be realized if they are constrained to take into account the problem of democracy.

Democracy as the maintenance and legitimation of difference can be understood as a means that becomes its own end and motivation. Difference is not naturally present in society; the right to democratic difference, and its legitimacy, depends on politics. Difference is not *in*difference, the dumb coexistence of inert objects examined by a neutral observer unaffected by them. Difference exists only against a backdrop of unity (such as the principle of an equality of rights). This is where the French republican (and socialist) political tradition comes to the aid of the fledgling democracy.[39] Neither the traditional political parties nor the elite of the *service public* can be expected to carry the democratic project. Nor can democracy as the affirmation of difference be identified with the direct popular participation of the street that has been traditional since the revolutionary *journées*. The hope that new social movements and new forms of self-management would provide the needed innovation has failed. Rather, when a univocal interpretation is avoided, it appears that the globalization feared by many also offers unexpected openings for democratic politics. The precondition of the present stage of globalization (which has gone beyond the multinational corporate age or the reciprocal lowering of industrial tariffs to foster the internationalization of culture, services, and finance) was the end of the cold war. That made possible a transformation of the relation of the citizen to the state. The republican ideal remains, but the absence of an enemy makes its logic less materially imperative. (The existence of real enemies of the post-1789 republic played the same role for the first republican logic.) The concept of republican unity can now appear for the first time as what it always was: the symbolic representation of society's own values. This symbolic role was incarnated by the absolute monarch; for the republic, it is represented by the principle of equal rights. The Revolution confused the incarnation with what it incarnated. Killing the real king, it gave new life to his symbolic role as a threat to a republican unity that, for the same reason, was doomed to repetition because the symbolic can never be fully realized.[40] But the symbolic is not without real effects, as French history constantly demonstrates.

As is so often the case, French history illuminates contemporary France. Concern with the corruption of the republic had an antecedent: worry about the corruption of the monarchy. The remedy offered then was appeal to the quasi-independent judicial bodies called the *parlements*. Their role in creating the climate of public opinion that led to the calling of the Estates-General was vital. Their disappearance after 1789 is explained by the unitary logic of French republican politics. To replace the monarchy, the Revolution had to speak with one voice and to create one unique and unified general will. Judicial autonomy was a threat to unity in the same way as was royal veto power.[41] But the independent lawyer did not disappear with the Revolution; indeed, the period from 1875 to 1920 is often referred to as "the Republic of Lawyers [La République des avocats]." These were lawyers who had gone into politics; they were not representatives of the law as such. The recent political scandals within the democracy of opinion have been produced by magistrates—public servants who were acting now in the service of the law.

The first appearance of a demand for the autonomy of the magistrates dates not surprisingly to their creation of an autonomous professional union in the wake of 1968. Another step occurred in 1971, with the judicial ruling that the preamble to the constitution—the Declaration of the Rights of Man—was part of the "bloc de constitutionalité." This opened a new flexibility in legal interpretation that was extended to include the idea of rights that, although not explicit, have "a constitutional value" (as the court ruled in 1994 concerning a right to housing). The cultural import of these developments was suggested by the creation in 1985 of a journal, *Droits*, whose premise was that "the science of law has its place among the human and social sciences and belongs more generally to the shared culture of society."[42] These developments challenged the traditional orientation of French legal thinking, both before and after the Revolution, which had been toward unified administrative law. From this point of view, the impact of globalization on the state encourages a political reflection on the symbolic status of republican unity that makes room for a rethinking of the autonomy of law and the right to difference within a democratic political culture.

The intervention of the judiciary can be understood as the production and legitimation of difference. When the magistrate was simply an arm of the (republican or absolutist) state, justice and the interest of that state were identical, while individual rights were a private matter whose protection was possible only by the state applying the law uniformly. Although the magistrates remain servants of the state (as opposed to the independent *avocat*, or lawyer), they are likely to win still more autonomy in the present political climate. When the magistrate serves the law by protecting individual rights, particular interest acquires an autonomy and a legitimacy that it previously lacked. The increased public interest in judicial matters has a further consequence. The clash of two interests (and their lawyers) in the judicial arena presupposes implicitly that both interests are potentially or in principle legitimate. The court renders a judgment, whereas the central state subsumes particular cases under general administrative rules. While a juridical society may become quarrelsome, it is also a society that recognizes a right to difference precisely because and insofar as that right is based on the assumption that there is a shared symbolic conception of justice that permits the (never final) adjudication of the coexistence of these rights and differences.[43] An autonomous judiciary cannot create a democracy, but a democracy cannot be maintained without judicial liberty, which not only prevents individual corruption but also challenges the corruption of the republic. Such a judiciary becomes a political institution precisely to the degree that it is not a politicized institution. The evaluation and legitimation of individual differences imply the recognition of the symbolic status of republican unity. The republic is not denied when it has to give up its pretension to define justice; it becomes a republican democracy.

If globalization can be understood as contributing to the possible realization of the French political project, can the same be said for the phenomenon of exclusion? The right to difference could be criticized for putting an ideological halo on what global capital does on its own. But societies are political bodies that determine for themselves, politically, the role of the economy; otherwise they would be corporations whose well-being is measured by their bottom line. If France has become a pawn in a globalized economy, this was the effect rather than the cause of the corruption of the republic. This means that the political treatment of the problem of exclusion (including its economic causes) presupposes the elimination of that corruption by the creation of a republican democracy. The independence of the judicial magistrate is a first step. Its effect is to guarantee that members of society are autonomous individuals whose rights are assured by law. Only such individuals have the ability to become members of a political society. It is not enough to provide all citizens with economic necessities; recognition of what Hannah Arendt called "the right to have rights" is fundamental to the integration of the members of a republican democracy. Only under these conditions can individuals organize themselves to make demands on a state that not only ensures their symbolic community by protecting their real rights but also—like the incarnate monarch—is expected to hear the needs of the society. The magistrates' ability to appeal to the law against the state, making the state just another particular interest, is essential for the state to acquire the legitimacy needed to play its unitary republican role (by being open to the society and to the economy while still uniting social diversity) without falling prey to the accusation of arbitrariness that, in the end, brought down the ancien régime. To be both unitary and yet diverse is the definition and the difficulty of democracy.

## APPENDIX: FRENCH ECONOMIC THEORY AS POLITICAL

Although its vanity has cost French theory some of its currency among literary and cultural critics, it could be usefully replaced by the contributions of a creative group of French economists working in the historical and political tradition described here. At a moment when rational choice theory in its various guises is attempting to lay claim to the status of a general theory of social (and even of private) life, the French approach could be seen as offering the foundation for a counterattack. They are returning to the old motifs of political economy to challenge the antipolitical, thick-headed attempt to maintain the purity of an imperious economic logic that is incapable of admitting its own limits. A successful counterattack would mark points in the attempt to set limits to those aspects of globalization that threaten the foundations on which the economy rests as well as the goals that it claims to pursue.

The French approach is composed of many threads, which I will try briefly to knit together. The authors who have contributed to it write in both technical-academic and more popular journals. Their work of course also takes into account the general debates in the field of economics as practiced across national frontiers. A recent review article that provides a useful overview, "Penser ensemble l'économie et la société: La sociologie économique," by Jean-Louis Laville and Benoît Levesque, cites nearly as many English-language authors as it does French in its seventy-five dense footnotes.[44] One note, however (n. 54) gives away the French strategy when it seeks to translate Karl Polanyi's key concept of "embeddedness." Polanyi's *The Great Transformation* (1944) sought to understand why the Great Depression that followed the 1929 crash was more than just a cyclical crisis. Polanyi tried to show the historical uniqueness of the autonomous market for goods and services (including the market for wage labor) as the foundation of a new and artificial type of society. This artificially maintained market distinguished capitalism from all other known human societies in which the economy was subordinated to other dimensions of social relations: it was *embedded*. The Great Depression could be seen as the revenge of real social relations over the artificial market that had sought to impose its logic without taking account of the resistance of the actual society and the people who made it work. It represented a civilizational crisis.

The concept of embeddedness poses a translation problem because Polanyi's insight can be read modestly or more radically. The modest interpretation simply points out that what appear to be purely economic phenomena—for example, prices or job creation—have a social dimension that needs to be taken into account. This social dimension is studied by economic sociology. It shows that prices are not natural, any more than demand is some fixed physical sum determined by unchanging human needs; otherwise there would be no advertising industry. As a result, economic sociology can criticize the assumption of neoclassical economics that economic agents are benefit-maximizing subjects provided with perfect information about the conditions and results of their choices. The modesty of this interpretation is suggested by the translation of embeddedness as *étayage*, which implies the existence of two independent factors whose interaction cannot be neglected by the analysis. This point has been evident to economic sociologists since Max Weber, whose "methodological individualism" did not ignore the environment in which the individual had to function.

A more radical translation of the concept of embeddedness goes back to the founder of French sociology, Emile Durkheim, for whom the individual, as well as the economy, is always, despite surface appearances, subordinated to the social whole. The concept should be translated as *encastrement*, suggesting that the economic can never dominate over its environment and that its apparent autonomy is an illusion that needs to be shown its limits. The priority accorded to the social does not exclude the individual; it does not strip the individual of its autonomy; nor is it incompatible with a market society. Durkheim's theory is called functionalist because it assumes that the kinds of individual encountered in every society are formed by—and function to ensure the preservation of—that society. For this kind of theory, the rationally choosing neoclassical economic actor is not a presupposition; the theory has to ask why and how that type of individual came to dominate in a given type of society.[45]

This French interpretation of Polanyi's concept of embeddedness has practical implications. Bernard Perret, the former head of evaluation for the French Plan, offered a simple suggestion in the very title of a 1994 book: *L'économie contre la société*.[46] Socialist prime minister Lionel Jospin drew the political and critical consequences in his reply to the June 2000 White Paper on European Socialism proposed by Tony Blair and Gerhardt Schröder: "Yes to the market, no to the society based on the market." Jospin's formula is eloquently terse; its practical implementation remains to be seen.

The early appearances of this French orientation date to the late 1970s, when what was called the school of regulation developed the concept of Fordism to designate a specific phase of capitalist social development that went beyond the nineteenth-century economic model analyzed by Marx. The concept of Fordism was intended to be more precise and analytic than competing categories such as welfare capitalism, postindustrial society, or Habermas's Weberian-Marxist concept of late capitalism. Since economies that are embedded in social relations obey forms of regulation that are both explicit and implicit, the task of economic analysis is to uncover and compare types of regulation. For example, Fordism designates a mode of social reproduction in which constantly increasing output makes it possible to pay increasing wages for jobs guaranteed over the long term. In exchange for these gains, the capitalists earn the cooling of class conflict, while workers pay the price of losing their claim to control the organization of labor. The appeal of this analytic approach to authors such as Michel Aglietta, Robert Boyer, or Alain Lipietz is that when patterns of capitalist accumulation change, this will result in a double crisis—on the side of labor and on the side of capital. Labor can no longer be bought off with better wages, while capital will have to invent a new ideology of deregulation in order to regain dominance.

The school of regulation can be seen as developing a twentieth-century version of Marxist political economy. But the approach is not narrowly Marxist. Its insights have been drawn more broadly as a theory of conventions, developed by Jean-Pierre Dupuy and André Orléan.[47] The notion of "conventions" refers to patterns of regulation that can be either explicit or implicit; these patterned relations form conventions that serve to coordinate anticipations and permit arbitration among conflicting interests. In this way, conventions (or regulations) permit a transition between the levels of micro- and macroanalysis without appeal to the artificial and abstract subject and the invisible hand of market economies. The conventional regulations are part of the everyday expectations of market participants, who for that reason are not just the disembodied actors portrayed by rationalist economic logic: they are embedded.

The advantage of this approach is that the relation of social to economic change can be studied without the risk of one-sided reductionism; each depends on and presupposes the other. Instead of talking about a general economic mode of production applicable in every society regardless of its history and its resources, the goal is to "explain both the geographical diversity of capitalisms and the variations in the temporal configuration of social forms. It thus produces a more precise periodization than those that previously existed and shows the specificity that has characterized postwar growth."[48] If one form of social regulation—say, Fordism—fails, another must be assumed to replace it if chaos is not to result. The new form may be more stable, but its costs and benefits have for their part also to be analyzed critically.

From this perspective, the global economy is not simply denounced as a "horror" (as suggested by title of the best-selling screed of Viviane Forrestier).[49] It is a form of regulation resulting from a series of compromises among social actors. "The notion of a mode of regulation that is supposed to explain a period of relative stability *and* the irruption of crises refers to a coherent ensemble formed by different social relations, institutional dispositions, productive techniques, and organizations that ensure regular economic growth and the stability of social functioning."[50] If Anthony Giddens has pushed Tony Blair to move "beyond left and right," French economists are proposing to their politicians the project of a new social contract that is not simply economic.[51]

This French holistic model suggests the need to analyze social movements politically. This approach differs from the American sociological analysis of such movements that reduces them to either the quest for identity by neglected interests or the opportunistic mobilization of power resources. Reductionist accounts, even when they intend to lend support to these movements, undermine them by adopting such an antipolitical view. The French proposal situates these movements within given forms of regulation while asking how they can culminate in the establishment of new types of regulation that can be as different as formal contracts, legislative decisions, or local and informal rules of the game that legitimate decisions politically. Whereas the sociological perspective reduces social movements to the ends they are assumed to seek and then judges them in terms of the criteria imputed to the movement by the analyst, the approach of French political economy avoids such means-ends judgments in favor of the functional analysis of an embedded socioeconomic self-regulation (from which, of course, crisis and conflict are not excluded).

The analysis of the welfare state as itself simply another form of regulation provides a counterpart to the account of social movements. The difficulties facing the modern state are not just the financial result of its ability to increase taxes in difficult economic times. If Fordism was the result of a compromise that promised good wages and job security in exchange for workers' nonparticipation, this implicit compromise was regulated explicitly by the old welfare state. The new social contract would be a compromise in which the workers—or perhaps the users of the services "produced" in what is increasingly a service economy—can play a more active role. One need not assume that the cost to the workers would be a loss of security or that the gains of the capitalists would be paid in the coin of deregulated globalism. When bureaucratic administrations are no longer expected to satisfy the needs of clients who are passive consumers, the need for nonmarket social relations to solve problems posed by the marketization of society becomes evident. The form that will be invented cannot of course be predicted in advance.

A final, more philosophical-political dimension of the French theory should be considered. Durkheim's most important successor, Marcel Mauss, developed his uncle's insights in a short essay on "The Gift."[52] The modern economy based on market-mediated exchange-values is embedded in more primordial social (and political) relations regulated by the giving (and receiving) of gifts. Indeed, we repeat the same archaic gesture when we offer our hosts flowers or a good bottle of wine. It would be short-sighted to interpret our gift as an exchange for the hospitality we are to be offered. Some relations are and can only be noneconomic; their logic or rationale is *antiutilitarian*, but without it our social relations would lose their coherence. This insight and its implications have been the theme developed over the past decades by Alain Caillé and the journal he edits, the *Revue du MAUSS* (whose title is an acronym for Mouvement anti-utilitaire en sciences sociales). Not surprisingly, many of the political economists to whom I have referred here have published in that journal. Perhaps more surprising is the fact that similar themes have been taken up by the liberal capitalist prophet of "the end of history," Francis Fukuyama, whose recent new book, *Trust*, is subtitled *The Social Virtues and the Creation of Prosperity*.[53]

This nonutilitarian (and nonmarket) dimension of the reproduction of social relations can also be applied to the proposal to treat the problems of the welfare state by noneconomic means. An example of that approach, coming this time from the state, can be seen in the decision of the then Socialist prime minister Michel Rocard to introduce the so-called RMI or "minimum revenue of [societal] insertion." Rocard, the leader of the so-called second left, made the assumption that social integration must be assured if the society, and therefore the economy, is to function to its fullest capacity. It should be noted, however, that the RMI has been criticized by those who see it as simply functional to the needs of the economy. These critics propose instead, for example, the notion of a "citizen wage," to which each is entitled, simply in order to ensure the continued functioning of the polity. Other critics contest the automatic nature of the benefit, which doesn't demand individual effort at self-betterment. The debate is both practical and theoretical, sociological and philosophical—for the good of all participants. Its importance need not be stressed here.

A final contribution to this constellation of French economic theory should be mentioned, although its author stands deliberately outside the mainstream (as he always has). Living in retirement outside Parisian debates and writing often in German rather than French, André Gorz has suggested arguments that fall within the new paradigm described here—but he has done so on the basis of his original, and critical, Sartrean reading of Marx. For example, his most recent book, *Misères du présent: Richesse du possible* (1997),[54] makes use of Marx's basic analysis of the commodity—as a dual phenomenon, having both use-value and exchange-value—to show how the capitalist stress on exchange-values alone robs society of the vast potential use-values that are produced by that same capitalism. The relationship to the original insight of Polanyi is evident. The Marx who thereby joins the new French political economy is not the economist but rather the social and thus political analyst of modern social relations in their uniqueness and in their inherently unstable form.

# CHAPTER 10

# Intersecting Trajectories of Republicanism in France and the United States

## The Concept of Republicanism: Historical Symmetries and Asymmetries

Like many inherited historical concepts, republicanism has been understood differently in different contexts and at different times. This has resulted in confusion, polemic, and, most often, paradoxes that also have the benefit of adding depth and richness to the concept itself. So it is today. As used in France, republicanism refers to the political project that found its idealized representation in a vision of universal citizenship that is identified with the achievements of the Third Republic. In the United States, the concept designates the social community needed to provide a meaningful identity to the participants in a liberal polity organized to ensure competition among people who benefit from equal but abstract individual rights. The paradoxical result of the French stress on the political form of republicanism as opposed to the American emphasis on its social implications is that in practice French republicans defend just the kind of formal abstract rights that American republicans denounce as liberalism, while American republicans praise the kind of identity politics that the French republicans criticize as a threat to the unity of the nation. This paradox is all the more frustrating because both sides seek the same result: inclusion. But the meaning of that concept too remains unclear. Is the system to include the individual, or does the action of the individual reproduce and validate (or transform) the system?

Republican political theory has served and continues to serve in both countries as a critique of the existing society. In France, the republican critique today focuses on the problem of exclusion rather than the old Marxist notion of class. The excluded are those whom society is unable to integrate not only into its economy—whose capitalist nature is often ignored or reduced to the euphemism "the market"—but into its political life as well. Republicanism and integration stand together as a political program.[1] In the United States, the concept is related to the (often vague) concept of communitarianism, which is invoked to denounce the abstract legalism and competitive egoism of an individualistic liberalism that both veils and rationalizes a self-denying society through the politics of what Benjamin Barber criticizes as "thin democracy."[2] It demands a participatory rather than a merely representative democracy and stresses personal virtue and "the good" rather than the individual rights that serve political liberalism as trumps in the game of life. The fact that American republicanism can come to imply the demand for more social—even socialist—measures returns to the initial paradox. It inverts the French quest for a political alternative to radical social—or socialist—demands.

This polar opposition of the French and American representations of republicanism has the virtue of identifying a problem but the weakness of remaining at a formal level. In both cases, republicanism can play a critical function because it represents a political solution to social problems.[3] In both cases, it proposes guidelines for eliminating exclusion and ensuring inclusion (although the community sought by the French is national and universal, while the American model is more limited and particular). As a political concept, republicanism represents the universal, which is always in a position to denounce the particularity and division (or individualism) that are characteristic of any modern society. But, for the same reason, social actors are always able to criticize the formal abstractness of the universal claims of the political sphere.

In its concrete form, this abstract opposition expresses the difference between social and political forms of exclusion and inclusion. The American republican treats social inclusion in a community as a political project; the French republican sees inclusion in the polity as the presupposition of a social politics. In the one case, social action is expected to have political consequences; in the other, political action is seen as the basis for social transformation. These Franco-American differences are not the result of conceptual predispositions, as if the French were innately Cartesian and the Americans inherently pragmatist.[4] The roots of the difference lie in the respective histories of these two model republics that cannot reconcile their differences or recognize their similarities.

The historical genesis of the concept of republicanism in both countries suggests that the duality between a social and a political interpretation of the concept has always been present in each of them. In both cases, the concept goes back to the revolutions that gave each nation its claim to being at once unique and a model to be universally imitated. In France, political republicanism made its vital appearance with the events of August 10, 1792, and the Jacobin dictatorship that followed. It is often seen as the rejection of the egoistic individualism (and provincial federalism) that was the product of the simple *liberté* achieved on the night of August 4, 1789, and consecrated in the work of the Constituent Assembly. The republic, legislated into being by the new convention, stood for the attempt to create a nation based on an *égalité* that would overcome the new forms of social exclusion that had resulted from the political abolition of the ancien régime. In this sense, republican politics and socialism could be unified for a moment, as Lenin himself had seen as early as 1904, when he described his ideal revolutionary as "a Jacobin who is inseparably bound together with the organization of the proletariat."[5] This identification of republicanism and socialism explains the passionate reception of the Bolshevik seizure of power in October 1917 by so many French republicans, at the time but also long after the event when they could have known better (such was the case, for example, of the dominant historians of the French Revolution, Mathiez, Lefèbvre, and Soboul). But the response to communism was far from unanimous. The dominant strand of French republicanism had remained political in 1848, and with the foundation of the Third Republic in 1875 the concept came to be represented by the brigades of republican *institueurs* bringing civilization to the French peasantry while directing a never-ending crusade against the old (clerical) order. This more traditional republicanism maintained its roots in the Enlightenment critique of prejudice and privilege, themselves an older form of exclusion to be overcome by the heritage of the Revolution. The French image of a *république des lettres* did not disappear with the ancien régime.

The third concept in the French revolutionary trinity, *fraternité*, might be assumed to represent the form of inclusion that could overcome the opposition of *liberté* and *égalité* that was implicit in the republican model. Mona Ozouf's brilliant sketch of the peregrinations of this concept and its critical afterlife in the nineteenth century is suggestive. It shows that *fraternité* could acquire the connotation of true *liberté* of the individual—for example, in Michelet's stress on the centrality of the Fête de la Fédération (commemorating July 14 and national unity) that joins together free individuals in a higher and quasi-mystical union that, however, does not demand the sacrifice of individuality. But it could also be understood as true *égalité* within the new social system—for example, in the Terror's attempt to unify society by excluding not just its visible enemies but also its lukewarm camp followers.[6] Yet such fraternity cannot be taken for granted in either case, and neither can it be imposed on the individual or on society: the political republic cannot guarantee social inclusion any more than the political guarantee of individual rights won in 1789 ensured social equality after 1792. *Fraternité* offers no mediation, only an incantation; indeed, there is always the danger that it will destroy the two poles whose apparent opposition called it forth.[7] The quest for inclusion that replaces the idealist vision of a revolution that overcomes all opposition demands a rethinking of the inherited categories of French republicanism. The curious symmetrical asymmetry of the French and the American forms of republicanism provides a framework for that project.

The American revolutionary model seems to start from social diversity and work toward political unity as something derivative, secondary, and perhaps even artificial.[8] This exposes it to the danger that social diversity—which a French republican would denounce as exclusion (and a socialist decry as social division), while the optimistic Americans adopt the benign label "pluralism"—will be preserved under the merely formal and abstract unity of the political society. This difficulty too has a history that helps clarify the issues at stake. Whereas the French had first to seize state power and use it in order to intervene into politically determined unequal social relations, America appears to have been a country already nearly equal and quite free whose self-governing society was threatened by British political interference after the Seven Years' War. To protect the self-governing society, such outside political intervention had to be rejected. This gave rise to the psychological perspective that still haunts American politics: that government is best that governs least. Its corollary is the demand for a government of laws, not of men, as if any political intervention at all were a danger because it potentially benefits one of the existing social groups over the others. In this way, the rights of the individual are supposed to be protected and equality before the law ensured. But how was this to make possible the participatory associative social life admired by observers since Tocqueville? Such free association would permit the natural development of fraternal relations on the basis of actions by individuals with no reference to or need for state intervention. This is just what market liberalism claims to provide, yet the competitive egoistic basis of market cooperation (where, as Adam Smith points out, my butcher does not provide me with meat out of beneficence) is hardly the kind of fraternal community sought by today's American republicans.

The American republican model is thus no more free of internal tension and conflict than is the French. The participatory republic that is said to be made possible by the rule of law and the protection of equal rights can effortlessly—and unthinkingly—be transformed into a liberal democracy where procedural justice guarantees formal individual rights that may only serve to make palatable economic competition that makes participation in shared associative projects unlikely. This inability to join in a shared project is encouraged by the multiplicity of private concerns that is ensured by liberal pluralism. It may lead to political turbulence at times when market dysfunction makes it impossible to satisfy all needs, and demands become louder as the inability to satisfy them becomes manifest. At that point, the call to sacrifice the pleasures of private life may be heard; the danger of democratic overload and the perils of ungovernability will be invoked to justify a return to republican discipline.[9] The republic is then no longer simply the formal rule of law; it becomes a political intervention to save society from itself.

This poses again the question of the relation of liberty to equality. Does liberty trump equality, such that equality before the law is the best that the republic can offer? That is the prevailing American interpretation, which accepts the resulting social inequality as the price that must be paid. The reason that inequality can be accepted so easily is, apparently, that it does not constitute a form of exclusion because, as I noted at the outset, the American republic is based on a *social* representation of what holds together a society.

The comparison of the American and the French models of republicanism is made more difficult by the fact that the concept itself fell out of favor in postwar American political discourse. This dominant self-understanding had been brilliantly expressed by Louis Hartz's account *The Liberal Tradition in America* (1955). Following Tocqueville, Hartz developed the old aphorism "no feudalism, no socialism" to stress the uniqueness of America's historical path. Yet the postwar dominance of Hartz, Hofstadter, and the liberal consensus historians was followed by the emergence of a republican interpretation represented by Bernard Bailyn's *The Ideological Origins of the American Revolution* (1967) and Gordon Wood's *The Creation of the American Republic* (1968). This republican reading benefited also from its seeming ability to provide a radical critique of American liberalism without having to invent a proletariat or to make a revolution. The huge success of John Rawls's *A Theory of Justice* (1971) was, in its own way, an incitement to rediscover republicanism. The abstract individual portrayed by Rawls's deontological liberalism encouraged a communitarian response that drew on republican themes to situate that individual. (In the process, the communitarians tended to make the problem of the identity of the individual into a new type of pluralism called multiculturalism.) The shared priority of the social system over the action of the individual in these reactions to America's social liberalism permitted them to identify themselves with the historical concept of republicanism. *Fraternité* was their presupposed solution; *liberté* and *égalité* the problems to be overcome. The solution has remained foreclosed, and the problems are still debated.

Meanwhile, the French had avoided the debate altogether by relegating liberalism to the domain of the economy while leaving it to republicanism to regulate political relations.[10] While this preserved their republican ideology, it did not protect their political life from the realities of liberalism in an increasingly global marketplace. Like it or not, they faced the problems that were felt more directly by the American republic (if not American republican theory), which did not shy away from the implications of liberalism. However, they did have another variant of republican theory that could be called on to reformulate these difficulties in a language more familiar to them. This was the doctrine known as *solidarisme* that had been developed on the basis of Emile Durkheim's sociology. The concept itself points to the central place of the question of exclusion for the French republican tradition.[11]

## SOME ELEMENTS OF THE DEBATE TODAY

The most recent sustained political-theoretical critique of American liberal democracy is Michael J. Sandel's *Democracy's Discontent: America in Search of a Public Philosophy*.[12] This study is useful in the present context because its two parts correspond to the dualities found in the concept of republicanism. Sandel presents first a conceptual critique of what he calls the "procedural republic," which guarantees an abstract, rights-based individualism that produces a series of jurisprudential decisions that threaten the very unity of the republic. Sandel has a good eye, and his examples can be multiplied from near-daily experiences of rights affirmed by courts that defy the pragmatic good sense of the normal citizen. Sandel follows with a provocative historical reconstruction of the devolution of the republican social institutions left by the the founders into the liberal abstractness that he descried in the first part of the book. He traces the historical narrative through which political life became subordinated to the formal and procedural interventions of the courts, whose presupposition of a rights-based individualism is then confirmed by the results of their judicial intervention. He retraces two centuries of crucial turning points where the values of the participatory social republic were defeated by the orientation to formal individual rights. Unfortunately, Sandel doesn't succeed in weaving the two parts of his book into a political-philosophical synthesis, which may be why his brief practical proposals for contemporary America are distressingly modest and stubbornly optimistic, as I will show. His historical-conceptual approach does, however, suggest the possibility of a comparison with the two centuries of French political evolution. The postrevolutionary French seem to have gone from political to social republican politics whereas the postrevolutionary Americans have passed from social republican politics to formal-procedural politics; the two seem to have inverted and exchanged their revolutionary trajectory. What can explain this inversion?

Sandel unfortunately makes no comparisons to other forms of republican politics. This lacunae is filled, however, by Sylvie Mesure and Alain Renaut's *Alter ego: Les paradoxes de l'identité démocratique*.[13] The authors reconstruct carefully and artfully the debates in Anglo-American political theory since Rawls and his communitarian critics began their quarrels (one of whose first shots was fired by Sandel's earlier *Liberalism and the Limits of Justice* [1982]). Two important assertions follow from their attempt to clarify the logic underlying the claims and counterclaims of the participants: while one cannot abandon the individual rights that are the foundation of any political or economic liberalism, this need not result in the formal procedural individualism denounced by communitarians. Taking the work of Will Kymlicka as a provisional starting point, they reject the social or cultural exclusion inevitably produced by the traditional form of French political republicanism (i.e., the version identified above with American liberalism). They propose to remedy this defect by what they call a "Copernican revolution" that accepts liberalism's basic claim that society exists to further the rights of the individual but then reinterprets this claim to include among those individual rights what they call "cultural rights."[14] The Copernican inversion, however, makes clear that these cultural rights are not to be confused with the "collective rights" that Kymlicka's liberalism tries vainly to defend. The concept of collective rights moves too close to a communitarian position, threatening the liberal foundation of rights. Rather, the Copernican revolution decenters the priority of the individual: the condition of the possibility of individual liberty in modern democratic societies depends necessarily on the freedom of the other. In this way, the defense of cultural rights implies the need to integrate a conception of political activity that protects and ensures the freedom of the other. Such cultural rights differ from the static, juridified conception of individual rights found in liberalism. Individual liberal rights can coexist with cultural

rights as long as these latter are not defined ascriptively by a prepolitical social identity of the type appealed to by communitarianism.
Renaut and Mesure's conception of cultural rights shows them to be
the result of a participation that takes the individual beyond his
atomized, prepolitical existence precisely because that existence presupposes the freedom of alter ego (i.e., the other).

This attempt to synthesize American liberalism and French
republicanism recalls the approach suggested by the subtitle of
Michael Walzer's *Spheres of Justice: A Defense of Pluralism and Equality*.[15] The difference, however, is that Walzer's concern is to develop
a theory of distributional justice, which he explicitly opposes to
"political prudence."[16] Politics for him is only another "sphere"
where the conditions of a just distribution must be analyzed and
eventually criticized. There is presumably a just distribution of
political power, as there is of the goods found in the other spheres,
such as money and commodities, free time, education, and membership. The difficulty is that Walzer does not explain the unity of
the society as a whole, the organization of its values, or the weight
to be placed on each of them. For this reason, it is not clear how his
useful attempt to delimit spheres and to determine criteria of justice
specific to each of them could be applied either to the problem of
exclusion or to the redefinition of political republicanism. Walzer's
theory would not so much solve the problem as dissolve it, denying
its political character by parceling it out to the different spheres.
And despite some shared communitarian affinities, someone like
Sandel or an earlier critic of liberalism such as Benjamin Barber,
would certainly find Walzer's theory too "thin" a description, pre-
ferring something more like a "strong democracy." But such prefer-
ences must be justified politically, rather than by a static theory of
distributive justice of the type proposed by Walzer. That is why Barber's recent work, since his *Macworld vs. Jihad* (1995), has focused on
the manner in which civil society (or "global civil society") can
mediate between market liberalism and nationalist fundamentalism.[17]

Mesure and Renaut's insistence that their Copernican revolution
retains the gains of rights-based liberalism makes their approach
more comprehensive than Sandel's vision of a classical participatory
republicanism that the American founders are said to have left as
their legacy. But Sandel's participatory orientation avoids the

potential slippage that transforms cultural rights into collective rights that are ascriptively based on an essentialist identity politics. Yet participation is itself a slippery concept that is not incompatible with either a populism or a nationalism that would trample the rights of the other. This is why Mesure and Renaut's proposal insists that the modern democratic individual has a cultural identity that can only be affirmed in concert with others: no individual has a culture alone. The others with whom this cultural identity is shared cannot, however, be wholly defined by their culture; in that case, they would not be other but identical to me and therefore incapable of affirming my cultural identity. As the title of Mesure and Renaut's book indicates, this cultural identity includes a relation to the other as both alter and ego: as an ego like me and thus equal to me but also as alter, different from me, and guaranteed an equal right to this difference. Their goal is to preserve a place for both the political determination of society (protecting cultural rights to overcome a type of exclusion) and the influence of that same society on political choices (avoiding the formalism of the liberal government of laws rather than of men).

Mesure and Renaut's reformulation of the republican challenge is more abstract than Sandel's, but it clarifies the (inter)relation of the concepts whose inversions I traced at the outset of this discussion. In doing so, it poses a new question: is the same society both the object of political intervention (to protect cultural rights and ensure inclusion) and the subject that acts on political choices (to produce the new, inclusive cultural liberalism)? In the first case, the society is passive and formally liberal; in the second, it is active and oriented to the primacy of the inclusive community. The formal-liberal social relations in the first instance are found to be unsatisfactory because they exclude the right to cultural identity that is necessary if society is to act on itself or even feel that it is lacking a basic cultural right. Mesure and Renaut have to assume that such a liberal society is only passive because it misunderstands a fundamental aspect of its own liberal rights; thus, when it comes to recognize the complexity of its own identity (by reading their book), it will act on its passive and formal state in order to orient itself toward community. This is a perhaps plausible philosophical reading of the dilemmas of modern liberalism,[18] but it depends on a complete delegitimation of the counterclaims of Sandel and the communitarians, who fall to the side of *égalité* in the model of French republicanism. As with the opposition of *liberté* and *égalité* in the case of the French Revolution, the intervention of a third term clarifies the issue. Instead of *fraternité*, the concept of *solidarité*, developed at the beginning of the century by the republican followers of Durkheim, helps to clarify the underlying presuppositions and difficulties.

*Solidarisme* claimed to be a social-scientific translation of French political republicanism. What Durkheim called the "social fact" of increased interdependence among the actors within complex modern societies transformed externally determined "mechanical" or "segmentary" forms of social interdependence based on resemblance (i.e., a sort of prepolitical or ascriptive identity) into internally motivated "organic" structures based on the increased division of social labor and the dangerous new freedom that it made possible. The organic metaphor did not serve only to unify the perspective of system and actor as a way to overcome the duality confronting French republicanism. It also meant that in the normal course of modern social reproduction, deviations from the norm would necessarily occur as the organism adapted to shifts in its environment. Some deviations could be normal and healthy, like the cold that I treat before it becomes pneumonia or even the increase in juvenile delinquency that may be a symptom of a deeper social malady. The question for politics was to determine when these normal deviations became "anomic" and thereby threatened social reproduction as a whole. The association of "anomie" with the idea of law and legislation (as a deviation from the *nomos*, the posited as opposed to natural-physical law) pointed to the place and problem of how and on what basis politics determines the stability and reproduction of the whole. But the dilemma that Mesure and Renaut clarified returns here. As Christian Ruby shows in *La solidarité*,[19] the society that results from political intervention is not identical to the one whose "anomie" called for that intervention. *Solidarisme* is ultimately just another *grand récit*, a seamless story with no dark spaces, obscurity, or contradiction that humanity tells itself in order to avoid taking responsibility for its own self-creation. Its sociological functionalism presupposes what it sets out to prove, making *solidarisme* a theodicy while leaving no room for the creative politics that it claims to found.[20] That is no doubt one reason why Mesure and Renaut do not return to this French tradition but introduce the concept of cultural rights in order to show that the only way to preserve the liberties ensured by rights-based individualism is by a political intervention that guarantees the equal right to cultural difference. The problem—as suggested by my criticism of Walzer's reduction of politics to simply another sphere—is how to relate a theory of justice to a political theory in the context of a modern democracy where the two senses of republican politics seem constantly to interfere with one another and where contemporary choice and the weight of history are knitted together by invisible threads.

## BEYOND THE POLITICS OF WILL

Despite their asymmetries, contemporary French and American republicanism agree that something must be done. The French tend still to expect the state to do it, but they are faced with the dilemma expressed by Socialist prime minister Lionel Jospin after the decision by Michelin (in fall 1999) to reduce drastically its workforce despite record profits, declaring that it is not the state's job to run the economy. Within days, the leader of his own party, François Holland, reminded Jospin of the old republican truth that state intervention is necessary in order to achieve a society of full employment. This little exchange indicates that the two republican visions remain with us. Granted, the prime minister referred to the economy while the party leader spoke about society. Does the difference make a difference? Does full employment depend on the economy or on political choices? The former option (for political inaction) appeals to the self-moving systemic laws of the market, while the political action sought by the latter is based on a voluntarism that denies to society the capacity to move on its own. Looking for a way out of this polar opposition, the prime minister might have recalled his earlier comment on the Michelin affair: that the trade unions should do the job for which they were created! In that way, apparently, the two positions would be reconciled in a version of *solidarisme*. In fact, the appeal to the unions introduces a new element into the discussion: its attempt to reconcile the republican duality is based on a model of society in which work is the basis of social solidarity. Yet neither form of republicanism—in France or in the United States— was based on this kind of socio-economic foundation: they were both political.[21] But the quest for a third way forces us to clarify what is meant by the political.[22]

Something must be done. But who will do it? That too is a political question, as Sandel constantly reminds his readers. The idea of a self-organizing society whose solidarity is based on work recalls the usual image of egalitarian America at the founding period. But that picture is not quite accurate. The republican historians following Bailyn and Wood, who challenged the liberal consensus, showed that the picture of a harmonious "state of nature" that needs politics only to avoid what Locke called "inconveniences" is misleading. In the second part of *Democracy's Discontent*, Sandel retraces the historical moments at which the republican state and its political institutions could either affirm the need for participation or opt for procedural, antipolitical solutions to the problems facing a maturing economic society. This implies that the task of republican politics is . . . the reproduction of the conditions of possibility of republican politics. This self-referentiality (or reflexivity) in Sandel's concept serves to avoid the reduction of politics to a means to realize an economic end. (The same distinction explains why Walzer maintains a strict separation among the spheres). But this does not explain who will be the agent of republican politics. Sandel's story becomes a *grand récit* that, like *solidarisme*, presupposes what it wants to prove. It is unable to explain how an apparently good republican beginning could devolve into the anomic procedural republic that reproduces an antipolitical liberalism rather than political republicanism. At one point, Sandel seems to intuit the root of the difficulty, when he notes that government action must work for (what it takes to be) the common good. This sets up a potential conflict between the self-reproducing participatory social conditions of republican politics and the governmental decisions that, as representing the common good, claim universal validity. This clash between the universal claims of the political state and the particular vision of its citizens seems to imply that there is a potential contradiction between what is to be done and who is in a position to do it.

Inconsistent or contradictory proposals need not result from sloppy analysis; the political world is not always amenable to philosophical logic. Jospin has tried to made a virtue out of necessity by labeling his inconsistency a "method": he affirms now the autonomy of the market, now the need for the state to intervene, and then the need to rely on some parastate actors to solve political problems. Sandel is more methodical, but he cannot face up to the implications of his intuition: the state must act, despite Sandel's preference for republican participation. But he is no more able than Jospin to recognize a structural feature of democratic political action that explains this inconsistency. In a modern democracy (which protects basic individual rights), there is no single unique and unified will that either can act on society from outside of it or can represent the self-conscious action of society on itself. Politics is neither fully autonomous nor wholly dependent on external conditions that it cannot affect. The imperative that something must be done presupposes the existence of a unified actor who will do the right thing. And it assumes further that there is—out there, somewhere, independent of politics—a right thing to be done. This attitude expresses what I call a politics of will. It presupposes the existence of a circumscribed political agent (and an end sought by politics) that in modern times is called "sovereignty" and is identified in and with the state. Rather than worry whether globalization has made this notion of sovereignty obsolete, it is important to see that sovereignty was never real; it was always only an imaginary representation.[23] But the imaginary is not arbitrary; it is called forth by a reality that is better explained by this representation than by any positive empirical account. In this case, the reality is composed of the sedimented history of the two republican traditions, to which it is necessary to return to understand the challenges to contemporary politics.

The French version of a politics of will appears in the very title of the Declaration of the Rights of Man and of the Citizen. Its silent assumption is that these two types of rights are compatible and mutually reinforce each other. The political logic of the Revolution makes clear the difficulty hidden by this presupposition. In the ancien régime, the King was the particular incorporation of the sovereign and universal will of the nation; after the Revolution, the people as sovereign had to step into his place. But the revolutionary elimination of the politically instituted hierarchies of the ancien régime meant that the individual as such was liberated, although no particular individual, even in association with his fellows, could claim the universality of the sovereign people. The oscillating history of the Revolution can be interpreted as the conflict of these two wills, that of the particular *homme* and that of the universal *citoyen*. Their clash prevented the establishment of a political sphere where individual autonomy is not reduced to a meaningless fiction. By definition, a politics of will can only be total; a divided will—be it that of the individual or that of the nation—would be incapable of willing. The rights of man had to become private if the virtue of the citizen was to triumph, but for the same reason republican virtue could not be transmitted to the private sphere, which remained outside of it. In the language of the revolutionaries, the *pouvoir constituant* can never be finally and completely expressed as *constitué*; no institution can once and for all incarnate the sovereign will of the nation; the past can no more determine the future than fathers can determine the freedom of their sons. As a result, as was seen already in the case of *solidarisme*, the very political conditions that made possible the French Revolution—the claim that the people and not the monarch incarnate the will of the nation—made impossible a successful republican conclusion to the Revolution. That is no doubt another reason why so many historians of the Revolution sought comfort in communism.

Proud of their revolutionary exceptionalism, the French tend to deny the radicality of what they call the American "War of Independence."[24] They are not wrong to do so; the intent of the struggle was surely not revolutionary in the same way as the French Revolution had to be. But its conclusion neither produced a harmonious union nor conserved an old Eden of social equality. In the national confederation, but even more within the individual states, disharmony reigned. Too democratic, too dependent on their constituents, the politicians—who once virtuously stood for office and were now forced to run for it—found themselves facing raging and transitory societal passions. Pennsylvania, the most democratic of the states, whose constitution is often compared to the radical Jacobin constitution of 1793, is the paradigm case. Laws passed during one legislative period were rejected the next; favors were courted; no one could know what tomorrow would bring. And this of course was not good for business, which needed formal legal certainties. But the feeling that anarchy was a threat had another, noneconomic signification, which explains why the needs of capital do not explain the creation of the new, stronger nation-state by means of a new constitution. This constantly changing legislative agenda of which Pennsylvania was only the extreme case proved, over time, that the will of the sovereign people was not one, that it could not be one, and that, it became clear, it should not become one. Politics had other tasks than those of a unifying and unique politics of will.

The practical lessons drawn from the experience of politics were always more important for the Americans than any political theory that purported to predict or explain them. So it was, for example, when the British imposed the Stamp Act in 1765, which the Americans somewhat nervously protested (using the slogan "No taxation without representation") only to find—to their surprise—that they could do business perfectly well without the stamp of state authority affixed to their private contracts. A similar learning process took place in the period between the Peace of Paris in 1781 and the meeting in Philadelphia in 1787 that led to the creation of a new federal constitution, when it became clear that no one, preexisting, and unified subject had to exercise its sovereign will. The Americans came to realize that the power accorded to government was not transferred to it by a contract with a preexisting social subject; they were painfully aware that their divisions excluded such an ideal vision of politics. Rather than proposing the republican political goal of creating such a subject, their experience showed that the place of political power must remain empty if society is to flourish. This was not a denial of the role of politics and political institutions. Power, or republican unity, was needed to hold together social diversity at the same time that such a unitary power was a threat to that diversity. Americans' new institutions incorporated the lessons of their practice. And it was this insight—rather than the political institutions invented by their so-called science or their naturally egalitarian society—that led them to go beyond a politics of will. Of course, the framers of the Constitution did appeal to a science of politics (as is explained, for example, in *Federalist* 51's presentation of the doctrine of checks and balances), and they took into account the nature of their society (as when *Federalist* 10 explains why neither despotism nor factious division threaten the new republic). Political scientists will no doubt continue to debate whether these two arguments are compatible; for our purposes, *Federalist* 63 is more important than either of them because it appeals to the American political experience while drawing conceptual lessons from it.

The choice of a bicameral legislature whose upper chamber bore the aristocratic title of "Senate" needed justification in a political society that had only just overcome the hierarchies of an old monarchy. Historians know that the creation of the Senate was the result of a compromise that permitted the smaller states to accept the Constitution. But *The Federalist* could not say that; it had to argue from principle. Number 63 explained that the Senate, like all the branches of the new government, was republican in the sense that it was representative of the sovereign people. But, the argument continued, this form of political representation differs from that of the ancients, which was based on popular participation; American institutions, on whose "modern" nature *Federalist* 63 insists, develop instead a new form of representation that is based on *"the total exclusion of the people, in their collective capacity."* Two points should be stressed in this surprising formula, which is italicized by its author. The people are excluded, after a comma, "in their collective capacity." They are not excluded—pace theories of liberalism—as individuals; that was also the point implied by *Federalist* 10's insistence that societal factions would nullify one another. More important still is the fact that the Senate, like all the branches of government, is representative—which implies that none of them can claim to incarnate the one, united, and sovereign will of the people. The sovereign people is everywhere and nowhere, which is why the institutional schema of *Federalist* 51 insisted that there be no political "will independent of society itself." In this way, what began as a pragmatic compromise between the small and large states in Philadelphia also can be seen as the theoretical formulation of a historical experience that showed the impossibility of a politics of will claiming to be the representative of, or having as its end the production of, the one sovereign people. That is why American pluralism is not based on the nature of American society (or on a naive optimism about good [Lockean] human nature that needs only to be left alone to bloom under a solitary sun); this pluralism is a political creation—and it depends on continual republican political action if it is not to become the kind of divisive pluralism that produces what the French rightly fear today: social division and political exclusion.

## REPUBLICAN POLITICS: ANOMIE AND JUDGMENT

The historical reconstruction of crossed republican histories that I have traced here can be tied together by the introduction of a final conceptual distinction. The philosophical debate between liberalism and communitarianism, and the historical analysis of the trajectories of the republican project, can be reformulated as the alternative between a democratic republic and a republican democracy. The former concept, which designated the societies of the former socialist bloc, is a generalization of the model of republican politics that stresses the pole of *égalité* and insists on the primacy of society or the community over the rights of the individual. Ideally, a democratic republic would be a direct democracy in which society literally translates itself (or its sovereign will) directly into the political sphere—which thereby loses its autonomy. The democratic republic illustrates the difficulties faced by a politics of will: the political sphere has no autonomy, politics is imaginary; more than an illusion, it is a self-delusion, but it is not without real effect. Because of the paradoxical self-abnegation of society, which wants only to affirm itself in its sheer positivity and cares nothing about what it could become, the really existing democratic-republican state becomes increasingly powerful precisely because its action is performed in the name and place of society. American historical experience, as reflected in *The Federalist*, showed the danger of this return to a premodern refusal of political representation. In the terms proposed here, it becomes a politics of will that denies the difference between society and its political representation while presupposing the existence (or desirability) of a real, or at least potentially real, unified sovereign. The opposite pole, republican democracy, appears to opt for simply the inverse form of a politics of will, defending individual rights by means of what Sandel denounced as the procedural republic. A politics based on the priority of the right over the good appeals to an abstract individual equality before the law, without asking how that law is made, by whom, and for whom. The communitarian critique of that vision cannot be ignored.

A clearer definition of the republican democracy emerges from the attempt to go beyond the repetitive debates between liberals and communitarians. Sandel's account of "democracy's discontent" and Mesure and Renaut's theory of cultural rights avoid the ahistorical ("normative") speculation that has dominated recent Anglo-American political theory. The Copernican revolution operated on rights-based liberalism integrates social considerations by stressing the cultural dimension of individual identity. This means that integration takes place in the political sphere, which is the presupposition for the kind of politics of distributive justice that concerns Walzer. Cultural identity is not sacrificed to the ascriptive prepolitical vision of communitarian identity politics. But how this politics integrates the other as other is not clear in the French philosophers' conclusions. This is where Sandel's intuitive recognition of the limits of his participatory politics that results from the fact that government differs from the republican social community is helpful to clarify one dimension of America's republican experience. Insofar as each branch of government is representative, the decisions of each have the force of law, which means that they are valid for the entire society. They may appear to result from the procedural formality that grates on the nerves of communitarians because it reproduces the opposition of the universal and the particular that American republicanism wants to overcome. Yet insofar as all branches of government are representative, none of them can claim always to represent or incarnate the reality of the sovereign people. Each of them relates to the republican community in the same way as does Sandel's "government." This relationship represents the structure of a republican democracy: its republican political institutions ensure that the society remains democratic, pluralist, constantly in movement, and resistant to fixation. As Tocqueville said of democracy, what counts in this republican democratic politics is not what it is but "what it leads people to do."[25]

The distinction between these two types of republican institutions is made clearer by the way in which each would define and confront the problem of exclusion. For the democratic republic, exclusion would be a form of anomie, whose remedy would be sought through social measures imposed by the state. It would attempt to create work for all in order to ensure that the old form of social integration based on productive labor was maintained. This approach ignores a difficulty, however: it abandons the more modern organic integration based on social division and individual autonomy in favor of a more segmental form of integration based on shared identity. As a result, it would treat manifestations of cultural identity— for example, wearing religious or ethnic signs—as threats to the unity of the society. But that society is based not on true social equality but rather on formal equality (or likeness) of all citizens as identical members of a legal republic. The paradox from which this investigation began returns: the democratic republic achieves the opposite of what it intends, a merely procedural equality. The explanation of this paradox was suggested by the antinomies of a politics of will that emerged from the French Revolution and still haunts its republican vision two centuries later. As was the case for *solidarisme*, the practical difficulty is that no criteria distinguish the anomic as a sign of illness from the healthy reaction of the body politic to a new challenge affecting its environment. After all, the cultural liberalism of Mesure and Renaut might well see the affirmation of religious identity not just as a healthy reaction to the leveling tendencies of modern mass democracy but also as a sign that modern society is sufficiently healthy to welcome and benefit from the affirmation of otherness.

If a republican democracy is to overcome the politics of will, its treatment of the problem of exclusion will have to distinguish the anomic from the healthy. Anomie is not a discrete real property that naturally belongs to a phenomenon; it is a political relation. Its etymology implies that the anomic is that which doesn't fall under the law. Since the law is posited as universal, the anomic is that which exists as a particular. But it is not just any particular phenomenon; rather, it is a particular that resists subsumption under a pregiven law. Such particular phenomena are not naturally present in the world; they too are the result of a political relation. Logically, a particular is only particular insofar as it is one among a plurality of particulars, without whose presence the particularity of any one of them could not be known as such. But the plurality of particulars in turn can only be recognized as particular insofar as it is related to a universal that is explicitly posed as universal. The concrete form of this logical figure is a republican democracy. As with Sandel's problematic relation of government to the republican community, a republican democracy exists insofar as the government posits laws valid for all at the same time that these laws (which are *nomoi*, not *physei*) are never posited as the irrevocable expression of the naturally existing sovereign will of the (in principle) united people. In this way, the particular phenomena that are the concern of politics are related to the universal claims of the state, but they are never defined exclusively or entirely by that political state. What counts as political is constantly open to redefinition. The anomic is not definitively the sign of a fatal illness. What one branch posits as valid for all may be contested insofar as some of the people appeal to another branch—which, after all, is equally representative of the people. In this way, the anomic can be integrated into a healthy polity—indeed, it can contribute to the health of that polity.

This practical consequence of republican democratic politics can be expressed as a political imperative: multiply the number of representative political institutions. This of course cannot be done by a simple act of will. Its presupposition is that a healthy polity is fluid and open to change. There is no reason to retain only the inherited tripartite logical division of (preexisting) powers.[26] Indeed, as opposed to the traditional interpretation (which wants to limit the role of government), the American republican vision of checks and balances stresses less the checks than the balances. Each branch has an active interest in maintaining itself that serves to ensure the dynamic counterbalancing of the others, which cannot pretend to be the sole incarnation of the sovereign popular will. A republican democracy needs to develop this kind of dynamic balance as its society becomes more complex, differentiated, and open to the world around it. Representative institutions can build on experience that appears to be "only" social, or they can draw from experience that transcends the frontier of the sovereign political entity. An example of the former concerns the role of trade unions in a society where the traditional solidarity through work is challenged by the global economy; the catalytic role of the European Union might illustrate the latter if it could get beyond rhetorical criticism of a democratic deficit, which is misleading because it is based implicitly on a democratic republican politics of will.[27] In the first case, the function of trade unions cannot be reduced to the direct representation of the so-called real interests of the working class, as if this class existed as a discrete natural being needing only to be examined by a scientific observer who could diagnose its needs. In the second, it cannot be assumed that new European institutions will spring up according to the so-called law of subsidiarity, which is only the translation into modern garb of the implicit hierarchical realism of the Catholic natural law tradition that restricts the inventiveness of the legislator and denies the autonomy of politics.

The corollary to the imperative to multiply representative institutions is the recognition that the society or polity that is to be represented is itself active, plural, and constantly producing innovation.

But this pluralism cannot be treated as the basis of an identity politics that insists representatives must incarnate a discrete essential identity that exists already on a prepolitical level. This slippage, which rightly worries many French republicans, who denounce American multiculturalism as the example to be avoided, is not a threat as long as the political search for inclusion of the anomic does not treat them as passive victims. This is how the anomic can be distinguished from the healthy. It appears at first that anomie exists because of the exclusion of a group from participation in the universal claims of the republican democracy.[28] But if the excluded seek to restore their relation to the republic, they are subjects whose very activity is a sign of the political distinction of the anomic from the healthy: the degree to which they are capable of making themselves heard at the representative level of one (or several) of the different representative institutions within the republican democracy.[29] The impetus to seek such a hearing is provided by the representative republican institutions that provide dynamic incentives to social action. In this way, by entering public debate, the particular that appeared to be anomic proves itself to be a legitimate actor with a claim to recognition as universal. It is then no longer anomic, outside the law; it has changed the law by changing its relation to the law. Of course, this recognition can be contested, and its validity is no more permanent than any measure passed by one of the branches of the republican democratic government. But because it comes from society even while claiming to belong to a lawful (nomic) universe of discourse, its mediation makes the intervention of the government no longer appear abstractly universal. Government action is not imposed but called for by the demand for representation. This republican democratic treatment of the problem of exclusion overcomes the limits of procedural liberalism.

The theoretical premise of this practical treatment of exclusion goes beyond the politics of will to what I have called a politics of judgment. The anomic structure of exclusion is simply another expression of the paradoxical trajectories of French and American republicanism. That which is anomic is outside the law, and yet it can only be defined in relation to the representative political institutions that posit the law. Although the anomic cannot be subsumed under an existing law, that does not mean that it cannot propose its own lawful claims to be heard and included as representative. This dynamic structure recalls the concept of the reflexive judgment proposed in Kant's *Critique of Judgment* as the means to understand the claim that a particular object gives rise to an experience of beauty that is universally valid for any and all individuals. There is no pregiven law that defines the beautiful in the way that physical laws explain occurrences in the natural world. The beautiful can be said to be anomic in this sense.[30] The same situation holds for the particular phenomena that call for political action; they cannot appeal to existing law even though they must demand recognition as themselves lawful. The process by which this political translation of the anomic takes place is suggested by the representative structure of the republican democracy through which the excluded seek to gain a hearing.[31] While the phenomena that designate exclusion—unemployment, homelessness, ethnic discrimination, and so on—are real and can be analyzed (and criticized) by empirical methods, the process of exclusion is a relation governed by a dynamic that defines the political. At what point any of these phenomena loosely said to denote exclusion becomes a political problem cannot be determined by preexisting laws.[32] That relation and its dynamic are the object of a politics of judgment that avoids the paradoxes of a republican politics of will.

The politics of judgment has in fact been at work throughout the construction of this analysis. It is not expressed as the willful insistence that something must be done (although the author's intent is certainly *not* that nothing be done). Rather, the politics of judgment comes into play when the attempt to do something has failed or would clearly lead to results that are undesirable (such as those promised consciously or not by the institution of a democratic republic). But the politics of will cannot be eliminated by an act of will; indeed, the politics of will always takes precedence over the politics of judgment. As Kant knew full well, everything that can be analyzed in terms of the pregiven, a priori laws of science and morality should fall into their purview. Similarly, if it is possible to intervene to solve a problem that is clearly technical or moral, that intervention is justified and necessary. But intervention in the modern globalized society is often complicated, faced with ambiguity, confronted by paradox, and therefore resistant to technical or moral solutions. That is no reason to abandon politics. These resistances call for a redefinition of the political by means of a confrontation with its limits. Those limits appeared in the intersecting trajectories of the French and American versions of republicanism, each of which found itself driven to affirm what the other claimed as central to its vision. Republican theory can too easily mistake itself for the positive model for a democratic republican politics of will. Only when it adopts the reflective form of a politics of judgment can it develop the institutions of a republican democracy in which the modern phenomena of exclusion can be overcome by Tocqueville's ideal of a politics that "leads people to do" more than just reproduce the formal republican structures. A self-organizing democracy becomes possible only within the limiting framework of a republican democracy that, paradoxically, motivates only by the formal procedures that ensure social indirection.

# CHAPTER II

# Reading U.S. History as Political

## THE PHILOSOPHER, THE HISTORIAN, AND THE POLITICAL MEANING OF REVOLUTION

Historians correctly warn their political scientist friends against the danger of an overly present-centered reading of the stakes of politics. For example, the issues roiling French politics must be understood within the symbolic framework inaugurated by the rupture begun in 1789. Seemingly unrelated actions, whose motivation seems to depend only on simple self-interest, may acquire a meaning that their authors have not consciously intended. Similarly, German politics is framed by the symbolic context created by both Frederick the Great's early legal codification of the Allgemeines Landgesetz and by the failure of the 1848 revolution to institute a liberal parliamentary regime that could unite the different German lands. The case is complicated by the fact that the formal legality of the Rechtsstaat is only potentially compatible with the material quest for national unity. The presence of this past is still felt today in the politics of German unification. The United States too is affected by such a symbolic historical matrix, despite its tendency to forget or deny the political significance of its revolutionary origins. This forgetting and denial are themselves significant. For example, when the Americans fought a civil war that was the most bloody in all previous history, each side claimed to be defending the basic principles on which the original union had been established. Indeed, the motives of each side were themselves mixed. President Lincoln, who fought to preserve the Constitution, began his famous Gettysburg Address with the phrase, "Four score and seven years ago," referring to the date of the Declaration of Independence as the founding moment.[1]

Americans act as if their revolution were preordained, viewing it as the logical outcome of principles of freedom developing naturally on a virgin continent among a people united by shared values. The problem is not so much that this vision ignores the existence of the native peoples, as well as that of the British (and French). The difficulty is that, however they interpret their origins, Americans do not consider their roots as political; their country is assumed to have been born liberal. The Revolution is not seen as a rupture with the past and the inauguration of a new history; it is called a revolution but treated as if its result were nothing but the restoration of existing rights. This should give the political historian pause at the same time that it challenges the philosopher: What was it, really, that American Revolution? Why call it a revolution? After all, one of its strong supporters in England was Edmund Burke, whose later critique of the French Revolution would make him the father of conservatism. The apolitical interpretation implies that the Americans engaged in political actions only in order to preserve their society from perceived threats to its continuity (whereas the French sought to change society itself). Despite its unquestionably radical political character, which produced more emigrés than the French Revolution, the American Revolution resulted in a paradoxical antipolitical orientation that has marked American self-understanding since the Revolution's successful conclusion. This political self-denial needs to be explained and its effects understood. The historian's study of the chain of real events must be supplemented by the philosopher's reflection on the symbolic framework in which the events acquire their sense—in this case, their antipolitical meaning. This symbolic framework is the origin rather than the cause of meaning; it originates a historical process whose significance transcends the immediate intentions and activities of its agents.

The path of the American Revolution can be divided into three distinct moments whose continuity and interdependence were not always evident to the participants. Its immediate context was set in 1763 by the end of the Seven Years' War, known in the colonies as the French and Indian War. The victorious Americans and English faced very different consequences of their victory. For the colonists, the defeat of the French meant they no longer needed the protection of English power; for the mother country, which was now at the head of an empire, it was necessary to govern the new possessions while also repaying the debt accumulated during the war. The English had to take initiatives, whereas the colonists were quite happy to be left alone. It was logical to try to make the colonies pay since the war had brought them benefits and peace would now bring new profits. This political initiative by the English was also suggested by the generally accepted mercantilist economic policy theory. While colonial resistance also had a material basis (many early rebels were smugglers, for example), this alone did not justify the risky process that would lead them to political independence. Their initial resistance spoke first of all the language of the times, denouncing a violation of "the rights of an Englishman." The English of course thought they knew quite well the nature of these rights. But the colonists contested their claims, and in the years of skirmishes that followed, new initiatives by both sides forced a constant redefinition of what these rights truly meant. The body of the Declaration of Independence in 1776 lists these stages and skirmishes in its justification of the need finally to separate, but the list is preceded by a short philosophical statement of those "truths" that the Americans had come to "hold" as "self-evident." To explain how the factual grievances and the truths came to be identified with basic rights that gave meaning to the imperative of independence, a method for reading history philosophically has to be made explicit.

The Revolution could not stop with a definition of rights; it was necessary to win national sovereignty in order to ensure their realization. Once independence was declared, it had to be given political reality.[2] That meant first of all winning the War of Independence, which was realized in 1783. Just as the long debate seeking to define American rights had changed the meaning accorded these rights, so the experience of the war changed the sense of the sovereignty that the Declaration affirmed. At the outset the thirteen colonies were so focused on their differences that many felt it necessary to include the Declaration of Independence in their state constitutions. But the War of Independence was the struggle of an entire nation. It was, however, a nation whose constitution, rightly named the Articles of Confederation, created a weak central government in order to protect the autonomy of the member states. This posed problems even during the struggle for independence, as states' pursuit of their self-interest threatened the collective future. When the war was no longer there to hold them together, centrifugal tendencies became more threatening. The challenge was to find a way to maintain unity while preserving difference. It became necessary to find a positive content for the concept of representation that the colonists had rejected when the English invoked it to justify their rule (on the specious basis of the colonists' "virtual representation" in Parliament). This search had further unintended consequences because of the abstract way in which representation was first understood. The relation of the represented to their representation put the accent on the former, such that the people who were represented could criticize the adequacy of their representation, while the representative had to demonstrate his own necessity. This meant concretely that relations between the sovereign nation and the sovereign states as well as the relation of the rights won in the earlier colonial struggle to the political institutions needed to ensure their realization were defined as representative. The struggle for rights of the first period could not be separated from the battle for sovereignty in the second. But the two had to be made compatible with one another.

It might seem at first that the opposition of the two concepts of representation (of rights and of the sovereign people) found a synthesis in the new constitution proposed in 1787. While this claim can be justified, it suggests that the political revolution culminated in an antipolitical society. The usual explanation of this result is that the Constitution guarantees only the kinds of liberal and capitalist rights that belong to the domain of private life.[3] This interpretation evades historical and philosophical problems by projecting contemporary values onto historical actors, assuming that they sought to realize the values that contemporary society attributes to them. Two silences in the Constitution rule out its interpretation as a successful synthesis whose results are antipolitical, socially conservative, or favorable to liberal capitalism. These silences open the space for the creation of a republican democracy. The two unforeseen institutions that the Constitution did not mention were the competitive coexistence of political parties and the practice of judicial review. These institutions emerged in the wake of what its contemporaries called the Revolution of 1800. Jefferson's electoral victory in that year was itself a historical innovation; it was the first time that political power passed peacefully from one party to another. Its significance was that American society admitted to itself that it was at once one and yet divided. That is why, three years later, when Jefferson appealed to his electoral majority to deny the legitimacy of an appointment by his predecessor, the public could accept the counterclaim by the Supreme Court that the Constitution stands above any temporary majority. The two aspects of representative politics are united as the democratic moment of party competition is joined to the republican constitutional framework. To reconstruct the political logic that led to these innovations, a method for the philosophical reading of history needs to be suggested briefly.

## PRINCIPLES FOR READING

Rather than interpret it in terms of its contemporary results, the reality of the American Revolution needs to be read from the standpoint of the self-theorization that was forced on it as it confronted new challenges that its previous principles could not accommodate. That constantly reformulated theory was doubly reflexive. At a first level, it articulates the three periods through which the Revolution was seen to develop; these can be interpreted respectively as the lived experience (*le vécu*) of the struggle for sovereignty, the conceptualized form (*le conçu*) of that social autonomy, and the political reflection (*le réfléchi*) of these first two moments.[4] The lived experience corresponds to immediate or prepolitical existence; the conceptualized form expresses the social relations instituted by that lived experience; what is reflected as the unity of these two moments makes explicit their political implications. This triadic articulation can be also seen to have been repeated within each of the three revolutionary periods. For example, the lived experience of the first period corresponds to the brute givens of colonization, including two crucial absences, the open frontier and the nonexistence of social orders, and one important presence, the habit of religious freedom.[5] The colonists were forced to conceptualize this immediate experience in the form of social rights only when the English intervened in this society, which had conceived of itself as self-regulating. The political reflection of that autonomous society that guaranteed the rights of its citizens occurred when the question of independence could no longer be avoided. This doubly triadic structure, among and within the periods of revolutionary development, explains why the final moment of political reflection is not a transcendence of the two previous moments, which find their true meaning and disappear into it.[6] Each moment is autonomous; there is no causal necessity at work in the movement from one to another; the meaning of any one of them may not be understood by its contemporaries or may even be misunderstood—as in the case at hand, concerning the political results of the Revolution.

This doubly reflexive structure explains how each period can take up anew and develop the theoretical and practical results of its predecessor. The moment of political reflection in which one period culminates institutes the lived experience of its successor. The way this logical pattern produces institutional results can be illustrated by a simple example. The Declaration of Independence, which is the political reflection of the moments of lived colonial experience and its social self-conception during the first phase of opposition, does not conclude the revolutionary experience. Independence had to be not only declared but given adequate institutional form. The members of the Continental Congress who voted the Declaration immediately left Philadelphia to return home; more important than the national struggle in their eyes was the need to invent constitutions adequate to the particular societies of their home states. The different constitutions created by the thirteen do not contradict the political unity proclaimed by the Declaration of Independence. Their diversity becomes a contradiction that cannot be ignored only when it is necessary to reflect the national sovereignty in a confederal constitution. That constitution had to incarnate unity while conserving diversity in the same way that the social experience of the struggle against England was reflected politically in the Declaration of Independence that unified a diverse country. But the political unification of social diversity was necessarily unstable in both cases because the reflective status of the political had not yet been given institutional form. That is why the Revolution could continue. The unstable political unity of the Confederation represents the lived experience of the third period just as the unrealized promise of the Declaration did for the second.

Before turning to the actual historical articulation of the third period and its relation to the Revolution of 1800, the conceptual paradox from which I began must be underlined: the American Revolution was a political movement and yet it was incapable of understanding itself politically. The moment of political reflection was regularly transformed into the lived experience of a new articulation of the original revolutionary structure. This self-critical relation in which temporary moments of reflective synthesis are immediately set into motion by the very process that led to their achievement needs to be explained. The political reflection of lived experience and its conceptualized social form is inherently unstable. Political reflection proposes categories (and institutions) that make sense of and give meaning to the moments that preceded it, but it thereby changes the sense that the participants had attributed to their own experience. That is why political reflection becomes in turn a new moment of lived experience, setting the cycle again into motion. This triadic structure cannot be imposed from outside on an already completed history; it emerges from within the constantly renewed attempt to make sense of a historical process that, because of this dynamic, can justly bear the title of revolution. The positive sense of experience is constantly challenged as society faces the need to explain its own legitimacy to itself—and to "a candid world," as the Declaration adds. This concern with political legitimacy—rather than personal need or interest—transformed the attempt to maintain what were at first only traditional rights (of the English) into a modern revolution that challenged previous political tradition.

If the results of the Revolution could not be understood politically, the instability of the synthetic moment of political reflection must be one of the grounds of this difficulty. The concept of political reflection expresses the interdependence between society and a political intervention that becomes necessary because modern societies can no longer appeal to external forms of legitimation—be they gods or the traditions of the ancestors; they have to legitimate themselves by means of their own internal resources. They can do this because, despite their difference from traditional societies, modern societies are also symbolically instituted. Societies are not simply defined by factual relations among entities that can be observed from outside by a neutral observer. They are sets of meaningful relations. Politics is therefore not an intervention whose legitimation lies outside society, and neither does the cause of political action lie in factual social conditions. The concept of political reflection expresses the interdependent relation between society and political intervention. Politics is thus the way that society acts on itself in order to maintain or transform its (meaningful) social relations.

Two inverse dangers threaten this political reflection. If society acquires the appearance of autonomy, such that political reflection appears unnecessary or even harmful, the ability of that society to reflect on itself and thus to open itself to change is threatened. Alternatively, if politics becomes separate from society, it may close itself to social experience and, in its illusion of absolute liberty, seek to impose a social perfection that makes future political intervention unnecessary since a perfect society has no more need to reflect critically on itself. The first error produces an antipolitics; the second a utopia that is also antipolitical. In this context, the two extraconstitutional institutions developed in the wake of the Revolution of 1800 acquire their full sense. Parties represent the political action of society on itself; judicial review prevents the separation of the political sphere from society while guaranteeing rights whose meaning is not fixed but allows for an expanded sense of social justice. Read this way, the results of the American Revolution only appear to be antipolitical; in fact, the results were and are quite political—as long as we know how to define the political.

## READING AMERICAN THEORY HISTORICALLY

The conceptual expression of the lived experience of the colonists was a demand for the "rights of an Englishman" that was at once historically rooted and open to interpretation. These rights were articulated with the help of concepts drawn from sources as diverse as natural and contractual law; Greek, Roman, and English history; and of course the Bible. When the English challenged their interpretations of these rights, the colonists fought back by appealing to their opponents' own conceptual-historical language drawn from Whig theory. The Whig vision of history begins from the premise that the existence of society depends on the presence of a power whose essential nature leads it to seek always to expand at the cost of social freedom, which must always be alert to defend itself. This theory could be interpreted in an optimistic or pessimistic vein. The optimistic view portrays freedom reconquering its rights after the Norman Conquest, first with the Magna Carta, then with the Declaration of Rights, and finally in the Glorious Revolution of 1688 that gave birth to a stable society organized around the new, limited, and balanced power called "the King in Parliament." The pessimists, on the other hand, argued that conquering freedom is not inevitably bound to be successful; the excesses that followed the Revolution of 1640 warned against naive optimism. Appealing to a stern Protestant theology, these pessimists became critics of the established order; their identification as Old Whigs suggests that the foundation of their critique of the corruption of the court party was an appeal to the traditional "rights of an Englishman," accompanied by a rejection of the kind of economic progress that was making England a mercantile empire.

When Old Whig theory is turned against the established power, its religious and biblical roots lead it to encounter classical political theory. If power can expand, the reason must be that freedom has been "corrupted"; freedom lacks the virtue necessary for good politics, which must be founded on the distinction between the common good and private interest. Thus the Old Whigs acquired the name "Commonwealthmen." Their version of Whig thought was taken over in the colonial struggle once the Americans were forced to define what they meant by the "rights of an Englishman." From this starting point, the colonial opposition could conceptualize its claims at the social level; resistance was justified by a critique of the "corruption" of the prosperous English society and by an appeal to colonial virtue. Although Burke famously took the colonists to task for their hypersuspicious mentality that "sniffed conspiracy in every tainted breeze," they proved that their own virtue was no abstraction; it was affirmed in the experience of popular resistance, which had the further benefit of instituting de facto forms of social self-government (for example, in the resistance to the Stamp Tax, or the refusal to wear clothing imported from England, and even the tar-and-feathering of

Loyalists). This movement, initiated by the merchant class, quickly passed to the direction of popular committees called Sons of Liberty. The social struggle became political once the question of sovereignty was posed. This passage to the political took time; it was based in the Old Whig political theory, which had to be led to reflect on the contradiction between the primacy of Old Whig freedom affirmed in colonial lived experience and the equally Old Whig affirmation of the social virtue manifested in the Commonwealth. That potential contradiction was hidden for a moment by the Declaration of Independence; it was only conceptualized in the second period, when independence had to be realized, and it was reflected finally in the constitutional politics of the third period.

The first Continental Congress met in 1774. This congress had no legitimate political status. It could only propose resistance to measures perceived as oppressive, then suggest compromises to a Parliament in London that refused to grant it any political status, and finally dissolve itself to return to the states. In this way, the first congress depended on social conditions (including the interests of the English merchants to whom the proposed compromises were in fact addressed). A second congress met in 1775, after the first battles at Lexington and Concord. Its delegates considered themselves still to be ambassadors from their states. But this time, under the pressure of events, the congress proposed a Declaration of the Causes and Necessity of Taking Up Arms. A year later, it opted for political independence after a final conciliatory gesture was unsuccessful; significantly, its action was now addressed to the king, since social pressure had not affected the attitude of Parliament.[7]

On the basis of what right did the delegates found their political claims? The Declaration of Independence incorporates two arguments: its proclamation of certain "self-evident truths" is followed by a historical recapitulation of the misdeeds accumulated since 1763. That second and longer part of the Declaration makes use of Old Whig logic: it shows that England had been "corrupted" and that American freedom must isolate itself from the Old World in order to protect its rights. The implication is that these rights are the basis of political sovereignty. But the Declaration did not propose political institutions to guarantee rights against the kind of anarchy that had followed the Revolution of 1640. This failure points to a latent contradiction in the American use of Old Whig theory. Neither the self-evident truths that found American rights nor the social relations expressing them suffice to explain the status of the political sovereignty declared in 1776.

The independent colonists drew on the concept of the commonwealth to define the republic as the reflected form of their new institutions. This catchall concept hid an issue that had been present during the first period and could now emerge as the lived experience of independence in the second period. The problem had been present earlier, when England had tried to legitimate its mercantile policies by means of the concept of "virtual representation." The thesis was simple. A good power is one that represents the common good of society; the "King in Parliament" is supposed to ensure such representation by the immediate copresence of the three estates of the kingdom in the elaboration of laws. This doctrine implied that the colonies had no more need to be represented than did the English citizens of Manchester. But self-government had defined the sense of their lived experience for the colonists; they had invented theoretical refinements to justify that experience, distinguishing, for example, between internal and external taxes in order to justify resistance to the latter. Now that they were free, their republican concept of representation of the common good had to take a form that was different from the English model. It was clear that the representation of social orders could not be adopted in a country that had none. How were sovereignty, freedom, and self-evident rights to be represented? Was representation even the proper form for the new political institutions? If so, what was to be represented, by whom, and how? The constitutions adopted by the independent states sought a social form adequate to the lived political experience of the first phase as it was now reflected by the question of political representation.

The contrast between the constitution of Pennsylvania and those of the other states illustrates the difficulty that confronted the newly independent Americans. The colonial political leaders of Pennsylvania had discredited themselves by seeking to slow the movement toward independence whereas the leadership in the other colonies had taken the direction of the movement. The authors of Pennsylvania's free constitution belonged to the middling or artisan strata of society. They assumed that the society their constitution would represent was based on a relative equality of conditions; as a result, they produced the most directly democratic of all the new constitutions. A society of equals would be best represented by a unicameral legislature flanked by a weak executive and an elected and revocable judiciary. All laws had to be made public and debated by the public before being adopted, a year later, by the legislature. A council of censors was to be popularly elected every ten years to function like a classical senate, permitting the people to repeal unjust or unpopular laws directly. Other popular democratic measures were added as well to ensure a direct and continuous representation of society in the political domain. This goal contrasted with the attempts made by the other states to filter representation in order to make sure that it had an explicitly (elite) political status.[8] All of them instituted bicameral legislatures, while some made either the executive or the judiciary more independent (with veto power), and none created a council of censors in which the people were given a voice in lawmaking. As opposed to Pennsylvania's, these latter constitutions were based on inherited English Whig theory. For it, representation is a technique for protecting social freedom by means of a system of checks and balances. But the absence of social estates, whose freedom is supposed to be guaranteed by their political power, meant that the division of the voice of the sovereign people into two chambers, much less the executive or judicial veto, could not be justified. As a result, the question of representation was not resolved any better in the more traditional states than it had been in Pennsylvania.

The problem of representation became explicitly political when the creation of a national constitution became necessary. The states had insisted on their own interests and prerogatives even when the presence of a common enemy in war had unified them externally. The Continental Congress had no real power; George Washington appealed vainly to it for military support. The Articles of Confederation, proposed in 1777, were not ratified until 1781, shortly before the decisive battle of Yorktown. A country that had insisted so strongly on rights and legitimacy made war without any legitimate political authority. There was no hope of a mobilizing appeal along the lines of the French Revolution's "la patrie en danger." Once independence had been won, the Confederal Congress remained without power. Its members were representatives of their states; they were bound by an imperative mandate, which meant that they were incapable of creating a national politics. This weakness posed the question of the nature and status of political action, which became the lived experience of the third period. The political impotence of the nation was a sign of the failure of both the politics of direct democracy in Pennsylvania and the traditional representation of political society in the other states. This third period thus reflects at one and the same time the prepolitical lived experience of self-evident rights and their representative conceptualization in the autonomous societies of the states. The Old Whig primacy of freedom and the republican insistence on the realization of the commonwealth had to be unified in a constitution whose structure makes explicit the political sovereignty expressed by the Declaration of Independence that the practice of the Confederal Congress was unable to conceptualize adequately.

The new constitution of 1787 was called "federal" in order to suggest to the states that it would not rob them of their social freedoms. The debate concerning its ratification made explicit at last the theory that lay at the foundation of the entire revolutionary process. The opponents of this constitution who criticized its lack of a declaration of rights posed a serious challenge because they appealed to the inherited theoretical assumption that power is a political threat to freedom. But what did they mean by a political threat? The political cannot be conceptualized as the guarantor of prepolitical freedoms (or self-evident rights) any more than social rights can be reflected as political either immediately or through the filter of representation. Those freedoms and those rights are born with and from the political of which they are the concrete realization. That is why the proponents of the new constitution had no difficulty, after ratification, in accepting the demand for a bill of rights. The difference is that this constitutional-political protection of freedoms and rights now took the form of the first ten amendments to the Constitution rather than appearing as the prepolitical premise on which that fundamental law is based. The Constitution reflects a different lived experience of freedom and another conceptualization of the society in which that freedom is manifested. It is concerned with a freedom and rights that are directed to a future in which they can acquire and adopt new forms fitting new visions of justice. In a society without estates or orders, freedom takes the form of equal and shared political rights; the constitution founds only what Hannah Arendt wisely called "the right to have rights." The primacy of these political rights permits an explanation of how the birth of political parties and the justification of judicial review form the culmination of the political revolution that created a unique republican democracy.

## READING THE FRAMERS' READING

This political reading of the implications of the American revolutionary experience can be developed further by an examination of the reflection on that experience produced by the authors of *The Federalist Papers*. This collection of essays, written to influence public opinion in favor of the ratification of the Constitution, sought to reassure those who saw the new constitution as a threat either to the freedom of the individual or to the social rights of the states. But the analysis has implications that remain actual. For example, Hamilton (in number 9) and Madison (in number 10) sought to reassure those who invoked the classical argument that an "extended republic" will necessarily fail to produce and maintain community and cohesiveness. The danger was the emergence of "factions," which would necessarily proliferate because of the sociological diversity of a large territory. The multiplication of these factions was assumed to create the kind of anarchy that classically is the prelude to tyranny. *The Federalist* accepts the sociological diagnosis but rejects its political implications. Factions are to freedom what air is to fire, insists Madison. Rather than seek to suppress them in the name of a wholly unified society, *The Federalist* sees in them the guarantee of freedom because, in the extended republic, each will provide the counterweight to the others. This argument was taken up again by the pragmatic pluralism of liberal sociology in the 1950s. It could also be used critically by progressive political theorists who denounced the apolitical nature of a society where political parties are condemned to be only coalitions of factional interests reduced to their lowest common denominator. But these sociological interpretations neglect the constitutional structure; they reduce political institutions—as did the state constitutions outside Pennsylvania—to a simple technique invented by political science to manipulate a society incapable of political self-organization.

A second analysis in *The Federalist Papers* has a contemporary relevance that illustrates the difficulty that arises from the treatment of the political structure of society as if it were distinct from the social (or that of individual rights). The authors have to explain and justify the system of institutional checks and balances set up within the Constitution itself. If the three branches of government were organized only to block each other reciprocally so that society can function according to its own immanent rules, government would be stymied, politics would be impotent, and, most important, the citizen would be left to the mercies of the law of the strongest. This is exactly the presupposition of both the contemporary right and its left-wing opponents. The former criticizes the checks and balances as the root of the government's inefficiency, wasteful spending, and inability to act decisively in the national interest; the latter see in this same institutional structure the expression of a social pluralism that prevents the state from intervening on the side of victims or less favored minorities because a weak state ensures the social dominance of wealth or capital. *The Federalist* takes up the problem in number 51. "In framing a government which is to be administered by men over men, the great difficulty lies in this: you must first enable the government to control the governed; and in the next place oblige it to control itself." But this is just what the sociological analysis of the role of factions in an extended republic was supposed to do. The authors now in effect recognize that the previously proposed sociological grounds are not sufficient in this explicitly political context. That is why number 51 adds that "whilst there being thus less danger to a minor from the will of a major party, there must be less pretext, also, to provide for the security of the former, by introducing into the government a will not dependent on the latter, or in other words, a will independent of the society itself." But how can this argument, which says not only that checks and balances protect minority rights but also that the voice of the majority must not be blocked by minority interests, be brought into harmony with the provision for a bicameral legislature in which the Senate has precisely the function of blocking the impetuous will of the majority?

The relation of the sociological to the political analysis is made explicit in the attempt to explain the need for a senate in number 63. The relation of majority and minority presented in number 51 could have been resolved by a sociological argument suggesting that the protection of the minority permitted it to develop its own interests until it could eventually become a majority, as when commercial interests come to replace agricultural ones or those of one geographical section later dominate another section. This is not the same as a political argument, in which a minority convinces a former majority of the justice of its cause. To accomplish that goal, the minority needs to pass through the system of political representation, as number 63 explains that concept. The Senate in classical republican theory represented the aristocratic branch of society—which of course did not exist in America. Number 63 proposes instead that the Senate stands as the federal instance since the senators are named by the states, whose concerns are thus represented at the national level. This practical solution to the worries of particularly the smaller states has theoretical implications that are easily misinterpreted. All three branches of government are republican, hence they all are representative. If the Senate represents the states while the House represents the people, how is the legislative branch as a whole representative? The answer is that *all* the branches represent, each in its own way, the sovereign people. But this representation is not conceptualized as if society imposed an imperative mandate on its political representatives (nor in terms of the older English concept of virtual representation). *The Federalist* distinguishes the classical notion of representation from the modern form proposed in the Constitution: "The true distinction between these [classical governments] and the American governments, lies *in the total exclusion of the people, in their collective capacity.*" This at first glance shocking assertion, italicized by its author, seems to confirm the view of those who saw the new governmental proposals as antidemocratic. But a closer reading in the historical context of the political experience of the Revolution shows it to be in fact the foundation of a political democracy. The sovereign people, in its collective capacity, is everywhere and nowhere: it is everywhere, in the sense that freedom will find always find its champion in one or another of the institutions of government, but it is also nowhere, in the sense that none of these institutions can claim to be the totality of the people, to speak the truth of the people, to represent the unified will of the sovereign nation. It is in this sense that the American federal republic constituted itself as a republican democracy.

This theory of political representation permits an explanation of the process by which the minority whose rights and interests are guaranteed can hope eventually to become a new majority. The justification of a theory of sovereignty that shows it to be everywhere and nowhere is not deduced from a science of politics but results from the political experience of the Revolution. The question of sovereignty had been posed at the outset of the revolutionary process as a theory of virtual representation that explained the relation between the parts of the British Empire and the general interest of the whole. When it was clear that the contradiction between the two would be resolved in favor of the whole and that English Whig theory could not imagine a federal solution, the colonists fell back on the Old Whig stress on the primacy of freedom. The identification of sovereignty with freedom from an encroaching and corrupt governmental power served to justify the demand for independence, but its limits became apparent when the social interests expressed in the state constitutions clashed with the need to assure the unity of the nation. The catalyst for a reformulation of republican sovereignty was Shays' Rebellion, a movement of small farmers who feared the loss of their land because of a lack of hard currency that prevented them from paying their taxes. This was the ultimate recourse of society against the state. It posed again the question of political power and its relation to society.

The Constitutional Convention that met in Philadelphia in 1787 had no explicit mandate to reformulate the institutions of government. Although the delegates did not appeal to the Revolution as the origin of their initiative, the fact that the framers insisted that their new constitution be ratified not by the existing state governments but by popular conventions specially elected for that purpose is a sign that they understood their legitimacy as depending on the political reflections of the revolutionary experience. The existing Confederal Congress had represented the nation in a way that gave the represented (i.e., the society in each of the states) power over their representative. Under its direction, society functioned, but without political foundation; left to itself, there were grounds to fear that it would descend into anarchy before becoming a tyranny.[9] As *Federalist* 51 argued, the framers had to invent a political foundation capable of protecting society against its own worst instincts, including the temptation to abandon hard-won individual rights and political sovereignty in exchange for social order. That foundation had to represent institutionally the sovereignty that was asserted in the

Declaration of Independence but left adrift in the unsteady relation of the Confederal Congress and the states; now its form had to be explicitly political. The sovereign people, everywhere and nowhere, exists in the mode of the symbolic; it is this political representation that permits society to act upon itself. The political medium established by the Constitution is neither the economy nor individual interest, and neither can it be their mediated existence in the form of social relations; democratic politics concerns rights,[10] the first and foundational right being the right to have rights, which in turn can be guaranteed only by a representative republican government.

## The Institutions of Democracy

An interpretation of the political implications of the American Revolution has to be able to account for the two radical innovations that followed immediately in its wake: the emergence of a stable yet fiercely competitive two-party political system and the constitutional jurisprudence by which the Supreme Court successfully introduced and legitimated the idea that the Constitution is the supreme law of the land whose sway dominates over any temporary legislative majority or any activity by the executive branch. The invention and coexistence of these two institutions are the foundation of a unique political structure that I have called a republican democracy in which the primacy of the Constitution ensures the republican dimension of the polity whereas the political parties serve to maintain and invigorate democratic activity. Both these historical innovations not only depend on but contribute to the maintenance and reproduction of individual and political rights. It is tempting to try to explain these two institutional innovations retrospectively, by reference to the socioeconomic interests they serve. But while there is no reason to deny the influence of socioeconomic factors, their function and salience can be understood only on the basis of the symbolically instituted framework that is the political reflection of the Revolution.

The emergence and legitimation of political parties was unexpected and not desired by the framers.[11] The classical vision of republican politics is founded on virtue, defined as the ability of the citizen to abstract from his private interests in order to devote himself to the public quest for the common good. The Puritans of New England as well as the Cavaliers of the South invoked frequently the need to defend their virtue in the struggle against the corruption of English society. They demonstrated the reality of that virtue during the first period of the Revolution, engaging in boycotts of English finery, to which they preferred homespun, and, more generally, risking their all for the sake of their rights and freedom. Once independence had been won and prosperity had returned, they began to doubt themselves. The existence of new fortunes, won sometimes by doubtful or speculative practices, contrasted with the frugal independents who joined Shays' revolt or made democratic Pennsylvania nearly ungovernable. Although all the state constitutions had contained provisions for protecting, even for creating, virtue, the idea has no place in the constitution of 1787, nor does *The Federalist Papers* accord it serious consideration. Some might see in this absence a sign of the modernity of the Constitution. But the absence of explicit reference to virtue does not mean that its presence wasn't felt; after all, even our modern world does not function as if it were a self-reproducing automaton divorced from its environment. The programs of the competing political parties may be only the rationalization of interests, but their appeal is ultimately moral—expressing a claim to just that virtue that finds no representative in the constitutional order.[12] This imperative implicit in the new system suggests the reason for which a two-party politics has prevailed in the United States (as opposed to other countries, where multiple interests have resulted in multiparty systems). The virtue that underlies the claims of the competing parties is of course not real and demonstrable in the content of party platforms. It is symbolic, like the popular sovereignty that is represented in all (but not incarnated entirely in any) of the branches of government.[13]

It remains to explain the birth of the political parties themselves, since another implication of the politics of virtue is that society is (or ought to be) one and that it is unified around the public quest for the common good. The polity that is divided, it was assumed, is condemned. The origin of the parties is often explained by the opposition between the protocapitalist commercial and fiscal policies of Hamilton and the agrarian democracy of which Jefferson dreamed. But this account treats relations that are in fact political as if they were first of all social (and it forgets that the much-praised farmer of

Jefferson was a small agrarian capitalist). There had been competing interests since the founding of the colonies; the crucial question is why those interests became political and potentially divisive. Both parties had supported the new national constitution;[14] they had worked together in Washington's government to give the new nation a content that could endure. The French Revolution brought their divergences to a head by forcing them to reflect on their visions of their own political future. Jefferson's supporters saw the Revolution as the successor and confirmation of their own struggles and hopes; the allies of Adams feared that its anarchical course would contaminate their own American republican experiment. Harking back to older political concepts, Adams's Federalists criticized the naive optimism that prevented the Jeffersonian Republicans from understanding the difficulty of governing a sinful and easily corrupted humanity; their hope was that the stable (mixed) institutions of England would gradually emerge in America. The Jeffersonians denounced these attitudes as aristocratic, monarchist, and antirepublican; they criticized such a vision of the future as showing no confidence in public opinion, which it sought to control rather than obey. Each of the parties of course claimed to represent the national interest that, it was assumed (correctly, because of its symbolic nature), exists above and beyond everyday politics.

A further step is needed to explain how the two parties gained their legitimacy. Treated as a system, this bipartite structure is essentially modern insofar as it accepts the fact of social division rather than decrying it as a defect to be remedied. Social division is not treated as a threat to unity, as in the classical conception of a republic. The acceptance of the idea that although the society is fundamentally divided it is nonetheless still one was possible because the Americans had gone beyond the classical conception of a republic that is founded on the reality of a res publica; they had come to understand that the unity of a modern republic is symbolic, like the sovereignty that it represents. The authors of *The Federalist Papers* had made this point implicitly when they moved beyond the sociological analysis of the implications of division in numbers 9 and 10 to a properly political account of division as represented by institutional checks and balances, analyzed in number 51. It could be argued either that the earlier social analysis suffices to conjure away the fears for freedom or that the political analysis suffices. If both are maintained, this could be taken to imply that the party system is needed in order to mediate among the branches of government, between the citizens and the government, and between the states and the nation, as well as to level regional differences as the parties agglomerate diverse interests. Again, this is not false, but it is still only political science, treating the parties as if they were just the expression of real social divisions. Such an account does not see the need to ask how society could conceive of itself as at once unified and also divided, with the result that opposition must be recognized as legitimate.

The modern nature of the system of political parties is explained by the way in which the Constitution articulates the symbolic nature of political sovereignty. This same symbolic nature of power explains how the Americans came to accept judicial review of legislative (and executive) actions by a nonelected branch of government as necessary to the defense of their republican democracy. Political parties exist in the same modality as do the branches of the federal government; none can claim to incarnate once and for all power, knowledge of the common good, or the definition of the law. Political parties represent interests in the same way that representation is present throughout the constitutional edifice. Their modernity is the same as the "modern" form of representation described in *Federalist* 63, whose arguments have to be added to the sociology of numbers 9 and 10 and the political science of number 51. The foundation of the peaceful transfer of powers during the Revolution of 1800 was the implicit recognition of the symbolic nature of the sovereign power. The same recognition explains the acceptance of judicial review, which reaffirms the basic republican political framework necessary to protect the rights that make democratic party politics possible. Only when a society recognizes that its essence is to be divided can it understand that there will always be a confrontation between different rights that claim to represent the common good and that these rights must be defended (or extended) politically as well as juridically. The birth of the party system and the practice of judicial review are bound together as part of the political reflection of the Revolution.

It remains to ask whether the political matrix that emerges from this philosophical reading of the legacy of the Revolution remains actual.

It would be difficult to try to fit a long historical chain of development into a categorical framework developed to account for the relatively condensed experience of the revolutionary origin of American politics. The categories of lived experience, its conceptualization, and its political reflection have to be treated with appropriate flexibility. Still, a brief effort may prove useful. The lived experience of American history is represented by and in the Constitution, which defines concrete rules of the game but whose symbolic character also opens it to possible changes in these rules (e.g., amendments). Its conceptualized form is the party system, whose changing nature is affected not so much by immediate social conditions as by the sedimentation of the lived political experience in the society. Constitutional rules determine what can affect the party system, but their flexibility makes possible reconstitution of the system and changed relations among its components (as with campaign finance laws). At the same time, the politics of the parties is also affected by the reflection of this system represented by the process of judicial review, which can expand, contract, or simply maintain the field of political experience (as with the relation of free speech to campaign finance). Two twentieth-century examples can illustrate this relation. The New Deal expansion of the state's role had to be imposed on a recalcitrant Court by the relation of party forces that forced it to cede after the 1936 electoral triumph of Roosevelt's party. On the other hand, during the civil rights movement it was judicial decisions that catalyzed political action. These illustrations point to the fact that the reflected form of the political is not the conclusion or the goal of political action. The civil rights cases after all were founded on amendments to the Constitution voted after the Civil War but joining the first ten amendments to make up the Bill of Rights. The fact that this great transformation of American life depended on the first and primary political right, which is the right to have rights, suggests that American politics since the Declaration of Independence has turned around the struggle to define those rights which are "held" to be "self-evident" truths.[15]

A second means of verifying the historical usefulness of this political matrix is offered by the interpretation of the symbolic nature of sovereignty presented in *The Federalist Papers*. If the sovereign people is represented everywhere and nowhere in American political institutions and if the system of checks and balances can perform its dual function only insofar as each institution of government must attempt actually to realize in itself that representation of the sovereign people, there will necessarily be a clash among the branches and institutions of government, since each can check the pretensions of the others only by making assertive counterclaims for itself. As a result, American history can be read as a continually changing series of relations among the actors on the political stage, each of which may at one point become dominant only to overreach by treating its symbolically representative function as if it were real, not just inciting resentment from the other branches of government but discrediting itself among the very real sovereign people it claims to represent. The actors in this political dynamic are not only the three branches of government—although historians are familiar with denunciations of congressional government, or an imperial presidency, or judicial activism, which are said to have dominated at different periods of American history. Other institutions, such as political parties, can become part of the same cycle, as can the federated states and even smaller units of government that have made popular the concept of the NIMBY;[16] even apparently nonpolitical agents, from business to the press, artistic institutions, or churches, become part of this dynamic that not only checks but also serves to balance. If these nonpolitical actors find themselves caught in the political game, this is yet another indication that the legacy of America's revolutionary foundation is a political one, that of a republican democracy, despite the self-conception of her citizens and her political scientists.

CHAPTER 12

# Fundamentalism and the American Exception

Despite the constitutional separation of church and state—which Jefferson considered his proudest achievement—religion has always played a role in American political life. And it has not always been the organized religious congregations that have been leaders in crossing the line that the Constitution tries to establish. Religion touches deeper; it affects the language through which people express themselves as well as their vision of the nation to which they belong. What is new in the last two decades is the rise of a religious right that has become an active voting bloc bringing into politics social and cultural (or moral) issues that had been left previously to the private sphere. To interpret this new role of religion, sociological considerations have to be joined to historical and philosophical analysis. It is not enough to cast anathemas on fundamentalism or to denounce its use by one's political enemies.

The first step in the transformation that has taken place was the democratization of the nominating process by which American political parties select their presidential candidates that followed the disastrous designation of Hubert Humphrey as presidential candidate by the party leadership at the Democratic Party's 1968 Chicago convention. This democratization by means of an extensive system of primary elections had an unintended consequence that has come to haunt the political process. Only the most engaged and partisan voters turn out for the primary elections, with the result that candidates have to slant their platforms toward the extremes of their respective parties in order to win the nomination and then have to seek to return to the center of the political chessboard for the November election. Thus, to take a recent example, the moderate Bob Dole had to move to the right in order to win the support of the Christian Coalition in 1996 and then seek vainly to return to the center in the general election. The same fate met then-president George H. W. Bush in 1992, who had to move to the right after his near-defeat by Pat Buchanan in the New Hampshire primaries and was unable to find his way back to the center for the general election against the moderate Bill Clinton. The current president, George W. Bush, faced a similar problem in his primary campaign, when he had to rally the faithful to hold off John McCain. It remains to be seen how he will redeem his debt to these groups while maintaining the support of the center.

These examples seem to indicate that religious fundamentalists play a crucial role especially in the Republican Party today. An article in *Time* magazine (May 11, 1998) is typical; headlined "The G.O.P. Mantra: Keep Dobson Happy," it explains that James Dobson is "the country's most powerful representative of conservative Christianity." But this manner of exercising influence marks a shift in the way religion had attempted to make its strength felt. A decade earlier, in 1988, the representative of the religious fundamentalists, Pat Robertson, ran personally in the primaries against the then vice-president George Bush. Robertson claimed to represent a moral majority and presented himself as a direct political challenge. Yet in the end Reverend Robertson could exercise only the traditional indirect influence on the process. The reverend's claim to represent a moral majority proved itself not to be a political claim; the role of religion is oriented to social reform. Indeed, if one watches the sermons of the media evangelists, of whom James Dobson is typical, their preaching is more pragmatic than political (and Mr. Dobson is a psychologist, not a pastor). Similarly, the rise and fall of figures like Jim and Tammy Baker or Jimmy Swaggert, testify to a traditional social orientation that is only indirectly political.

But what then explains the political strength of the religious fundamentalists? One can't say that they manipulate their followers, since their followers have to be already receptive to their message. Moreover, their message is not unambiguously found on the political right. True, it is shocking for those who believe in progress through scientific enlightenment to read in the *New York Times* (March 6, 1996) the surprising headline, "70 Years After Scopes Trial, Creation Debate Lives."[1] But it should be recalled that when Scopes, a high school biology teacher who was put on trial in 1921 in Tennessee for violating that state's law forbidding the teaching of evolution, the lawyer for the state was none other than William Jennings Bryan, formerly the populist candidate for president, who later became Woodrow Wilson's secretary of state. Bryan's argument was both that the majority has the right to vote whatever laws it wishes and that religion is central to democratic society. "If it is necessary to give up either religion or education," he argued, "then it is education that should be abandoned."[2] But Bryan's appeal to the democratic rights of the majority was not without echoes. His attempt to bind together democracy and religion was not a solitary venture; he had previously made his mark nationally with a speech denouncing attempts of the wealthy "to crucify us on a cross of gold."

It should not be concluded hastily that religion influences only right-wing politics. After all, the civil rights movement of the 1960s can hardly be imagined without the spiritual support its participants derived from their faith and the material aid brought by the churches (black and white, united). Martin Luther King Jr. was a pastor, and his organization was called unambiguously the Southern Christian Leadership Conference. But it is also worth noting that, at the time of his assassination, the Reverend King was in Memphis to support striking municipal garbage workers. This was no anomaly. Going further back in American history, Richard Hofstadter points out that one of the most anti-Darwinian counties in the United States—Kanawha County in West Virginia—voted more heavily for the socialist Eugene Debs in the 1924 elections than did any other county in the United States.[3]

This radical populist role of religion should not be surprising any more than is the aid religion offers to conservatives. Did not the liberating word of Luther inspire the militants of Thomas Münzer as well as the rigorous but republican institutions of Calvin's Geneva, while Luther himself took the side of the princes? Thus it is not surprising that one of the most forceful advocates of creationism in contemporary America is Pat Buchanan, who, in his primary races against George H. W. Bush and Bob Dole, made himself the advocate of the working class against the untamed forces of the global economy and free trade. In short, religious fundamentalism is not a univocal political phenomenon. Its relation to the political needs to be examined more carefully.

## The Roots of Fundamentalism

In order to see the novelty of the recent rise of religious fundamentalism and its relation to politics, it is useful to recall the role of religion in the work of the two founding fathers of contemporary sociology, Durkheim and Weber. Although Durkheim was a friend of the socialist leader Jean Jaurès and a practicing republican, his Cartesian spirit did not in the least incline him to deny the contribution of religion to modernity. What he called the "elementary form" of religion was based on a distinction between the sacred and the profane that arises when the individual is forced to recognize that society is greater than the individual and that social experience takes men and women beyond their everyday secular experience. But Durkheim understood that this definition did not yet suffice to distinguish religion from magic, which gives rise to a similar experience that transcends the everyday private world of the individual. For this reason, he added a further criterion: since religion is not something individual but is by its very nature social, a church is also necessary to give stability to the religious experience.

At the time of the Dreyfus affair, in 1898, Durkheim developed the political implications of this conception of religion in a modern society. He argued that what he called the modern form of religion is based on the critical spirit of science and the sanctity of the individual; its church is the republic, which must protect the members of its congregation, whose faith in turn provides the ties that bind them together in a community. Those who refused to consider the possible innocence of Captain Dreyfus claimed that to question the verdict condemning him (and, even more, to question the army that prosecuted him) was a threat to the national community. But their refusal to accept the criticisms of the evidence, Durkheim replied, was itself a violation of the critical and individualist "religion" that was the very foundation of the republic. The nature of this modern individual who has become "sacred," as well as that of his republican church, will concern me later. For now, it suffices to note that Durkheim's modern religion leaves no room for fundamentalism; its individualism is critical and self-critical.

Another aspect of the religion of the modern individual is suggested by Max Weber's study *The Protestant Ethic and the Spirit of Capitalism*. Weber analyzes the genesis of an "inner-worldly asceticism" that is the basis of an activism whose results led to the modernization of traditional society. The strict doctrines of predestination and of the incomprehensibility of the grace to be accorded by a *deus absconditus* throw the individual into doubt, anguish, and the fear of eternal condemnation. Three implications follow, although the first, which will be important for the discussion later on, is only implicit in Weber. First, no sign permits an individual to know his destiny or that of other men. Hence Calvinism will have to give way to a religion of toleration that will give birth to a plurality of beliefs and practices. Second, a methodical behavior is meanwhile adopted, reflecting the will to act in this world in a way that is at least compatible with the Divine Will. This is a way to confront the doubt and fear, but it will become also the basis on which the "spirit" of capitalism—and only then its material reality—will arise. But, finally, the success of capitalism tends to destabilize the religious premises on which it was built. This explains Weber's pessimism and his famous thesis concerning the "disenchantment of the world." The inner-worldly asceticism that sought to avoid self-doubt by doing the will of God can begin to think of its success as a visible sign that it has been chosen. With that changed perspective, the taut springs of willful action begin to loosen, and the spirit cedes to the desires of the flesh.

Today, we seem to be living in the world that Weber foresaw and feared. An all-powerful economic logic has replaced the methodical rationalization of the Calvinist's inner-worldly asceticism. Speaking of the United States, which he knew well, Weber described "a race for wealth stripped of its religious or ethical sense," which has become a "sport." And he concludes his study with the famous lines:

"No one knows . . . whether at the end of this fantastic development there will arise new prophets or whether there will be a great renaissance of old ideas and ideals—or, instead of either of these possibilities, we will not undergo a mechanical petrification embellished by forms of behavior that take themselves too seriously."[4] Does this mean that rationalization—which for Weber coexists with the modern (and capitalist) world—ends with its own self-negation? In that case, the present return of the religious would be a kind of "charismatic" new beginning of a history that has become petrified. Such a reading would be compatible with Weber's broad use of the term "charisma," whose roots in the religious sphere spread across the different domains that he analyzes methodically in his masterwork *Economy and Society*. But it is also tempting to follow Weber's later distinction, in "Politics as a Vocation," between a politics of conviction—whose essence is in a sense religious—and a more secular and sober politics of responsibility. It is too soon to draw either conclusion—although we should recall that Weber himself predicted a "war of the gods" that no rationality can bring to an end.

## Roots of the Present Religious Renewal

Leaving aside Durkheim for the moment, this brief recall of Weber's sociology of religion points to one of the most innovative aspects of Protestant fundamentalism in the United States. The American theologian Harvey Cox has recently published a new study, *Fire from Heaven*, that, together with his 1968 study *The Secular City*, which predicted an accelerating secularization of modern society, shows that the ambiguity seen by Weber is still present today.[5] The new book's subtitle explains its purpose: *The Rise of Pentecostal Spirituality and the Reshaping of Religion in the Twenty-First Century*. Cox introduces the reader to the Pentecostal world by returning to two roughly contemporaneous events at the end of the nineteenth century whose social and religious signification reflect what I have presented as the Weberian dilemma. The first is the Great Colombian Exposition held at the World's Fair in Chicago in 1893, at which the organizers convened what they proudly called a "parliament" of all the world's religions for a discussion of the foundations of their doctrines. The local newspapers could count on the religious literacy of their readers, so they could not help invoking the metaphor of a "pentecost" uniting the world's "languages" and overcoming the division that resulted from the human hubris that dared construct the Tower of Babel. The results of the meeting, however, were simply formal, academic, and in a way even secular. The second event, in 1906, took place in an informal church that began meeting in a former stable in Los Angeles. Here, on Azusa Street, the Spirit seemed truly to descend on a gathering of simple and poor people of both sexes and all races. Whereas the meeting in Chicago was a formality, the spirit of the stable on Azusa Street gave birth to the Pentecostal movement, the religious denomination whose worldwide growth has surpassed that of all others. This is the theme of Harvey Cox's exploration.

Without referring to Weber's distinction between a church and a sect, Cox distinguishes fundamentalism, which fixes the identity of the faithful by recourse to a churchlike, formal, and written set of rules, from a Pentecostal experience that, like a sect, opens to a future based on hope. The two are radically opposed. Fundamentalists insist on doctrinal purity and attack modern forms of religion such as Bible criticism, scientific Darwinism, or the idea of a church that intervenes in society. Pentecostals refuse the coldness and formality of a church that has become foreign to the individual experience of religion while it consecrates established social divisions. The opposition, in a word, is between the letter and the spirit.[6] It follows from this opposition that fundamentalism lends itself to a conservative reading of social-political life; in the United States, it yearns for the simple and believing country that formerly united homogeneous families in a moral and hard-working society.[7] On the other hand, Pentecostals, moved by millenarian expectations, look to a future that will realize their hopes and whose arrival seems to be confirmed by the intensity of their own intimate religious experiences. This, concludes Harvey Cox, explains the attractiveness of Pentecostalism to the 87 percent of the world's population who live beneath the threshold of poverty.[8] It explains Cox's own enthusiasm as well, but also his inability to understand the American manifestations of this new type of religious engagement.

Harvey Cox's post-Weberian analysis points to the ambiguous role of religion in American political life. For him, fundamentalism would stand on the right, Pentecostalism on the left. But the United States proves to be the exception to the rule. That is why, after having offered his readers a guided tour across the Pentecostal world and shown how this new form of religion seems to incarnate a populist-democratic revolt capable of displacing the Marx-inspired theology of liberation, Harvey Cox returns to the United States. Here, he has to admit that his Pentecostals can also be drawn to reactionary politics, to megalomaniacal or paranoiac forms of nationalism, and to anti-Semitism and that they can be manipulated by false prophets using the mass media to create the illusion of a personal religious experience. The groups of whom he is speaking are called the "Third Wave." They have invented a new theologico-political cosmology—what Cox, always academically à la mode, calls a new narrative—according to which, without being aware of it, Jimmy Carter, the Masonic Lodges, the Council on Foreign Relations, and even George H. W. Bush—in alliance with Wall Street and the Communist International—are doing the work of Lucifer while working for the creation of a "new world order."[9] At the end of his chapter, Cox admits to "truly regretting" what he has just described; he says he is "disillusioned," "furious," "exasperated," and "truly fearful" for the future if such people are to come to power in the United States. His only consolation, he says, is that if such theories—or theologies—exist, they have taken root only in white society.[10] In an America that has long been divided by the racial question, that is a rather meager consolation. I will return to it in a moment.

## Why Politics?

What needs to be explained first is the move from religion to politics. Doesn't the Christian tradition (the doctrine of the two swords) teach us to render unto Caesar that which belongs to him? After all, these are people for whom the Bible is the Word of God and, in the case of the Pentecostals, people who stress the personal experience of the Spirit. Indeed, until quite recently, studies of electoral participation by all types of so-called fundamentalists showed that they tend to abstain from politics. What counts for them is the sacred, preparation for the other world, obedience to the divine commandments, as well as the humility of God's creatures in this world. It might be thought that this new concern with politics can be explained as a sort of secularization of the Protestant spirit, analogous to Weber's "inner-worldly asceticism." These are people who are living a return of the religious while endowing their secular participation with a sacredness that confirms their faith despite (or sometimes because of) the frustrations that result from this secular and political practice. It is this latter fact that invalidates the analogy to Weber's Calvinists who created the "spirit of capitalism" before its reality could be materialized. The new Christian concern with politics seeks to influence an already existing field of modern life.

It is tempting to fall back on an economic explanation that connects the new political-religious spirit to the long economic crisis that began in the wake of the oil shock of 1973 (and only seemed to end in the second Clinton term). A sociological account of the effects of this slow and now more rapid economic decline on the "little people" who are its victims could explain their resentment of an unleashed speculative spirit that has enriched the already wealthy. This would explain the narrative that sees a new world order emerging. The Luciferian hypothesis in turn would be confirmed by the fact that this new order emerged during the eight-year presidency of one of their own: Ronald Reagan. Recalling Harvey Cox's "consolation" that this paranoid style seems to affect only whites, one could explain this as the result of lower-class whites thinking that the government is increasing their taxes in order to subsidize welfare for the needy whom they think—wrongly—are mainly minorities.[11] As a result of this spectacle of the enrichment of some and the impoverishment of others, what are called social and moral questions come to play a political role. People say to themselves that at least in this domain they can make themselves heard, impose their values, feel that they are participating in society. And moreover the values they are defending are not relativist; they are the Word of God, immutable across the ages, beyond the tides of fortune.

Such a socioeconomic analysis is certainly not false, but it is incomplete. It doesn't explain the phenomenon that concerns me here: the appearance of a politics based on religion. In effect, just as Weber's "spirit of capitalism" cannot be explained in terms of an already existing capitalist economy, so too the politicization of religion cannot be explained by a political analysis of socioeconomic reality. That doesn't mean that the analysis is irrelevant; it can serve to explain the use to which the politicization of religion is *then* put by private interests (who benefit disproportionately from the tax reductions won in the name of small government). But the problem with such reductionist demystification is that its results often reinforce the feeling of powerlessness and the resentment of victimization by forces too great to be mastered. Indeed, it is this feeling of powerlessness (that earlier analysts such as Hofstadter or Bell attributed to "status anxiety" in a modernizing world) that explains in part the cosmological political paranoia of the "Third Wave." Its theologico-cosmological narrative confirms their conspiratorial theses and simultaneously reinforces their beliefs. This latter aspect seems specific to the new movements.

If one must render unto Caesar, one must also render unto God. Harvey Cox points to an important theological transformation: the shift from a premillinarian theology to a postmillinarian eschatology. The premillinarian theology assumed that the Last Days will be announced by a series of catastrophes that are the sign that Christ will return. In other words, Christ will return before the establishment of His Kingdom. This implies that there is no reason to be concerned with the secular and profane world. On the other hand, the postmillinarian theology assumes that justice will slowly but surely be established on earth and that this will prepare the return of Christ, who will sanctify a purified world. This version of the religious narrative encourages political engagement. The fact that this postmillinarian doctrine contradicts the Pentecostal appeal to immediate spiritual experience is ignored by Harvey Cox.[12] Rather, he points to the biblical passage (Genesis 1:27) on which the postmillinarian thesis is based: "Be fruitful and multiply, and fill the earth and subdue it; and have dominion over the fish of the sea and over the birds of the air and *over every living thing that moves upon the face of the earth*" (the italics are Cox's, not the Bible's, from which the passage is paraphrased). From the postmillinarian standpoint, this passage commands man to impose his law here and now upon everything in this world—institutions as well as those who refuse to obey the Divine Law. Only then will the earth be ready for the return of Christ; only then will the millennium come.

The practical consequences of this theological reorientation are illustrated by the decision of Pat Robertson—a candidate for the Republican nomination for the presidency in 1988—to shift his field of activity and rebaptize the university he had founded Regents University. A regent is someone who governs on earth during the absence of the true sovereign. The change of names is hardly benign.[13] In his book, published in 1991 under the title *The New World Order*, Pat Robertson explains that "there will never be world peace until God's house and God's people are given their rightful place of leadership at the top of the world. How can there be peace when drunkards, communists, atheists, New Age worshipers of Satan, secular humanists, oppressive dictators, greedy moneychangers, revolutionary assassins, adulterers, and homosexuals are on top?"[14] This is the creed of the new fundamentalists, the truly politically correct of today.[15] How can we understand what moves them? Why have they appeared specifically in the United States? To answer, one has to return to American history.

## A VERY AMERICAN KIND OF POLITICS

The fact that Pat Robertson founded a university in order to propagate his faith is not an innovation in American history. Yale University was created by religious dissidents who believed that Harvard had given too much freedom to Unitarian temptations. A few years later, Princeton University owed its birth to a similar pattern; it was followed by Oberlin College in Ohio and a series of others throughout the nineteenth century. This phenomenon points to one of the crucial elements of American religion (and of religion in America): its relation to a sometimes confusing democratic vision that is at once individualist and populist. Fleeing European social hierarchies, Americans rejected the idea of an established church whose existence would consecrate a social elite.[16] American denominational religions were (in Weber's terminology) sects that maintain themselves by the unity of a belief whose questioning they forbid. One does not enter such sects ascriptively, by birth or inheritance, but from a free individual choice based on a private spiritual experience. But the very individual freedom that makes for the strength of the sect also explains its weakness. In order to maintain itself, it has to rationalize and fix its liturgy because individual faith cannot endure without the help of rules and institutions accepted by all. But sooner or later this makes the sect into what Weber called a church. At that point, the formal liturgy that replaces the experienced spiritual unity of the believers comes to be felt as a fetter; it not only justifies the domination of the letter over the spirit but also consecrates a social hierarchy that is resented by those in the lower ranks. Those at the bottom (in terms of their status in the group, not simply in economic terms) will tend to leave,[17] to create or join a new sect that in its turn will eventually feel the necessity of dictating rules, rigidifying doctrines, closing itself off from the living sources of spirituality. Each sect appeals to the Bible, but each reserves to itself the right to interpret it according to its own lights—or its enthusiasms. And yet each of the new sects will consider biblical criticism and free debate a threat to the faithful.

This fissiparity of religion in the United States has often been pointed out. It is said to explain the exacerbated individualism of Americans as well as their populist antistatism. The particular form of American egalitarianism also has its source in the stress on the equal validity of the (spiritual) experience of each person. Hence the American goal is not the creation of a real equality but simply to ensure that each has the possibility of entering life's race without pregiven handicaps. The populist anti-elitism that results from this attitude has a darker side. It is based on the idea that each person can—and therefore must—perfect himself . . . and that a person who is unable to do so is responsible for his own failure. More than that: such a person is condemnable for not having made sufficient efforts. Worse: he is the incarnation of immorality and does not merit either our compassion or our aid. After all, just as he was free to choose his denomination, so he is free to choose the path to salvation. (The only state aid that is considered legitimate on this account is that given to education, since each individual needs a minimal education in order to combat sinfulness, and everyone can benefit equally from such education—an attitude that helps explain the mediocrity of the precollege student in America, because the goal of education is not to create an elite but to educate the average citizen.)[18]

These characteristics explain why conservative politics in the United States is quite compatible with laissez-faire, deregulationist economics. After all, the rich man is considered to be a person just like me; I could find myself in his place tomorrow, for we do not live in a hierarchical or caste society. Hence there is no reason to sacrifice my interests for the common good, since the common good is nothing but private and individual liberty and equality interpreted in this very American manner. But this still does not explain why people with such attitudes should take part in politics. To understand that further step, it is necessary to look at what makes up the exceptional characteristics of American political life itself. While many criticize Americans for their denial of the importance of politics in their own national development, a closer look suggests that in its own way America is a deeply political nation. This is true not only of its founding moments or its republican-democratic institutions but also of the social experience that forms what Durkheim called an "elementary form" of religious life.

The ambivalent individualist and populist way of living religion in America affects what can be called the religion of America (which should not be equated with a banalized popular version of Rousseau's notion of a "civil religion"). America was the first Protestant nation;[19] it conceived of itself as a new Israel: Europe represented Egypt, America was the Promised Land. Or, varying the narrative themes, America is the return to paradise lost; its religion must thus be a sort of natural faith that cannot lose itself in the arcana of theory; all that is needed is a new trinity: to believe, to give witness to one's good faith, to share an experience of common wealth (rather than of the artificial and formal government of the commonwealth). It follows that the independent United States itself would become a sort of sect whose sacred text is the Declaration of Independence.[20] But that sect is peopled by individualist and egalitarian Protestants. Hence it is experienced as the incarnation of Good, which cannot be compromised in negotiations with Evil. That is why, as Seymour Martin Lipset notes, it is only in the United States that one can accuse a fellow citizen of disloyalty by calling him "un-American" (in France, for example, "un-French" is not used to suggest deviation from the nationally accepted norm).[21] In effect, "America" represents a unique and unified experiential system of belief, a sort of living and lived ideology that one chooses in the same way that one chooses to enter into a denominational sect. One believes or one doesn't: it is as simple as that. But, since belief expresses an act of will, it follows that evil is also the result of an act of will—of ill will—that has to be fought. And since the will is expressed by a yes or a no, everything that falls into the domain of the uncertain, the ambiguous, or the undetermined has to be rejected. The paradoxical result is that the populist and democratic individualism that was expressed in the plurality of sects becomes messianic: rigid, exclusive, and doctrinaire.

It is not necessary to stress the consequences of such a moralizing religiosity for domestic or foreign politics; the crusading spirit that from time to time takes hold of American political life is well known. The second volume of *Democracy in America* is rich with illustrations of this type of behavior, most strikingly in the chapter entitled "What Makes Democratic Armies Weaker than Others at the Beginning of a Campaign but more Formidable in Prolonged Warfare" (part 3, chap. 24). The resulting inability to take account of the role of accident, of human weakness, and of uncertainty is accompanied by a self-critical spirit founded on the perfectionist individualism that takes responsibility for the choice of salvation. That is why, significantly, as Seymour Martin Lipset notes, there have been movements opposing every American war.[22]

More important for my purposes is the fact that this American form of religiosity can explain the reason that the Pentecostal movement acquires a reactionary and paranoiac form in the United States. The American religion of the nation helps us understand the transition from pre- to postmillinarianism. If it is not to be arbitrary (or based on empirical accident), the explanation of such a transformation has to show the existence of a mediation that is present at the starting point as well as at the conclusion. In the present case, the individualist and egalitarian spirit manifested in the denominational life of American sects seeks to institutionalize virtue; in so doing, it makes religious passion into a kind of political morality. But the voluntarism that is inherent in the religiosity of the Protestant sects and the perfectionism that it presupposes and accentuates give a utopian orientation to that political morality by forbidding any compromise with Evil. In this way, the Pentecostal spirit in America is made into a new variant of fundamentalism. This explains the appearance here of all the reactionary elements that Harvey Cox thought the future-oriented Pentecostal spirit could avoid. The question now is whether this transformation is a new expression of what is called American Exceptionalism.

## On the Proper Political Use of Religion

I stressed at the outset of these remarks that religion can lead to a right or a left orientation in politics and later demonstrated how the premillinarian orientation can also lead to an abstention from politics. What political role can religion play today? What role ought it to play?

Newt Gingrich was convinced that his liberal enemies had made politics into a secular religion; his riposte was the 1994 Contract with America that promised a return to the true values of the nation. On the other side of the spectrum, others tried to counter capitalism's harshness with what Hillary Clinton espoused for a moment as a "politics of meaning," while her husband preached the need for a "new Covenant"—in the biblical sense of the term—that he also called an "Alliance with the American Family." American politics was reduced to the agitation of two sects incapable of communicating with one another. Politics was reduced to a choice of values.[23] Such a politics of will is total and totalizing, as I have suggested. The politicization of religion leaves no room for politics—that is the weakness of fundamentalism, of whatever color and in whatever sphere of social life. It results only in sermons about political correctness that leave no place for the properly political work of seeking means to permit modern individuals to live together autonomously, without becoming dependent on the will of the others.

But fundamentalism exists, and in the United States its politicization is not accidental. Perhaps the question should be reformulated: what can this religious form of politics teach us about the political? This is where the double definition of the "elementary form" of religious life according to Durkheim becomes a useful analytic tool. With Durkheim, one must first distinguish the sacred from the profane and then go beyond individual belief to take into account the social and socialized practice of religion. As distinct from the sacred, the profane is not determined once and for all by the religious or moral will. This means that is is necessary to create conditions that make possible political deliberation about daily life. That is why I suggested earlier that—although he did not make the point explicitly—Weber's Calvinists would necessarily have to become tolerant. If the sacred cannot be identified with the profane, the plurality of choices in society must be tolerated at the same time that the validity of each of them can be put into question because none of them can incarnate fully the sacred. No one can therefore claim to know the truth; each has only his own lived experience. But that experience has no meaning unless it is recognized, communicated, and shared; purely individual experience would lead to the paranoia that American historians like Hofstadter worried about. That is why Durkheim stressed the role of the church and recognized the political republic as its equivalent for modern individuals. But American social and cultural experience was not formed by the existence of a church; its basic experience was the denominational existence of the sects. Should one conclude that Durkheim's vision of modern individualism makes sense only within the secular church that is the French type of (democratic) republic?

The role of religion in the civil rights movement in the United States suggests another possibility. The intervention of religion there adopted a unique political form. It was a nonviolent movement characterized by individual acts of witness. These acts expressed the strength of a belief and the choice of its individual expression in order to communicate with others and to bear witness before them. That expression took a specific form insofar as it sought to use instances of particular oppression to communicate a message that was universal and formulated in terms of rights. As opposed to the all-or-nothing politics of will engaged in by the fundamentalism of the religion of America, this was an attempt to communicate a form of judgment. Such a communication will be received only if it awakens in others a common experience; in other words, if it makes evident that each and all belong to a common church and share a common belief—a common sense. This communicational structure explains why Martin Luther King Jr. did not only appeal to an individual or moral faith but also to the Constitution of the church that America incarnates. This constitutional foundation of the civil rights movement made clear that it (as well as its allies who were seeking to create a new left) recognized that individual moral faith cannot survive without the public rights that ensure the difference of the sacred and the profane and guarantee in this way a principle of tolerance that contemporary fundamentalists who have turned to politics can neither accept nor even understand.

We can conclude that there are two fundamentalisms in the United States and that they represent a double threat: they can give rise to a political religion or to a religious politics, both of which are dangerous. A politsical religion would excommunicate some of its citizens from the shared political life; it would become rigid, dogmatic, and sclerotic. A religious politics would leave no room for individual choice; it would pursue the individual into the depths of private life, which would dry up as a result, becoming conformist, incapable of communicating.

This double threat cannot be avoided by a politics that ignores religion. Religion, like fundamentalism or Pentecostalism, is not just an illusion that can be debunked by materialist or positivist criticism. Weber has to be joined to Durkheim. Religion, as Durkheim knew, is only an expression of social life. Anyone who wants to better social life has to understand it in *all* its expressions. This means that fundamentalism in America can be avoided only if its two manifestations are avoided. This is what Weber understood: that, at least in the United States, an ethics of responsibility must be joined to an ethics of conviction in order to avoid the fundamentalist dead end that seems to be the only manner to avoid the "war of the gods" that he predicted and feared. Responsibility to the church that is America is only possible insofar as one accepts the egalitarian and antinomian individualism whose result is a critical spirit founded on the idea that no secular institution can pretend to possess once and for all the truth (and that the sacred, because it is sacred, remains beyond our ken). In the last resort, what was for Weber an antinomy—the ethics of conviction versus the ethics of responsibility—becomes, in the American (and Durkheimian) perspective, a complementarity. The vicious circle becomes a virtuous dialogue that enriches all participants and that cannot, in principle, ever be completed.[24]

# PART 3

# Back to Marx?

# CHAPTER 13

# *Philosophy by Other Means?*

## POLITICAL PHILOSOPHY AFTER *1989*

Paradoxically, after 1989 Marx's political philosophy can be read not only as philosophical but also as political. If Marxism is not (in Sartre's famous phrase) the "unsurpassable horizon of our times," it remains a rigorous confrontation with modernity and a challenging attempt to understand its novelty.[1] This is because, despite Marx's intention to provide a theory *of* the revolutionary proletariat that would serve *for* the praxis of that world historical agent, he was and continued to be a philosopher; despite his critique(s) of idealism, Marx remained under its spell. Indeed, this philosophical intention ultimately vitiates his attempt to surpass philosophy by its own means in the practice of political revolution. For just this reason, a reevaluation of the critical potential of Marx's philosophical theory permits new insight into the way a certain form of economic liberalism has apparently triumphed by denying its own political nature. Its conception of the individual and of individual rights as natural givens rather than as dependent on the prior choice of a political framework is put into question when Marx's mature economic theory is read with the eyes of philosophy. If this critical philosophical reformulation is not undertaken, Marx's economic theory unintentionally puts into question the philosophical premises that guided his analysis. It is these premises that must be reclaimed in order to make sense of Marx's potential contribution to our political self-understanding in the new contemporary world.

Marx's work in its entirety can be seen as an attempt to do philosophy by other means. Although his early passage from philosophy to political economy attempted to go beyond Hegel's claim that Reason or Spirit governs the course of world history, Hegel's historical vision remained the foundation of Marx's theory. The dialectical process in which a subject seeks to actualize itself in the world, finds that its manifestation or appearance is inadequate to its own essence, returns to itself enriched from the experience, and sets out once again to find a superior and more adequate actualization recurs in each of the phases of Marx's development. The 1843 discovery of the proletariat as the key to overcoming Hegel's "merely political" theory became the foundation of a new phase, in which Marx tried to articulate a materialist philosophy for which Revolution became the subject of political history. As in Hegel, two sides had always to be examined. A phenomenology that describes the appearing forms of the historical subject had to be joined to a logic that explains the necessity that underlies these appearances. But the account remained only theoretical; it was not adequate to the practical role that concerned Marx. The 1848 revolution in France forced Marx to confront the limitations of his theory. The successive political appearances that progressed from the political revolution of February, to the (failed) social revolution of June, and then to the stalemated republican compromise seemed to confirm Marx's phenomenological expectations. But the economic logic that he assumed would lead to the next stage proved inadequate. Confronted with Bonaparte's seizure of political power in 1851, Marx was forced to recognize another logic, that of politics. The coexistence of two logics forced Marx to expand his categorical framework.

The first volume of *Capital* completes this phase of Marx's work. Now the philosophical subject whose actualization he attempts to explain is the history of the relations of production, a history that is supposed to culminate in the overcoming of the contradictions inherent in capitalist social relations. But the history of economic relations cannot be reduced to a quasi-mechanistic determinism; such a reduction ignores the social-normative dimension that the logic of Marx's systematic ambitions requires. It became clear that an adequate account of the development of the relations of production must supplement the phenomenological and logical moments of the analysis with an account of the genesis and normativity of the phenomena that are being analyzed. In this way, the critical dimension that was crucial to Marx's refashioned Hegelianism could be made explicit.

The categories of genesis and normativity were implicit in Marx's early attempts to go beyond the Hegelian paradigm. Genesis designates the practice by which something comes into being; normativity refers to the framework within which that phenomenon enters into legitimate and meaningful relations with other entities. An adequate account must not only describe the phenomena and their dialectical necessity; it must also show how that necessity is concretized historically in the form of normative demands that in turn impel the genesis of new phenomena. Although Marx at times abandons this categorical framework for a misguided economic reductionism, the categories of genesis and normativity can be used to explain the central role of the commodity form in all three volumes of *Capital*. From this perspective, *Capital*'s subtitle—*A Critique of Political Economy*—acquires a contemporary relevance. Marx's trajectory is now seen to pass from a critique of the separation of the political sphere from its socioeconomic basis through a reductionist attempt to show that political economy represents "the anatomy of civil society"—and can be considered to be the realization of philosophy by other means—on to a critique of the separation of the economic from the political and a recognition of the proper place of the political. This trajectory permits a reinterpretation of the utopian revolutionary vision of the unpublished manuscript of 1857 known as the *Grundrisse*, showing that in fact the other means for realizing philosophy cannot replace the philosophical project. Realized philosophy, from this perspective, is neither the idealist nor the materialist end of philosophy. Realized philosophy is the renewal of the philosophical project.

Political philosophy after 1989 finds itself in an absurd situation where a humanity that has been defined historically by its quest to overcome the dictates of blind nature accepts as natural—and even glorifies—a set of artificial and harmful restrictions on its freedom, denying the creative autonomy of its own reason and subordinating this autonomy to the dictates of market forces whose political premises it denies. Yet if there is one theme that Marx emphasized from the beginning to the end of his work, it is that humanity's own production—be it the mechanisms of the market, the unintended consequences of social relations, or the science that has apparently subordinated nature to its own "one-dimensionality"—has become alien and must be reclaimed. This quest remains his most valuable and enduring legacy. By recapturing the sense of Marx's original project, as philosophy and as political philosophy, it becomes possible to reclaim that legacy and to rejoin the historical project that took form when the Greeks discovered that philosophy and democratic politics implied one another mutually. Rereading Marx, taking seriously his philosophical attempt to do philosophy by other means, has contemporary political implications—although not those claimed by pre-1989 Marxists of whatever stripe.

## From Philosophy to Political Economy

### Realizing Hegel

Marx's trajectory began, and concluded, in a conflictual embrace with Hegel. He joined with the Young Hegelians in opposing the heirs of the master. What distinguished the orthodoxy of Hegel's heirs was their insistence that philosophy constitutes a system, a totality whose content is expressed in Hegel's famous aphorism in the preface to his *Philosophy of Right*: "What is rational is actual and what is actual is rational." Although he opposed the orthodox heirs, Marx's earliest work did not abandon the systematic philosophical project. A note to his doctoral dissertation indicates his intent. Marx's editors have accurately titled this note "The Becoming-Philosophical of the World as the Becoming-Worldly of Philosophy."[2] The qualification "as" must be emphasized. The aphorism claims that the world will only become philosophical—that is, rational and autonomous—insofar as philosophy abandons its speculative separation from that world. This means that when the world has become philosophical, philosophy will thereby have become worldly—that is, material and sensible. The aphorism is not simply philosophical; it is programmatic. Its systematic demand is that the world and philosophy, genesis and normativity, phenomenology and logic must be integrated in order for each to realize truly what it is yet only potentially.

Marx knew that it was not sufficient simply to will that the world become a better place. The foreword by the orthodox editor of Hegel's *Philosophy of Right*, Eduard Gans, had denounced that sort of voluntarism as reflecting a merely subjective and thus arbitrary freedom; only systems can refute other systems, insisted Gans. Marx therefore had to make a double claim: (a) it had to be shown that philosophy as philosophy could realize itself only by becoming worldly—in other words, philosophy could be systematically complete and normatively necessary only through this turn to the world; and (b) it had to be demonstrated that the world as world could be stripped of its accidental immediacy to become rationally actual by becoming adequate to the demands of philosophy. Only this doubly systematic imperative explains how material conditions dependent on external forces could generate social relations that can achieve normative autonomy. Expressed in the metaphorical language of the will that Marx sometimes adopted, the world had to strive to become philosophical just as philosophy had to strive to become worldly. In contemporary philosophical terms, the genetic material moment has to be shown to be also normative, in the sense of being driven by a normative goal, and the normative philosophical moment must on its side be genetic, in the sense of impelling this transformation. This aphorism of the young Marx forms the kernel of his entire philosophical and political development.

The systematic imperative that Marx underlines from the outset of his work does not prevent him from claiming simultaneously that his theory is critical. When it became clear that political conditions in Prussia would prevent him from pursuing a university career, Marx became the editor of a newspaper in Cologne. The empirical reporting that he undertook in this capacity, as well as the need to defend his journal from reactionary enemies, led to his dissatisfaction with the rash and rhetorical criticism of many of his Young Hegelian friends. Criticism that stood outside of its object and applied to that object standards that could not be justified had to be rejected. In its place, Marx developed what can be called a theory of immanent critique. If philosophy that had not become worldly was inadequate as philosophy and if a world that had not become philosophical was an unrealized world, then immanent critique of either was justified. It could expect to find within its object not only elements of inadequacy but also signs pointing toward the true realization of the object of immanent critique. Marx developed this notion of immanent critique first in his critique of Hegel and then in his critique of the social world of capitalism. Nearly all his writings were titled or subtitled *A Critique of . . . ,*" although it is only with *Capital*, as will be seen, that the concept was fully elaborated.

### Criticizing Hegel

Marx's unpublished "Critique of Hegel's Philosophy of the State" (1843) has two primary aims. The first is simply to refute claims for the autonomy of the political sphere; only then could philosophy's turn to the social world be justified by the systematic imperatives of philosophy as Marx understood it. This was a first step toward the quest for other means. The second aim of the critique is presented in a published essay of the same year, the "Introduction to a Critique of Hegel's *Philosophy of Right*." It argues that insofar as Hegel's theory is an accurate (phenomenological) reflection of actual German society, its refutation provides a "critique of the *oeuvres incomplètes*" of that society, which appears as a not-yet-rational world to which philosophy is shown to relate uncritically.[3] This essay is also important because Marx develops in it a critical concept of democracy, whose apparent replacement by the self-realization of the revolutionary proletariat marks a turning point.

Marx criticizes Hegel's political idealism for its inversion of subject and object. "Hegel makes all the attributes of the contemporary European constitutional monarch into absolute self-determination of the *will*. He does not say that the will of the monarch is the final decision, but rather the final decision of the will is—the monarch" (OM, 6). Marx inverts this claim: the monarch "is sovereign in so far as he represents the unity of the people, and so he himself is just a representative. . . . The sovereignty of the people does not derive from him, but he from it." In this way, Marx can affirm that democracy is "the generic constitution. Monarchy is a species, and indeed a poor one. Democracy is content and form. Monarchy *should* be form only, but it adulterates the content." As content and form, democracy is thus philosophy made worldly and the world made philosophical; it "is the resolved mystery of all constitutions" (OM, 7). But the nature of this democracy is not explained further. To develop his analysis, Marx has to explain how democracy can be at once social and a human product and at the same time political and universally valid. Until Marx answers this question, his critique of the speculative nature of Hegel's state is only normative; the genetic component has yet to be developed explicitly.

The modern individual described by Hegel's theory is caught between the public and the private spheres, between bureaucratic and social imperatives. There is an opposition between the formal universality of the state and the material existence of the individual. To realize his nature as a citizen, man must abandon his civil life, withdrawing into his abstract universality bereft of any particular content. But Marx notes that this is historically a progress; it entails the abandonment of that medieval "democracy of unfreedom" (OM, 11) where the individual was defined and thus limited by membership in a particular estate. This transformation was brought about under the absolute monarchy that was accompanied by the triumph of the formal imperatives of the bureaucracy. What social differences remained were eliminated by the French Revolution, whose political egalitarianism considered distinctions among men to be purely social, private, and without consequences for political life. But this political life was now separated from civil society. When civil society has become private, social distinctions no longer have any universal or normative legitimation; they appear changeable, accidental, external to the individual, and in principle arbitrary. But this, interjects Marx in a note to himself, should be developed in the discussion of Hegel's treatment of civil society (OM, 18). From the point of view of the state, and of democracy, what counts is that this emancipation from determination by his estate liberates the individual from the medieval "*animal history* of human kind, its zoology" (OM, 19–20). But this liberation turns into its opposite; "it separates man's *objective* being from him, as something merely *external* and material. It does not consider the content of man to be his true actuality." But, interjects Marx again, this too is left for the discussion of civil society (OM, 19–20).

Why did Marx never write his critique of Hegel's theory of civil

246 | *Back to Marx?*

society? The answer is suggested by his discussion of universal suffrage. Hegel's objection to democracy was that it has no form; the participation of all as equals is possible only through abstraction from all particular content (as Marx had noted). Instead, Hegel used the concrete material determinations of the estates (and guildlike corporations) to ensure that all interests found representation. Marx rejects this anachronism. He wants to draw out the positive potential as well as the critical implications of universal suffrage. Voting is said to permit civil society to raise itself to political existence, which is its true, because universal form of existence. Granted, this form of existence is an abstraction, but Marx sees it also as the dialectical transcendence of that abstraction. In voting, civil society makes its political existence into its true existence, and by this very gesture it makes its civil existence inessential. Separated from one another, the interdependent opposites dissolve. "The *reform of voting* is therefore, within the *abstract political state*, the demand for the *dissolution* of this state, but also the *dissolution of civil society*" (OM, 27). This dialectical conclusion fulfills the two systematic goals: (1) it explains the genesis of the democracy whose normative legitimation Marx had provided at the outset of his analysis; and (2) it is a critique of the separation of the political sphere from actual society that also—importantly—criticizes the basis of that separation as being due to the self-alienated structure of civil society itself. The conditions for philosophy's becoming worldly thus coincide with those needed for the world to become philosophical. The overcoming of the abstract political state shows the self-alienated character of its foundation in civil society. It remains to find within civil society the key to overcoming this self-alienation.

Democracy as the "resolved mystery of all constitutions" would soon be replaced in the third of the *Economic and Philosophical Manuscripts of 1844* by communism as the solution to "the riddle of history" (OM, 431). What is the relation of these two proposals? If Hegel's idealism was criticized for its uncritical accommodation to the existing world, for mystifying the real by embedding it in a normative system of rationality of which material reality is but an appearance, Marx will have to be able to show how the analysis of the existent world contains within itself a contradiction that explains why the world strives toward philosophy as philosophy opens itself to the world. Hegel's theory of the modern state presented the culmination and completion of his political theory; Marx's critique of Hegel's idealist program leads him to invert the path, moving from the political toward its material foundation. But what is at issue for Marx is more than simply a materialist inversion; Marx's claim is also historical. Hegel's theory explained the existent political structures of his time and showed why they were necessary to the progress of modernity over the Middle Ages, but the inconsistencies in the theory when confronted with modern social conditions implied that history had not yet ended and that the imperatives of philosophy remained to be realized. That is why Marx noted that the critique of the political illusion opens the path toward the analysis of civil society.

### Revolution Replaces Spirit as the Foundation of the New Philosophy

Marx's essay "On the Jewish Question" develops the implications of his critique of the "merely political" emancipation that seeks to replace monarchy with a republic. The French Revolution that overthrew monarchy and constituted a truly political state, independent of civil society, simultaneously dissolved civil society into a formless mass of egoistic individuals relating to one another only externally. Marx criticizes this merely "political revolution [that] dissolves civil life into its constituent elements without revolutionizing these elements and without subjecting them to critique" (OM, 49). As a result, the rights of man serve to consecrate a kind of egoistic individualism. The rights to equality, liberty, security, and property are victories over monarchy that serve only to protect man as an "isolated monad, withdrawn into himself"; they guarantee the right to exist as a "*limited* individual limited unto himself," whose freedom becomes "the right of private property" (OM, 45), whose "security" is guaranteed by a legal "equality" whose empty formality means that it protects the actual inequality existing in civil society (OM, 46). But Marx does not stop with this reductionist critique of the rights of man (which a conservative such as Edmund Burke or Marx's beloved Balzac could share).

Despite its call for material social change, "On the Jewish Question" also argues that the separation of political from social life makes true democracy impossible. To overcome this division, alienated, egoistic individual life must be replaced by "generic being [*Gattungswesen*]." This critique is normative; it is a prefiguration of the analysis of alienation developed in the *Economic and Philosophical Manuscripts of 1844*. But philosophy as normative must acquire a genetic efficacy, a power to impel transformative action and thus to become worldly. This has not yet been demonstrated. At best, Marx could claim to have shown how philosophy becomes worldly and why the world must (ideally) become philosophical; he has not shown that philosophy becomes worldly *as* the world becomes philosophical. This may explain why he does not return to his favorable evaluation of the advance of the modern state over the "democracy of unfreedom" to consider the positive aspects of the new rights won by the revolution. Instead, the "Introduction to a Critique of Hegel's *Philosophy of Right*" continues the systematic philosophical critique.

Marx now "declares war" on a world that is "beneath all critique" but remains "an object of the critique just as the criminal who is under the level of humanity is still the object of the executioner" (OM, 59). The occasion for this "war" is offered first by Marx's normative critique of religious alienation, which he insists must be supplemented by a an "irreligious critique" whose ground is "man makes religion" (OM, 57). Critique is now "no longer an end in itself but simply a *means*" (OM, 59). Its task is suggested by the fact that religion appears also as an active protest against unhappiness (rather than passive alienation); this offers the genetic moment of the critique. As a means, critique "must make these petrified relations dance by singing before them their own tune" (OM, 60). This metaphorical definition of the critical task was given a more philosophical form in a letter that Marx published in the same issue of the *Deutsch-Französische Jahrbücher*. He insisted there that "reason has always existed, but not always in a rational form."[4] The genetic moment cannot be separated from its normative complement. This is clear in Marx's critique of two "parties" seeking German liberation, each of which accomplishes the opposite of what it intends. The "practical party" demands the negation of philosophy and concentrates on the world. But "you cannot transcend [*Aufheben*] philosophy without actualizing it" (OM, 62). The "theoretical party" is equally one-sided, concentrating on the "critical struggle [against idealist philosophy]" without seeing that it too exists in the world. It "thought that it could actualize philosophy without transcending it" (OM, 63). Once again, the world's becoming philosophical must be understood as philosophy's becoming worldly.

This context explains the philosophical role of the proletariat and Marx's turn to political economy as the way to do philosophy by other means. Normatively, "the critique of religion ends with the doctrine that man is the highest being for man, hence, with the categorical imperative to overthrow all conditions in which man is a degraded, enslaved, contemptible being" (OM, 64). Genetically, "theory is only actualized in a people inasmuch as it is the actualization of their needs. . . . It is not sufficient that thought should seek its actualization; actuality must itself strive toward thought" (OM, 65). The two moments come together when "a particular class by virtue of its particular situation undertakes the universal emancipation of society" (OM, 67). This demands "the formation of a class with radical chains," which is

> a class of civil society which is not a class of civil society, . . . of a sphere which has a universal character because of its universal suffering and which claims no particular right because no particular wrong but unqualified wrong is done to it; a sphere which can invoke no historical title but only a human one; a sphere, finally . . . which, in a word, is the complete loss of humanity and can only redeem itself through the complete redemption of humanity. This dissolution of society as a particular Estate is the proletariat. (OM, 69; italics omitted)

The key to this first formulation of the demand for proletarian revolution lies in the notion of the formation of such a class. The proletariat is not simply the poor; Marx insists that the poverty of the proletariat is *"artificially produced"* (ibid.). The demonstration of the logical necessity of this artificial production falls to political economy.

After introducing the proletariat as the genetic material basis for revolution, Marx turns to the normative moment necessary to his systematic account. "As philosophy finds in the proletariat its material weapons, so the proletariat finds in philosophy its spiritual weapons, and once the lightning of thought has struck in this naive soil of the people the Germans will complete their emancipation and become men" (ibid.). Philosophy thus becomes worldly as the world becomes philosophical in the revolutionary proletariat. Marx repeats his systematic intention at the conclusion of his argument: "The head of this emancipation is philosophy, its heart is the proletariat. Philosophy cannot be actualized without the transcendence [*Aufhebung*] of the proletariat; the proletariat cannot be transcended without the actualization of philosophy" (OM, 70). The philosophical problem, however, lies in Marx's metaphorical appeal to the "lightning of thought" that is supposed to awaken the proletariat to its normative vocation. The metaphor refers to what came later to be called class consciousness. But the concept itself remains to be analyzed—normatively in the second of the *Economic and Philosophical Manuscripts* and genetically in the third manuscript. The philosophical result of this systematic claim for the proletarian revolution is that *Revolution replaces Spirit as the subject whose process of appearance and self-recognition was the foundation of the Hegelian system.*

The first of the *Economic and Philosophical Manuscripts* uses long excerpts from classical political economy to demonstrate the "artificial" formation of the proletariat by capitalist economic relations. Political economy presupposes the existence of private property rather than analyzing critically its systematic political presupposition, which Marx shows to lie in alienated labor. By showing the mutual dependence of private property and alienated labor, Marx illustrates the genesis of internally contradictory socioeconomic property relations that are at war with their own premise and thus open to the weapon of immanent critique. But this first manuscript breaks off before drawing conclusions, and the second manuscript seems to recognize that the task could not be accomplished by genetic means alone. The presence of a contradiction does not mean necessarily that it will be overcome. Hence the second manuscript returns to the opposition between alienated labor and private property, proposing this time a normative account. At first, alienated labor and private property relate to one another positively; the action of each (unintentionally) improves the lot of the other. Capital's search for greater profit increases social productivity, while labor's demand for better wages and conditions forces capital to invent more efficient machines. This positive relation appears to make the interests of labor and capital identical, yet each also comes to recognize that its relation to the other implies that it is dependent on something external to itself. Each then seeks to affirm its independence: capital becomes exploitative, while labor engages in industrial struggle. But both strategies are fatally flawed since the two *are* related to one another, and the pretense of acting independently works against what each nonetheless is. This leads to a third stage in which the two poles collide—and where Marx's manuscript breaks off, unable to say more about the forms this normative collision would generate. Nonetheless, this normative account conceptualizes the "lightning of thought" that would make the proletariat conscious of its revolutionary destiny. It complements the genetic account of the first manuscript.

The third and longest of the *Economic and Philosophical Manuscripts* confirms Marx's critical Hegelianism while proposing a method for doing philosophy by other means and justifying his passage from philosophy to political economy. Marx argues that the "greatness" of Hegel's *Phenomenology* is due to his having understood the positive, creative function of labor.[5] Since Hegel was concerned only with mental labor, however, he neglected the negative side (the alienation) that prevents actual labor from realizing itself. Adopting other means, Marx proposes to actualize what Hegel did only in thought. "The entire so-called world history," explains Marx, "is only the creation of man through human labor and the development of nature for man" (607). New needs are generated in this process; these needs become normative demands that spur the process forward. The panorama that emerges shows "how the history of industry . . . is the open book of man's essential powers" (602). The relation that in the first manuscript entailed a contradiction between alienated labor and private property now becomes positive as society and its laboring subjects are enriched. The opposition between subject and object is overcome; "natural science will lose its abstract tendency and become the basis of human science" (604). This claim clarifies the result expected from the clash of opposites in the incomplete second manuscript. The concept of communism is presented as "the completed naturalism = humanism and . . . the completed humanism = naturalism," and as such it is "the true resolution of the conflict between man and nature and between man and man" (593 f.). With this communist solution in view, Marx has accomplished the passage from philosophy to political economy; philosophy has become worldly in the new and modern science that reflects on a world that is, apparently, becoming philosophical.

The third manuscript provides a cautionary note before turning to the new means for doing philosophy. Communism "is the riddle of history solved, and it knows itself to be this solution" (593 f.). The phrase is familiar; Marx had used a similar formulation when describing democracy as "the resolved mystery of all constitutions" (OM, 7). Its reappearance here suggests that the first phase of Marx's political theory has been completed; he has rid himself of the illusory separation of the political that vitiated Hegel's theory of the modern state. The price to be paid for this philosophical liberation remains to be calculated. If the political economy with which Marx replaces philosophy becomes as separated from the other social relations as did the state in Hegel's idealistic view of political life, the price may be too high. Marx will have to show that his new theoretical standpoint also makes room for the revolutionary democratic practice of politics that Marx had pointed to as "the modern French" alternative to Hegel's merely political transformation (OM, 10). This need to make room for politics became clear with the outbreak of the 1848 revolutions.

## FROM POLITICAL ECONOMY TO POLITICS

### Economics and the Proletariat

An illustration of the normative dimension of Marx's critique of the "artificial formation" of the proletariat is offered by the claim in the *Economic and Philosophical Manuscripts* that the opposition between the propertied and those who lack it is an "indifferent opposition," whereas the clash of capital and labor presents a truly dialectical opposition that must develop toward a resolution (590). This distinction is justified by a dialectical sketch of the development of political economy as it becomes scientific. The mercantilists saw the objective essence of wealth in precious metals, becoming thereby "fetishists, Catholics." Adam Smith—whom Marx's new friend, Engels, had called "the Luther of political economy" (584–586)—made labor the essence of wealth, thus introducing a subjective dimension. This labor was abstract, free of all individual qualities, and able thereby to overthrow earlier modes of production because it was universal whereas they were only particular and thus limited. This development culminated with Ricardo, whom his contemporaries accused of amoralism because he described the conflict of capital and labor openly. Those who followed Ricardo were forced to become apologists, for it was now evident that the reality behind the abstract labor that constitutes wealth was a negative principle, abstract man considered only in the formal universality of his being: the worker. The resulting figure recalls the form of alienation encountered in religious consciousness; like religion, political economy claims a normative universality that it cannot justify. Marx's critique has to find the immanent foundation of this alienation so that his own normative dialectical critique can be realized.

The theory of alienated labor provides the necessary genetic complement. Marx analyzes four aspects the worker's condition as wage laborer. (1) He is alienated from his product; the more he produces, the less he receives; the product in which he has invested his labor belongs to another, is external to him, and exercises a power over him—much as in religious alienation, where the more power is attributed to god, the less remains for man. (2) The worker is alienated from nature, which is necessary for the objectification of his labor and for the reproduction of his own life. Nature has become a commodity; the worker depends on the capitalist to provide him with it—to work on and to consume. As a result, he is alienated in the act of production; his labor does not belong to him, does not permit his self-affirmation, and constrains his freedom. (3) Since labor has become merely a means, the worker is reduced to the status of an animal; the consciousness and freedom specific to man are denied him. In this way, the worker is alienated from his own generic being; he is not free to become that which he is. It follows (4) that the worker is alienated from other men. Since the relation of man to man (and, in the third manuscript, to woman [592]) is the index of man's relation to himself, to his world, and to his own activity, alienation reaches here its pinnacle. The conclusion of this analysis of alienated labor is radical. Reformers like Proudhon who want to raise wages produce only better-paid slaves. Wage labor must be abolished. But this is a return to the normative standpoint; it explains that the system of capitalist relations must be overthrown, but it does not show how this can take place.[6] Indeed, Marx's manuscript breaks off inconclusively shortly after this argument is proposed. Before returning to the different path offered by the third manuscript, it is necessary to look at the economic grounds of Marx's political hope.

Marx's economic theory before 1848 did not build on the unity of philosophy and the proletariat, of normativity and genesis. The lectures presented in Brussels in 1847 that were revised and published as "Wage Labor and Capital" only in April 1849 began by claiming that the defeats of 1848 show that however remote a renewal of class struggle may appear, the political forms have been tried and found wanting; it is time to return to the economic logic that grounds bourgeois rule and proletarian slavery. Not all labor is wage labor, insists Marx, and neither is capital a suprahistorical reality. "A Negro is a Negro. He only becomes a slave in certain relations. A cotton-spinning jenny is a machine for spinning cotton. It becomes capital only in certain relations."[7] Not every sum of commodities or exchange-values is capital. Capital comes to exist "by maintaining and multiplying itself as an independent social power, that is, as the power of a portion of society, by means of its exchange for direct, living labor. The existence of a class which possesses nothing but its capacity to labor is a necessary prerequisite of capital" (DM, 257). This means that capital is the domination of accumulated past labor over the direct living labor of the proletariat.

Marx does not draw from his argument any conclusions that bear on political strategy or suggest a course of political action. His concern is to establish the inevitable necessity that the proletariat overcome the socioeconomic relations in which it is confined. The expected economic crisis will be the catalyst for renewed class struggle, which Marx wants to show is vain if it is not total. In his 1847 polemic against Proudhon, *The Poverty of Philosophy*, Marx draws the normative political implication of his economic analysis. The proletariat is "already a class over against capital, but not yet for itself." The genetic complement is said to be found "in the struggle" (DM, 214). But this voluntarism needs to be justified in its turn; the genetic political moment cannot stand alone. A reconciliation of the economic and the political perspectives was suggested in the third of the *Economic and Philosophical Manuscripts*: the insertion of the logic of the economy into a conception of history. The success of this approach depends on one difference between the analysis of alienated labor in 1844 and the simple economic logic of "Wage Labor and Capital." The alienation analyzed in 1844 and at the outset of "Wage Labor" presents a phenomenology of the abstract individual worker, whereas the economic logic of wage labor concerns labor as a social relation that—like the proletariat—is an "artificial formation."

### Economics and History

The communism described in the *Economic and Philosophical Manuscripts* is said to be the product of "the entire movement of history" (594, see also 618) The communist revolution—like Hegel's Spirit—plays a teleological role; it is the realization of the revolutionary subject. Marx's phenomenological premise is that "the entire so-called world history is only the creation of man through human labor and the development of nature for man" (607). Whereas "Wage Labor" stressed the negative effects of increasing industrialization, in 1844 Marx had insisted that "the history of industry and the present objective nature of industry is the open book of man's essential powers, the sensibly present human psychology" (602). He criticized what he calls "crude" or "leveling" communism, whose notion of equality is based on a "return to the unnatural simplicity of the poor and wantless man who has not gone beyond private property nor even yet achieved it" (592). Communist man's relation to his objects will no longer be a "one-sided" possession for use as a means to an externally given end; as in his earlier vision of democracy, Marx describes communist possession as "all-sided" (598). In this way, the "development [*Bildung*] of the five senses is the work of all past world history." As a result, "the fully constituted society produces man in this entire wealth of his being, produces the rich, deep, and entirely sensitive man as its enduring actuality" (602). The antagonism of wage labor and capitalism must be overcome not by returning to a simpler past but by using critically the achievements of the present to transcend the conflict.

The objective development of capitalism prepares this communist future in which "in the place of the political and economic wealth and poverty steps the rich man and the rich human need" (605). But while capitalism prepares this possible future, it does not produce it merely by the logic of its own breakdown and demise. The "lightning of thought" has not been explained. Marx must show concretely why communism is not merely a normative ideal to which reality must adapt but represents also the "entire movement of history" (594), which is its genetic complement. Only then will communism not be susceptible to the critique Marx levels against the idealism of "merely political" solutions. But because such ideals do play a role in history, he has also to explain what might be called the production of consciousness, showing how circumstances make men just as much as men make circumstances. This is the task Marx takes up in *The German Ideology*.[8] The production of consciousness and the production of capitalism are historically interdependent.

The subtitle of Marx's account of the historical rise of capitalism is significant: *Natural [naturwüchsig] and Civilized Instruments of Production and Forms of Property* (GI, 65). "Civilized" production is the product of human activity—which, however, turns against its producers in the alienated form of capital. The workers who produce capital are subordinated to its dictates; their autonomy is reified by its imperatives. The proletariat can also truly "civilize" production, however, because it has no particular class interests that would prevent the generalization of the new productive forces. Marx's critical analysis tries to show that in producing capitalism the proletariat has produced also the means of its own liberation. The philosophical anthropology that forms the framework of the analysis–tracing the successive phases of economic development that have led to capitalism and its "ideological" self-representation—articulates a dialectic that begins with production, passes through its objectification in a world where it is subject to determinations that were not intended by the conscious producers and become barriers to them, and finally ends with a negation of this externality in the communist revolution, whose abolition of (externally determined) labor liberates an autonomous and enriched humanity. The problem with this dialectical logic is suggested by Marx himself, however, when he asserts that revolution is necessary not only because it is the only way to overthrow the ruling class but also "because the class *overthrowing* it [the ruling class] can only succeed through a revolution in ridding itself of the muck [*Dreck*] of the ages and become thus capable of a new grounding of society" (GI, 70). This means that it is not simply the production of capitalist social relations that makes the proletariat capable of inaugurating truly human history. The metaphorical "lightning of thought" remains to be explained.

### Economics and Philosophy

The importance of *The German Ideology* lies in its attempt to situate the capitalist economy in the context of a history that illustrates materially the progress of humanity toward its own emancipation. At times, Marx seems to think that an immanent critique of the historical process that produced capitalism could also point to the latent normative potential for transcending that social formation (at times on material-logical grounds, at others for anthropological-phenomenological reasons). Sometimes, his critique seems intended more to enlighten the potential revolutionary subject about its own situation, following the insistence in the 1843 "Exchange of Letters" that "consciousness is something it must acquire even if it does not want to."[9] On yet other occasions, Marx's materialism becomes less a critique and more a positivist reductionism pointing to a mechanically functioning productivist logic of history. In each case, critique seeks to explain the passage to action, as social transformation or as political change. The account oscillates between two poles suggested by the distinction between a phenomenological and a logical account of the "lightning of thought": in the former, the proletariat must see through the world of appearance and understand the logic of its situation; in the latter, the proletariat must become aware of its own practice and reappropriate consciously the production of its social life. In the one case, the world becomes philosophical; in the other, philosophy becomes worldly. The challenge is to unite the two poles.

Marx's *Theses on Feuerbach* (1845) provides another illustration of the ambiguity of his conception of philosophy following his discovery of the primacy of political economy. The second paragraph of the third thesis, which posed the question "who will educate the educator," now describes "revolutionary practice" as "the coincidence of the changing of circumstances and of human activity or self-changing."[10] In other words, "revolutionary practice" would on its own realize Marx's demand that philosophy become worldly as the world becomes philosophical. This claim permits Marx to avoid the voluntarism that is apparently suggested by the famous eleventh thesis: that the philosophers have only understood the world whereas the point is to change it. By contrast, *The Communist Manifesto* (1848) brings together the strands followed to this point in a different manner. The critical reader is struck here by Marx's ability at once to sing a hymn to capitalist civilizing processes and to denounce their nefarious effects. The contradiction between the forces and relations of production develops while stripping the veils from past traditions and fixed relations. "All that is solid melts in the air" as capitalism continues its self-revolutionizing process.[11] In the end, the worker is brought face to face with his lot, which is made "manifest" by history itself. But the concept of alienated labor is not invoked to explain the next step. Instead, Marx introduces the activity of the Communists. They are not a separate party; they have no separate interests, and they do not seek to impose (as doctrinaires) their own sectarian ideas. To this practical universality corresponds the theoretical superiority that comes from their "clearly understanding the line of march, the conditions, and the ultimate general results of the proletarian movement."[12] As the communists carry out the dictates of history, Marx has returned to the idealism of Hegel: *Revolution has replaced Spirit as the philosophical subject of history.*

## FROM POLITICS BACK TO POLITICAL ECONOMY

### *The Phenomenology of Politics*

The realization of the revolution as subject of history must unite the normative and genetic moments that guided Marx's analysis. The philosopher has the phenomenological task of following this subject's appearing forms in order to recognize and articulate the immanent logic of their manifestation. The French revolutions of 1848 provided a practical illustration, since the political revolution of February was followed by an attempted social revolution in June. That is why the introduction to *Class Struggles in France* (1850) asserts that a victory in February would have been in fact a defeat. It would have been that "merely political" revolution that Marx criticized in his youth. The apparent failure in June, by unifying the enemies of the proletariat, makes possible the emergence of a truly revolutionary party. While the demand for a "social republic" revealed the "secret of 19th century revolution," its neglect of class antagonisms was based on an illusion of *fraternité* that had to be destroyed.[13] The "specter of communism" that Marx had recently invoked at the outset of *The Communist Manifesto* could become reality only if this phenomenological movement culminates in the self-consciousness of the proletariat.

But the proletariat is not alone on stage; Marx has to explain also the appearances and illusions of bourgeois politics. He now must treat the state as a "power" rather than criticize its impotence. This implies that society is not a homogeneous body needing only to be liberated from politics to realize its essential democratic nature; the economic critique that sought to actualize philosophy by other means needs a political supplement. But the status of the political in Marx's analysis is ambiguous. The phenomenology of revolution that he describes in *Class Struggles* concludes with an affirmation of the priority of the logic of revolution, proclaiming "The Revolution is Dead, Long Live the Revolution" (CSF, 62). This is why the politics Marx describes is a politics of illusion. Succeeding classes come to power only to be caught between their claims to universality and the particularity of their own interests. The first victim of this illusion was the proletariat, whose decisive role in February led it to "lower the *red* flag before the tricolour" in the belief that the social republic could be achieved peacefully (CSF, 46). At the same time, however, the bourgeois republic showed itself for what it truly is: a state whose purpose is to perpetuate the rule of capital. By destroying the proletariat's illusions, the defeat proves to be a victory. But this complicates the situation; there are now three moments in Marx's phenomenology: the imperatives of the political sphere, the claims of particular interest, and the omnipresent logic of the "specter" that haunts the political stage. In the strategic maneuvering and the shifting class alliances that characterized the drama of 1848, the republic became the political form to which all parties had to appeal, despite their differing goals. It was the political form in which their contradictory interests could coexist. The imaginary republic denounced by the young Marx's critique of Hegel's state thus acquired political reality.

The republic is of course only a political form; the particular business of society continues on its own. Had the monarchist factions recognized their real interests rather than dreaming of political restoration, they would have seen that their old division as representatives respectively of landed and financial interests no longer existed. Both benefited from the national debt, which the Party of Order continued to increase as it tried to defend the state against society. Although the manufacturers opposed this policy, their economic weakness at this stage of the development of French capitalism meant that they could have political influence only in alliance with the proletariat. But June had taught them the danger of this, and so they too were forced to support the Party of Order. The political situation appeared hopeless. Marx predicted stalemate, with the Party of Order and Bonaparte joining together against their common enemy, the people, "until the new economic situation has again reached the point where a new explosion blows all these squabbling parties with their constitutional republic sky-high" (CSF, 142). This economic crisis would produce the objective destruction of the illusion of the political that the phenomenological progression described by Marx had produced on the side of the revolutionary subject. The unity of the two moments would mean that revolution was not only possible; it could now become actual.

## The Logic of Politics

Instead of the expected revolution based on economic developments, French politics took an unexpected turn with the coup d'état of Louis Napoleon Bonaparte. Marx sought to explain this new turn in *The 18th Brumaire of Louis Napoleon* (1852). He repeats many of the earlier arguments from *Class Struggles* but adds new elements to his theory of the political. The best known, presented in the preface to the second edition (1869), seems to appeal to economic reductionism, suggesting that a stalemate in the class struggle permits the rise to power of a mediocre individual like Bonaparte. The political can achieve an autonomous position, independent of the economic infrastructure, only in such exceptional conditions—whose very exceptionality seems to confirm the general validity of a reduction of the political to the economic. But Marx's systematic theoretical goals suggest a different reading. The theme of Revolution as the subject of history suggests the need to supplement the phenomenological critique of the illusion of the political presented in *Class Struggles* with a logical critique of political illusions. This goal explains the use of theatrical metaphors in Marx's analysis; the political is the stage on which illusion must appear, and the failure to understand this symbolic element of politics dooms its practitioners. Understanding this political logic was the key to Bonaparte's seizure of power, just as failure to understand it doomed his opponents, leaving the field, Marx expected, to the revolutionary proletariat.[14]

The different logical foundations of bourgeois and proletarian revolution mean that each will be accompanied by different phenomenological appearances. "Bourgeois revolutions . . . storm quickly from success to success. They outdo each other in dramatic effects; men and things seem set in sparkling diamonds and each day's spirit is ecstatic. But they are short-lived; they soon reach their apogee." In contrast, continues Marx, proletarian revolutions "constantly engage in self-criticism, and in repeated interruptions of their own course. They return to what has apparently already been accomplished in order to begin the task again . . . ; they shrink back again and again before the indeterminate immensity of their own goals, until the situation is created in which . . . the conditions themselves cry out: *Hic Rhodus, hic salta*."[15] This self-critical proletarian political project implies that no objective or economic determination ensures success. The political process is not simply superstructural or illusory, and the theatrical metaphors are more than simply metaphorical.

The need to understand the logic of politics resulted from the failed expectations to which the phenemenological account of *Class Struggles* gave rise. Marx had expected that the passage through the series of political appearances that followed the February revolution would be complemented by the intervention of economic crisis. This infrastructural logic that explains the succession of political forms was treated as separate from these political appearances. In contrast, *The 18th Brumaire* offers a logic of politics that is immanent to the political, so that Marx can conclude that "this parody of the empire was necessary to free the mass of the French nation from the burden of tradition and to bring out the antagonism between the state power and society in its pure form" (18th, 244). This does not mean that the economic is irrelevant, but it implies that its place has to be evaluated from within a political logic that must be accounted for in its own terms. The phenomenology of political illusion was presented from the participant perspective; its logic has now to be analyzed from the standpoint of the observer. That external analyst, as was implicit in *Class Struggles*, is none other than the proletariat, that specter whose defeat in June meant that it "passed into the *background* of the revolutionary stage"(18th, 154).

After the inadequacy of an account focused on political illusions has become clear, Marx turns to a critique of the illusion of politics. The problem is to understand the relation of these two analyses. Marx notes the irony that, having deified the sword, the bourgeoisie came to be ruled by it; after destroying the revolutionary press, it has lost its own; after sending out spies and closing the popular clubs, it finds its salons are watched by the police. This may have protected its purse, but it cost it "the appearance of respectability" (18th, 235). Napoleon's coup replaced the parliamentary force of words with force without words, destroying the illusion of politics. But Marx's explanation does not appeal only to economic interest. "The opposition between the executive and the legislative expresses the opposition between the nation's heteronomy and its autonomy" (18th, 236). The origin of this antipolitical executive power has to be explained. Its source is the triumph of the absolute monarchy over feudalism, a triumph that centralizes power in the state. The French Revolution took this centralization a step further, and the first Napoleon and then his restored successors perfected the system. The result is the kind of political alienation the young Marx had denounced abstractly in the Hegelian state. "Every *common* interest was immediately detached from society, opposed to it as a higher, *general* interest, torn away from the self-activity of the individual members of society, and made a subject for governmental activity" (18th, 237). Indeed, the parliamentary republic's attempts to ward off the threat of revolution led it to further centralization. "All political upheavals have perfected this machine instead of smashing it," concludes Marx (18th, 238). Bonaparte's coup completes the separation of the state machine from society; the political illusion now has its proper logical foundation.

This analysis of the role of the absolute state and its successors in creating the conditions necessary for the rise of bourgeois relations of production is the crucial insight of *The 18th Brumaire*. Marx had previously assumed that the transition from feudalism to capitalism took place according to a sheer economic logic defined by the contradiction between the growing forces of production and the outdated relations of production. Now his analysis of the illusion of the political and of political illusions led him to abandon his previous theory of the subject of history on which that model was based. He had assumed that Revolution replaced Hegel's Spirit as the motor and telos of historical development. Now political experience had shown that it is not sufficient to trace the phenomenological process by which revolutionary appearances supersede one another until they come to coincide with their essence. The triumph of world capitalism (in which Bonaparte's new empire was an active participant) had defeated the bourgeois political revolution after the latter had defeated the social republic. Marx had to find a different subject. Not capital—which is only an appearance—but capitalist social relations, as reflected in the mirror of the commodity form, became the new standpoint from which to show how the actualization of philosophy as the making philosophical of the world can realize philosophy by other means.

### The Capitalist Economy as Political Subject

Marx himself published only the first volume of *Capital* (1867), whose subtitle explained that it presented the "theory of the immediate production process."[16] This fact explains why Marxists often misunderstood the kind of theory that Marx was proposing—although the subtitle alerts the philosophical reader, since immediacy is only the first form of appearance and does not reveal the essence that makes it possible. The less alert reader would pay greater heed to the concern with economic production. Yet it is only after nearly 150 pages of logical analysis of the commodity form and a general description of capital's logic that chapter 6 proposes to leave the "Eden of the innate rights of man" that will bring a change "in the physiognomy of our *dramatis personae*."[17] The theatrical metaphor and the demand to leap to a new perspective are familiar from the political account of *The 18th Brumaire*. Their presence suggests that Marx has not changed his method but rather its object. The phenomenology of appearing forms and the logic that governs their necessary articulation are still present. The new theory of political economy will join together those moments, which had remained side by side as separate texts in the *Economic and Philosophical Manuscripts*. The commodity form—uniting use-value and exchange-value—becomes the basis of their unity. Its full development as realized capitalism is summarized at the end of volume 1 in chapter 25, "The General Law of Capitalist Accumulation." But this "law" leads neither to socialism nor revolution; at most, it shows that capitalism produces increasing (relative) misery for an increasing part of the population. Perhaps to convince humane readers to reject such a system, the following chapter's description of "original accumulation" demolishes the argument of apologists who claim that capitalism is something natural. But Marx's stress on a systematic, philosophical, and immanently critical theory is more rigorous.

The economic theory of *Capital*'s first volume can be explained relatively simply, once one accepts the labor theory of value.[18] Marx presupposes that capitalism functions fairly: all commodities are sold at their (exchange) value, which is determined by the amount of average socially necessary labor contained in each of them; this includes the labor necessary to produce all their components, raw materials, an aliquot value of machinery consumed, and the labor added. The trick, and the source of surplus-value, is that one commodity involved in the process of production is the worker, who is purchased as the commodity called "labor-power." The worker's exchange-value is determined, like any other commodity, by the amount of average socially necessary labor needed to reproduce him (and his family). But as opposed to other commodities, purchased for their use-value and consumed privately, the consumption of labor-power consists in putting it to work. And it can be put to work for a longer period of time than is necessary to reproduce it. The excess that results goes into the pocket of the capitalist, who has fairly purchased a commodity on the market and used it freely, as is his right.

This economic description is at first formal. It follows the appearance of capital as money goes through a cycle at the end of which more money emerges. In its immediacy, this appearance of profit making as dominating all social relations within capitalist society explains nothing. Just as the biologist cannot begin with the immediacy of the human body, so the political economist must find the "cell form" that permits the explanation of the phenomena that concern him. This cell form is the commodity. Commodities have not only use-values–which are inherently subjective, personal, and thus not comparable with one another—but also exchange-values, which, as socially established, appear to define the economic sphere as objective and measurable. If a coat is regularly exchanged for a given amount of cloth, we assume that something equal is being exchanged on both sides, something shared by both commodities. It appears at first that this property shared by both commodities is money, but the value of money itself can change—for example, at the beginning of the capitalist era with the discovery of Latin American gold. This is where the labor theory of value enters. The labor incorporated in a commodity is average socially necessary labor; it is not the concrete labor of the particular tailor who produced the coat that is exchanged. *Capital* thus presents an economic theory of the social relations that engender this process.

The social production process of capitalism is based on a series of commodity exchanges. The capitalist appears immediately as a person having the money needed to buy means of production (machinery and raw materials, as well as the labor-power to work them). These means of production have to be available on a free market, which is not the case, for example, in the feudal "democracy of unfreedom." Not only must restrictions on the use of land and its products be eliminated; guild rules that regulate production must be overcome. Most important, however, is the emergence of the free worker, whose freedom is due to his separation from the land and the community that formerly ensured his subsistence; this abstract freedom leaves him no choice but to sell his labor-power on the market. Marx's reconstruction of the historical process by which these necessary commodities came onto the market can be left aside, but two implications should be stressed. First, capitalism is a historical creation rather than a natural development inherent in human social relations; second, for the theory as simply economic, it is the purchase of the commodity labor-power that permits the capitalist to realize surplus-value. *This historical specificity of capitalism is what makes the economic theory implicitly a political theory.* At the same time, one sees here how Marx presents his earlier theory of alienated labor in a new guise. The concrete and particular labor of any particular worker counts not for itself but only as the abstractly universal form of average or general socially necessary labor.

The political implications of the economic theory become clearer in "The Production of Relative Surplus-Value" in part 4. Capitalism now appears as more than a system for the production of surplus-value; it is also a political relation that divides society into two opposed but mutually interdependent classes: those who own the means of production and those who must sell their labor-power in order to maintain their physical existence. The process begins with what Marx calls the "formal subsumption" of the worker under capitalism, at first through forms of simple cooperation in which formerly autonomous artisan producers are brought together to realize a single task. While each may work with the same tools and in the same manner as before, the result is still increased productivity of the whole. Since it was the investment by the capitalist that brought them together, it appears that capital is responsible for this benefit and that the additional (or "relative") surplus-value that ensues rightfully belongs to the capitalist. This is of course only an appearance, since it is the joint labor of the workers that has produced the surplus, which has been alienated and is now found in the pocket of the capitalist. Nevertheless, workers as well as capitalists are taken in by the appearance, which is indeed a progress over the patriarchal, political, or religious forms of exploitation that existed previously insofar as labor, while still dependent, is nonetheless freed from external bonds imposed by force.

The political illusion grows in the next stages, when the capitalist first introduces a division of labor into the workshop and then, on the basis of this division of labor, begins to modify the production process itself. This leads to the development of what Marx calls "manufacture." As the labor process is increasingly divided, the workers' tools are modified, rendered more efficient, and adapted to new types of production. At this point, it also becomes possible for science to enter into an increasingly rationalized production process, which is adapted to its formal and mathematical reason. The use of science is also encouraged by the rationalized production process, which no longer depends on accidental human skills. Once again, the alienated illusion attributes the new gains to the "genius" of the capitalist or to his managerial skills. The contribution of the workers is neglected; they are paid simply for their labor-power— whose exchange-value decreases as work becomes simplified and the skilled are replaced by the unskilled or by women and children.

The division of labor and the advance of manufacturing production transform the workers' formal subsumption under capital into a "real subsumption." The worker cannot produce without selling his labor-power to the capitalist. The small artisan who seeks to maintain the old ways that ensured his independence finds himself undersold by more efficient capitalist manufacture. And whereas the manufacturing worker still needs skill to work with the new and more adapted tools, a further shift occurs with the advance to "machinery and large scale industry." The specificity of the machine lies in the fact that it has incorporated into itself the tools formerly used by the worker, such that the worker is transformed from the agent of production to simply a cog in the functioning of a machine that, increasingly, seems capable of running on its own. With this, the process of alienation is complete; the worker's subjectivity as agent has been transferred to capital, which now appears in the form of gigantic, interconnected machinery running on its own.

It is difficult to see how this description of the complete alienation of the working class through its real subsumption under capital can justify Marx's earlier argument that this class would become the agent of world historical transformation. The economic has replaced the political as the locus for a change that, however, the self-contained production process seems to exclude by its very (artificial) nature.[19] Marx seems to be aware of the problem. In the penultimate chapter, "The Historical Tendency of Capitalist Accumulation," Marx asserts that "the mass of misery, oppression, slavery, degradation and exploitation grows; but with it grows the revolt of the working class, a class constantly increasing in numbers, and trained, united and organized by the very mechanism of capitalist production." The contradiction between capitalism's monopoly and the relations of production to which it has given birth is revealed by this action. "The integument is burst asunder. The knell of capitalist private property sounds. The expropriators are expropriated." This "inevitable" revolution is justified in a final footnote, which is simply a self-citation from *The Communist Manifesto*. How could Marx simply return to the old standpoint, as if the theory of *Capital* changed nothing? Marxists, who took volume 1 to represent Marx's final theoretical position, found here a simple theory of economic determinism. But even if philosophy becomes "worldly" with "the inexorability of a natural process," it is not clear how this makes philosophical the economic world that Marx has described. Indeed, if it is only natural (*naturwüchsig*), then it is not rational or civilized. Perhaps this is why, in the paragraph preceding his final self-citation from *The Communist Manifesto*, Marx describes the "inexorable" revolution in the Hegelian terminology according to which capital-ism is a "first negation of individual private property" that will be in its turn negated to establish a superior form of property built "on the achievements of the capitalist era" (1:929). It remains to see what Marx might have meant by this new form of property.

## FROM THE CRITIQUE OF POLITICAL ECONOMY TO THE DISCOVERY OF THE POLITICAL

### Critique as Immanent

The persistence of Marx's systematic theoretical goal in *Capital* is suggested by a letter he wrote to Ferdinand Lassalle in which he describes his economic theory as "a presentation of the system, and through the presentation a critique of that system."[20] By starting from the commodity form as the unity of use- and exchange-value, Marx is able to present a phenemenology of capitalism, whose foun-dation is this commodity logic. In this way, he can show the necessary illusions into which the apologists of capitalism are led.[21] The diffi-culty, however, is that this dialectic can slide into a kind of reduc-tionist positivism that is typified by Marx's frequent recourse to metaphors of revolutionary midwives lessening the birth pangs of a society pregnant with its own future. This positivism can also trans-form revolution into evolution, as when Marx cites favorably in the postface (1873) to the second edition of volume 1 a Russian reviewer's comparison of his work to "the history of evolution in other branches of biology" (1:101). This neglects the role of consciousness, the real-ization of philosophy through the lightning of thought.

If capitalism is an economic process whose development ulti-mately makes obsolete its own presuppositions at the same time that it produces the conditions for new and truly human relations, it must be a theory of social relations that only appear to be economic. The opening theme of *The Communist Manifesto* has not been abandoned: all history is a history of class struggle. The economic development described in volume 1 as if it were simply the evolution of alienated labor determined by the logic of commodity relations does not func-tion on its own. The process that led to the "real subsumption" of labor was the result of struggles by workers to better their wages and conditions, to which Marx devotes over eighty pages in chapter 10, "The Working Day." The relative success of such struggles is one of the factors driving capitalism constantly to modernize work conditions in order to ensure the subordination of the workers while producing relative surplus-value. Those who doubt the revolutionary potential of the proletariat make the same errors as the apologists for capitalism who look only at the side of exchange-value. They do not recognize the "civilizing" element of capitalism as doubly conflictual, producing advances in the forces of production but also inciting progress on the side of the workers. Marx's immanent dialectic avoids such one-sided reductionism; his recognition of the doubly "civilizing" aspect of capitalism escapes the temptation to idealize or romanticize precapitalist conditions as is often done by reactionary critics of capitalism.

The immanent critique of the commodity form and of the social relations that it presupposes and reproduces explains why Marx considered his theory both a presentation of the immanent logic of capitalism and a critique of that logic. The place of immanent critique is clear in a passage from the *Grundrisse* that introduces the notion of alienated labor into the economic theory in a way that is only implicit in *Capital*:

> The recognition [*Erkennung*] of the products as its own, and the judgement that its separation from the conditions of its own realization is improper—forcibly imposed—is an enormous [advance in] awareness [*Bewusstsein*] that is itself the product of the mode of production resting on capital and as much the knell of its doom as, with the slave's awareness that he *cannot be the property of another*, with his consciousness of himself as a person, the existence of slavery becomes a merely artificial, vegetative existence, and ceases to be able to prevail as the basis of production.[22]

It is not economic exploitation but the alienation of the human from what he can become—in the case of developed capitalism, what he has become in an alienated manner through its conflictual "civilizing" process—that makes possible and necessary the overthrow of capitalism.

The immanent critique thus restates Marx's philosophical problem while making it possible to avoid dead ends, which, unfortunately, are also present in his text. Immanent critique does not only or principally condemn capitalism in its own productivist terms—stressing capitalism's inefficiencies, the costs resulting from its need to hire overseers in order to discipline rebellious workers, or its indifference to the ecological results of production oriented only to exchange-value. It does not only or principally denounce capitalist exploitation and the immiseration of the working class but starts from the assumption of a fairly functioning capitalist system in order to develop its critique. It is not only or principally moral or rhetorical criticism that hopes to awaken sympathetic souls to the good cause. It is not only or principally a theory of crises whose result is the destruction and devaluation of productive capacities and workers' lives. It is not even only or principally a critique of the domination of the commodity form and the subsumption of all spheres of life to the domination of that form's logic. Rather, critique as immanent seeks to reveal what capitalism's "civilizing" function has also created: the socialized worker, a use-value that is abusively reduced to an exchange-value, and the possibility of using science to escape the curse of mere physical labor.[23] In this, the project of *Capital* is not different from the task that Marx set himself in the *Economic and Philosophical Manuscripts*. The difference lies in the nature of the political project that emerges from *Capital* once we go beyond "the immediate production process" and look at the *re*production of capitalism as a system of social relations. It will be clear that Marx does not reduce the political to the logic of the economy. His arguments make plain that understanding capitalist economic relations presupposes a theory of the political. It is capitalism's inability to understand its own political presuppositions that ultimately condemns it.

## Capitalism as Political

Volume 2 of *Capital* analyzes the circulation process through which capitalist relations are *re*produced. The account traces the metamorphoses through which a produced commodity finds a buyer, who acquires its use-value by paying the equivalent of its exchange-value; the money thus acquired must find on the market the machinery, raw materials, and labor-power necessary to begin the production process whose result will put the capitalist in possession of a new commodity, which will in its turn trace the same cycle. The importance of this analysis for political theory is suggested by an unpublished chapter, "The Results of the Immediate Production Process," which explains the transition to volume 2. As often in his manuscripts, when he is groping for the proper formulation of his questions, Marx has recourse to Hegelian language. While the immediate production process began with money and commodities as preconditions, at the end of the cycle these have now been, as Hegel would say, "posited" as capital. This means that the nature of the ingredients in production has changed because they exist in a different set of social relations. The use-value that was put to work by the capitalist is now relevant only as the exchange-value of the commodity. This means that the work of the worker is only apparently the production of a product, since what counts as reality in capitalism is the valorization (*Verwertung*) of the means of production. The "real subsumption" of the worker under capital has now become inscribed in the process of capitalist *re*production. The domination of past labor over the present, the subordination of living labor to objectified value, the inversion of producer and the object produced that were first seen in religious alienation are now part of the process of capital's self-realization.[24] Capital is value existing for itself and maintaining itself. "In the labor-process looked at purely for itself the worker utilizes the means of production. In the labor process regarded also as a capitalist process of production, the means of production utilize the worker. . . . The labor process is the *self-valorization process* of objectified labor [i.e., of capital] through the agency of living labor" (R, 1008). What was in itself or potentially capitalism at the outset of the process has now become for itself or actual because it now reproduces (or posits, in Hegel's language) its own conditions of existence as capitalist.

This self-positing of capitalist relations and their reproduction transforms the economic process of immediate production into a political process of social reproduction. For itself, capital is simply self-valuating value whose purest and most absurd form is described in the third volume of *Capital* as interest-bearing capital—money that immediately produces more money, as if no social mediations were necessary. Capitalism takes itself to be the universal mode of productive relations, but its inability to recognize its own preconditions makes it only a particular, historically situated mode of human production. Thus, even though it is in a particular business, each capital takes itself as an end in itself. The resulting competition at first has positive effects: it stimulates the development of the forces of production, the increasing application and development of science, and the creation of a more versatile socialized worker. But these benefits concern the use-value of capitalism (and of competition), whereas the capitalist—capital personified and possessing a will—is concerned with exchange-value. The paradox that emerges is that capital as self-reproducing value posits itself as particular in the person of each capitalist and yet also posits the general social relations that permit it to reproduce itself. As posited, capitalist social relations entail a political dimension, but, as particular, none of the competing capitals can take this dimension into account in running their particular businesses. This explains why, in *The 18th Brumaire*, the bourgeoisie was seen to be willing to abandon its political power in order to preserve its economic interests.

This political dimension of capitalism is not developed in the posthumously published volumes 2 and 3 of *Capital*. Instead, an economic demonstration of the "law of the tendential fall in the rate of profit" is often taken to imply that Marx predicted the necessity of a breakdown (*Zusammenbruch*) of capitalism. Yet his next chapter presents six "counteracting factors" that could limit the law's effects. Among these factors are a more intense exploitation of labor, the reduction of wages below their value, and the presence of a relative surplus population—but not the effects of class struggle. Granted, the further "development of the law's internal contradictions" asserts that "the true barrier to capitalist production is capital itself" (3:358). But this lapidary phrase need not be read as demonstrating an economic contradiction. Although the rate of profit may fall, profit can still be made, surplus-value extracted. The problem lies in the realization (*Verwertung*) of this surplus-value or profit, and that depends on the sphere of circulation, where capitalist social relations have to be *re*produced. The two spheres exist, notes Marx, independently in time, in space, and in theory.[25] As the rate of profit falls, the drive for accumulation by each competing capitalist continues; the market must be expanded constantly, following "a natural law independent of the producers and ever more uncontrollable. The internal contradiction seeks resolution by extending the external field of production. But the more productivity develops, the more it comes into conflict with the narrow basis on which the relations of consumption rest." And, adds Marx, "it is in no way a contradiction, on this contradictory basis, that excess capital coexists with a growing surplus population" (3:353). The contradiction may be occasioned by the dominance of the particular mode of capitalist production, but its effects are felt at the level of human social *re*production whose political implications are not developed in these posthumous volumes.

The attribution to Marx of a theory of necessary economic breakdown also leaves open the question of why volume 3 continues for more than six hundred pages after the formulation of the "law" that is supposed to foretell capitalism's demise. What is the status of these considerations of commercial capital, interest-bearing capital, and the forms of rent on land? A purely economic interpretation is possible. It would show that, from the standpoint of the logic of capital, these phenomena are remnants of an earlier period that have become barriers in the present advanced conditions. But such a criticism of capitalism's irrationality remains on capital's own, economic terrain. It is productivist in its logic and leaves no place for conscious political intervention. And it neglects the earlier explanation of the "absurdity" of interest-bearing capital that forgets that money doesn't beget money without intervening social relations that explain this appearance.

The final part of volume 3, "The Revenues and Their Sources," opens the space for a more political interpretation. Marx criticizes the "Trinity Formula" for its ahistorical reification that identifies each of the factors of production (land, capital, and labor) with its owner, claiming thereby to explain the source of the revenues of each. His explanation of the origin of this "bewitched and distorted world" in the capitalist relations of production is familiar. At first, with the struggle to limit the working day, the proletariat knows immediately that it is being exploited. But with the development of relative surplus-value, the "growth of the forces of social labor . . . appear[s] in the immediate labor process as shifted from labor to capital. Capital thereby already becomes a very mystical being" (3:966). Then, in the sphere of circulation, the conditions of production are left behind; it now appears that surplus-value is not simply realized but actually produced in circulation. Volume 2 unveiled the actuality behind this appearance, but it neglected the effects of competition; this explains why capitalism's true nature remains veiled for its agents. When competition was introduced in volume 3, its lawful results (in the form of the technical calculations of real prices and the average rate of profit) were engendered only behind the backs of the individual agents. The mystification reappears at a still deeper level "as the capital fetish, value creating value, so it now presents itself once again in the figure of interest-bearing capital as its most estranged and peculiar form." Finally, a part of surplus-value appears to be completely asocial, bound "rather with a natural element, the earth, [and now] the form of mutual alienation and ossification of the various portions of surplus-value is complete" (3:968). The attribution of revenues to land, labor, and capital "completes the mystification . . . the reification of social relations." Thus "it is also quite natural . . . that the actual agents of production themselves feel completely at home in these estranged and irrational forms of capital . . . for these are precisely the configuration of appearance in which they move, and with which they are daily involved" (3:969). An immanent critique that demystifies this consciousness does not, however, show the possibility of overcoming the social relations that gave rise to it. The question of political agency, or the role of class struggle, remains open.

The domination of capital over labor is "essentially different from authority on the basis of production with slaves or serfs." A theory of domination is of course a political theory, based on the notion of authority. Thus capital's authority and legitimacy depend on the social relations of production that create the illusion that it is capital that produces the constant amelioration of the productive apparatus; the capitalists acquire this authority as "personifications of the conditions of labor vis-à-vis labor itself, not . . . as political or theocratic rulers." But the competition among the many capitals means that "the most complete anarchy reigns among the bearers of this authority" (3:1021). Each particular capitalist imagines himself to be autonomous, thinking that he could reproduce his relations of production on his own. Yet his profit is the result of a historically specific process of social distribution. But, cautions Marx, to criticize only the relations of distribution is "still timid and restrained" and does not see that these relations correspond to a particular form of production (3:1023). Valid change will come only through crisis, which is now defined as "the contradiction and antithesis between, on the one hand, the relations of distribution, hence also the specific historical form of relations of production corresponding to them, and on the other hand, the productive forces, productivity, *and the development of its agents*" (3:1024; my emphasis). Clarification of the last clause might be expected from the next, and final, chapter of volume 3, which presents Marx's theory of "classes." However, the manuscript breaks off before that theory is developed.

This attempt to clarify the place of the political in the economic theory of *Capital* permits an interpretation of what Marx's theory of classes may have intended, despite the fact that the actual manuscript seems to fall into a kind of descriptive sociology for which Marx is unable to find a unifying thread. By becoming a commodity, the productive worker is involved in the paradoxical structure of alienation through which capitalism develops its "civilizing" process. In principle, this productive worker has become "all-sided" and "rich in needs" in the same way that capital has done so.[26] Considered from the standpoint of use-value, he has retained and developed his own human needs. It is this that makes him in principle a political agent, capable of transforming not only the relations of distribution but also those of production. Considered as human, rather than as a commodity or as exchange-value, he sees what the capitalist, caught in his illusions and a prisoner of competition, is unable to see: that capital "is the existence of social labor . . . but this existence as itself existing independently opposite its real moments—hence itself a *particular* existence apart from them" (Gr, 471). The imperative of the class struggle is to overcome this particularity that claims falsely to be the natural, and thus universal, mode of human productive relations.

### Politics and Class Struggle

The place of the political in Marx's economic theory apparently inverts the relation between the political and the social that he had criticized in Hegel's theory of the state. Rather than consider the political as the locus of change, he suggests that the domination of capital means that the economic has become both the locus and the agent of change. From this perspective, Marx's later work would be a critique of the economic illusion that parallels his early critique of the political illusion. This does not contradict the assertion that the agency of change lies in the developed human capacities of the working class considered not in its alienated existence as wage labor but from the perspective of its noncapitalist humanity. The challenge is to establish the proper relation between these two aspects of Marx's theory of the political. Marx never developed this theory, but two essays from the 1870s suggest what he might have been able to draw together from the questions that had animated his philosophical project. The first, *The Civil War in France* (1871), develops further his phenomenological analysis of politics in the land of the political illusion. The second, *The Critique of the Gotha Program* (1875), contains Marx's most general statement on the political process that would make it possible to move beyond the logic of economic capitalism. Taken together, these essays are a reprise of the phenomenological and logical moments of Marx's analysis.

*The Civil War in France* was presented to a meeting of the General Council of the First International on May 30, 1871, two days after the repression of the Paris Commune. Marx insisted that the salvation of France depended on the proletariat, whose regeneration is "impossible without the revolutionary overthrow of the political and social conditions that had engendered the Second Empire."[27] The political tool for that overthrow had been discovered by the Communards themselves. Marx's description of the Commune presents it as the complete negation of existent political institutions. A new political form was necessary because "the working class cannot simply lay hold of the ready-made state machinery and wield it for its own purposes" (CWF, 206). It appears at first that Marx sees the positive "working" existence of the Commune as a form of direct democracy. It suppressed the standing army and made public officials responsible and revocable, with short terms of office paid at workers' wages. It eliminated the separation of executive and legislative functions, in effect uniting particularity with universality. The church was disestablished, and its role in education—which would now be free for all—was eliminated. The judiciary was made elective and revocable, and thus "divested of that sham independence which had but served to mask their abject subservience to all succeeding governments." Decentralization was achieved by the imperative mandate to ensure that "universal suffrage was to serve the people, constituted in communes, as individual suffrage serves every other employer in the search for the workmen and managers of his business" (CWF, 210). This sudden reduction of politics to business gives pause; it recalls a terrible phrase that Lenin adopted from Engels: the government over men is replaced by the administration of things.[28] The administration of things and the process of reification by which exchange-value comes to dominate capitalist relations are uncomfortably close to one another. The fact that Marx does not notice this difficulty suggests the need to look more closely at the political innovations of the revolutionary Commune.

Marx's description of the "true secret" of the Commune is ambiguous. On the one hand, it is "essentially a working-class government, the product of the struggle of the producing against the appropriating class," while, on the other hand, it is "the political form at last discovered under which to work out the economic emancipation of labor" (CWF, 212). The first clause implies that Marx saw the Commune as the realization of direct democracy; the second suggests that the role of this political form is to permit the (phenomenological) class struggle to develop to its full dimension, to recognize itself for what it truly is, to free itself from the mystifications of capitalist alienation. The two clauses need not be contradictory, as long as the capacity for direct democracy proposed by the first clause is not assumed to be already prepared under capitalism and simply waiting to be liberated by the revolutionary midwives. A democratic government that makes possible the struggle to realize the economic emancipation of labor can permit a process of political learning through which the working class becomes conscious of its own human potentiality.

This political interpretation of Marx's argument recalls his insistence in *The German Ideology* that class struggle is needed to eliminate "the muck [Dreck] of the ages" (GI, 70). In this sense, "the great social measure of the Commune was its own working existence" (CWF, 217), which "did not pretend to infallibility, the invariable attribute of all governments of the old stamp. It published its doings and sayings, it initiated the people into its shortcomings" (CWF, 219). This fits the picture of the Commune as a political form that permits the working class to learn to understand its capacities in the process of realizing its own potential. This interpretation is confirmed when Marx insists that the working class has "no ready-made utopias to introduce *par décret du peuple*. They know that in order to work out their own emancipation and along with it that higher form to which present society is irresistibly tending by its own economic agencies, they will have to pass through long struggles through a series of historic processes, transforming circumstances and men." But the next sentence flatly contradicts this political interpretation when it asserts that the workers "have no ideals to realize, but [need only] to set free the elements of the new society with which the old collapsing bourgeois society itself is pregnant" (CWF, 213). The creative potential of the political sphere is denied by such democratic bravado.

The concluding section of *The Civil War in France* does little to clarify the ambiguous relation among direct democracy, economic determinism, and the invention of the "political form at last discovered under which to work out the economic emancipation of labor." Although there are passages that lend credence to the deterministic viewpoint, the political interpretation is not excluded. The Commune is said to be the political form "at last discovered," just as democracy and then the proletariat were identified by Marx's earlier writings as solutions to the "riddle of history." As usual, Marx's first draft uses more Hegelian language. Its reconstruction of the development of political centralization underlines the state's "supernaturalist sway over real society" (CWF, 247). The Commune's revolution against "this supernaturalist abortion of society" (CWF, 249) and against the alienation that makes "administration and political governing . . . mysteries, transcendent functions only to be trusted to the hands of a trained caste . . . absorbing the intelligence of the masses and turning them against themselves" (CWF, 251) is "the *political form of the social emancipation* . . . of labor" (CWF, 252; Marx's emphasis). Now, however, Marx does not appeal to direct democracy as realizing social emancipation: the Commune "is *not* the social movement of the working class and therefore of a general regeneration of mankind, but the organized means of action. The Commune does *not* do away with class struggles . . . but affords the rational medium in which that class struggle can run through its different phases in the most rational and humane way" (CWF, 252; my emphasis). Granted, other phrases in the draft are more economistic, and a few also point toward direct democracy as a solution. Philology cannot solve the systematic problem. If the Commune is the discovery of "the political form of social emancipation," *The Critique of the Gotha Program* (1875) should help understand what Marx means by this affirmation.

Marx develops the political importance of the economic distinction between use-value and exchange-value, between labor in capitalist society and human labor, in his critique of the theories of Ferdinand Lassalle that had been incorporated in the draft program of a unified German Workers Party. The apparently self-evident assertion that because labor is the source of all wealth and culture and since it can be performed only in and through society, all members of society have a right to all its products is only true—Marx admonishes—in capitalism. If there were cooperative ownership of the means of production, then labor would no longer be the measure of the value of what is produced, and relations of distribution would not be governed by commodity exchange. The error is not only a matter for theory; the program's proposals do not deal with communist society "as it has developed on its own foundations"—as it has posited itself and as it reproduces itself through a dialectical process of class struggle and overcoming of opposition—but are applied to a society that still bears the "birth marks" of capitalism.[29] As a result, equality seems to demand that each individual receive from society the equivalent of what he has contributed in terms of labor time. But this is still a capitalist form of equality that treats the individual as a worker, as exchange-value, and neglects all other aspects of his work and life needs. Even though there is no class inequality, since all are workers, this formal equality based on the treatment of individuals as wage laborers legitimates real inequalities that are rooted in other dimensions of social relations. At the same time, it neglects that which is unique to the individual as a human person independent of the commodity market.

Marx's vision of real equality is well known: in the advanced phase of communism, when the antithesis between intellectual and physical labor is overcome and "when labor is no longer just a means of keeping alive, but has become a vital need, when the all-round development of individuals has also increased their productive powers and all the springs of cooperative wealth flow more abundantly—only then can society cross the narrow horizon of bourgeois right and inscribe on its banner: From each according to his abilities, to each according to his needs" (Gotha, 347). Marx's adoption of this slogan of the utopian followers of Saint-Simon and Fourier is surprising, and his affirmation that freedom is achieved within the labor process challenges the vision of *Capital* that sees science as making possible forms of freedom outside labor. More important, the solution of the political problem of equality by the leap beyond social scarcity is philosophically a petition of principle. Marx's earlier argument, in *The German Ideology*, that historical progress is accompanied by the production of new needs should have alerted him to the problem. Perhaps this utopianism is explained by the suggestion in *Capital* that the worker as human—not as exchange-value—develops new, "civilized" capacities. But another passage from *The Critique of the Gotha Program* stresses the value of political autonomy in a way that recalls the earlier critique of Proudhon, which was repeated in the *Grundrisse* (Gr, 463). "It is as if," Marx writes, "among slaves who have finally got behind the secret of slavery and broken out in rebellion, one slave, still the prisoner of obsolete ideas, were to write in the program of the rebellion 'slavery must be abolished because the provisioning of slaves in the slave system cannot exceed a certain low minimum' " (Gotha, 352). Again, this insight is left undeveloped.

*The Critique of the Gotha Program* was written for strategic reasons by a political revolutionary. But class struggle also played a role for Marx as political philosopher. His mature economic theory analyzes the conditions in which that "artificial" revolutionary proletariat whose historical role was discovered in 1843 is formed, but the other necessary moment, designated by the metaphor of the "lightning of thought," is still not explained. Marx's critique of capitalism's creation of a world regulated by the logic of exchange-value could no longer assume, after the experiences of 1848 and 1851, that Revolution is the subject of history. The subject of history whose logical appearances are analyzed in *Capital* is capitalist social relations reified in the commodity, whose use-value as laboring humanity remains a silent spectator to the "civilizing" development of the capitalist economy, just as the proletariat was the absent presence haunting the political illusions whose logic was traced in *The 18th Brumaire*. The realization of Marx's systematic philosophical project demands that this other moment become "for itself," consciously and actually, what capitalism has made it potentially. The logic of the commodity form developed in *Capital* is only the appearance of a deeper reality, which is the class struggle between labor and capital. What happens if this appearance is transcended? *The Critique of the Gotha Program* gave only a negative answer: the reign of real equality will not be inaugurated immediately; individual difference will remain—and the place of politics as the conscious regulation of social relations will persist, along with the need to continue to do philosophy in order to understand, justify, and critique the choices and judgments that have to be made.

## PHILOSOPHY BY OTHER MEANS

If Marx's mature theory of capitalism represents philosophy as worldly, it remains incomplete without its complementary moment. That representation of the world as philosophical reappears explicitly at different points in the *Grundrisse*. Although the distribution of life chances in a given society appears to be the result of historical accident, the fact that all societies must *re*produce themselves means that relations of production are the foundations on which other relations are built. But this does not make them causally or materially determinant; they express a relation that, while it may appear as a unitary force, is nonetheless itself the result of social interaction. Societies must reproduce the social relations that make them the specific societies they are. This framework permits the reintroduction of the categories of genesis (in the form of the reproduction process) and normativity (in the form of the relations that get reproduced). Neither can exist in isolation. Thus Marx criticizes Smith and Ricardo for presupposing that the individual is the agent of production rather than recognizing that, before the eighteenth century, the community was the subject and the individual only its appearing form (Gr, 84). Private interest as the apparent basis of social relations emerges only with the dissolution of communal societies; it then, with the development of the money form, becomes the abstract bond uniting society. The private individual and the monetary bond are historical products "whose universality produces not only the alienation of the individual from himself and from others, but also the universality and the comprehensiveness of his relations and capacities" (Gr, 162). This contradictory unity must, again, undergo "dissolution."

Once again, a solution is first offered in the claim that, stripped of its bourgeois form, wealth is only "the universality of individual needs, capacities, pleasures, productive forces etc., created through universal exchange . . . the absolute working out of his creative potentialities, with no presuppositions other than the previous historic development" (Gr, 488). But this resolution lacks mediation. The genesis of the primacy of the relations of production must be explained and its normative status clarified. Property, which was originally simply the expression of man's relation to nature as the objective form of his subjective existence, undergoes a *political* development that must be explained. Property, in other words, is not a natural given; property is posited in a political process. Marx reconstructs the process by which communal and collective forms of ownership typical of earlier societies gradually break down and the individual is liberated. The result of this process (whose details can be left aside here) is that the individual appears as that "free" worker who brings himself to the market as labor-power, the only commodity he owns. At this point, Marx forgets that the formally free worker is nonetheless in a different situation from the slave or serf. Instead of asking what can be done with this freedom, Marx transforms the political process into an economic logic whose "dissolution" he tries to interpret in economic terms. But the systematic nature of his construction, which satisfies the philosophical imperative posed at the outset of his path, suggests that the argument cannot be simply economic.

To be complete, the account of the necessary dissolution of capitalism must have four distinct moments corresponding to the genetic and normative expressions of use-value and exchange-value. From the side of capital, the demonstration must show that (1) capital develops use-values whose realization is blocked by its one-sided stress on exchange-value; and that (2) even on its own terms it produces economic crises caused by the pressure of competition that drives it to expand beyond its own limits. This dual contradiction must be accompanied on the side of labor by the demonstration that (3) within the alienation of capitalist production, "civilizing" processes produce a new wealth of needs and capacities that form the basis of a new form of social relations; and that (4) the labor theory of value is made obsolete by economic development itself such that alienated labor can no longer reproduce capitalist social relations. Enough has been said about the economic problems in capitalism's self-realization; while it will not break down on its own, the crises that plague its process of reproduction cannot be denied. The other three moments are developed in a brief but lucid—even prophetic—

account of fully realized capitalism at the beginning of notebook 7 of the *Grundrisse*. While its arguments explain Marx's expectation in *The Critique of the Gotha Program* that, in the second phase of communism, the "springs" of wealth will flow freely, they also suggest the need to reconstruct a normative notion of the political that can replace capitalism's apparent reduction of that domain to the economic sphere.

The complete development of capital takes the form of modern industry based on machinery. In these conditions, it is not the "direct skillfulness" of the worker but "the technological application of science" that is the crucial productive force. At first, this appears to produce a "monstrous disproportion between the labor time applied and [the value of] its product." And "the human being comes to relate more as watchman and regulator of the production process itself," inserting "the process of nature, transformed into an industrial process, as a means between himself and inorganic nature, mastering it." From the standpoint of exchange-value, the worker simply stands at the side of the process; he is present "by virtue of his presence as a social body" (Gr, 699). But this is where the process inverts itself. "It is, in a word, the development of the social individual which appears as the great foundation-stone of production and of wealth." And, Marx continues, *"the theft of alien labor time on which present wealth is based* is a miserable foundation in the face of this new one" (Gr, 705; Marx's emphasis). This account goes beyond the abstract individualist view of alienated labor formulated in 1844. Its economic premises have systematic philosophical consequences.

Beginning from the side of labor, the development of productivity by the application of science that makes nature work for man means that labor time ceases to be the measure of value. Production based on exchange-value breaks down of its own accord. The growth of the power of social production increases the disposable time available to society, which at first falls to the capitalists and their class. But as this disposable time grows, it becomes clear that "real wealth is the developed productive power of all individuals. *The measure of wealth is then not any longer, in any way, labor time, but rather disposable time*" (my emphasis). Capitalism thus contains a "moving contradiction" (Gr, 708) that leads it to reduce labor time to a minimum even while postulating labor time as the measure and source of wealth.

On the other hand, since work has become supervisory and regulatory, the worker recognizes that "the product ceases to be the product of isolated direct labor; rather it is the combination of social activity that appears as the producer" (Gr, 709). Individual labor has now become "civilized" as social labor—as producing not exchange-value but use-value. In addition, "free time—which is both idle time and time for higher activity—has naturally transformed its possessor into a different subject, and he then enters into the direct production process as this different subject" (Gr, 712).

As for capital, it seeks to limit the new human possibilities in accord with its own concept of wealth. Even if it succeeds, this will only lead to surplus production that cannot be sold, and necessary labor will be interrupted because the surplus labor already produced cannot be realized as capital.

On the other hand, capitalism's normative orientation to exchange-value may slow the development of new productive techniques because it refuses to admit the priority of "the free development of individualities" rather than "the reduction of necessary labor time so as to posit surplus labor"; as a result, it does not see that "the general reduction of the necessary labor of society to a minimum . . . then corresponds to the artistic, scientific etc. development of the individuals in the time set free, and with the means created, for all of them" (Gr, 706).

The four moments necessary to the transcendence of capitalism on its own basis are now present. What does this apparently economic account tell us about Marx's final vision?

The communist "world as philosophical" portrayed in *The Critique of the Gotha Program* was based on a postscarcity utopia whose economic possibility has now been made concrete. What will follow this self-dissolution of capitalism? Earlier in the *Grundrisse*, Marx criticized Adam Smith's conception of work as a curse and of tranquillity as happiness. "It seems quite far from Smith's mind that the individual, 'in his normal state of health, strength, activity, skill, facility,' also needs a normal portion of work, and of the suspension of tranquillity." Smith doesn't see what Marx had called in 1844 "the greatness of Hegel's phenomenology": that overcoming obstacles is a liberating activity and that external aims are "stripped of the semblance of merely external natural urgencies, and become posited as aims which the individual himself posits—hence as self-realization, objectification of the subject, hence real freedom, whose action is, precisely, labor." Marx's alternative vision is heroic but troubling. It implies that "labor which has not yet created the subjective and objective conditions for itself . . . in which labor becomes attractive work, the individual's self-realization," is unfree. Freedom is not "mere fun, mere amusement, as Fourier . . . conceives it." Truly free work, such as musical composition, is "at the same time precisely the most damned seriousness" (Gr, 611). Material productive work becomes free only "when its social character is posited," made explicit, and reproduced consciously and "when it is of a scientific and at the same time general character, not merely human exertion as a specifically harnessed natural force, but exertion as subject, which appears in the production process not in a merely natural, spontaneous form, but as an activity regulating all the forces of nature" (Gr, 612). This return to the vision of the third of the *Economic and Philosophical Manuscripts* is inconsistent with Marx's systematic critique of capitalism, which was based ultimately on capitalism's necessary failure to recognize itself as political because of the blinding effect of competition that makes each capitalist universalize his particular interest. Marx's postcapitalist "world as philosophical" appears to make a virtue out of that necessity, returning to the Young Hegelian premises from which he began. His goal seems in effect to be a direct or transparent democracy with no place for individual difference or particularity.

The source of the difficulty can be traced back to Marx's critique of the political illusion and the illusion of politics. The systematic argument for the dissolution of capitalism began from two mutually interdependent poles, capital and labor, each of which was itself marked by the duality of the commodity form. The use-value of capital produced conditions in which the basis of its existence as exchange-value (the labor theory of value) was negated; on the other hand, its orientation to exchange-value led to cyclical economic crises that threaten its social reproduction. Meanwhile, the exchange-value of labor-power was negated by the new working conditions (automated machinery, science) that at the same time created the free time and social working conditions in which human values replaced exchange-values as defining the condition of the worker. A similar dual contradiction of mutually interdependent poles and their self-dissolution can be seen retrospectively in the analyses of *Class Struggles in France* and *The 18th Brumaire* that led Marx to return to the study of political economy. The political state and the society were related in terms of political illusions and the illusion of politics; politics could not achieve the social revolution that was claimed to be nonetheless inevitable. But Marx did return to politics, both in *The Civil War in France* and in *The Critique of the Gotha Program*. Insofar as the Commune was not a direct democratic solution but rather provided only the framework in which class struggle could be waged, politics retained its autonomy. And insofar as *The Critique of the Gotha Program* admitted that even in a post-capitalist society individuals will not be all equal and problems of social distribution will remain, the political retains a normative role that provides the framework in which social relations can be generated and reproduced consciously.

Marx never thematized the place of the political in his mature theory. The present reconstruction of his path suggests that he passed from a critique of the separation of the political from society, to a social analysis that reduced the autonomy of the political, on to a political economic theory that replaced the political, and finally to a recognition that the absence of the political from the capitalist economy condemned that mode of social relations because it is unable to recognize its own presuppositions and therefore its own limits. The source of this uncertain quest for political understanding lies in the systematic project that has been shown to motivate Marx's theory. The philosophical moments of genesis and normativity and the methodological moments of phenomenology and logic are invoked in order to demonstrate the world's becoming philosophical *as* philosophy's becoming worldly. But this philosophical synthesis cannot be achieved; it is an idealism that ultimately denies to both philosophy and the world the autonomy that Marx's systematic quest shows each of them to need in order to play its critical role. The phenomenological cannot become identical to the logical; genesis and normativity must remain distinct if each is to retain its critical potential. But, as Marx saw in the second of the *Economic and Philosophical Manuscripts*, these two moments cannot remain indifferent to one another. For them to find an adequate relation, the *political* (which need not be identical with the state, as *Capital* makes clear) has to provide their shared ground and mediate between them. As a result, both moments are in a perpetual competition for the power to define the political.

This critical theory of politics is the result of a rereading of Marx's theoretical trajectory. Just as the problematic nature of democratic politics could only become clear after the experience of its radical negation—in the guise of a claim to be the realization of true democracy—by what can be called totalitarian idealism,[30] so too Marx's systematic and rigorous pursuit of an idealistic philosophy by other means was needed in order to recognize the political force of critical theory. This realization has a practical consequence as well, insofar as it permits recognition and critique of another form of idealism: the one confronting the post-1989 world that wants to replace political choice by submission to the "natural necessity" of the market. The economy is not neutral; social relations are not natural but historically produced; and whatever our vision of the good society, its justification can be in the end only political. As a "critique of political economy," *Capital* is not a guidebook to running a society; it is the demonstration of the political presuppositions that underlie economic choices. Marx does not and cannot provide a philosophical legitimation for political choices. What he does do is to demonstrate that the failure to think politically brings with it a form of alienation that, as in the logic of *Capital*, leaves the citizen in thrall to a society that, like it or not, is the product of his own activity.

# *Notes*

Unless otherwise specified, all translations are mine.

Introduction

1. Karl Marx and Friedrich Engels, *The Communist Manifesto*, with an introduction by A. J. P. Taylor (Harmondsworth: Penguin, 1967), pp. 82–83.

2. The role of the French intellectuals is important for my argument because, as is seen in part 2, French history illustrates one of the two basic types of democratic politics. When I turn to the work of the first generation of the Frankfurt School, it is to suggest one way in which a critical theory that starts from Marxist premises can lose sight of its original political goal (and become identified with a kind of cultural theory that, in the United States, is often identified as French). On the other hand, the recent work of Jürgen Habermas, representing the second generation, shows how those same concerns can develop toward a unique vision of what a chapter in his newest book (which I received too late to address in this text) calls a "democratic *Rechtsstaat*." See Jürgen Habermas, *Zeit der Übergänge* (Frankfurt: Suhrkamp, 2001).

3. Consistent with the theoretical goals of this book, I have eliminated most material that is either anecdotal or dated historically. The two experiences described here, as well as some brief introductory remarks to chapter 7's discussion of Castoriadis, are the exceptions that, I hope, justify the rule.

4. Of course, the real reason for the invasion had nothing to do with defending true socialism against a heretical Third Way; the invasion was an expression of the so-called Brezhnev doctrine, which insisted that no state could leave the Soviet bloc—recognizing that if one were permitted to deviate from Moscow's line, others would soon follow—as indeed they did in 1989.

5. See, for example, Marc Morjé Howard, *The Weakness of Civil Society in Post-Communist Europe* (Cambridge: Cambridge University Press, 2002).

6. The concept of the symbolic institution of society is developed particularly by Claude Lefort. It is explained in detail in chap. 8, "From the Critique of Totalitarianism to the Politics of Democracy." It should be noted that the distinction between symbolic and cultural meaning implies a distinction between the goals of political science and those of political theory. The political scientist assumes that he can stand above a given world and describe from without its structures and relations, as if meanings were always the same, never open to change. In this, the political scientist is making assumptions typical of a traditional rather than a modern democratic society.

7. Another way to explain this point is to distinguish between the political and politics. The political refers to the symbolic institution of meaning within which different issues gain (or lose) salience for practical politics. Transformations of the political make possible political change. How else can one understand the importance, for example, of feminism or the rights of various minorities (or indeed of rights themselves)? Issues that were not the concern of practical politics suddenly become fair game because of such changes.

8. I should stress that the category of antipolitics is not restricted to totalitarianism and that neither are the two identical. I have described elsewhere the history of what I call "two hundred years of error" that came to an end with the downfall of communism. The French Revolution of 1789 overthrew the old hierarchical and traditional society, liberating the individual and making possible democratic politics. But it produced as well conditions in which democracy became a threat to itself: individualism and the reign of private interest along with political instability and social inequality. For two centuries, appeals to an invisible hand, to a social plan—or to some variant of the two—competed in the *anti-political* quest for an end to democratic instability. See Dick Howard, "Rediscovering the Left," *Praxis International* 10, nos. 3–4 (October 1990–January 1991): 193–204.

9. This is the picture painted most memorably by Hannah Arendt's *On Revolution* (New York: Viking, 1963).

10. Chapter 9 suggests some reasons why, in contemporary conditions, these characteristics may be changing.

11. Many examples, from all periods of Marx's work, are offered in

chapter 13. From his doctoral dissertation, when he called on "philosophy [to become] worldly as the world [becomes] philosophical," to the eloquent insistence that "reason has always existed, but not always in a rational form," published in a letter to Ruge in the issue of the *Deutsch-Französische Jahrbücher* in which he announced the proletariat as the agent of revolution, down to the very project of *Capital* as an immanent critique of political economy, Marx's materialist rationalism is the red thread crossing through his work.

12. Need I stress that it is an achievement? This philosophical project is what separates Marx from even the most philosophical of his disciples—such as Lukács, whose *History and Class Consciousness* is no doubt the pinnacle of Marxist theorizing. The disciples had to reconstruct what they assumed to be a systematic philosophical project; Marx had to invent that project, through many false starts and misleading way stations, with no certainty that he would come to the end of the road.

13. See chapter 7 for Castoriadis's development of the implications of the Marxist imperative: no revolutionary practice without revolutionary theory.

14. See Dick Howard, "Quand l'Amérique rejoint tragiquement le monde," *Esprit* (October 2001): 8–14, published in German translation as "Krieg oder Politik?" *Kommune* 19, no. 10/01 (October 2001): 6–9.

## 1. Marxism in the Postcommunist World

1. For example, the belabored and ultimately inconsistent schemata that Marx uses to explain the circulation of capital in volume 2 of *Capital* seem to have dictated the choice of massive investment in heavy industry at the expense of consumer goods. Of course, there were nonideological reasons for the Soviet choices, but most of these too imitated earlier capitalist models of economic development. Rosa Luxemburg had warned of this difficulty before the Bolshevik seizure of power. In her *Accumulation of Capital* (1913) and more strongly in her posthumous reply to her critics in the *Antikritik* (1921), she insists that Marx's categories are not transhistorical; they apply only to the historically specific mode of production called capitalism.

2. The first sentence of Adorno's *Negative Dialectics* explains that philosophy remains radical in a reified capitalist society precisely because it is theory, while Marcuse's vision of a totally administered capitalist society leaves no place for any positive political agency that could be discovered by immanent critique; all that remains is the Great Refusal popularized in the 1960s in the old Frankfurt School adage: *Nicht mitmachen!* See chapter 3 for a further discussion of the Frankfurt School.

3. See John Lewis Gaddis, *We Now Know: Rethinking Cold War History* (New York: Oxford University Press, 1997) for a summary of recently available materials from former Soviet archives.

4. See the article-petition published under the ironic title "Le spectre du trotskisme," in *Le Monde*, June 21, 2001. The authors stress, "We were Trotskyists, some of us are still Trotskyists, and others could become Trotskyists." The occasion for this intervention was the admission by French prime minister Lionel Jospin that he had remained a Trotskyist not only after he joined the Socialist Party but after he became its first secretary and indeed a minister in the government of François Mitterrand. He apparently left the "Lambertist" branch of the Fourth International only in 1987. For details, *Le Monde*, June 6, 2001, which headlines "The Political Secret of Lionel Jospin," as well as see *Le Monde*, June 7, 2001, and the analysis of the varieties of French Trotskyism in *Le Monde*, June 13, 2001.

5. Trotsky's ability to understand the dynamics of revolutionary action is clear in his accounts of both the 1905 and the 1917 revolutions, in which he was a leading actor. This is what I refer to as his phenomenology. On the other hand, his structural dogmatism resulted in an inability to put into question the role of the Bolshevik party in supposedly making the revolution. As a result, as Claude Lefort shows, he could never understand Stalinism as other than the product of Stalin's petty personality. See Claude Lefort, "The Contradiction of Trotsky," in *The Political Forms of Modern Society* (Cambridge, Mass.: MIT Press, 1986). On Lefort, see chaps. 5, 6, and 8, below.

6. Rosa Luxemburg, *Selected Political Writings*, ed. and trans. Dick Howard (New York: Monthly Review Press, 1972), p. 369. It was the recognition of Luxemburg's contradictions after I had edited and translated this work that led me to the critical account that I presented in *The Marxian Legacy* (1977; 2d ed., Minneapolis: University of Minnesota Press, 1988), whose first chapter deals with both the continued attractiveness of Luxemburg and these internal contradictions.

7. In *Die nachholende Revolution* (Frankfurt: Suhrkamp, 1990). Habermas's arguments are discussed in chapter 4, below. The idea that the West, or western democracies, have nothing to learn from Eastern European and Soviet experience implies that more than seventy years of history in that part of the world can be written off as simply an unfortunate accident. It implies as well that there is no relation between Western democracy and the development of totalitarianism. I will return to this point below—indeed it is a theme that runs throughout this book.

8. There are other grounds for the turn to cultural studies, as I suggest in chapter 3.

9. I develop this argument in more detail in chap. 13, "Philosophy by Other Means?"

10. It is a sign of the consistency of Marx's philosophical concerns that he made a similar point more than thirty years later, in *The Critique of the Gotha Program* (1875), this time with regard to the difference between equal rights under capitalist conditions and the future equality that would be brought by communism. But, as will be seen in chapter 13, his self-understanding had matured in these thirty years.

11. In this sense, Marx is proposing what I will call in the final part of this chapter a political theory. It is an account of how individuals relate to one another and to their society as a whole. This is not always, however, Marx's own self-understanding; it was emphatically not that of Engels, who edited the second and third volumes of *Capital*, which may not follow the logic that Marx would finally have found. On the other hand, the passages from the *Grundrisse* (the unpublished thousand-page manuscript written in 1857) that I cite can be interpreted in a more political light; they do reflect Marx's own systematic conception.

12. The passages to which I am referring are from notebook 8 of the *Grundrisse* (New York: Vintage, 1973), esp. pp. 699–712. More detail is presented in chapter 13, below.

13. In Karl Marx, *The First International and After* (London: Penguin, 1992).

14. See Dick Howard, "Rediscovering the Left," *Praxis International* 10, nos. 3–4 (October 1990–January 1991): 193–204.

15. The ideas of responsibility and judgment as well as the previous suggestion that when theory claims to pierce beneath appearances it assumes a risk point to a significant political problem for democracies: the right to be wrong is the precondition of democratic choice. There are of course different types of error and different ways to assert this right. Further discussion of this matter recurs throughout this book, as well as in my two studies of political judgment: *Political Judgments* (Lanham, Md.: Rowman and Littlefield, 1996), and *Pour une critique du jugement politique* (Paris: Cerf, 1998).

16. Many have criticized Arendt for her faith in the emergence of revolutionary moments, particularly in *On Revolution* (New York: Viking, 1965). I will return to her analyses in the comparative discussion of the American and French Revolutions, and the democracies they created, in chapter 10.

17. This paradoxical circularity also means that democracy is necessarily incomplete. The attempt to realize democracy was the step that misled Marx and became one of the justifications of his totalitarian successors. The idea that the proletariat had only "its chains" to lose connects Marx to a predemocratic political (or romantic) ethos.

18. One cannot even appeal to a weaker form of historical logic, such

as the social-democratic progression sketched by T. H. Marshall as the progress from civil rights to political rights and finally to social rights. See the recent reprint of Marshall's *Citizenship and Social Class* (London: Pluto, 1992).

19. As did Georg Lukács, and the Frankfurt School after him. But in both cases the philosophical quest led them to misunderstand its political implications.

20. Karl Polanyi, *The Great Transformation: The Political and Economic Origins of Our Time* (1944; reprint, Boston: Beacon, 1957). As previously indicated, I am talking about politics in the classical sense, as the determination of the principles that govern a social order, that give meaning to the relations existing within it (for example, those of men and women, parents and children, the living and the dead), and that define in this way what the Greeks called a "political regime." Politics in this sense institutes a domain of symbolic meaning. Thus one might ask why the Greeks considered the *oikos* (household, or sphere of production) to be insignificant, leaving it to women and slaves, whereas modern capitalism privileges the economy as a domain of freedom (at least for some)?

21. *Democracy in America*, trans. George Lawrence (New York: Doubleday, Anchor, 1969), p. 243. Translation modified.

22. In this sense, as Castoriadis points out, political theory can be said to be "materialist" because it defines "what matters" (*ce qui matière*) in a given society at a particular moment. Castoriadis's wordplay is found in "La question de l'histoire du mouvement ouvrier," in *L'expérience du mouvement ouvrier* (Paris: UGE, 1974), 1:63. On Castoriadis, see chapter 7.

23. Recall the earlier citation from *The Critique of the Gotha Program*, which can be considered to be Marx's other or more mature *Manifesto*. Marx criticized Lassalle's economism by pointing to the slave who criticizes slavery because wages will never exceed a fixed minimum. That is economism, implies Marx; the issue is freedom, which is political.

## 2. CAN FRENCH INTELLECTUALS ESCAPE MARXISM?

1. When I label people "Communist," I am not referring to their programmatic or policy choices but rather to a more general political attitude that colors the way they give meaning to their world. Readers too often neglect the third section of the *Manifesto*, which describes "Socialist and Communist Literature" in a dialectical progression whose culmination is of course Marx's own position. This then leads to the short final section that describes the "Position of the Communists in Relation to the Various Existing Opposition Parties." Communists are said not only to support "the attainment of the immediate aims . . . of the working class," but, more

important, to "represent the future of that movement." Therefore they "support every revolutionary movement against the existing social and political order of things," including "the democratic parties of all countries," who are seen as participating in "the forcible overthrow of all existing social conditions." Just as communism will overcome all opposition within society, so the Communists and their theory represent the truth that unifies all oppositional standpoints. An analysis of the historical reasons that made Marxism so influential in France is found in chap. 9, "The Burden of French History."

2. See Dick Howard, *Pour une critique du jugement politique* (Paris: Cerf, 1998); and idem, *Political Judgments* (Lanham, Md.: Rowman and Littlefield, 1996).

3. François Furet, *Le passé d'une illusion* (Paris: Calmann-Lévy, 1995).

4. One should, however, note the attempt of the pseudonymous Épistémon [Didier Anzieu] to show, in *Ces idées qui ébranlèrent la France* (Paris: Fayard, 1968), that May '68 was its translation into action. See my discussion of Sartre's contribution in *The Marxian Legacy*, 2d ed. (Minneapolis: University of Minnesota Press, 1988).

5. I refer of course to his essay on the Revolution of 1848, *Class Struggles in France*; his analysis of the seizure of power by Louis Napoleon Bonaparte, *The 18th Brumaire*; and his glorification of the struggle of the Paris Commune in *The Civil War in France*.

6. Lefort's essay "Rereading *The Communist Manifesto*" was originally published in François Chatelet, Evelyne Pisier, and Olivier Duhamel, eds., *Dictionnaire des oeuvres politiques* (Paris: PUF, 1986). The English translation is found in Claude Lefort, *Democracy and Political Theory*, trans. David Macey (Minneapolis: University of Minnesota Press, 1988).

7. The results of this interest politics are cheapened because the rewards offered are generally more symbolic than materially real. (It should be noted that the use of the term "symbolic" here refers to something that is real and is won but whose value is only symbolic, acquiring its meaning from the political way in which meanings are instituted in a given society. This political function of giving meaning is referred to often in the following chapters as "the symbolic.")

8. See my essay "The French Strikes of 1995 and Their Political Aftermath," *Government and Opposition* 33, no. 2 (spring 1998): 199–220. An earlier version appeared in "The French Strikes of 1995," *Constellations* 3, no. 2 (October 1996): 248–260. The essay explains the different positions taken by the groups associated with Bourdieu, on the one hand, and the journal *Esprit*, on the other.

9. See Reinhart Koselleck, *Kritik und Krise* (Frankfurt am Main: Suhrkamp, 1973); and François Furet, *Penser la Révolution française* (Paris:

Gallimard, 1978). Further discussion of this point is found in my essay "The Origin of Revolution," in Dick Howard, *The Politics of Critique* (Minneapolis: University of Minnesota Press, 1988).

10. The English translation of this essay, which was first published in the *Revue bleue* in 1889, can be found in *Emile Durkheim on Morality and Society*, ed. Robert N. Bellah (Chicago: University of Chicago Press, 1973), pp. 43–57. All quotations in the text are from this translation.

11. The argument sketched here is developed by means of a contrast to the "methodological individualism" of Max Weber in Dick Howard, "Individu et société," in Christian Delacampagne and Robert Maggieri, eds. *Philosopher 2* (Paris: Fayard, 2000), pp. 419–432.

12. See "L'idée française de la révolution," *Le Débat*, September–October 1997. I quote passages from pp. 25, 28, 28, 29, and 30, respectively in this discussion. The citations from Furet at the beginning of thesis 9 are from pp. 30 and 29.

13. Furet's critique of the "edifying" discourse concerning the French Revolution is formulated in his critique of the Marxist interpretations in the first chapter of *Penser la révolution française*. See my discussion in Howard, "The Origin of Revolution."

14. The essay was published in the August–September 1997 issue of *Esprit*, on pp. 131–151. The citation is from p. 146.

15. This distinction also alludes to the subtitle of Claude Lefort's remarkable analysis of Machiavelli, *Le travail de l'oeuvre* (Paris: Gallimard, 1972).

16. Since most French intellectuals had been schooled in the theories of critical doubt begun by Marx, pursued by Nietzsche, and brought to a peak with Freud—and Jacques Lacan, the Parisian master awaiting his Thomas Mann—there is a strong tendency to speak the language of Lacanian psychoanalysis, with its distinction of the imaginary, the symbolic, and the real. The symbolic in this context expresses what classical political philosophy designates by the idea of a political regime. It marks the moment when the individual subject separates from the immediacy of the infant's relation to the world and learns how meaning is attributed to things and relations.

### 3. THE FRANKFURT SCHOOL AND THE TRANSFORMATION OF CRITICAL THEORY INTO CULTURAL THEORY

1. Published in 1937, in the exiled *Zeitschrift für Sozialforschung*, these essays became available in Germany in the 1960s only in pirate editions easily found in radical bookstores. They were soon translated into English. See Max Horkheimer, "Traditional and Critical Theory," as well as "Postscript"

in *Critical Theory* (New York: Herder and Herder, 1972); and Herbert Marcuse, "Philosophy and Critical Theory," in *Negations: Essays in Critical Theory* (Boston: Beacon, 1968). Marcuse was not shy about his past work; Horkheimer was. It was only the existence of the pirate editions that led him to republish (some) of his early work.

2. This is from the first sentence of Kant's "What is Enlightenment?" in *Kant's Political Writings*, ed. Hans Reuss (Cambridge: Cambridge University Press, 1970), p. 65. The italics are mine.

3. This sentence appears in the introduction, under the heading "The Possibility of Philosophy," in T. W. Adorno, *Negative Dialectics*, trans. E. B. Ashton (New York: Seabury, 1973), p. 3.

4. The dislikes in question concern particularly American jazz. I should stress that I am not claiming that there is a direct line of filiation linking the Frankfurt School to the kinds of literary and cultural theory that are identified in the university today as critical theory. My concern here is with the suggestive similarities of the two—and their inability to deal with politics. The fact that many of today's cultural critical theorists appeal to Adorno (but not to Horkheimer or to the Frankfurt School) seems to me to be merely coincidental. Moreover, the other member of the Frankfurt School who wrote extensively on aesthetics, Herbert Marcuse, is more nuanced (or less consistent) politically than Adorno. Although he sometimes wanted art to take to the street and lose its aesthetic form, Marcuse titled his final work *Die Permanenz der Kunst* ("The Permanence of Art," though its title in English translation is *The Aesthetic Dimension*). For a discussion and analysis of Marcuse's oscillating aesthetic theory and its political implications, see Dick Howard, "Out of the Silent 50's," *Defining the Political* (Minneapolis: University of Minnesota Press, 1989), pp. 21–30.

5. A full-scale reconsideration of the vogue enjoyed by the politics of theory would have to take into account its French variants (which often build on Gramsci's concept of hegemony), starting no doubt with Louis Althusser's employment of the term in his February 1968 lecture "Lenin and Philosophy," published as Louis Althusser, *Lénine et la philosophie* (Paris: Maspero, 1969). See chap. 2, "Can French Intellectuals Escape Marxism?" The final thesis, which suggests they have tried too hard to change the world, whereas the point rather is to understand it, is congruent with the critique of a politics of theory here.

6. I suggested this point in the first edition of *The Marxian Legacy* (Minneapolis: University of Minnesota Press, 1977), and amplified it in the second (1988). See in particular the chapter dealing with Horkheimer, as well as the afterword to the second edition.

7. Rolf Wiggershaus's meticulous social history was published in German in 1986; its English translation appeared in 1993, at a time when

another "post" led to a more critical approach to the old theory: the challenge of postcommunism. See *The Frankfurt School: Its History, Theories, and Political Significance*, trans. Michael Robertson (Cambridge, Mass.: MIT Press, 1993).

8. Cited from Rolf Wiggershaus, *The Frankfurt School*, p. 127. The parallel to the above citation from Adorno's *Negative Dialectics*, published more than thirty years later, in 1966, is a sign of a continuity that some would deny.

9. One of Horkheimer's most famous remarks was the lapidary observation that "the pill" killed love. Here, one is tempted to see the romantic heritage of critical theory. But before condemning new reactionaries, it should be noted that the rebellious offspring of critical theory were not innocent of all charges; even Jürgen Habermas was driven at one point to attack what he called their tendency toward a "left-wing fascism." See n. 18, below.

10. Wiggershaus, *The Frankfurt School*, pp. 536, 537. Translation slightly modified.

11. Ibid., p. 537.

12. The issues raised here, and their theoretical roots, are nicely dealt with in William E. Scheuerman, *Between the Norm and the Exception: The Frankfurt School and the Rule of Law* (Cambridge, Mass.: MIT Press, 1994).

13. Wiggershaus, op. cit., p. 320.

14. This essay is discussed at some length in the chapter treating Horkheimer (without Adorno) in *The Marxian Legacy*. It marks the high point, and a turning point, in Horkheimer's work far more than does the better-known collaborative essay he wrote with Adorno during his California exile, *The Dialectic of Enlightenment*. The critique of the two totalitarianisms leaves unquestioned the place of capitalism in Horkheimer's analysis; it seems to disqualify the sphere of politics rather than, as it might have, calling into question the relation between the socioeconomic infrastructure and the cultural or ideological superstructure that is said to depend on it.

15. The concept of a politics of critique is rendered ambiguous by the genitive, which could suggest that it is the critique that is political (or replaces the political, as I am claiming here) or that there is a critical politics that has its own specific structures and imperatives (as I try to suggest in my book of the same title). This is not the place for a discussion of the latter usage.

16. Helmut Dubiel, *Wissenschaftsorganisation und politische Erfahrung: Studien zur frühen Kritischen Theorie* (Frankfurt am Main: Suhrkamp, 1978). The English translation, by Benjamin Gregg, was published as *Theory and Politics: Studies in the Development of Critical Theory* (Cambridge, Mass.: MIT Press, 1985).

17. Wiggershaus's account of the kind of research undertaken by the Institute for Social Research after its return to Germany is surprising to Frankfurt hero-worshipers. This bread-and-butter work was at first carried out in connection with the trade union movement but soon lost even this political justification. Questions of theory disappeared from the Frankfurters' concern—with the exception of several doctoral dissertations (including those of Oskar Negt, Rolf Tiedemann, and Alfred Schmidt) published in the short-lived book series that the Institute edited. In its place came practical field research that Wiggershaus describes under the title "Farewell to independence: research in Mannesmann factories." In effect, the research seems unambiguously to have taken the side of management. Although Adorno continued the theoretical work of negativity, Wiggershaus recounts the now well known story that all the old copies of the *Zeitschrift für Sozialforschung* were kept locked away in the basement of the institute's Frankfurt offices, as if to lock away the political concerns that underlay the radical theoretical stance of the founders. This explains why the new left first encountered most of these texts in pirate editions, including the eight volumes of the entire life of the *Zeitschrift*, whose last year's issues appeared in English.

18. Habermas, even then, was hardly a hard-line leftist. He attacked the illusions of the student left at a congress of the SDS in 1968, publishing his theses under the heading "Die Scheinrevolution und ihre Kinder," which provoked an immediate counterattack in him in the book *Die Linke antwortet Jürgen Habermas* (Frankfurt: Europäische Verlagsanstalt, 1968). That Habermas would later develop his own version of a critical theory that has culminated in the formulation of a radical theory of democracy could of course not have been treated in Wiggershaus's 1986 book. See chapter 4, below, for a discussion of Habermas's more recent work.

19. Max Horkheimer, *Eclipse of Reason* (New York: Oxford University Press, 1934; Reprint, New York: Seabury, 1974, p. vi.

20. Marx makes this point in the "Exchange of Letters" with Ruge, Bakunin, and Feuerbach, originally published in the *Deutsch-Französische Jahrbücher* and reprinted in Karl Marx, *Frühe Schriften I*, ed. H-J Lieber and Peter Furth (Stuttgart: Cotta, 1962), p. 448.

21. See Marx, *Frühe Schriften I*, p. 104.

## 4. HABERMAS'S REORIENTATION OF CRITICAL THEORY TOWARD DEMOCRATIC THEORY

1. Published in Cambridge, Mass., by the MIT Press in 1989.

2. The work published under this title by the Beacon Press in Boston in 1973 is an abridged version of the German original. It excludes particularly the more philosophical discussion of Marxism.

3. "Zur philosophischen Diskussion um Marx und den Marxismus," *Theorie und Praxis: Sozialphilosophische Studien* (Neuwied: Luchterhand, 1963), pp. 261–335.

4. The controversy is documented in *Die Linke antwortet Jürgen Habermas* (Frankfurt: Europäische Verlagsanstalt, 1968). There is no editor of this volume; "the left" that is answering Habermas takes itself as a collective subject—as Habermas no doubt feared.

5. Published in Boston by the Beacon Press in 1971.

6. Published by the Beacon Press in 1975.

7. Published in two volumes by the Beacon Press in 1984 and 1987.

8. Published by the MIT Press in 1996.

9. Martin Jay's *The Dialectical Imagination* (Boston: Little Brown, 1973), which was the first to treat the school as a whole, did discuss both Neumann and Kirchheimer. His study, however, considers only the period 1923–1950. It was not until 1994 that a full-length theoretical analysis of their contribution was proposed by William E. Scheuerman, in *Between the Norm and the Exception: The Frankfurt School and the Rule of Law* (Cambridge, Mass.: MIT Press, 1994). See also the collection of their works edited by Scheuerman, *The Rule of Law Under Siege* (Berkeley: University of California Press, 1995).

10. Frankfurt: Suhrkamp, 1990.

11. This second appendix, titled "Popular Sovereignty as Procedure," was originally a lecture published in a volume titled *Die Ideen von 1789 in der deutschen Rezeption*, ed. Forum für Philosophie Bad Homburg (n.p., 1989).

12. The interview was published in *Die Zeit*, no. 53 (1993). It is cited in a recent article by Dany Cohn-Bendit, who plays on the famous phrase of Horkheimer in his title, "Wer vom Totalitarismus schweigt, sollte auch nicht über die Freiheit reden," *Kommune* 19, no. 3/01 (March 2001): 6–10. (Horkheimer's phrase, written at the outset of the war, was "He who refuses to speak of capitalism, should say nothing of Fascism." It appeared in "Die Juden und Europe," *Zeitschrift für Sozialforschung* 8 [1939–1940]: 115.)

13. This suggestion is most clear in chap. 9, "The Burdens of French History," which traces the difficult emergence of the autonomy of the law and its impact on the practice of democracy in contemporary France.

14. In the French way of dealing with such issues, these norms would be called symbolic: they institute the meanings that we collectively attach to the sounds that we utter, and they socialize us to recognize that the world is not composed simply of neutral and self-identical or objective facts that present themselves to a neutral or disincarnated consciousness.

15. The "proceduralist paradigm" may confuse the Anglo-Saxon reader, for whom proceduralism refers to a strictly neutral, value-free

jurisprudence. As Kenneth Baynes has pointed out, Habermas makes explicit on his concluding page what is clear to the careful reader throughout: for him, autonomy is the value underlying his proceduralism. See Kenneth Baynes, *Democracy and the Rechtsstaat*, in *The Cambridge Companion to Habermas*, ed. Stephen White (New York: Cambridge University Press, 1995), pp. 201–231.

16. See the preceding note, concerning Habermas's notion of proceduralism, the problem of neutrality, and the value assumption that Habermas makes concerning autonomy. He would of course claim that autonomy is necessary in order for the democratic processes he is describing in *Between Facts and Norms* to function fully.

17. Habermas indicates his debt to Ingeborg Maus, whose acute critique of Carl Schmitt (and his left-wing admirers) is also developed in her brilliant reading of Kant as a theorist of radical democracy in *Zur Aufklärung der Demokratietheorie* (Frankfurt: Suhrkamp, 1992). I have discussed Maus's contribution in the article "Just Democracy," *Constellations* 2, no. 3 (January 1996): 333–353.

18. "Reply to Symposium Participants," *Cardozo Law Review* 17, nos. 4–5 (March 1996): 1545.

19. The only Frenchman truly to engage Habermas at this level has been André Gorz (an Austrian by birth). I should thank him here for years of critical correspondence on these matters, which are sedimented in this chapter as elsewhere. As he once dedicated an essay on these matters to me, I should like to do the same with this chapter.

## 5. The Anticommunist Marxism of *Socialisme ou Barbarie*

1. Lefort and Castoriadis are discussed elsewhere in this book (see chaps. 6 and 7). Lyotard joined the group in the mid-1950s; his experience teaching in North Africa led to his assuming responsibility for much of the journal's analysis of France's long colonial war against Algerian independence. The journal supported the independence movement, without, however, giving in to the apocalyptic hopes of many French leftists that an Algerian victory would bring socialism to the former colony and even inaugurate a revolutionary process in France. Castoriadis claims that it was Lyotard who was most resistant to the need to break with Marxism in order to remain on the side of revolution (as presented in Castoriadis's long article series in the last issues of the journal, under the title "Marxisme et théorie révolutionnaire," which is reprinted as the first part of *The Imaginary Institution of Society*, trans. Kathleen Blamey [London: Polity, 1987]). If that is the case, Lyotard's development in the ensuing years demonstrated his capacity to learn from experience.

Daniel Mothé (a pseudonym) was the "worker" among the journal's contributors; he was employed at the Renault factory at Billancourt (the famous center of communist militancy) until he was forced to retire because of an on-the-job injury in the 1970s. During the May '68 uprising, he tried to bring together young workers with students occupying the university (including a visit to an "Action Committee" of young Americans of which I was a founder). The work that he published in the journal gave rise to two books: *Journal d'un ouvrier* (1958) and *Militant chez Renault* (1965). While following a new career as a sociological researcher, he has continued to publish political analyses under the name Mothé, particularly in *Esprit*, while publishing his sociological work under his given name, Jacques Gautrat.

2. The theory of bureaucratic state capitalism started from the premise that the Bolshevik Party had to do in Russia what the indigenous capitalist class had been unable to do: industrialize the country and bring it into modernity. This would in turn prepare the conditions for proletarian revolution (and create a proletariat in a largely agricultural and backward land). There are many difficulties with this theory, as the journal's authors came to recognize over time. Among the most important are that capitalism supposes the existence of a market society and free laborers whose juridical and personal freedom is the only good they have to sell in it. The "dictatorship of the proletariat" created neither a free market nor free laborers.

3. This is exactly the way Marx reasoned in both his analyses of Bonaparte's seizure of power after the failed 1848 revolution in France. See note 4 in chapter 6 and especially chapter 13, below.

4. Paris: Galilée, 1989.

5. Published in *Esprit*, February 1998.


## 6. Claude Lefort's Passage from Revolutionary Theory to Political Theory

1. The text of the *laudatio* can be found in *Festschrift zur Verleihung des Hannah-Arendt-Preises für politisches Denken, 1998* (Bremen: Heinrich Böll Stiftung, 1999). Unfortunately I never saw the page proofs of the text, and the printed version has numerous unfortunate errors.

2. I should stress that to say democracy poses problems is not to say that it doesn't also solve others and it is emphatically not to oppose to it some better or more stable form of political life.

3. See "La résurrection de Trotsky?" reprinted in Claude Lefort, *Eléments d'une critique de la bureaucratie* (Geneva: Droz, 1971).

4. This is of course the same argument that Marx suggested in *The 18th Brumaire*. The confiscation of the revolutionary activity by a bourgeois

government is a negation of workers self-activity that results from their lack of self-conscious initiative; when they recognize and in turn negate that negation, their activity then becomes self-consciously revolutionary. Cf. chapter 13.

5. See chapter 5 for a discussion of *Socialisme ou Barbarie*.

6. Claude Lefort, "Organisation et parti," *Socialisme ou Barbarie*, no. 26 (1958).

7. Claude Lefort, "Qu'est-ce que la bureaucratie?" in *Eléments d'une critique de la bureaucratie* (Geneva: Droz, 1971).

8. Lefort is a remarkable reader of philosophers and philosophy, for reasons that I will suggest in a moment. It is worth noting here that he returns frequently also to Machiavelli, Michelet, Tocqueville, and Guizot.

9. Claude Lefort, *Les formes de l'histoire: Essais d'anthropologie politique* (Paris: Gallimard, 1978).

10. I discuss Lefort's concept of ideology in more detail in chap. 8, "From the Critique of Totalitarianism to the Politics of Democracy."

11. Claude Lefort, *Le travail de l'oeuvre: Machiavel* (Paris: Gallimard, 1972), p. 776.

12. Edgar Morin, Claude Lefort, and Jean-Marc Coudray (a.k.a. Cornelius Castoriadis), *Mai 1968: La brèche. Premières réflexions sur les événements* (Paris: Fayard, 1968).

13. Lefort's article began with an expression of relief: "We are a small number who have been waiting for such a book for a long time, a book telling what it is like in the Soviet prisons and labor camps, telling of the terror that not only in times of danger but continuously accompanied and reinforced the edification of the bureaucratic regime in the USSR." His next paragraph then asked "Why were we waiting for it?" And although he recalls his earlier critique of totalitarianism, *Un homme en trop* further develops that critique by integrating it into the democratic political theory that would remain his central concern. In this sense, Lefort was "waiting" for an occasion to develop further his own theory.

14. Lefort was also involved in the debates within and around the diverse psychoanalytic groups that, in the wake of Lacan's break with Freudian orthodoxy and the schisms among Lacan's followers, were particularly rich during this period. Some of his important essays, such as "The Image of the Body and Totalitarianism," were originally lectures to these groups before being published in their journals.

15. This terminology is of course also indebted to Lacanian psychoanalysis, which distinguishes among the symbolic, the imaginary, and the real.

16. It should be noted that Habermas refers to this transcendent symbolic institution of society as metaphysical thought that must be overcome

by postmetaphysical theory. See the brief discussion of this point in chapter 4.

17. This implies that religion is not a form of ideology. One should recall that when the young Marx criticizes religious alienation, especially in "Toward a Critique of Hegel's *Philosophy of Right*. Introduction," he sees that religion is *also* a struggle against demeaning social relations. Cf. chapter 13.

18. In Claude Lefort, *L'invention démocratique* (Paris: Fayard, 1981). Lefort is referring to the 1978 alliance between the Socialist and Communist Parties, which were to run in the parliamentary elections on the basis of the Common Program. When it became clear to the Communists that this would not work to their advantage (despite the high figures that the polls were registering), the party raised absurd demands that were clearly aimed at breaking the alliance. Of course, the 1981 victory of François Mitterrand that reactivated that alliance (and much of its program) showed that the Communists were right to worry. However, one should not blame the subsequent loss of Communist influence on this alliance with the Socialists; its causes run deeper, as I suggest in my discussion of French political culture, especially in chap. 9, "The Burden of French History."

19. Such a claim would itself be ideological, naturalizing the indeterminacy typical of democracy. This remark is important for understanding the present situation in the former Soviet bloc.

20. Lefort has returned once again to the question of totalitarianism in *La complication: Retour sur le communisme* (Paris: Fayard, 1999). I discuss this volume briefly in chap. 8, "From the Critique of Totalitarianism to the Politics of Democracy." Its title suggests another formulation of the structure of democratic indetermination: it proposes that the reduction of totalitarianism to an "illusion" (Furet) or an "*idéocratie*" (Malia) oversimplifies; the philosophical analysis of the political institution of society to which Lefort was led by his critique of totalitarianism cannot neglect the actual power politics that are also involved. That may be why Lefort's subtitle refers to communism rather than to totalitarianism.

21. Volume 2, for example, points out that the original condition of the Americans was not only that of material equality but characterized by the fact that the original settlers had fled the old world in a quest for religious liberty—such that the desire for liberty can be said to be generative also.

22. This lecture was part of the program organized in 1982–1983 by the Center for the Philosophical Study of the Political, directed by Jean-Luc Nancy and Philippe Lacoue-Labarthe; it is published in Philippe Lacoue-Labarthe and Jean-Luc Nancy, eds., *Le retrait du politique* (Paris: Galilée, 1983), pp. 71–88. On this center, see my discussion "The Origin

and Limits of Philosophical Politics," in Dick Howard, *The Politics of Critique* (Minneapolis: University of Minnesota Press, 1988).

23. Alain Montefiore, ed., *Philosophy in France Today* (Cambridge: Cambridge University Press, 1983).

24. Both essays are reprinted in Claude Lefort, *Essais sur le politique: XIXe–XXe siècles* (Paris: Seuil, 1986); the first was originally published in *Libre* in 1978, the second in *Passé-Présent* in 1982. Lefort does not explain why he placed the second before the first in *Essais*.

## 7. From Marx to Castoriadis, and from Castoriadis to Us

1. I purchased my first copies of Marx's *Capital*, as well as the three volumes of Lenin's *Selected Works*, in the edition of Progress Publishers, Moscow, in 1965; they were not yet easily available in U.S. editions. I found them not in bookstores but in the trunk of the car of the San Antonio Communist Party member who came weekly to peddle his wares on the campus of the University of Texas at Austin. This is of course not an endorsement of the Communist Party's openness; the manuscripts of the young Marx that explore such "bourgeois" themes as alienation were translated late and reluctantly by the party (in the German edition, they appeared as supplementary volumes to the forty-volume edition of the *Complete Works*). Louis Althusser's immensely popular philosophical claim that there was an "epistemological rupture" between the humanist theory of the young Marx and the scientific discoveries made by the mature Marx were published at the same time. See Louis Althusser, *Pour Marx* (Paris: Maspero, 1965); and Louis Althusser, Jacques Rancière, and Pierre Machery, *Lire le Capital*, 2 vols. (Paris, Maspero, 1965).

2. Published in New York by Basic Books in 1972.

3. Neither of them had time to write the chapter, and the person they asked to do so did not deliver. Lefort was finishing his massive study *Le travail de l'oeuvre: Machiavel* (Paris: Gallimard, 1972) and preparing the publication of a first collection of his essays, *Eléments d'une critique de la bureaucratie* (Geneva: Droz, 1971); Castoriadis was completing the second part of *L'institution imaginaire de la société* (Paris: Seuil, 1975) and preparing the publication of his collected essays, which would begin to appear in 1974.

4. Herbert Marcuse's *One-Dimensional Man*, published in 1964, had already made suggestive references to Husserl; Marcuse had studied with Husserl's successor, Heidegger, whose abstract theorizing he rejected in favor of the more concrete Marxist concept of alienated labor. Marcuse's personal influence on the editors of *Telos* was important, and many of his earlier essays from his Frankfurt School days were translated in the journal,

306 | 7. From Marx to Castoriadis to Us

providing philosophical substance to his growing public image as a guru for the new political left.

5. They were published with my introductions (which had been subjected to what the journal's chief editor called "constitutive editing"), which later were republished in modified form in *The Marxian Legacy*, most of whose chapters had their origin in work done for *Telos*.

6. Originally published in *Textures*, nos. 12–13 (1975).

7. It is really a turn to the Greeks, who had not played a significant role during Castoriadis's earlier development but would become increasingly important for him. There is not room in this chapter to do more than call attention to these later essays that look increasingly to Greek democracy as a model of the autonomy central to his concerns. That the Greeks invented simultaneously not just philosophy and democracy but also tragedy (whose role—for example, in *Antigone*—is to warn against the hubris that threatens autonomy) is not only a historical demonstration of Castoriadis's theses (recalling Marx's wager on history) but also a sign that history follows no linear or progressive path (rejecting the metaphysics that underlies Marx's wager).

8. The details of this claim, and the notions of a phenomenological and logical moment to the analysis, are elaborated in the discussion of Marx's theory in the final chapter of this book.

9. Castoriadis, *L'institution imaginaire de la société*, p. 157.

## 8. From the Critique of Totalitarianism to the Politics of Democracy

1. The term appears to have been used already in 1923 by anti-Fascists; Mussolini laid claim to it in 1925, when he ascribed to his new regime a "fierce totalitarian will" and then, a few months later, defined his goal in a famous aphorism: "Everything in the State, nothing outside of the State, nothing against the State." For details, see Enzo Traverso's useful introduction to the well-selected anthology *Le totalitarisme: Le XXe siècle en débat* (Paris: Seuil, 2001), pp. 19–20. Traverso suggests that the first appearances of the concept were during World War I, which was seen as the first "total war."

2. I argue this point from a different perspective in chap. 9, "The Burden of French History," where the new independence of the judiciary is seen as legitimating the idea of a plurality of interests, which in turn challenges the unitary French vision of their political republic. In the present context, the modern legitimacy of interest derives from its contrast to premodern societies in which the individual is subordinated to the community.

3. There are of course cases where totalitarianism has been imposed by

force, for example, in postwar Eastern Europe. But even in those cases, if the regime is to be established, it must find some witting collaborators, or it quickly becomes simply a dictatorship. The normative claim and the political reality have to have an overlapping structure from the standpoint of the participant.

4. Rosenberg's aphorism is cited by Claude Lefort in a lecture that he, as a prior recipient of the Hannah Arendt Prize of the City-State of Bremen, gave in honor of Helena Bonner, the winner of the prize in 2000. Lefort's lecture (in German translation) was published as "Die Weigerung, den Totalitarismus zu denken," *Kommune* 19, no. 5/01 (May 2001): viii–xiv.

5. I will not present Lefort's philosophical development as if it were somehow part of a necessary or logical path or as if it somehow resulted from a sudden lucidity that, finally, permitted him to gain a knowledge of the truth. Rather, I use Lefort in order to explain why the critique of totalitarianism remains necessary for anyone who wants to be involved with political theory today. Thus I do not propose a complete reading of Lefort's work here; I rather use him for my own goals. I do hope, however, that the reader will want to return to Lefort's work, whose philosophical and political implications do not cease to intrigue me each time I review them anew. I should note that I have reconstructed the earlier evolution of Lefort's work in *The Marxian Legacy*, 2d ed. (Minneapolis: University of Minnesota Press, 1988).

6. See William David Jones, *The Lost Debate: German Socialist Intellectuals and Totalitarianism* (Urbana and Chicago: University of Illinois Press, 1999).

7. See chapter 3, which discusses the transformation of Marxist critical theory into critical cultural (or literary) theory. A sad legacy of Horkheimer and Adorno's totalizing "dialectic of enlightenment" was the remark of Roland Barthes (in his inaugural lecture at the Collège de France) that all language is totalitarian. On the other hand, Michel Foucault never expressed publicly his obvious debt to the same source.

8. See Carl J. Friedrich and Zbigniew K. Brzezinski, *Totalitarian Dictatorship and Autocracy* (Cambridge: Harvard University Press, 1956). It is true that this definition is static and structural, and it was seriously challenged empirically by the beginning of de-Stalinization in the Soviet Union. But the process of de-Stalinization could also give rise to the impression that the communist system would "converge" with the political life of the Western democracies, giving rise to a world composed of similar "industrial societies." This latter thesis, like the totalitarianism thesis of the social scientists, ignores the dynamics of political experience. As a result, not only is the understanding of totalitarianism oversimplified; so too is the understanding of democratic politics, as I shall show.

9. On the Congress for Cultural Freedom, see my essay, written while writing the first draft of the present book, "L'anti-totalitarisme hier, aujour-d'hui et demain," *Critique*, no. 647 (April 2001): 259–278. An enlarged English version appears in *Government and Opposition*, summer 2002.

10. The term "slippages" (*dérapages*) was used in the pathbreaking work of François Furet and Denis Richet, *La Révolution française* (Paris: Hachette, 1965), which marked the first serious break with what Furet was to denounce later as "the [Marxist] revolutionary catechism" in what became the first chapter of his *Penser la révolution française*. "Slippages" was of course a lame way of expressing the fact that the political course of the revolution could not be determined simply by its material infrastructural necessities. In a sense, the rich work of Furet in the succeeding years, down to his *Le passé d'une illusion*, was an attempt to understand more precisely the status of these political "slippages."

11. It should be recalled that Lefort was Merleau-Ponty's student and his posthumous editor; he has returned constantly to that of Merleau-Ponty's work, as one sees in his collection *Sur une colonne absente: Ecrits autour de Merleau-Ponty* (Paris: Gallimard, 1978). Lefort saw quite early the difference between the existential phenomenology of Sartre and that of Merleau-Ponty; his polemic's with Sartre in the early 1950s in *Les Temps Modernes* turned around the difference between his analysis of the "experience" of the proletariat, which stood richly in contrast to Sartre's paradoxical insistence on the "idea" of the proletariat, and its incarnation in the Communist Party. For details, and the critique of Sartre's positivism, see Howard, *The Marxian Legacy*.

12. One cannot always rely on good instincts. The other popular anti-totalitarian critique from the 1970s was that of Michel Foucault. Trying to elaborate a new conception of the intellectual, Foucault's activity with regard to prison reform set one parameter, while his more general critique of repressive society took a very different form, one that lent itself to the transformation of critical theory to cultural theory. And of course Foucault's instincts could mislead him, as with his early support not just for the movement against the shah of Iran but specifically for the ayatollahs of Khomeini.

13. This thumbnail sketch, whose methodological implication I will draw in a moment, leaves out the role of those associated with the monthly journal *Esprit*. That is in part because *Esprit* was one of the places where Lefort published and developed his analysis. Nonetheless, any larger historical picture of French antitotalitarian criticism should not ignore *Esprit*. I discussed its history and general orientation in chapter 8 (pp. 135–149) of *Defining the Political* (Minneapolis: University of Minnesota Press, 1989).

14. It should be noted that this faith in the proletariat will reappear as the more general phenomenological question of the body. Here, the prole-

tariat represents the positivity of revolution, whereas it will later be taken up in a sort of dialectical movement between incorporation and disincorporation that is constitutive of democracy and its possible slippages. I will return to this question later in this chapter, in the section entitled "The History of Meaning."

15. "What Is Bureaucracy" starts from a confrontation of Marx with Weber, who apparently is able to understand this modern phenomenon better. However, the formalism that permits Weber's ideal typical account to encompass the variety of modern social structures comes at the price of inadequate differentiation within the bureaucracy. More precisely, Weber cannot distinguish between technically necessary functions and those that are the result of the need for the bureaucracy to reproduce itself in order to legitimate its presence (as Lefort had shown for the Soviet bureaucracy). The political role of the totalitarian-Stalinist bureaucracy then proves to be a key to understanding the ambiguities of industrial capitalist social bureaucracies. Lefort is also still concerned with the critique of capitalism. What appeared to Weber to be the most efficient and rational mode of modern social relations is seen to depend on the existence of a quantitatively leveled—Tocqueville would say egalitarian—form of social relations. Although Lefort does not refer to Tocqueville at this time, he already suggests that democracy is not a solution but a problem: it can lead to self-management (*auto-gestion*), or it can present the conditions that make possible its own totalitarian elimination by a bureaucracy that claims to act in order to realize the very equality that is its own premise.

16. Indeed, it is telling that Lefort had seen this problem when he wrote "The Contradiction of Trotsky," but he did not recognize that the same critique applied to Socialisme ou Barbarie.

17. As suggested in chapter 5, concerning Socialisme ou Barbarie, its ability to recognize the new and its attempts to thematize the importance of historical novelty were nonetheless among its strong points.

18. Lefort asks these questions explicitly in the concluding essay to *Eléments d'une critique de la bureaucratie* (Geneva: Droz, 1971), titled "Le nouveau et l'attrait de la répétition." This is significant, since *Eléments* republishes his most important essays from the first period of his work. The English translation is found as chapter 4, "Novelty and the Appeal of Repetition," in *The Political Forms of Modern Society* (Cambridge, Mass.: MIT Press, 1986).

19. This was published in François Chatelet, Evelyne Pisier, and Olivier Duhamel, eds., *Dictionnaire des oeuvres politiques* (Paris: PUF, 1986), pp. 671–682.

20. The first of these significant essays, which repay reading today, was "L'échange et la lutte des hommes" (1951), which takes its starting point

from Marcel Mauss's essay on *The Gift* and challenges Lévi-Strauss's reading of his anthropological predecessor; the second (1952) takes up the question of "sociétés 'sans histoire' et historicité"; while the third, also published in 1952, is entitled "Capitalisme et religion au XVIe siècle: Le problème de Weber." For a discussion of these precocious works, see Howard, *The Marxian Legacy*.

21. I will return to this point below, in the section titled "The Meaning of History."

22. There is nonetheless an important difference between the two: Religion is articulated around the question of meaning; it represents explicitly the symbolic element that gives reality its identity while making clear the difference between the secular and the religious. Precapitalist society, on the other hand, is interpreted by Marx as if it were a real reality that presents itself as such, with no need for a symbolic mediation. Since the meaning of the precapitalist or premodern world is given once and for all by an origin that is external to that world, such a society cannot be put into question or become self-critical; that is why it is closed to the new.

23. See Claude Lefort, "Outline of the Genesis of Ideology in Modern Societies," in *The Political Forms of Modern Society*. The essay was originally published in the *Encyclopedia Universalis* and reprinted as "Esquisse d'une genèse de l'idéologie dans les sociétés modernes,"in Claude Lefort, *Les formes de l'histoire: Essais d'anthropologie politique* (Paris: Gallimard, 1978), pp. 278–329.

24. The claims made in these two sentences appear to contradict one another. How can totalitarianism integrate otherness while totalitarian ideology claims that society carries its own legitimation within itself? The contradiction is overcome, as will be seen in a moment, by the activity of the totalitarian party—the same party that was responsible for "the contradiction of Trotsky" analyzed in Lefort's still-Marxist first phase. The difference between totalitarian ideology and really existing totalitarianism is crucial.

25. The English translation appears in *The Political Forms of Modern Society*; the French was reprinted in *L'invention démocratique: Les limites de la domination totalitaire* (Paris: Fayard, 1981).

26. I will return to the politics of the rights of man in the last part of this discussion. It is worth noting here Lefort's insistence on the presumption of innocence, which he calls an "irreversible gain for political thought." (*The Political Forms of Modern Society*, p. 71).

27. The capital letters indicate that here "King" and "Nation" do not refer to particular incarnations of empirical realities; the claim concerns the symbolic meaning of the terms, as will be seen in a moment. Absolutism as a form of regime is the opposite of the arbitrary domination of an empirically existing power holder.

28. One sees here the return of the structure called bourgeois ideology, which is now explained by a non-Marxist theory of history. Whereas its first description, above, situated it within a world that is dominated and determined by capitalism, now that ideology is determined by its relation to what Lefort will call "the democratic invention" (or the imperative to invent democracy).

29. This is where Shakespeare becomes more relevant to the argumentative strategy than Darwin—although of course Marx seems to appeal indiscriminately to both of them.

30. This temptation toward what Merleau-Ponty called a "pensée du survol" is illustrated in Lefort's massive study *Le travail de l'oeuvre: Machiavel* (Paris: Gallimard, 1972), which presents first an 80-page demonstration of the historical inability to come to a common understanding of the label "Machiavellian" and then a 160-page survey of eight types of interpretation of Machiavelli's works, each of which is in itself convincing but ultimately assumes for itself a position outside the work that claims somehow to observe it in its neutral totality. In other words, the problem of political science's positivism is philosophical.

31. The crucial analysis is found in "The Image of the Body and Totalitarianism," which is translated in *The Political Forms of Modern Society*; originally published in *Confrontation* (1979), it is reprinted in *L'invention démocratique*. In the following discussion I will allude to other essays of Lefort, sometimes without citing them directly.

32. This problem is of course at the roots of modern social contract theory. I suggest a historical-political solution to it in chapter 10 by distinguishing a republican democracy from a democratic republic.

33. This is why in 1989 the older, still-believing Communists could not understand what was happening to them, as was typified by the plaintive cry of the old East German head of the secret police, Erick Mielke: "Wir lieben euch doch!" (But we really love you).

34. The contribution of Lefort's essay on *The Gulag Archipelago*, whose character as a "literary investigation" he underlines, should be stressed, particularly in the context of the sudden French "discovery" of totalitarianism. Also worth noting is Lefort's concern with the philosophical and political status of works of literature. His most striking statement in this regard is found in the attack on those who claim to defend Rushdie's right to publish a work like the *Satanic Verses* on the grounds that it is only a novel—as if it was not necessary to take seriously the way in which a novel creates a symbolic world.

35. One might imagine that, for a time, this structure can succeed in presenting itself in the symbolic mode and thus exercising a symbolic power. That would explain why totalitarian power is, obviously, not simply

imposed by force. But, as I will demonstrate in a moment, this symbolic power falls to the level of reality once the active party member has really to exercise his power. That is why the image of society as a body will be doubled by the image of society as an organization—both organized and organizable.

36. One recalls here the arguments of Lefort's 1956 article, "Stalinism Without Stalin," *Socialisme ou Barbarie*, no. 20 (1956–1957).

37. In fact, Lefort distinguishes a contemporary form of ideology that marks a transcendence of bourgeois ideology; he calls this new form the "invisible ideology" and describes it as the reign of the trivial, of the anything-goes, a relativism where everything is equivalent to everything else and nothing has a particular or critical value. Since this idea, presented in the "Outline of the Genesis of Ideology," has not been developed further by Lefort, who has in the meanwhile spent much time writing on Tocqueville (among others) and the question of the rights of man, I only allude to it in this footnote. The similarity of this "invisible ideology" to what has come to be called postmodernism suggests that it would be worth returning to this matter since at least some postmodernists claim to be heirs to a radical political project that avoids the snares of ideology.

38. The justification of this interpretation of Marx as theorist of the political (and critic of the domination of the economic) is suggested in the discussion of Marx in chapter 7 and developed in chapter 13's rereading of Marx.

39. It is necessary to underline again what I said previously: ideology and the democratic revolution go together; ideology is made necessary by the revolution it seeks to legitimate at the same time that the fixity of the legitimation it proposes is constantly put into question by the dynamic inherent in the new democratic society. Thus ideology is both produced by the democratic revolution and thrown into doubt by it. But ideology is not by itself totalitarianism: the latter is an existing reality. That is why I speak here of a "totalitarian temptation" that attracts many people who, if they were faced with the reality of totalitarianism, would reject it with horror.

40. My favorite example of this tendency is the clause written into one of the Brazilian constitutions (I do not remember which one) produced at the end of their long dictatorship that decreed "real inflation shall not exceed 8 percent." Surely a laudable goal, and one that could be defended politically, but does it belong in a constitution?

## 9. THE BURDEN OF FRENCH HISTORY

1. The French are captivated by their own history, seemingly unable to look at the present in its own terms and for that reason always in danger of

repeating the old rather than facing the new. Mark Twain underlined this tendency in an amusing portrait of a French political speech in *Innocents Abroad*. A more scholarly argument making the same point is Robert Gildea's *The Past in French History* (New Haven: Yale University Press, 1994).

2. In fact, quarrels over legitimacy existed ever before 1789, in the form of religious conflict (as when Henri IV famously decided that "Paris is worth a mass" and converted), conflict between the aristocracy and the monarchy (the Fronde), or shortly before the Revolution, with Boulainvilliers and the claim of the Frankish origin of French nobility. These quarrels antedated the emergence of modern politics.

3. The phenomenon denotes first of all the increased numbers of unemployed, but its connotation extends to the broader problem of maintaining the social solidarity envisioned by the republican project. Traditional unemployment was temporary; the individual's social self-conception as a worker remained. Exclusion eliminates such social ties, creating a climate of dependence that compounds isolation. Welfare payments and other social benefits permit survival but not integration. The result is what Jean-Paul Fitoussi and Pierre Rosanvallon call the "corruption" of the republic, a term to which I will return later. See their *Le nouvel âge des inégalités* (Paris: Seuil, 1996), p. 197.

4. The most famous case is the affair of contaminated blood transfusions, which cost former prime minister Laurent Fabius his chance to achieve the highest political office. His public affirmation that he was "responsible but not guilty" could only further discredit the authority of the republican state. At the same time, Denis Salas points out that the number of court cases in general had risen from 6 million in 1962 to 10.5 million in 1972 and then to 14 million in 1993. Whether the two phenomena are connected demands further investigation. See Denis Salas, *Le tiers pouvoir* (Paris: Hachette, 1998), p. 275 n. 2.

5. I have included a separate appendix at the end of this chapter in which I sketch some of the orientations in contemporary French economic theory. The reader will see that the historical and political structures analyzed here are present there as well.

6. It was this culture whose deracinated triumph was denounced and whose necessary demise was predicted by Fichte's *Reden an die deutsche Nation*. The abstraction and formalism achieved in France permitted at first great advances, but its separation from the soil of the nation would ultimately weaken it. The subtlety of Fichte's account is often missed by hasty dismissals of his "nationalism." For an account, see the introduction to the second edition of my *From Marx to Kant* (New York: St. Martin's, 1993), pp. 25–30.

7. See Bronislaw Baczko, *Comment sortir de la Terreur: Thérmidor et la Révolution* (Paris: Gallimard, 1989). Baczko points to accusations that Robespierre sought to install himself as the head of a new monarchy—an accusation that makes sense in light of the conflict between the will of the monarch and that of the Revolution. Marcel Gauchet speaks of "the enigma of Thérmidor" that consists in the inability of its agents, who were clearly marking an end to the revolutionary order, to break with the underlying unitary logic of the revolution. See his *La Révolution des pouvoirs: La souveraineté, le peuple et la représentation, 1789–1799* (Paris: Gallimard, 1995), pp. 154–155.

8. The Commune united republican claims at the national level (refusing to accept defeat by the Prussians) and the social level (in its working-class composition and demands).

9. See especially François Furet, *La révolution, 1770–1880* (Paris: Hachette, 1989).

10. See François Furet, *La gauche et la révolution au milieu du XIXe siècle: Edgar Quinet et la question du Jacobinisme, 1865–1870* (Paris: Hachette, 1986), which also reprints the essential documents. Furet of course knew that his own publication also had contemporary echoes: did support for the goals sought by socialist revolution mean that one had to support—however "critically"—the USSR?

11. The celebration of the bicentenary of the Revolution was marked by a series of clashes between the followers of the actual holder of the chair, Michel Vovelle, and François Furet. The often comic but quite serious competition is chronicled in Stephen Kaplan, *Adieu 1789* (Paris: Fayard, 1993).

12. Robert Gildea's *The Past in French History* has an excellent chapter on this ambiguous legacy. The standard French history of the right remains René Rémond, *La droite en France de 1815 à nos jours: Continuité et diversité d'une tradition politique* (Paris: Aubier, 1954), which distinguishes between ultras, Orleanists, and nationalists.

13. That is why the Constituent Assembly voted the Le Chapelier law forbidding the formation of trade unions. Indeed, the Le Chapelier law forbade even petitions from organized groups of any kind Although I will return to this issue below, it is perhaps worth noting here that even the constitution of the Fifth Republic (article 4) subordinates political parties to "the principles of national sovereignty and democracy." Guy Carcasonne's commentary notes that this means that parties "have no true status, nor are they bound by obligations that can be validated, as opposed to the situation in Germany" (*La Constitution*, 3d ed. [Paris: Seuil, 1999], p. 49).

14. This also explains why most political parties in France refer to themselves as movements, or unions, or reunions, rather than identifying themselves with particular causes. Thus one finds today on the right side of

the political spectrum the Rassemblement pour la République (RPR) and the Union des Démocrats Français (UDF)—as well the the far-right Front National (FN); on the left are the Socialists, who, in the recent past, were called the Section Française de l'International Ouvrier (SFIO), and a "republican" splinter group, the Mouvement des Citoyens (MDF). The shifts on the left are explained below.

15. The priority placed on the rights of man results from the same revolutionary need to replace the unity of the absolute monarchy with the nation by an equally powerful synthesis. Marcel Gauchet suggests that the revolutionaries were not, at the outset, seeking to overthrow the monarchy; they appealed to natural law and the doctrine of rights in order to establish their own claim to legitimacy. As the contest with the monarchy advanced, the transformation of the former Estates-General from a national assembly to a constituant assembly would eventually force them to recognize that the implicit logic of their own claim implied the need to reconstitute a regime of a very different type. See Marcel Gauchet, *La révolution des droits de l'homme* (Paris: Gallimard, 1989).

16. This attitude may explain why much of the French left saw 1917 as the realization of the project of 1789 and 1793, ignoring the antidemocratic practices of the Bolsheviks while believing their promises concerning their (professed) results. See chap. 10, "Intersecting Trajectories of Republicanism in France and the United States," for a comparison of the French republican and American democratic variants of these themes. It should be noted here that one variant of the French republican vision would be the creation of a formal or procedural state whose universality is the guarantee of individual rights. In this, the republic realizes the Rousseauian vision of the law—but not the substantial vision animating the Genevan's republican political idea of the general will.

17. The idea of realizing the republic by means of educational reform had been part of the original project of the French Revolution. The present-day bastion of the intellectual elite, the Ecole normale supérieure, was created in 1794 to train teachers. The presence of the revolutionary project in Ferry's reforms is evident. He had been a participant in the political debates begun by Quinet's refusal to accept the inevitability of a repetition of all phases of the originary revolution. His name remains associated not only with educational reform but with the colonial *mission civilisatrice*, which could be justified by appeal to the Declaration of Rights, arguing the need to extend these rights to non-French as well. The best discussion of the actuality of this republican theory remains Claude Nicolet's *L'idée républicaine en France* (Paris: Gallimard, 1982), which stresses the recurrence of the republican motto: "The [political] form will produce the [social] basis" (La forme tirera le fond).

18. The concept of a *republican* elite should be underlined. The republican goal is not a leveling down but rather the raising of all. This no doubt explains another phenomenon that is peculiar to French political culture: the role of the petition, signed by intellectuals acting not in the name of their specific science but rather as the conscience of the nation that is concerned with the best interests of that nation.

19. See François Furet, Jacques Julliard, and Pierre Rosanvallon, *La république du centre: La fin de l'exception française* (Paris: Calmann-Lévy, 1988).

20. The attempt to eliminate the Catholic schools led to massive demonstrations recalling the revolutionary *journées*, this time on the right, with over a million people in the streets of Paris in June 1984, and to the replacement of the minister of education, Alain Savary (who had cofounded with Mitterrand the new Socialist Party) by the very republican Jean-Pierre Chevènement. Quilès's exhortation is cited from the useful compilation by the staff of the journal *Le débat*, *Les idées en France*, *1945–1988* (Paris: Gallimard, 1989), p. 377.

21. Indeed, the present Socialist Party was created only at the Epinay Congress of 1971. Its ancestor was the SFIO, an organization whose name—the Section Française de l'Internationale Ouvrière—reflects the unitary and universal goals of republicanism. François Mitterrand, who had never been a socialist, needed to give himself ideological credibility by means of the new label.

22. This is no doubt another origin of the practice of using petitions signed by intellectuals and appealing to the good sense of public opinion. While this aspect of French political life could be traced back to the activity of Voltaire, his "écrasez l'infame" was considered a founding slogan, and its author an honorary ancestor, of the revolutionary republican tradition.

23. This is at least the principle repeated on all sides. The post-1945 control of the Communists over their affiliated union, the CGT, is clear to most observers, particularly after the CIA managed to join with a faction of Trotskyists to split that union in April 1948, creating the rival organization Force Ouvrière (FO). This obeissance was ideological as well as political. For example, when the Communist Party leader Maurice Thorez insisted in May 1955, despite all evidence, that "absolute pauperization" characterized the situation of the working class, the CGT Congress meeting in June adopted the identical thesis. See *Les idées en France*, pp. 132, 134.

24. This is of course a modern political appearance, not to be identified with the older category "reactionary" that come from the antirepublican struggles. The modern far right appears in the context of democracy. As Furet points out in *Le passé d'une illusion* (Paris: Calmann-Lévy, 1995), the idea of a revolutionary right emerges only in the wake of World War I.

See chap. 8, "From the Critique of Totalitarianism to the Politics of Democracy."

25. There was another, realpolitik reason for the alliance. As Mitterrand explained in *Ma part de verité* (Paris: Fayard, 1969), he considered that social change was making his party into the "sociological" majority; the new alliance would weaken the communists and make the socialists then also the "political" majority.

26. The success of this strategy would have depended on a similar choice by the German Social Democrats, as I suggested at the time. See "France, Germany and the Problem of Europe," reprinted in *Defining the Political* (Minneapolis: University of Minnesota Press, 1989).

27. Some see Gaullism as a return to a form of Bonapartism because of its plebiscitary character. Yet François Furet remarks perceptively (in *La république du centre*, p. 18ff) that whereas de Gaulle left behind a relatively firm set of institutions, Bonaparte left only a name.

28. Yves Mény, *La corruption de la république* (Paris: Fayard, 1992). Paul Jankowski points out that worry about this kind of corruption dates at least to the Cahiers de doléance of 1789, which complained of the confusion of public and private interest involved in the sale of offices by the king. See Paul Jankowski, "Méry de Paris," *French Politics and Society* 19, no. 1 (spring 2001: 61–69.

29. Other possibilities for corruption were provided by the policy of nationalizations and denationalizations that followed the initial measures of 1981. It is only fair to note that a first law governing party finance was passed in 1988, after the scandals had become too evident to ignore. It had to be revised again in 1990 and 1993. The absence of legal regulation was not the result of political scheming; its origin lies in the fact that the unitary representation of the republic implies that there is in principle no place for particular interest and hence no one thinks of the need to regulate it.

30. The recent revelations concerning these types of practices by the former mayor of Paris, Jacques Chirac, make clear this mutual complicity: although Chirac's RPR party got a larger part of the loot, parts of it went to all the parties. Politicians say that as long as money is not taken for personal reasons but for the good of the party, this is acceptable. And they are surprised when the public is outraged by their voting themselves an amnesty law for this reason. This is another aspect of the corruption of the republic. See Mény, *La corruption de la république*, pp. 282–292. Even the *New York Times* recognized finally that something new was afoot in France; see Suzanne Daley's "In France, the Wink at Corruption Gives Way to Scrutiny" (January 11, 2001, p. A3).

31. The most optimistic argument is presented by Denis Salas, who subtitles *Le tiers pouvoir, Vers une autre justice.*

32. Consistently republican, French laws represent the general will in its generality and universality, as opposed to American laws, which, although also claiming universality, take into account particular conditions—for example, a tax bill will exclude "all" corporations incorporated on such and such a date in this or that state when the tax favor is in fact being offered to only the one corporation that happens to fit that description. The *décrets d'application* are needed for a law that has been duly voted to become effective, giving the state bureaucracy significant autonomous power.

33. Mény explains this practice in chapter 3 of *La corruption de la république*, "Pantouflages: Le compromis historique de l'administration française." According to *Le Monde*, March 5/6, 2000, for the first time more than 50 percent of graduates of the Inspection des finances would prefer a career in private industry. An illustration of the dangers of this system is seen in the (temporary) downfall of former finance minister Dominique Strauss-Kahn, who was in charge of privatization of industries from 1991 to 1993, went into private business, and then returned as finance minister when the Socialists came back to power in 1996, only to fall victim to an accusation of corruption. What some call a functional synthesis, others see with a different eye. Yet *Le Monde*'s Thierry Bréhier (March 24, 2000) still applies the logic of the *synthèse* to find Strauss-Kahn's activity quite justifiable.

34. See my analysis in "The French Strikes of 1995 and Their Political Aftermath," *Government and Opposition* 33, no. 2 (spring 1998): 199–220.

35. Claude Lefort's *Un homme en trop* stressed the political arguments that many readers of Solzhenitsyn missed because they were concerned only with its sensational revelations. Lefort also stressed the threat that the book posed to the cultural power of the Communists. The importance of the theoretical argument is suggested by the fact that its publisher, Les Editions du Seuil, republished Lefort's book in a paperback edition in 1986, a decade after its first edition, when there was no shock value—only theoretical interest—to justify this project.

36. This project, which François Mitterrand tried to appropriate for his own purposes by calling for an "administrative provisional government," is still debated. See "Mendès-France voulait-il prendre le pouvoir en mai 68," *Le Monde*, June 29, 2001, which reports on a conference organized at the National Assembly to discuss this theme.

37. This is the argument suggested by François Furet, Antoine Liniers (a.k.a. Olivier Rolin), and Philippe Reynaud in *Terrorisme et démocratie* (Paris: Fayard, 1985). Liniers-Rolin's participant account of the one attempt at terrorism (a kidnapping) is fascinating. One might note, however, that Italy and Germany had also previously had popular fascist gov-

ernments, which could partially explain their more violent options. See also Paul Berman, "The Passion of Joschka Fischer," *New Republic*, nos. 4519 and 4520 (August 27 and September 3, 2001): 36–59.

38. Did ethics replace politics? Did it destroy it? Or was the demise of the political the precondition of the emergence of ethics? The verdict is not yet rendered, but the argument here favors the last alternative. The student strikes of the 1980s seemed to argue for the priority of ethics. However, see my essay "Ethics and Politics," reprinted in *Defining the Political* 294–304, where I take issue with this thesis concerning the massive strikes of 1986. On the other hand, it should be noted that the sense of political action of course changed. The idea of a historical vanguard was no longer plausible. This transformation in turn had effects in another sphere—the aesthetic— as Marcel Gauchet has noted. Experimental literature and poetry, even the cinema, which had been so important for the generation who still had an experience of the vanguard political temptation played little role for the new generation that came to maturity in the eighties. See Marcel Gauchet, "Totalitarisme, libéralisme, individualisme," in *Les idées en France*, pp. 513–515.

39. The other solution, borrowing from Tocqueville on America, would make democracy into a social condition and suggest that France could live without its political culture. But then France would be America!

40. This argument is developed at length in Claude Lefort's discussion of Michelet's argument against the killing of the king in "Permanence du théologico-politique?" in *Essais sur le politique: XIXe–XXe siècles* (Paris: Seuil, 1986). The notion of the symbolic as employed here comes from Lefort, whose use of this concept to understand the nature and limits of the totalitarian project is discussed in chaps. 6 and 8.

41. The disappearance of the *parlements* is not so strange when one takes into account the difference between lawyers who are members of the *barreau* and whose essential function is defense against the interventions of the state and those lawyers who are state employees and are known as *magistrats*. The latter, because they are dependent on the state and presumably work to fulfill its goals (and are under its administrative control) are given great powers. In the passages that follow, however, I am following the ideas proposed by Salas, *Le tiers pouvoir*, in proposing that present-day developments suggest these magistrates can free themselves from the control of the state and play a crucial role in democratization. On the other hand, the same globalization and democratization that favor the magistrates can be seen as a threat to the *barreau*. Concerning the latter, see Lucien Karpik, *Les Avocats: Entre l'Etat, le public et le marché, XIII–XX siècle* (Paris: Gallimard, 1995).

42. Cited in *Les idées en France*, p. 418.

43. The judiciary increasingly protects the rights of individuals or groups against the weight of societal demands. In so doing, it does not so much solve problems as pose new ones. The recognized rights still have to be integrated into the web of differences that make up a modern society.

44. Published in *Esprit*, June 2000, pp. 207–222. *Esprit* has devoted a number of special sections to the problems raised by the new economy. In an afterword to a new edition of his study of the past twenty-five years of French intellectual life, *Face au scepticisme* (Paris: Hachette, 1998), *Esprit*'s director, Olivier Mongin, tries to explain why he sees political economy acquiring a centrality on the intellectual agenda that had previously escaped its more technical-administrative orientation. In a series of developments culminating with the massive strike wave of 1995, it became clear that the old compromise between labor and capital—consecrated by the mutualization or sharing of risks through a form of social and generational solidarity based on the logic of insurance policies—could no longer hold. Structural and long-term unemployment made it impossible to ensure social integration through work, and especially through lifetime work in one firm. Then, as the consequences of the end of the cold war (which had permitted clear delimitation of the so-called enemy) came together with globalization, those who sought to renew the old compromise were clearly defeated. The shape of a new compromise remains to be seen.

45. A more complete discussion of Durkheim can be found in my article on him that will appear in Lawrence D. Kritzman, ed., *The Columbia History of Twentieth-Century Thought* (New York: Columbia University Press, forthcoming).

46. Bernard Perret and Guy Roustang, *L'économie contre la société* (Paris: Seuil, 1994).

47. See, for example, André Orléan, "L'individu, l'opinion et le capitalisme financier," *Esprit*, November 2000; and Jean-Pierre Dupuy, "Le détour et le sacrifice: Ivan Illich et René Girard," *Esprit*, May 2001.

48. Laville and Levesque, "Penser ensemble l'économie et la société," *Esprit*, p. 214.

49. Viviane Forrestier, *L'horreur économique* (Paris: Fayard, 1996). For a brief critical summary, see Pierre Rosanvallon, "France: The New Anti-Capitalism," *Correspondence*, no. 7 (winter 2000/2001): 34–35. See also Vincent Tournier, "L'apocalypse économique selon Viviane Forrestier," *Esprit*, March–April 1997, pp. 231–235. The Forrestier phenomenon is a part of the reaction of old French political logic to the new world of global economics. Along with *Le Monde diplomatique*, the acolytes of Pierre Bourdieu who call themselves "the left of the left," and an undeniably present and justified worldwide protest against the results of economic globalization, the plea in favor of the victim will—and should—always find support. Whether

this support can be translated into a political project is another, and more important, question. And still another is whether such support in the last resort is harmful to forming just the political project that it would need to realize its own goals. A brief but incisive presentation of the Forrestier affaire and its implications can be found in Pierre Rosanvallon's ironically titled essay, "France: The New Anti-Capitalism."

50. Laville and Levesque, "Penser ensemble l'économie et la société," p. 214.

51. Anthony Giddens, *Beyond Left and Right: The Future of Radical Politics* (Cambridge: Polity, 1994). See G. Roustang, J.-L. Laville, B. Eme, D. Mothé, and B. Perret, *Vers un nouveau contrat social* (Paris: Desclée de Brouwer, 1997).

52. See "Essai sur le don: Forme et raison de l'échange dans les sociétés archaïques," in Marcel Mauss, *Sociologie et anthropologie* (Paris: PUF, 1950).

53. Francis Fukuyama, *Trust: The Social Virtues and the Creation of Prosperity* (New York: Free, 1995).

54. André Gorz, *Misères du présent: Richesse du possible* (Paris: Galilée, 1997). For a discussion of Gorz's earlier work that led him to these position, see my essay on the new workign class in Dick Howard and Karl Klare, eds., *The Unknown Dimension: European Marxism Since Lenin* (New York: Basic, 1972), as well as the afterword to Dick Howard, *The Marxian Legacy*, 2d ed. (Minneapolis: University of Minnesota Press, 1988).

## 10. Intersecting Trajectories of Republicanism in France and the United States

1. Of course the excluded don't represent a threat to overthrow the system, as did the working class, but the republican's working class was never seen as the kind of social-revolutionary threat that was represented by Marx's proletariat. I will examine the ground of this difference below, when I consider the French notion of *solidarisme* and its Durkheimian roots.

2. See Benjamin Barber, *Strong Democracy: Participatory Politics for a New Age* (Berkeley: University of California Press, 1984).

3. As will be apparent, one of the roots of the paradoxical trajectories of the concept is that the French and the Americans have a different understanding of what counts as political.

4. Indeed, Tocqueville points out that "of all countries in the world, America is the one in which the precepts of Descartes are least studied *and best followed*" (chapter 1, "Concerning the Philosophical Approach of the Americans," *Democracy in America*, 2:429; emphasis added).

5. See V. I. Lenin, "One Step Forward, Two Steps Back" (1904), in *Selected Works* (Moscow: Foreign Languages Publishing House, 1960),

1:443. Note that Lenin speaks here of the "organization" of the proletariat, not the proletariat itself.

6. See the article "Fraternité," in *Dictionnaire critique de la révolution française*, ed. François Furet and Mona Ozouf (Paris: Flammarion, 1989), pp. 731–741.

7. In "Fraternité," Mona Ozouf recalls Jean-Paul Sartre's attempt to reconcile his existential philosophy with his Marxist ideology by inventing the concept of "Fraternité-Terreur." She doesn't mention that Sartre's concept has further implications, in effect justifying Stalinism. I have tried to show why the existentialist lover of freedom could find himself going to this extreme in *The Marxian Legacy*, rev. ed. (Minneapolis: University of Minnesota Press, 1988).

8. The Great Seal of the United States, printed on the back of every U.S. dollar, features on one side the revolutionary motto "Novus Ordo Seclorum" and on the other the unitary imperative "E Pluribus Unum."

9. Although this conflict between private interests or private rights and the public good has become increasingly evident, it is worth noting that its first appearance can be traced to the earliest stages of the American Revolution, when John Adams expressed his alarm at the democratic implications of Tom Paine's *Common Sense* in his explicitly republican *Thoughts on Government*. Similarly, as a president faced with the democratic opposition of the Jeffersonians, Adams would justify for the same reason the repressive Alien and Sedition Acts of 1798.

10. Rawls was translated into French only in 1987. Another reason for the French lack of concern with these issues is suggested in "Toward a Republican Democracy?" in chap. 9, "The Burden of French History." The French tradition of administrative law is republican and unitary, with no place for the kind of legitimate conflict of competing rights' claims that Rawls's theory seeks to legitimate.

11. A useful examination of this French history is found in Jacques Donzelot, *L'invention du social: Essai sur le déclin des passions politiques* (Paris: Fayard, 1984).

12. Michael J. Sandel, *Democracy's Discontent: America in Search of a Public Philosophy* (Cambridge: Harvard University Press, 1996).

13. Sylvie Mesure and Alain Renaut, *Alter ego: Les paradoxes de l'identité démocratique* (Paris: Aubier, 1999). It should be noted that among Renaut's work are studies and translations of Kant and Fichte as well as polemical debates with what he and Luc Ferry denounced as "'68 Thought." He also recently edited a five-volume history of political philosophy. Renaut and Mesure also published together the excellent study *La guerre des dieux: Essai sur la querelle des valeurs* (Paris: Grasset, 1996), while Mesure is the author of a study of Raymond Aron.

14. See, e.g., ibid., pp. 255–256.

15. Michael Walzer, *Spheres of Justice: A Defense of Pluralism and Equality* (New York: Basic, 1983).

16. See especially the discussion under the heading "Property/Power," in ibid., p. 292.

17. Since the index of Barber's *Strong Democracy* contains no references to republicanism, however resonant his account may be with some of the categories under consideration here, I leave aside any discussion of its detailed proposals. I have discussed Barber's more recent work in "Le déficit démocratique: Débats américains, questions européennes," *Transeuropéennes*, nos. 6–7 (winter 1995–1996): 7–14.

18. This interpretation does, however, fall back on the old Hegelian-Marxist model of immanent critique by assuming that there exists—but in alienated form—a solution to the dichotomies and antinomies that render bourgeois thought so unstable. I doubt that Mesure and Renaut had this version of immanent critique in mind, but the presence of this *Denkfigur* is worth noting.

19. Christian Ruby, *La solidarité* (Paris: Ellipses, 1997).

20. Donzelot, in *L'invention du social*, stresses its Rousseauian presuppositions that identify the state of nature with Reason and leave no room for political deliberation—that is, for error—on the part of democratic individuals.

21. This is not strictly true in the American case, as John Patrick Diggens has noted frequently and eloquently, most recently in *On Hallowed Ground: Abraham Lincoln and the Foundations of American History* (New Haven: Yale University Press, 2000). Lincoln's opposition to slavery was not simply moral; it expressed also a political philosophy that was rooted in the republican tradition but integrated the role of free labor. A discussion of this strand in American history is unfortunately not possible here. For the French case, the influence of Proudhon as well as that of the utopian socialists starting from Saint-Simon would also constitute an exception.

22. Challenged from his left in his own party and by his Communist Party coalition partners, Jospin tried to have his cake and eat it too in his September 26, 2000, speech to the Socialist deputies of the European Parliament meeting in Strassburg: "The market economy does not spontaneously work in harmony. It needs ground rules to function effectively." In our context, Jospin's claim would be to combine procedural liberalism with socialism while ignoring the question of social solidarity and inclusion that is, however, the true challenge to modern republican politics.

23. Something that is imaginary is not therefore either stripped of any real effects or an unnecessary illusion or fiction. It is necessary to appeal to the concept of sovereignty when analyzing modern democratic politics.

Sovereignty represents the symbolic unity of society. If one or another social group or political institution could actually incarnate this symbolic sovereignty, the democratic basis of society would be lost. See the discussion in "Republican Politics: Anomie and Judgment," later in this chapter.

24. In the following paragraphs, I am summarizing some implications of my book *The Birth of American Political Thought*, which I also discuss in chap. 11, "Reading U.S. History as Political."

25. The citation is found, significantly, in the chapter entitled "The Activity Present in All Parts of the Political Body in the United States: The Influence that It Exercises on Society," which stresses the influence of the political republic on the social activity of the individual. The citation is found in *De la démocratie en Amérique, I* (Paris: Gallimard, 1961), 1:254.

26. Indeed, one recalls that for many of the early modern political theorists, the judicial branch did not represent an independent representative power, and its independence is still questioned in many modern nations (such as contemporary France!). One might also recall that, in the *Second Treatise of Civil Government* (1689), Locke suggests that the so-called Federative Power "which deals with foreign policy" should be considered to represent an autonomous function of government. But there is of course no reason to look only to the past. The important point that needs to be developed further is that this imperative pertains to political institutions. If, as will be seen in a moment, one wants to treat trade unions as political, this means that their job is not simply (as Prime Minister Jospin suggested) to represent real (i.e., corporate) interests.

27. Still another example is offered by the development of international law, as suggested in the provocative study by Agnès Lejbowicz, *Philosophie du droit international: L'impossible capture de l'humanité* (Paris: PUF, 1999).

28. The excluded are excluded from something, after all. For example, French observers point out that the second generation of immigrants from the Maghreb differ from their parents in that they reject discrimination not simply because of its harmful and degrading personal effects but because they consider themselves to be first of all French.

29. This metaphor of "being heard" is used effectively in Jürgen Habermas's *Between Facts and Norms* (Cambridge, Mass.: MIT Press, 1996), which also uses the interesting metaphor of society "laying siege" on the state to which I am also alluding here. See chap. 4, "Habermas's Reorientation of Critical Theory Toward Democratic Theory."

30. Of course, this is not Kant's terminology. Moreover, it should be noted that Kant is talking about laws of the natural world rather than conventional laws, *physei* rather than *nomoi*. Nonetheless, in the political world of democratic republicans, there is a constantly present temptation to think

of the sovereign will as if it also existed *physei*, as a natural given. In this context, it might be noted that the justification of the politics of will recalls the Greek notion of the *oikos*, the household world of production that is restricted to women and slaves and governed by laws of necessity, as opposed to the *polis*, which is the public domain in which freedom can be realized.

31. I cannot develop the technical arguments for this structural analogy further here. See Dick Howard, *Political Judgments* (Lanham, Md.: Rowman and Littlefield, 1996), as well as the systematic philosophical treatment in idem, *From Marx to Kant*, 2d ed. (New York: St. Martin's, 1993).

32. Who would have thought, in the 1970s, that European societies could live with 12 percent rates of unemployment? At what point does racial discrimination become exclusionary? When and under what conditions do the poorly housed represent an instance of exclusion? These are not questions for an objective social science; there are no pregiven laws under which they can be subsumed and in terms of which their weight can be measured. They are political questions.

## 11. READING U.S. HISTORY AS POLITICAL

1. It is worth noting that most progressive movements in U.S. history have appealed to the values of the Declaration rather than to the constitutional mechanisms and procedures that are supposed to ensure democratic political action. This could be one explanation for the absence of organized progressive political movements—and for the repeated recurrence of populist politics that is often tinted with reactionary overtones. I will try to suggest here why the Constitution does in fact offer progressives political possibilities for making social change. As for the reactionary overtones, see chap. 12, "Fundamentalism and the American Exception."

2. That is why the definition of rights that are held to be self-evident is followed by a sentence that begins: "That to secure these rights, Governments are instituted among Men."

3. On this reading, it took the incorporation of the post–Civil War amendments, particularly the fourteenth, in order to nationalize the rights proclaimed in the Declaration of Independence. Of course, the incorporation of those amendments took another hundred years with regard to race relations, and it continues in other aspects of American life.

4. I indicate the original substantive form of the French wording to stress that I am referring here not to actual historical events but to their symbolic meaning. I am summarizing briefly here the method I used in *The Birth of American Political Thought*, trans. David Curtis (Minneapolis: University of Minnesota Press, 1989), which was originally written in French.

5. This is true mainly for the New England colonies, whose dissenting traditions and habits of ecclesiastical self-government made their churches more like what Weber designates as sects. Tocqueville stresses this habit of religious freedom particularly in the second volume of *Democracy in America*, where it seems to form a potential counterweight to the "tyranny of the majority" that he feared in the first volume and whose basis was the social fact of equality whose implications preoccupy him in that volume. Claude Lefort has stressed this latter point in several of his essays on Tocqueville, to which I am indebted. See also chap. 12, "Fundamentalism and the American Exception."

6. I have inverted the Hegelian structure in which the concept integrates the moments of the immediate (being) and its reflexive mediation (essence) because Hegel's system is not capable of thinking the autonomy of the political, as I tried to show in *From Marx to Kant*, 2d ed. (New York: St. Martin's, 1993). For Hegel, social problems make necessary political institutions, whereas the case of the American Revolution suggests that it is the political that gives meaning to the social.

There is a Hegelian aspect to the philosophical method for reading that I use in *The Birth of American Political Thought* (but not in the present discussion). In that book, a fourth section tries to interpret the various historical interpretations of the phenomena analyzed in order to demonstrate the validity of my arguments. This confirms the basic theoretical analysis in the same way as did Hegel's nonsystematic works, such as his *History of Philosophy; or, History of Religion*. (It might be noted that Marx proposed the same method in *Capital*, whose three volumes relate as a triad, moving from the immediacy of a single capitalism to the mediation through the circulation of capital, and culminating in the analysis of the many capitals, to which a fourth volume, *Theories of Surplus Value*, was added in a similar attempt to confirm the basic argument.) See the discussion of Marx in chapter 13, below.

7. It is worth noting that it is the king rather than Parliament, against which previous protest had been addressed, who is declared to be the author of the "long train of abuses and usurpations, pursuing invariably the same Object [that] evinces a design to reduce them [the colonists] under absolute Despotism," which gives the colonists "a right" [and a] duty, to throw off such Government." The colonists hoped to reason with (or appeal to the interests of) members of Parliament, perhaps even achieving something more than mere "virtual representation"; attacking the king meant that the question of sovereignty was now the only issue to be addressed.

8. This does not contradict the earlier assertion that the constitutions of the states intended to represent society. The explicitly political form of representation incorporated in these state constitutions was assumed to be

necessary in order to guarantee that the essence of society, its common good, would be correctly recognized. In this sense, the constitution of Pennsylvania and those of the other states do not differ; each assumes that there exists something called the common good, although they differ about the political institutions necessary for its discovery. I shall show that the federal constitution of 1787 works in terms of a different, properly political, logic.

9. No doubt an economic interpretation can be offered here. Lack of unity in the laws prevented interstate commerce from developing, while the overly democratic constitutions (not only in Pennsylvania) along with frequent renewal of the legislatures made for constantly changing laws that also worked against commercial growth. My point is not to deny the role of interest; it is to understand its place and its limits. Given their experience with English tyranny, the Americans' concern was above all political.

10. To avoid misunderstanding, rights are not a thing that an individual has, the way one possess an object; rights exist in and as social relations. To say that the object of democratic politics is rights does not mean that the increase (or loss) of rights is the content of politics; it means only that, whatever issues are addressed, the results will also affect the rights of those concerned. An increase in the minimum wage is not only an economic gain.

11. Readers will recall having learned in high school Washington's condemnation, in his farewell address, of "the baneful effects of the spirit of party," as well as Jefferson's first inaugural address, which insisted that "we are all Republicans, we are all Federalists." The interpretation of the emergence of parties as a *system* was developed most convincingly by Richard Hofstadter, *The Idea of a Party System: The Rise of Legitimate Opposition in the United States, 1780–1840* (Berkeley: University of California Press, 1969). Hofstadter of course belongs to the literal school of consensus historians. His argument is nonetheless fundamental.

12. This argument is illustrated by Martin Van Buren, the first professional politician to reach the presidency, in his *Inquiry into the Origin and Course of Political Parties in the United States* (1867; reprint, New York: Augustus M. Kelley, 1967). Although a fully pragmatic politician for whom party loyalty was the most important of all political principles, in his *Inquiry* Van Buren appeals to a contrast of good and evil that is typical of premodern politics.

13. The appeal to virtue can be seen not only in the cultural politics of the new left of the 1960s; it is also present in the cultural revolt that was symbolized in the antiestablishment cultural politics that made Barry Goldwater, the "conscience of a conservative," into the Republican Party presidential candidate in 1964 before it eventually brought Ronald Reagan to the presidency. See This point has recently been made again in Sam Tanenhaus,

"The GOP; or, Goldwater's Old Party," *New Republic*, June 11, 2001, which reviews among others Rick Perlstein's *Before the Storm: Barry Goldwater and the Unmaking of the American Consensus* and Lisa McGirr's *Suburban Warriors: The Origins of the New American Right.*

14. The anti-Federalists who opposed the new constitution did not think of themselves as a political party (indeed, they were opposed to parties as a threat to social unity). Nor did the relation of anti-Federalists to Federalists constitute a party system, as was the case later.

15. The argument for the priority of rights in American politics can be applied to the example of the New Deal and the role of political parties as well. Bruce Ackerman's provocative suggestion, in *We, the People*, vol. 1 (Cambridge: Harvard University Press, 1991), that the politics of the New Deal illustrates a second way in which the Constitution can be amended opens the way for such an interpretation—which is admittedly controversial and would demand a more historical analysis than can be offered here.

16. NIMBY is an acronym for "Not in My Back Yard."

## 12. FUNDAMENTALISM AND THE AMERICAN EXCEPTION

1. The *New York Times* of November 10, 2001, notes that all biology texts in the state of Alabama will include a warning that evolution is a "controversial theory." It is perhaps encouraging that the *Times* adds that Alabama has the "distinction" of being the only state to take such measures.

2. Cited in Richard Hofstadter, *Anti-Intellectualism in American Life* (New York: Vintage, 1962), p. 129. Hofstadter's discussion of Bryan is found in chapter 5, "The Revolt Against Modernity." His entire book remains a valuable warning for those who unthinkingly identify democracy with enlightenment and modernity.

3. Hofstadter points out later that Debs too had his anti-intellectual side. See the examples in ibid., p. 291.

4. *Die protestantische Ethik und der Geist des Kapitalismus*, in *Gesammelte Aufsätze zur Religionssoziologie* (Tübingen: J. C. B. Mohr [Paul Siebeck], 1986), 1:204.

5. Harvey Cox, *Fire from Heaven: The Rise of Pentecostal Spirituality and the Reshaping of Religion in the Twenty-First Century* (Reading, Mass: Addison-Wesley, 1995).

6. Ibid., pp. 74–75.

7. This fundamentalism is not new, nor is its relation to the politics of the far right. It was analyzed by liberal intellectuals worried about the rise of Goldwaterism in the 1960s, for example, in Daniel Bell's study "The Dispossessed," in *The Radical Right*, ed. Daniel Bell (1963).

8. It is difficult to accept Cox's claim that the birth of Pentecostalism can be compared to the Protestant Reformation (p. 118–119). Richard Hofstadter already observed a distinction similar to the one described by Cox at the time of the Great Awakening in the nineteenth century. But for Hofstadter, this opposition is at the root of a strong antiintellectual current in American history. See his *Anti-Intellectualism in American Life*.

9. Once again, this does not seem to be a new historical invention. Richard Hofstadter's attempt to explain McCarthyism and the rise of a new right-wing politics around Barry Goldwater and the John Birch society led him to analyze the recurrence of what he called a "paranoid style" of politics in American history. See Richard Hofstadter, *The Paranoid Style in American Politics and Other Essays* (New York: Vintage, 1964).

10. Cox, *Fire from Heaven*, p. 297.

11. See Thomas Byrne Edsall and Mary D. Edsall, *Chain Reaction: The Impact of Race, Rights, and Taxes on American Politics* (New York: Norton, 1992), for the reasons that this view of welfare is wrong—and why it nonetheless remains popular.

12. It is worth noting that the other manifestations of Pentecostalism described by Cox do not manifest this shift from pre- to postmillinarianism. Nor does Cox explain its appearance in the United States. I will try to do so below, by looking at what historians call the "exceptional" character of the United States.

13. Describing his visit to the new university, Cox tries to put the best face on it—but doesn't really convince. See Harvey Cox, "The Warring Visions of the Religious Right," *Atlantic Monthly*, November 1995, pp. 59–69.

14. Cited by Cox, *Fire from Heaven*, p. 291.

15. Another, more liberal, interpretation of the idea of regency is proposed by Seymour Martin Lipset, who uses the term "stewardship" to explain the exceptional role of philanthropy in America: everything that exists in the world belongs truly to God, and we are only the temporary stewards and thus have an obligation to aid those in need (*American Exceptionalism. A Double-Edged Sword* [New York: Norton, 1996], p. 68).

16. Richard Hofstadter notes that the Puritan clergy was "as close to being an intellectual ruling class—or, more properly, a class of intellectuals intimately associated with a ruling power—as America has ever had" (*Anti-Intellectualism*, p. 59). But he also notes that it was guilty of the error that is typical of intellectuals, imagining that it "might be able to commit an entire civil society to the realization of transcendent moral and religious standards, and that they could maintain within this society a unified and commanding creed" (p. 62). On the other hand, Tocqueville notes that these Puritans had also been dissenters at home, seeking liberty more than

economic equality. This may be one reason that, as I will suggest, they could initiate a kind of civil democratic tolerance and republican pluralism.

17. They may not leave on their own, but they will be liable to follow charismatic leaders who will find the room to emerge as the experienced unity of the believers becomes formal and bureaucratic as its liturgy is rationalized.

18. The sects that become churches often justify their transformation by pointing out that a poorly educated clergy typical of the sect is unable to face up to the challenges of modern life (including its secularism). The sects reply that experience of the spirit is more important than knowledge of the letter; worse, the educated man risks falling victim to the sin of pride.

19. Of course, there were other Protestant nations before the creation of the United States, but they were converts. America was born Protestant, so to speak.

20. From this perspective, the Constitution of 1787 (and Supreme Court judgments based on it) marks the transformation of the sect into a church. Radical movements, of the left and of the right, have appealed historically to the Declaration of Independence. Lincoln's Gettysburg Address begins "Four score and seven years ago, our forefathers founded. . . ." Lincoln's reference point is 1776, not 1787.

21. Lipset, *American Exceptionalism*, p. 31. In an article written in December 2001, reflecting on the impact of September 11, 2001, I suggested that American forms of anti-Americanism are particularly significant. (Cf. *Esprit*, janvier 2002.) The United States is founded on values, which of course can serve to put into question any given political claim to instantiate those values. While no one would talk about un-French attitudes, Hitler and his cronies did talk about *Un-Deutsch* behavior. But Germanity here referred to something essential, or substantial. The American values are of a different coin. I suggest that they have four distinct roots, all published in English language texts in 1776. The Declaration of Independence, of course, but also Adam Smith's *Wealth of Nations*, Bentham's *Fragment on Government*, and especially Gibbon's *Decline and Fall of the Roman Empire*. The article is also available on the Web site indicated in the introduction; a German translation is in *Kommune*, January, 2002.

22. Lipset even argues that Lyndon Johnson's error during the Vietnam War was his refusal to make it a moral crusade (because he feared that this would give rise to a renewed McCarthyism). The result was that the antiwar movement had the monopoly of morality (ibid., p. 66).

23. The best illustration of these developments was written before the peak of incomprehension; see E. J. Dionne Jr., *Why Americans Hate Politics* (New York: Simon and Schuster, 1991).

24. The reconciliation of Weber and Durkheim around the problem of

democracy is suggested in my essay "Individu et société," in *Philosopher 2* (Paris: Fayard, 2000).

## 13. PHILOSOPHY BY OTHER MEANS?

1. It should be noted that Sartre made this claim in the essay "Marxism and Existentialism," which appeared as a hundred-page introduction to the incomplete but still fascinating *Critique de la raison dialectique* (Paris: Gallimard, 1960), in which he attempted to offer a philosophical foundation to Marxist theory (p. 29). The remark follows a denunciation of the stagnation of Marxist theory, which Sartre hoped to renew. A discussion of Sartre's theory appears in Dick Howard, *The Marxian Legacy* (1977; rev. ed., Minneapolis: University of Minnesota Press, 1988).

2. "Das philosophisch-werden der Welt als weltlich-werden der Philosophie," in *Frühe Schriften I* (Stuttgart: Cotta, 1962), p. 70.

3. Citations from Joseph O'Malley's edition of Marx's *Early Political Writings* (Cambridge: Cambridge University Press, 1994) are given in parenthesis as OM, followed by a page number, here OM, 62. I have occasionally modified the translation but have always given the English source in OM.

4. The 1843 "Exchange of Letters" among Marx, Ruge, Bakunin, and Feuerbach is cited here from the *Frühe Schriften I*, p. 448. Two other passages from the exchange should be noted. "We do not," writes Marx, "face the world in a doctrinaire fashion, declaring, 'Here is the truth, kneel here.' We merely show the world why it actually struggles; and consciousness is something the world must acquire even if it does not want to." And, at the end of the letter, Marx notes that "mankind does not begin any *new* work but completes its old work consciously" (449, 450).

5. The *Economic and Philosophical Manuscripts* are quoted in my translation from the Cotta edition cited in n. 3, above; parentheses indicate the page numbers, here 645.

6. The critique directed here at Proudhon was a constant concern for Marx, whose goal was not simply to better the material conditions of "wage slaves." The political implications of this critique emerge in Marx's *Critique of the Gotha Program*, which I discuss under "The Capitalist Economy as Political Subject," below.

7. Citations from "Wage Labor and Capital" are from David McLellan, ed., *Karl Marx: Selected Writings* (Oxford: Oxford University Press, 1977), indicated by DM and a page number, here DM, 256.

8. Citations from this text are translated from the German, published in volume 3 of the *Marx-Engels-Werke* (East Berlin: Dietz, 1962), and are indicated in the text by GI followed by a page number, here GI, 35.

9. *Frühe Schriften I*, p. 449.

10. *Marx-Engels-Werke*, 3:6.

11. Karl Marx and Friedrich Engels, *The Communist Manifesto*, with an introduction by A. J. P. Taylor (Harmondsworth: Penguin, 1967), pp. 82–83.

12. Ibid., p. 95.

13. Citations from the English translation in *Political Writings*, vol. 2 (New York: Penguin, 1992), are indicated in the text as CSF, followed by the page, in this case 47.

14. Ironically, the concept of Bonapartism was adopted by the Fourth International (the Trotskyists) to offer a "materialist" explanation of Stalin's rise to power.

15. Citations from the English translation in *Political Writings*, vol. 2, are indicated in the text by 18th followed by the page, in this case 150.

16. *Capital* as a whole was subtitled *A Critique of Political Economy*. Each volume had its own subtitle in Marx's overarching conception. Encouraged by the economic crisis of 1857, Marx wrote a draft of his entire theory in 1857; this manuscript, which became widely available only in 1953, under the title *Grundrisse der Kritik der politischen Ökonomie*, supports the interpretation of Marx's economic theory as a whole that will be offered here. The failure of the crisis of 1857 to lead to revolutionary action may explain why the preface to the 1859 publication of *Toward a Critique of Political Economy* returns to the more determinist and reductionist theory that Marx and Engels had developed in *The German Ideology*.

17. Citations from the Penguin edition (London, 1967) are indicated in the text by volume and page number, here 1:280.

18. One need not treat that theory as the metaphysical claim that there is a kind of substance called labor that enters into the composition of each commodity; the theory can be understood instead as a critical theory of social relations. For a critique of the labor theory of value, see chapter 7's discussion of Cornelius Castoriadis, above.

19. It is only in volume 3 that Marx tries to show that a "law of the tendency of the rate of surplus-value to fall" interferes with capitalism's smooth reproduction process. This is because it is only in that volume that he introduces the competition among the capitalists that blinds them to the need to maintain the social formation on which their profits are based. That is when the "artificial" domination by the economic takes on a different connotation, that of being historically specific and thus transitory.

20. The phrase is found in a letter of February 22, 1858 ("Es ist zugleich eine Darstellung des Systems und durch die Darstellung eine Kritik desselben"). I first encountered it in Roman Rosdolsky's pathbreaking study of the *Grundrisse, Zur Entstehungsgeschichte des Marxschen "Kapital"* (Frankfurt:

Europäische Verlagsanstalt, 1968), p. 18n. On Marx's relation to Lassalle, see the discussion of *The Critique of the Gotha Program* in the section "Politics and Class Struggle," later in this chapter.

21. This systematic intent is evident in the amount of space Marx devotes to explaining not just that but how and why the economists were led to err. The fourth volume of *Capital, Theories of Surplus-Value*, is essential to Marx's project: his systematic demonstration is complete only if he can show the necessity of these illusions.

22. Citations from the Vintage edition (New York, 1973) are indicated as Gr, followed by a page number, here, Gr, 463. The reader will recall the earlier critique of Proudhon's politics as simply making for better-paid slaves. The same notion returns below in the critique of Lassalle in *The Critique of the Gotha Program*.

23. This latter point is subject to debate. Sometimes Marx seems to think that truly human relations lie outside the sphere of production, as in the Greek understanding of democratic citizenship; sometimes he is tempted by the romantic German model of self-fulfillment through the labor process. I will return below to his vision of human fulfillment as it is presented in the *Grundrisse*.

24. The manuscript of this chapter was first published in Russian and German in Moscow in 1933; it became accessible in the West in the late 1960s. Citations are from the English translation, printed as an appendix to the first volume of *Capital*, indicated as R followed by a page number, here R, 990.

25. This thesis, stated in the first part of chapter 15's discussion of the "internal contradictions" of the law, is not consistently maintained. The other claim is that relations of production determine relations of distribution. In fact, both theses can be maintained if care is taken to distinguish capitalist relations of production based on exchange-value from social relations based on human or use-values.

26. *Frühe Schriften I*, 598.

27. Citations from the English translation in the Penguin edition, *Political Writings*, vol. 3, are given in the text as CWF followed by a page number, here CWF, 200.

28. Engels's phrase is cited by Lenin in "State and Revolution," in *Selected Works* (Moscow: Foreign Language Publishing House, 1960), 2:314.

29. Citations from the English translation in *Political Writings*, vol. 3, are indicated as Gotha followed by a page number, here Gotha, 346–347.

30. See the arguments developed particularly in chapter 9, above. This reconstruction of Marx's project helps explain also the attraction-repulsion of critical intellectuals to Marxism that was illustrated throughout the first part of this book.

# Index

Scopes Trial, 222
SDS, 47
Second Empire, 147–48, 276
Section Française de l'Internationle Ouvsiere (SFIO), 156, 316n.21
*Secular City, The* (Cox), 225
self-criticism, 21, 34, 47, 63, 160, 261–62
self-evident rights, 199, 206–10, 218
self-organization, 74, 84, 110, 185, 196
self-realization, 277–78, 282; labor and, 284–85
self-willed servitude, 102
Senate, 188–89, 211–12
Seven Years' War, 177, 199
SFIO (Section Française de l'Internationle Ouvsiere), 156, 316n.21
Shays' Rebellion, 213, 215
siege/sluice metaphors, 58–59
Sieyès, Emmanuel-Joseph, 141
situationists, 68–69
slavery metaphor, 14, 88, 96, 254, 280
Smith, Adam, 16, 177, 252, 281, 284
Social Democratic Party, 44, 47, 84
social diversity, 176–77, 202–3
socialism, xiii, 4, 26, 84, 91, 150–51; antipolitical implications of, 19–20; really existing, 6, 54, 105, 160; utopian, 8, 19–20, 145–46
*Socialisme ou Barbarie*, 27, 63–72, 108–10; aesthetic function, 68–69; as bureaucracy, 112–13; bureaucracy, view of, 64, 66–70; creativity, view of, 67–70, 84; Lefort and, 63–65, 72, 74; membership, 64–65; revolution, view of, 66–67
Socialist International, 152
Socialist Party, 79–80, 144, 149–56, 292n.4, 304n.18
social movements, 29, 57–58, 159–60, 170; direct democracy, 276–78
social relations, 4, 20, 201, 256, 263; democratic, vii–ix, xi, 22, 132, 147;

meaning and, 203–4; normative expectations, 55–56
social reproduction, 15–16, 94, 123, 169, 271–75; genesis/normativity and, 281–82
social science, 25, 32, 55
society, 290n.6; individuality and, 78–79; as organization, 129–30, 312n.35; passive *vs.* active, 182–83; repetitive structure, 115–16; source of legitimacy, 78–79, 203–4
sociological analysis, 216, 220–21
*solidarisme*, 183, 187, 192
*Solidarité, La* (Ruby), 183
Sollers, Philippe, 86
Solzhenitsyn, Alexander, 26, 37, 77, 127, 128, 160, 303n.13, 311n.34, 318n.35
Southern Christian Leadership Conference, 222
sovereignty, 186–89, 200–202, 206, 323–24n.23; collective, 212–13; monarchy and, 244–45; symbolic nature of, 214–19
Soviet Union, 22, 160, 162–63, 291n.1, 307n.8; bureaucracy, 72–73; demise of, xiii, 26, 58; totalitarianism, 109–10, 118. *see also* Russian Revolution
*Specters of Marx* (Derrida), xiii, 27
*Spheres of Justice: A Defense of Pluralism and Equality* (Walzer), 181
Stalin, Joseph, 6, 35, 73, 80, 100, 118, 123, 292n.5
Stalinism, 18, 64, 69, 74, 109, 110, 112, 160, 292n.5, 307n.8, 322n.7
"Stalinism without Stalin" (Lefort), 73, 110
Stamp Act, 188, 205
Starnberg research institute, 52, 53
state, 17, 81, 200, 202, 259; authoritarian, 44–45; Hegel's theory of, 246–47, 275; language of, 58–59; nation-state, 139, 187. *see also* sovereignty